THE OVAL WORLD

THE OVAL WORLD

A Global History of Rugby

Tony Collins

BLOOMSBURY

LONDON · NEW DELHI · NEW YORK · SYDNEY

For John Collins, my dad

Bloomsbury Sport
An imprint of Bloomsbury Publishing Plc

50 Bedford Square
London
WC1B 3DP
UK

1385 Broadway
New York
NY 10018
USA

www.bloomsbury.com

BLOOMSBURY and the Diana logo are trademarks of Bloomsbury Publishing Plc

First published 2015

British Library Cataloguing-in-Publication Data
A catalogue record for this book is available from the British Library.

Library of Congress Cataloguing-in-Publication data has been applied for.

ISBN: HB: 978-1-4088-4370-3
TPB: 978-1-4088-4371-0
ePub: 978-1-4088-4372-7

2 4 6 8 10 9 7 5 3 1

Typeset in 12pt Adobe Garamond Pro by Deanta Global Publishing Services, Chennai, India
Printed and bound in Great Britain by CPI Group (UK) Ltd, Croydon CR0 4YY

MIX
Paper from
responsible sources
FSC® C020471

To find out more about our authors and books visit www.bloomsbury.com.
Here you will find extracts, author interviews, details of forthcoming events and
the option to sign up for our newsletters.

CONTENTS

CONTENTS

LIST OF ABBREVIATIONS

AFRF	Association Française de Rugby Féminin
ARL	Australian Rugby League
ARU	Australian Rugby Union
EARFU	East African Rugby Football Union
FFR	Fédération Française de Rugby
FIR	Federazione Italiana Rugby
FIRA	Fédération Internationale de Rugby Amateur
GAA	Gaelic Athletic Association
IB	International Rugby Football Board
IFA	Intercollegiate Football Association
IFA	Irish Football Association
IFU	Irish Football Union
IGRAB	International Gay Rugby Association Board
IRFU	Irish Rugby Football Union
JRFU	Japanese Rugby Football Union
LFRT	Ligue Française de Rugby à Treize
NFUI	Northern Football Union of Ireland
NIFC	North of Ireland Football Club
NRL	National Rugby League
NSWRFL	New South Wales Rugby Football League
NZRFU	New Zealand Rugby Football Union
PIRA	Pacific Islands Rugby Alliance
RFU	Rugby Football Union

SANZAR	South African, New Zealand and Australian Rugby
SARB	South African Rugby Board
SARFU	South African Rugby Football Union
SRU	Scottish Rugby Union (formerly SFU – Scottish Football Union)
UFRA	Union Française de Rugby Amateur
USFSA	Union des Sociétés Françaises de Sports Athlétiques
WPCRFU	Western Province Coloured Rugby Football League
WRC	World Rugby Corporation
WRFU	Women's Rugby Football Union
WRU	Welsh Rugby Union
YRF	Yugoslav Rugby Federation

INTRODUCTION
A BOY AND AN OVAL BALL

I can remember the precise moment I realised that I would never achieve my dream.

It was late 1973; I was just 12 and a few weeks into my first term at secondary school. The school had a wide catchment area and every year there were about 150 new boys. Rugby was the local game and playing it, knowing it and even being able to talk about it brought varying levels of adolescent prestige. I knew about it – my dad even worked alongside some of the top players – and I spent hours playing the game in the street with my best friend, Steve. Since the age of seven, when Dad took me to watch my first big match, I had set my heart on playing international rugby.

So when it came playing to rugby in PE lessons Steve and I thought we could show our new schoolmates what the game was really all about. The boys would defer to us and the girls would bestow their favours on us; it was just a matter of time.

We hatched a plan. At the next match, we would display our tactical insight and superior skill with a series of perfectly executed set-plays. The first would be audacious and daring. As scrum-half I would pick the ball up from the base of the scrum, feign to pass it out to the three-quarters standing to my right, but instead run around to the left and through the narrow gap between the scrum and touchline.

Steve, playing out on the left wing, would shout for me to pass him the ball. I would dummy it to him, the opposing defenders would fall for it, leaving me in the clear to romp through to the try line unopposed. We'd seen it done on television, practised at home, and knew it would work.

Ten minutes into the match, a scrum was formed just 25 yards from our opponents' try line. Our plan kicked in. Everything went like clockwork. The undefended try line beckoned to me. Just 20 yards and I would be over. Glory was within my grasp.

But as I tried to accelerate, the try line did not get closer. My feet seemed to be getting heavier and my legs shorter. I sensed movement to my right – and almost immediately the air was knocked out of my lungs as I crumpled under the weight of two of the school's fattest boys. I fell face first into the mud and the ball squirted out of my hands.

'Knock-on,' shouted Mr Miles, the PE teacher. Steve picked up the ball and stared at me, still on the ground trying to catch my breath.

'I knew you should have bloody passed it to me,' he said, his voice full of contempt.

I could have cried.

But although I knew then that playing rugby in front of tens of thousands of people or touring foreign lands was not to be for me, my interest in rugby did not disappear.

If anything, freed from the burden of having to play the game successfully, its fascination increased. The geometric perfection of a cut-out pass, the split-second timing of the bone-shuddering tackle and the spectacular artistry of the side-stepping three-quarter still continued to enchant me.

What's more, rugby seemed to be a game of unanswered questions and unsolved mysteries. It was played in exotic places like Fiji and Papua New Guinea, but countries like Germany and Brazil didn't seem to play it at all. Soccer, for some reason unfathomable to me, was infinitely more fashionable all over the world, but in towns like the one I grew up in, rugby was the most popular sport.

More confusingly, I also discovered that there were two types of rugby. Each had a different number of players in a team, separate rules and even reverse methods of numbering players' jerseys. When I watched the other rugby on television, I couldn't really understand what was going on. Of course, my dad and I would never bother going to watch it. I would later discover that neither type of rugby was very much interested in the other at all.

So although my interest in playing rugby evaporated, my curiosity about it expanded. There seemed to be many questions for which no one quite had an answer, and if it was my lack of athletic ability that ruined my dreams of a rugby career, my inquisitiveness about rugby and the wider world was stimulated and developed, and that ultimately led me to become a historian.

The Oval World is a book whose genesis lies in the muddy playing fields of early 1970s Britain. The stories it tells, the questions it answers and the mysteries it tries to solve are those that have occurred to most people who have ever watched a game of rugby, whether as fans or as casual observers.

As the tiredest of sporting clichés tells us, rugby is much more than a game – so this is a history of the life and times of the game and the world that created it, from *Tom Brown's Schooldays* to digital television, from Hull's docklands to Sydney harbour, from Welsh miners to a Russian prince.

Rugby is the story of the world we live in and how it was made.

PART I

KICK-OFF

In almost every part of the world, across centuries and civilisations, humanity's instinctive joy in catching, throwing and kicking a ball has meant that games which resemble rugby have long been played.

For the origins of rugby as we know it today, however, we must look to Britain. The rough and tumble games played in the fields and villages of pre-industrial times were taken up by the boys of Rugby School in the English midlands and transformed into a game of rules, regulations and morality.

Soon, the thrill of the try and the crunch of the tackle were gripping the imaginations of great swathes of the population. The game spread beyond its public school founders and became a passion of the industrial workers who were crowded into the great cities of the Victorian age.

Rugby was now a game played and watched by all …

1
THE TRADITION

It is a cold, sharp, sunny day in February, a sense of anticipation in the air. Small groups of people gather, some laughing and joking, others deep in serious conversation about the afternoon's prospects. They break up, moving, meeting and merging with other groups, a tide of multicoloured shirts, freezing breath and boisterous conversation.

As the crowd grows and snakes its way closer to the scene of the afternoon's action, the pace quickens and the chatter becomes louder. The familiarity of the ritual does nothing to diminish the growing sense of excitement.

And then, as they reach their destination, the crowd once more becomes individuals, some taking their usual places, others staking a claim for a good vantage point and newcomers wandering in search of somewhere to watch the day's proceedings.

The stage is set.

The match begins. The crowd lets out a convulsive roar. The players tear into each other, desperate to get hold of the ball and drive through, around or even over their opponents. The match is locked into a succession of surges, counter-attacks, surges. Eventually, as the game wears on, the two sides begin to tire and taut defences become slack and baggy.

Suddenly, the ball squirts free of the pack and is kicked through into open space. It is picked up and moved rapidly and precisely from player to player as they scythe deeper and deeper into enemy territory. The decisive score seems unstoppable. Supporters bellow encouragement, while their opponents grit their teeth.

Then it happens. The ball reaches its destination. Time momentarily stops. Encouragement becomes ecstasy. The thrill of triumph has momentarily abolished the cares of the world. And then the game ends, and the crowd begins to drain away, some to celebrate, others to commiserate.

But whether winner or loser, player or spectator, each will be back, week after week, year after year, in search of that sublime everlasting moment that only this game can bring.

Mauls and mardi gras

Such a scene is experienced whenever and wherever rugby is played, from Sydney to Swansea, Perpignan to Pretoria, and all points in between. This isn't a modern rugby match, however: it's a description of the Shrove Tuesday 'folk football' match played annually between the Up'ards and Down'ards of Ashbourne in Derbyshire, the rural heartland of England, one of a handful of such games that survive from the rural past.

Like most of these games it is open to all inhabitants of the town, whose allegiances are divided according to whether they were born north (the Up'ards) or south (the Down'ards) of the River Henmore, which not only divides the town but also provides the two goals. These are three miles apart, the southerly goal at Clifton Mill and the northerly at Sturston Mill.

Play takes place through streets, fields and the river as hundreds of men, young and old, and occasionally women, seek the honour of scoring the decisive goal – which results in the scorer's name being inscribed on the ball and it being presented to them.

In contrast to the complex rules of today, the Ashbourne game has never had many. The winner is the side that gets the ball to their goal and taps it three times against the remaining stones of the long-demolished mills. If no goal is scored, play finishes at 10 p.m., although if a goal is scored before 5 p.m. another ball is provided to prolong the game. Beyond that, whatever it takes to score a goal is acceptable.

Ashbourne is by no means unique or exceptional. Like a throwback on the evolutionary ladder of rugby, there are more than a dozen similar games still played today, from St Ives on the furthest reaches of Cornwall's west coast to Kirkwall, the capital of Orkney off the north coast of Scotland. Neither soccer nor rugby, like all pre-20th century team sports involving a ball, goals, hands and feet these games were known simply as 'football' and are now referred to as 'folk football' by historians.

This type of game can also still be found in Europe. In France, the first written reference to a game resembling folk football dates back to 1147. *La soule*, also known variously as *choule* or *cholle*, was played among the villages of Normandy, Picardy and Brittany in northern France up until the first half of the 20th century. In Italy, versions of football known as *calcio* emerged during the 16th century. Calcio Fiorentino was revived under Mussolini and is still a major tourist attraction in Florence today. Countless similar games were born and died without troubling the historical record.

Each one was more than just a game. Each was part of the cycle of festivals and celebrations that punctuated everyday life in pre-industrial, agricultural society. Shrove Tuesday, traditionally the last day before the fasting period of Lent in the Christian calendar, became the most popular day for folk football.

Across the Christian world, Shrovetide was a festival of indulgence and licence. Sports and games – ranging from pancake-racing to cock-fighting – were an essential part of the festivities. When Shrovetide football games took place, entire villages would close for the day while huge scrums of men and youths struggled to carry the ball to their goal.

Normal customs and rights would be suspended. Occasionally, women would play, as they did in the 1790s in Midlothian in Scotland. And, just as today, alcohol was always an essential lubricant.

Today, there are state-of-the-art stadiums, highly paid athletes and complex rules, but despite the distance of time and place, modern rugby stands firmly in the tradition of its medieval forebear.

'Football', rugby and soccer

The historian Barbara Tuchman once suggested that the invention of the ball was as important to the history of human leisure as the wheel was to the development of technology.[1] She was undoubtedly right.

Across all continents and cultures, people have played ball games since the dawn of human civilisation. As early as 300 BC the Chinese appear to have played a game called *cuju* that involved kicking a ball over a silk net suspended between two bamboo poles. The Greek writer Athenaeus of Naucratis described *harpastum*, a Roman game in which a ball was seemingly carried and passed by the participants – and which some have speculated as being the forerunner of rugby, despite there being no hard evidence.

The first recorded description in Britain of a game called football, by William Fitz Stephen in 1174, chronicles its popularity in London: 'After dinner all the young men of the city go out into the fields to play at the well-known game of football. The scholars belonging to the several schools have each their ball; and the city tradesmen according to the respective crafts, have theirs.'[2]

The emergence of folk football games like this may have been linked to the growth of towns, trade and the economy during the later Middle Ages that intensified local rivalries, the crucial competitive impulse for sporting contest. The word 'goal' seems to share some common heritage with the word 'boundary'. It may also be linked to a ritual called 'beating the bounds', where local people would walk the boundaries of their parish to share the knowledge of where they lay and to ensure that they were remembered in the future.

Perhaps because of such contests, folk football was often seen as a sport of the common people. Joseph Strutt's 1801 epic *The Sports and Pastimes of the People of England* describes the game as 'formerly much in vogue among the common people of England'. It was also suspected, sometimes with justification, of being a cover for the organisation of protests, or worse. It was banned in Ireland in 1719 by the British as being nothing more than a 'pretence' for 'tumultuous and numerous meetings'.[3]

The various ways a ball could be handled, kicked and passed were as diverse as the regions in which ball games were played. Some were far more organised and based on clearly defined rules. Teams of 22-a-side representing Cumberland and Westmoreland played each other for 1,000 guineas on Kennington Common in London in 1789. A four-a-side match was played in Ashbourne in 1846. Even one-a-side matches, based on the idea of cricket's single-wicket contests, were not unknown.[4]

The game of camp-ball, which was played across Norfolk, Suffolk, Essex and Cambridgeshire from at least the 15th to the 18th centuries, had a sophisticated set of rules and specialised playing fields, known as 'camping closes'. Teams of ten or 15 players would carry the ball upfield supported by 'sidemen' who would act as American football-style blockers. When a sideman's progress was halted, the ball had to be thrown to another player.[5]

Cornwall's 'hurling to goals' game was played between teams of 15 to 30 players and allowed similar forms of blocking. When tackled, the ball-carrier had to pass it backwards to a teammate. Forward passes were not allowed and when a player was tackled he would shout 'hold' and pass the ball back. If any rule was broken, wrote the 17th-century Cornish MP Richard Carew, players would 'take for a just cause of going together by the ears, but with their fists only, neither doth any of them seek revenge for wrongs or hurts, but at the like play again'.[6]

No matter how different or diverse these early games of folk football, the descriptions of matches make one thing clear – most resembled modern rugby far more than they did soccer.

You don't have to be a time traveller to see the connection. All you need is a map. Many of these early 'football 'games were played in areas that would later become hotbeds of rugby. In the area around Twickenham in south-west London, Shrove Tuesday matches were part of a well-established tradition. As well as Twickenham itself, matches were played in other outlying parts of London, at Teddington, Bushey Park, Richmond, Hampton Wick, East Molesey and Thames Ditton. The annual game at Kingston-upon-Thames did not finally end until 1868, just three years before the Rugby Football Union (RFU), the English game's governing body, itself was founded.[7]

In today's rugby stronghold of Leicestershire, matches were recorded from at least 1790, when the village of Ratby staged a match. On Shrove Tuesday 1852, a 15-a-side match was played between Blaby and Wigston in a field that is today just 15 minutes' drive from today's Leicester Tigers' training ground.[8] Enderby, another village in the district of Blaby, gained such a strong reputation that they played a team from Holmfirth, near Huddersfield, on Good Friday 1852 at the neutral ground of Sheffield's Hyde Park.[9] Fifteen miles from Leicester in the village of Hallaton, its traditional Easter Monday 'Bottle-Kicking' match (a misnomer: no bottles are used but three small barrels are carried but not kicked) is a remnant of an 18th-century mass folk football match that continues today.[10]

Further north, in today's bastions of rugby league, the East Yorkshire town of Hornsea could boast of its own 'football grene' from the 1680s. In the 1820s Primitive Methodists would gather to try and stop the annual match between the villages of Hedon and Preston. Even as late as the 1890s, one Hull FC rugby player claimed that he learned his rugby skills by playing traditional 'football' in the local village of Sutton.[11] In Yorkshire's West Riding, games were played at Keighley,

Pudsey, and most regularly at Holmfirth, the birthplace of Harold Wagstaff, arguably the greatest centre three-quarter to play either code of rugby.[12]

Across the border in Lancashire in the 1840s, Rochdale hosted a number of matches between short-lived clubs boasting names such as the 'Body Guards' and the 'Fear Noughts', prefiguring the town's later rugby club adoption of the moniker of Hornets in 1871.[13] In Orrell, a 30-a-side challenge was thrown out to local villages in 1841.[14] And in Cumberland, the mass folk football 'Uppies and Downies' game survives today in Workington's Easter game. Its neighbour Whitehaven also staged a match in which shipwrights would do battle with quarrymen.[15]

In Wales, a game called *cnapan* was apparently played by thousands in Pembrokeshire in the far south-west, in which men on foot and horseback would struggle for possession of a ball. It appeared to flourish in the 16th century and was being played on the River Teifi in West Wales in 1740.[16] In the Scottish Borders, folk football games flourished, most notably at Jedburgh.

This roll call of rugby precedents raises an obvious question. Why were these games given the name 'football' if they weren't played with the feet? The plain truth is, as with the origins of many words, we simply don't know for certain. Soccer's omnipresence in today's world can lead us to assume that football means a sport that is played exclusively with the feet. This was never the case. Even the Football Association in its early years allowed the hands to be used by outfield players to catch a ball. And, of course, the feet *are* used extensively in rugby. Place kicks, drop kicks, chip kicks, punts, bombs and grubbers are part of the armoury of every rugby team that takes the field. It is a game played with both hands and feet.

In fact, soccer's insistence that *only* the feet can be used by outfield players makes it the exception to the rule. This was widely recognised by the Victorian apostles of modern football. Writing in 1887, the first serious historian of the game, Montague Shearman, pointed out that 'there is no trace in the original form of [football] to suggest that nothing but kicking is allowed'.[17] Far from being a partisan of rugby, Shearman was a member of Wanderers FC, the first ever winners of the FA Cup.

Which game is the true inheritor of the traditions of early football? Indirectly, all of them. Directly, none of them. Viewed in terms of human evolution, folk football is related to modern soccer, rugby and the other types of football in same way that apes are the common ancestor to chimpanzees, bonobos and humans.

One simple fact remains, however. The sport most firmly rooted in the tradition of the football games played across Europe for centuries in which the ball is handled and kicked, and in which players are bodily tackled, is not soccer.

It is rugby.

2

A SCHOOL CALLED RUGBY

Early in 1856 a former pupil of Rugby School named Thomas Hughes sat down to write a book for his eight-year-old son Maurice. It was to be a story about what the boy could expect when he followed in his father's footsteps to Rugby. Hughes wanted it to be both entertaining and educational, preparing the boy for daily life at the school and introducing him to its principles. It would teach him the importance of character, how to become a gentlemen and, no less importantly, the valuable lessons to be learned from playing sport.

When it was finally published in April 1857, *Tom Brown's Schooldays* was an instant bestseller: 11,000 copies were sold in its first year and it went through almost 50 editions by the end of the century. It would become one of the most important novels of the Victorian age, establishing the genre of school stories, providing a model for schools around the world and inspiring countless thousands to play the game of rugby. But perhaps the accolade that the doting father Thomas Hughes valued most was that of the anonymous reviewer in *The Times*, who pronounced that the book was one that 'every English father might well wish to see in the hands of his son'.[1]

Sport, and particularly Rugby School's own version of 'football', was a crucial element of *Tom Brown's Schooldays*. As soon as he arrives at the school, Tom is thrust into the midst of a ferocious match. Thanks to a mixture of bravery and a sense of duty, he hurls himself into the fray and emerges a hero when, in the last minute of the game, he throws himself on a loose ball to save a certain try and ensure victory for his team. In doing so, he became rugby's first role model.

Rugby School itself had been established almost two centuries before in 1567 by a London grocer, Lawrence Sheriff, to 'teach grammar freely' to local boys. By 1818 it was the second largest public school in England, boasting almost 400 pupils and 'football', as rugby is called even today by its pupils, had become embedded in the daily fabric of school life.

The town of Rugby was no stranger to games of football. Nestled on the banks of the River Avon in the region known by the tourist brochures as the 'Heart of England', the area had a tradition of 'football' games stretching back to at least the mid-18th century. In the 1700s a match was played in Rugby town centre every New Year's Day. It was so popular – or such a nuisance, depending on your point of view – that on New Year's Eve in 1743 the town crier, Mr Baxter, was paid twopence by the local constable to cry 'no football play in ye street' to discourage potential players.[2]

As late as 1845, the same year that the school published the first printed rules of the game, 'six tailors of Rugby' issued a challenge to any other team of six men within five miles of the town to play them for a prize of five pounds.[3] The nearby villages of Flecknoe, Grandborough and Staverton also played regular matches in the 1840s. In 1843 local bookmakers offered odds of 100-1 on Flecknoe beating the undefeated Grandborough team. It was to be a memorable day for the village, and especially its gamblers. 'After playing eight hours, much to the surprise and mortification of the knowing ones,' reported the sporting weekly *Bell's Life*, 'Flecknoe succeeded in gaining two games, and therefore came off victorious.'[4]

None of these games or teams would survive into the 1850s. The growth of industrial manufacturing and the rigid discipline of the factory system left neither the space nor the time for traditional folk football matches. Profit overrode pleasure when it came to traditional sport. 'It is not a trifling consideration that a suspension of business for nearly two days should be created to the inhabitants for the mere gratification of a sport at once so useless and barbarous,' complained one Derby businessman in 1832 about the town's traditional Shrovetide match. In 1846 Derby's mayor read the Riot Act and called out troops to make sure that the match was not played. 'It is all disappointment, no sports and no football. This is the way they always treat poor folks,' complained one former Derby footballer.[5]

But if the traditional forms of the game played by ordinary people were withering on the vine, the game survived, and thrived, in elite public schools such as Rugby.

Tom Brown's world

By the time Thomas Hughes began to write *Tom Brown's Schooldays*, football at Rugby School had become far more than just another sport: it had become a symbol of the school's unique style of education. Unlike its more socially prestigious rivals like Eton and Harrow, Rugby emphasised the development of a boy's character. The leaders of British society, industry and empire had to be educated in the competitive spirit that drove the engine of economic expansion onward. And how better to do that than to play rugby?

This explains why the true hero of *Tom Brown's Schooldays* was not actually Tom Brown but Thomas Arnold, Rugby School's headmaster from 1828 to 1841, whose presence towered over the book. He believed that the active struggle for Christian principles was an essential part of everyday life. 'What we must look for here is, first, religious and moral principle; secondly, gentlemanly conduct; thirdly, intellectual ability', he taught.[6] Although not a phrase used by Arnold, this was the philosophy of Muscular Christianity.

Under Arnold, Rugby acquired an overwhelming sense of moral purpose. The school became a vivid reflection of the seemingly irresistible self-belief of the middle classes in the first half of the 19th century. Writing in 1846, one pupil described the school as:

> the image of that most powerful element in modern English society, the Middle Class ... In a late stage of civilisation, like the present, the idea of trade comes prominently and almost exclusively into notice, being able at length to connect itself with that from which it has long been kept apart, education and enlightenment. Even so, we feel that our power has of late begun to be acknowledged; and that feeling shall animate us to proceed, holding fast the birthright of moral thoughtfulness which our great teacher [Arnold] bequeathed to us ...[7]

The importance of Rugby School was confirmed in 1864 by the report of the Clarendon Commission, which the government had set up to examine education in England's seven leading public schools. Comparing it favourably to Eton, Harrow and Winchester, the commission declared that Rugby had:

> risen from the position of a provincial school to that of a public school and in efficiency and general reputation is second to none ... it has become in fact a national institution, as being a place of education and a source of influence for the whole Kingdom. ... It instructs everywhere, is known everywhere, and exercises an influence everywhere.[8]

The Clarendon Commission's seal of approval for Rugby School and the huge sales of *Tom Brown's Schooldays* brought Thomas Arnold's principles to a new and wider audience. And, for the first time, it gave sport an importance above and beyond the intrinsic enjoyment of chasing a ball around a field. Rugby football was no longer merely a game. For its disciples, it was a guide to life.

Playing the game

What type of a game did Rugby School play? As can be seen in *Tom Brown's Schooldays*, it differed little from those games of folk football that had taken place for centuries. The number of players was unlimited but usually numbered around 50- or 60-a-side. There was no time limit to matches, the contest being won by the first side to score two goals, although the first set of written rules from 1845 also stated that 'all matches are drawn after five days, but after three if no goal has been kicked'. And, like traditional Shrove Tuesday games, play was based on almost continual scrummaging, usually followed by kicking to set up more scrummages.[9]

Strange as it may seem to us today, a try scored no points at all. It merely provided an opportunity to try to kick a goal, hence the term 'try'. As in modern soccer, only goals counted in the score. And goals were not easy to score. Firstly, 'goal-keepers', usually younger boys in the school, were spread out along the goal-line to prevent the ball going over the line or being touched down. If a player managed to avoid these hordes and touch the ball down, the procedure to kick at goal was elaborate and time-consuming. The player who had made the touchdown punted the ball back from where he had touched down to a waiting player in the field of play. He would catch the ball and make a mark in the ground with his heel. But the moment the ball was kicked to the catcher, the defending side could rush forward to stop him catching the ball. If he caught the ball successfully, the catcher was allowed to place it on the ground for the try scorer to kick over the bar and between the posts of the goal.

Not surprisingly, this arcane procedure was not incorporated into the first set of rules drawn up by the Rugby Football Union in 1871, but it did have one piece of historical significance. The fact that the opposing side could charge the kicker meant that goals at Rugby School were scored by kicking the ball over the crossbar rather than under it.

As well as the goal-keepers, teams consisted mainly of 'quarters', whose job it was to kick the ball back downfield when it came to them, and 'players up', the forwards who would take part in the scrum or dribble the ball forward to the opposition goal-line. The scrum itself bore little relation to its modern incarnation. Forwards stood straight up and pushed, kicking the ball or, more usually, their opponents' shins, a practice known as hacking. Their aim was not to heel the ball backwards out of the scrum but to drive the opposing forwards back and dribble the ball forward towards the goal. Hooking the ball out of the scrum was viewed as a form of cheating.

Toughness was everything. A player who put his head down in a scrum would be accused of cowardice, because it indicated that he was concerned for the safety of his shins. For the Victorian public schoolboy there was no greater test of manliness than the ability to give and to take hacking on his shins. 'We all wear white trousers, to show 'em we don't care for hacks,' East explains to Tom Brown before his first school match. White trousers showed the blood and confirmed the wearer's imperviousness to pain.

Even the tradition of caps, still awarded today to international players, can be traced back to these adolescent trials of masculinity. Crimson caps were worn by boys of the School House team to distinguish themselves from their opponents. As old boy Sydney Selfe remembered, 'the *mot d'ordre* was "whenever you see a [bare] head, hit it"'.[10]

Boys would even adapt their boots specially for hacking by adding thick soles and filing the toes to a sharpness that could slash the shins of an opponent. Another Rugby old boy described in 1860 how 'fellows did not care a fig for the ball except inasmuch as it gave them a decent pretext for hacking … My maxim is hack the ball on when you see it near you, and when you don't, why then, hack the fellow next to you.'[11]

Even in the 1870s, rugby was a game played predominantly with the feet, literally 'foot-ball' as it was often spelt at the time. Handling the ball was severely limited. If the ball was caught from a kick before it hit the ground – a 'fair catch' – the catcher was allowed to kick the ball unhindered by the opposing side, known as a free kick. Running with the ball was only permitted if the ball was bouncing when caught – a stationary or even a rolling ball could not be picked up by hand and had to be kicked.

No one would have been more surprised than William Webb Ellis himself by the claim that he 'invented' rugby by picking up the ball and running with it during a match at the school in 1823. Ellis, who became an Anglican clergyman in later life, died in Menton in France in 1872 oblivious to his apparently historic achievement. Even the inquiry that was set up by the Old Rugbeian Society in 1895 to investigate the origins of Rugby football could not find any evidence – direct, circumstantial or even hearsay – to support the story. This did not deter it from proclaiming Ellis to be the 'originator' of the sport.

We do know for certain, however, that Jem Mackie, a Rugby pupil in the late 1830s, was renowned for running with the ball, but not long after he was expelled following an unexplained 'incident', a general meeting of the school formally legalised running with the ball in 1842. But for his expulsion, Mackie may have gone on to occupy William Webb Ellis's position in the mythology of rugby.[12]

Stories about boys like Mackie were passed down the school from one year to another. So, too, were the rules of the game. For decades rugby had no formal rule book. Disputes were resolved by discussion, argument and occasionally by a general meeting of the senior boys. But as the number of pupils increased and the game became more complex, it was decided in 1844 to set up a committee to agree a definitive version of the rules and in August 1845 three pupils were elected to compile the first written version of the rules. They were William Arnold, son of the recently deceased headmaster, W. W. Shirley, a future Regius Professor of Ecclesiastical History at Oxford University, and Frederick Hutchins, who would become a London solicitor. A mere three days later they submitted their draft, which was endorsed and printed.[13]

At just 20 pages, including the front and back covers, and only nine by six centimetres in size, *Football Rules* was a tiny book that could be slipped into the pocket of a player's white trousers and pulled out whenever a dispute arose. The 37 rules made no attempt to explain how the game was played; they were designed for pupils who already knew how to play. Instead they laid down the decisions and rulings on points of dispute or controversy. The first four introductory pages were taken up with the vexed question of boys who did not want to play – those seeking to be excused had to submit a note signed by a medical officer and countersigned by the recalcitrant boy's head of house.

A revised edition was published in 1862, but by that time the rules were no longer just the concern of boys at the school. Thanks to the unparalleled success of *Tom Brown's Schooldays*, Rugby football had begun to inspire and excite tens of thousands of boys and young men across Britain. Sadly, the child for whom the book was intended would neither read it nor play the game that the book so lovingly described. Just two years after *Tom Brown's Schooldays* was published, Thomas Hughes' son Maurice died.

3

WHAT TOM BROWN DID NEXT

The Victorians worried about many things. The Empire. The working classes. Status. Morality. Sex. The French. But as much as anything else they worried about their health.

This was especially true for the young men educated in the spirit of Thomas Arnold's Rugby and *Tom Brown's Schooldays*. After they left school and university, the vast majority entered a world of white-collar work and office life. The new industrial society had created hundreds of thousands of new jobs in the law, medicine, finance and management, all of them desk-bound jobs offering little opportunity for exercise or fresh air.

The dangers of this sedentary lifestyle were widely recognised. Scottish rugby's most determined advocate, H. H. Almond, the headmaster of the prestigious Loretto School in Musselburgh, near Edinburgh, worried about its effects on the health of the nation:

> The tendency of the population to congregate in large towns, the multiplication of artificial means of transit, the increased strain and competition of modern life, the calamitousness change by which business hours have begun [earlier] and ended later, till crowds of sallow clerks are now released from offices *after* the expiry of daylight for many months in the year, are all causes antagonistic to the prime necessity of a nation which is to be long vigorous.[1]

He was not the only one to feel this way. Concerns about the health and fitness of the professional classes led to the creation of gyms and athletics clubs in numerous industrial cities from the 1850s. 'Practical philanthropists are organising clubs for working men,' wrote a Mr Lascelles Carr to the *Yorkshire Post*. 'Why, then, should not we, the essentially middle class, possess ourselves of the same advantages?'[2]

It was another of those great Victorian anxieties, the threat from France, that gave a major boost to this new health and fitness movement. In 1858 Felice Orsini, an Italian political refugee who had spent considerable time in England, tried to assassinate Napoleon III in Paris. Fearful of an invasion by France, in May 1859 the British government created the Rifle Volunteer movement, a forerunner of the Home Guard. Spurred by patriotic duty, young middle-class men flocked to join. Once the threat of invasion had passed, the Volunteers quickly widened their activities to include athletics, gymnastics and other sports.[3] Their training grounds and fields would provide the first playing pitches for many early rugby, soccer and athletics clubs.

Enthusiasm for rugby slowly spilled out of the schools and universities and into the adult world. The first rugby clubs began to be formed in the 1850s, most notably at Liverpool in 1857 and at Blackheath in 1858, organised by boys who had learned the game at Rugby School and Blackheath Proprietary School respectively.[4] Numerous other clubs were formed at the same time by players keen to continue with the game they had enjoyed so much at school. The evangelical zeal of the young men who had been educated in the spirit of *Tom Brown's Schooldays*, whether at Rugby School or elsewhere, would be the catalyst that caused a rugby explosion.

Beyond the school

The burgeoning popularity of rugby could be seen in the way that the game spread to other public schools. *Tom Brown's Schooldays* was regarded as almost a handbook for the numerous private schools that were established in the second half of the 19th century and they naturally took up the rugby game. The authority that Rugby School commanded can be seen at Wellington College, Berkshire, which adopted the game in 1860 and where the first rule of football was 'in case of any dispute arising during a match, the rules are the same as those used at Rugby'.[5] But as the sport expanded, its rules began to be amended and altered according to the tastes and needs of schools and the numerous adult clubs that were established to play it.

No one used Rugby School's convoluted method of converting a try into a goal. The school's rule forbidding the picking up of the ball unless it was bouncing was ignored by Blackheath, Woolwich and Sandhurst. At Blackheath Proprietary School forwards were allowed to run downfield in front of the ball-carrier, obstructing opponents who attempted to tackle him, something that would soon become a feature of American football.[6] Sizes of teams differed, too. Schools tended to play with large numbers – for example, at Clifton 40-a-side was common – but clubs played anything from 20-a-side to 12-a-side, as Hull did against Gainsborough in the early 1870s, although 15-a-side had become the norm for club matches by the mid-1870s.

Unsurprisingly, one of the most common changes that was made to the rules was to ban hacking: bloodied shins acquired on a Saturday afternoon were not ideal preparation for work the following Monday morning. Richmond campaigned against hacking and were credited with persuading the RFU to outlaw it. They were not the only ones. The Hull Football Club, founded in 1865 by local Old Rugbeians, allowed tripping the man running with the ball but not hacking. Rochdale Hornets and Preston Grasshoppers both played Rugby School rules without the hacking.

Not every adult club shied away from hacking. When York played the shinguard-wearing York Training College in the late 1860s they tried to convince their opponents to remove their shinguards, but the College players took to the field wearing them and so York simply proceeded to hack away at their opponents' shins. By the end of the match, a York player recalled, they had managed 'to make them look a good deal worse for wear'. The original rules of St Peter's School in York also allowed hacking, but did specify that 'no player may stand on the goal bar to prevent [the ball] going over', one of the game's more unusual rules.[7]

Initially, the only matches these new clubs played were between their own members. Members of Liverpool played matches between teams of those who had been to Rugby; Cheltenham schools against those who had not. Bradford saw the Captain's side take on the Secretary's side, and many clubs played A–M versus N–Z or some other alphabetical combination. In the early 1870s St Helens even played fair-haired versus dark-haired.

Such contests soon lost their appeal and as the number of clubs grew so too did the desire to play matches against other teams, especially those seen as representatives of rival towns or regions. 'We saw reports in the papers of football matches being played at Leeds, Bradford and elsewhere, and we thought that Halifax ought to have a club also,' remembered the founder of the Halifax club, Sam Duckitt.[8]

The wide variety of rules used by clubs in different towns presented an obvious problem. Which rules to play under? When inter-club matches began, the understanding was that the home team's rules would be played. In 1864 the rugby-playing Leeds club played against the soccer-inclined Sheffield side, unsurprisingly winning at home and losing at Sheffield. Four years later Manchester brushed aside Sheffield by a goal to nil under rugby rules but lost the return match in South Yorkshire by two goals to nil.

Such an unsatisfactory state of affairs could not continue and talk about developing 'universal' rules became widespread. The issue had already arisen at Cambridge University when in 1848 students arriving from Eton, Harrow, Rugby and other public schools had attempted to draw up a common set of rules so matches could be played at the university regardless of schooling. But the Cambridge rules existed only for its students and were not played beyond the university.

By 1863 there were so many adult clubs playing different types of rules across the country that the matter acquired a new urgency. It was this need for an answer to this problem that led to 11 London-based clubs meeting in October 1863 to discuss the formation of a 'football association' that would draw up a common set of rules that could be played by all footballers, regardless of schooling.

It was not quite that simple. Pride in the rules that they had played at school caused many of the delegates to reject compromise. Debates dragged on into the small hours, political manoeuvring dominated the proceedings and it took six meetings for the new Football Association (FA) to agree on a set of rules. In fact, at the end of the fourth meeting on 24 November 1863, the meeting voted for a set of rules that included the following:

> 9. A player shall be entitled to run with the ball towards his adversaries' goal if he makes a fair catch, or catches the ball on the first bound; but in the case of a fair catch, he makes his mark, he shall not run.
> 10. If any player shall run with the ball towards his adversaries' goal, any player in the opposite side shall be at liberty to charge, hold, trip or hack him, or wrest the ball from him; but no player shall be held and hacked at the same time.[9]

In short, they voted to play football along the lines played at Rugby School.

Ebenezer Morley, the Hull-born solicitor who had just been elected secretary of the FA, then proposed a motion to endorse the most recent version of Cambridge University's rules, which did not allow carrying the ball or hacking. Eight delegates supported Morley and a committee was set up to discuss this with the Cambridge footballers. The meeting was adjourned amid confusion about what exactly had been agreed.

Morley seems to have been a man who believed that the purpose of democracy was to allow everyone to vote until they agreed with him. At the following week's meeting, attended by only eight clubs, he omitted from the minutes the previous decision to endorse hacking. C. W. Alcock, who would eventually become the secretary of the FA and of Surrey County Cricket Club, proposed a motion to delete the previously agreed rules that allowed hacking and running with the ball. Like Morley, he favoured the Cambridge rules. Alcock's motion was carried, meaning that the FA had approved two counterposed sets of rules in consecutive meetings.[10]

Faced with such blatant manipulation, the clubs favouring rugby rules didn't bother to show up at the following week's meeting, which endorsed Morley and Alcock's non-carrying and non-hacking rules. The newly founded FA claimed 18 clubs as members but it seems that at least six of them, such as Blackheath, played rugby rules.[11] What's more, the FA's new rules still allowed outfield players to catch the ball before it bounced and take an unimpeded kick. Even the Royal Engineers, who played in four of the first seven FA Cup finals, still played their own code of football that allowed running with the ball.

In truth, the formation of the FA made little immediate difference to rugby or soccer clubs. It did lead to its game being called 'soccer', a shortening of 'association' in the same way that 'rugger' was derived from the word rugby, but by and large its formation was ignored by most clubs. Four years after it had been founded, the FA had just ten member clubs, nine in London plus Sheffield FC, which had its own rules anyway.

Rugby-playing clubs significantly outnumbered their rivals inside and outside the FA. In the first issue of C. W. Alcock's *Football Annual*, published in 1868 and the leading annual of the game for the next two decades, 45 of the 88 football clubs listed played according to the Rugby tradition. Thirty others played FA rules and 13 played the Sheffield version. And, of course, some clubs played both or a combination of both. Such was the dominance of the rugby code that in January 1871 *Bell's Life*, the premier sporting weekly of the time, pointed out that 'every year has increased the superiority in point of numbers and popularity of the rugby clubs over those who are subject to the rule of the Association'.[12]

The birth of the RFU

Why did rugby eclipse soccer and the other types of football? Alone of all the public school games, Rugby's was the one that flourished among adult clubs. The Eton, Winchester and Harrow football games did not become adult sports. The FA rule book was a compromise of rules and preferences that had no direct link to any public school game. Rugbeians stood firm in their absolute belief in the superiority of their rules.[13] They were so self-confident about the merits of their own game that they had no use for the FA – or any other organisation.

This supreme self-reliance only began to be questioned in 1870, and it was sparked by the Victorians' concern for health. In November 1870 *The Times* published a letter complaining about the numerous injuries caused by hacking during games of football at Rugby School.[14] Current and former pupils rushed to the defence of the school – and of hacking: one Old Rugbeian now at Trinity College, Oxford, called it 'entirely legitimate'. In early December public disquiet had become so vociferous that Rugby School's medical officer, Dr Robert Farquharson, admitted in a letter to *The Times* that a boy had been killed playing football at the school; the cause of death was not hacking but an abdominal injury caused by a collision with another player. Hacking, he claimed, was not responsible for any major injuries.

For the first time, rugby was the focus of public condemnation, and this criticism could not be dismissed as the carping of rival schools. As we have seen, many adult rugby clubs were also critical of hacking and refused to allow it. Clearly rugby had to put its house in order.

At the same time, the game also found itself challenged by an unexpected source: the Football Association. In 1870 the FA had organised two international games between England and Scotland. Outraged that soccer could claim to represent the English and Scottish nations, rugby players in Scotland challenged their English counterparts to a representative match. To organise an international match, however, a governing body was required.

In December 1870 Blackheath secretary Benjamin Burns and his Richmond counterpart Edwin Ash published a letter in *Bell's Life*. It read:

> An opinion has for some time prevailed among the supporters of Rugby Football that some fixed code of rules should be adopted by all clubs who profess to play the Rugby game, as at present the majority have altered in some slight way the rules as played at Rugby School by introducing fresh rules of their own. Each club plays according to its own rules on its own ground, and consequently the strangers in each match, finding themselves at once at a disadvantage through not knowing the rules of the ground, confusion and disputes are generally the result. We therefore hope that all clubs playing the Rugby game will join with us in framing a code of rules to be generally adopted.

It ended with an appeal for all those in agreement with its contents to contact the authors, who would arrange a meeting to establish such a code of rules.[15]

The sense of common purpose that existed in the rugby fraternity can be gauged by the fact that, while it took the FA six long meetings to reach a somewhat hollow agreement, the founding meeting of the Rugby Football Union (RFU) on 26 January 1871 lasted a mere two hours. Edwin Ash welcomed the attendees by explaining that their goal was to 'frame a code of football based upon the Rugby system of play'. The 32 delegates representing 21 clubs agreed a constitution and appointed a sub-committee of three, all former pupils of Rugby School, to draw up the grandiosely titled 'Laws of the Game'.[16]

The committee reported back promptly and in June the new code was agreed. To answer rugby's critics, law 57 of the new rule book outlawed all forms of hacking and law 58 forbade the use of 'projecting nails, iron plates or gutta percha' on boots.[17]

The first committee of the RFU drew its members from a narrow and close-knit stratum of south-east England's professional upper middle classes. All 14 had attended public school: six had gone to Rugby and the others to Wellington, Tonbridge, Lancing and Marlborough. Seven were solicitors, two were brokers and the others were a doctor, accountant and military instructor. All lived in central or south London, except the Wellington College representative who lived at the school. The eldest was 29 and the youngest 20. In essence, this was a young gentlemen's club, one of the many that emerged in mid-Victorian Britain.

It proved to be remarkably successful. By 1875, the RFU was staging regular internationals against Scotland and Ireland, held an annual North versus South match and its membership had grown fivefold to 113 clubs, 21 of them in the North of England.[18] As with the school from which its sport emerged, the RFU was now exerting an influence throughout the 'whole Kingdom'.

The birth of a ball

The Victorians' concern for health had one other notable consequence for rugby. The importance of the game for Rugby School created a minor industry of ball manufacturing in the town. William Gilbert was a local cobbler whose boots and shoes were favourites of the pupils, not least because his shop was just across the road from the school. By the 1820s he was also making balls. The quality of the Gilbert football became so well regarded that in 1851 he exhibited two Rugby School balls, or 'educational appliances', as they were catalogued, at the Great Exhibition in London.[19]

Gilbert's early balls were not shaped in the way we know them today. Rugby balls tended to be much rounder than modern ones. Neither were soccer balls the perfect spheres of today. Both rugby and soccer balls resembled the shape of a plum more than they did their later distinctive shapes. Indeed, the shape of the rugby ball did not become settled until uniformity was forced on clubs by the emergence of inter-city matches and cup competitions in the 1860s and 1870s, and it was not until 1892 that the RFU's rules officially specified that an oval ball should be used for matches.

The manufacture of a uniform oval ball only occurred as the result of a major technological breakthrough, not from Gilbert but from his great local rival, Richard Lindon. Lindon may have begun his working life as Gilbert's apprentice, but in the spirit of competition that rugby itself taught he set up a shop a few doors down from his former employer.[20] By 1861 he had become so successful that he was supplying balls to Oxford, Cambridge and Dublin universities.

Lindon's success came at great personal cost. The first balls were made from a pig's bladder encased in leather panels. Inflating the ball had to be done by mouth – a dangerous procedure given the risk of infection from the dead animal. The task of blowing up the balls fell to Lindon's wife, Rebecca, in addition to her duties as the mother of his seventeen children. She eventually contracted a lung disease, fell ill and died.

Perhaps driven by his wife's tragic death, in 1862 Lindon invented a way to use a bladder made from rubber rather than a pig. His innovation was based on one of the great discoveries of the Victorian industrial age, vulcanisation, which made rubber more pliable and adaptable for a huge range of uses. At the same time, Lindon also developed a brass inflator which made it easier and much less dangerous to inflate balls. It also made it possible to produce standardised shapes for balls. The modern oval ball had been invented.

Richard Lindon's crucial place in the history of rugby is almost forgotten. He failed to understand the rules of the game of the intensely competitive world of business and did not patent his inventions. He did not become enormously wealthy. His quest to create a modern rugby ball not only lost him his wife, but left him devoid of the riches to which his inventions should have entitled him.

Yet he was the man who quite literally shaped the future of rugby.

4

RUGBY'S GREAT SPLIT

Dicky Lockwood was on trial. Again. For the second time in less than two years he faced charges so serious that they threatened to end his rugby career.

And what a career it was. He had made his first-class debut on the wing for Dewsbury at the age of 16. He was selected for England at 19. He captained Yorkshire to three successive county championships and introduced the Welsh four three-quarter system to England. In 1894 he captained England to victory against Wales, scoring a try and kicking three conversions.

Lockwood was a sporting superstar before the word was invented. Just five feet four and a half inches tall, he was acclaimed as 'Little Dick, the World's Wonder' and 'the Little Maestro'. Leaving Dewsbury's ground after a blinding display against Wakefield Trinity, he was, local newspapers reported, 'mobbed by a vast crowd which, contracting as the road narrowed, actually pushed down a strong stone wall and then shoved a hawker and a little lad through the aperture into the field below'.[1]

His photograph was sold outside grounds and in shops for one shilling, one penny, almost one-eighth of the nine shillings a week that Dicky was paid as a woollen printer in a local textile mill. When he was carried from the field with a broken collarbone playing for England against Ireland in Dublin in February 1887, Dewsbury was flooded with wild rumours that he had died. Hundreds waited through the night at the railway station to see him come home, just to reassure themselves that their 'Little Wonder' was still alive.

Now all that was in jeopardy.

His crime was the most serious in the rugby rule book. The punishment could be suspension or even complete banishment from the game he loved. If there was enough evidence, the Rugby Football Union (RFU) could expel his club from the sport permanently. He was facing the sporting equivalent of the death penalty.

His offence? He had been accused of professionalism – and if found guilty faced expulsion from the game he loved.

'A people who are one and all enthusiasts at the game'

Lockwood was a symbol of how dramatically rugby had changed since the RFU was formed in 1871. By the early 1880s the game had become the passion not merely of those with a public school background, but of great swathes of the population, from dockers to doctors, labourers to lawyers, factory workers to financiers, and almost everyone else in between.

Clubs were formed all over England. Manchester (1860), Bradford (1863), Leeds (1864), Bath (1865), Exeter (1871), Wigan (1872), St Helens (1873), Gloucester (1873), Coventry (1874) Leicester (1880) and Northampton (1880) were just some of the most prominent teams that have survived to the present day. There were hundreds of other local teams, often based on streets, churches, pubs and workplaces that did not enjoy such longevity or fame. Rugby, as *The Times* pointed out in 1880, was on the crest of a wave: 'the players of the rugby union game are probably twice as numerous as those of the [Football] Association ... In the North, the Leeds, Wakefield and Manchester clubs are prominent among a people who are one and all enthusiasts at the game.'[2]

Much of this interest was stimulated by the growing number of county cup competitions that began in the late 1870s: in Cheshire in

1877, in Durham and Northumberland in 1881, and in Cumberland in 1882. In Cornwall in 1877 Penryn were proclaimed county champions after losing only one match all season, a Devon cup began in 1887 and a cup competition was organised by the Midland Counties Rugby Union in 1882. In 1888, 14,000 watched the Midland Counties cup final between Coventry and Burton. Cup tournaments began in 1889 in Hampshire and in Kent in 1891. More often than not, the organisation of a cup competition coincided with the formation of a county rugby union. By 1885 there were more than a dozen county unions affiliated to the RFU.[3]

But the most successful county cup competition was undoubtedly the Yorkshire Cup. It kicked off in 1877 and crowds poured into grounds to watch it. In the first round, 8,000 people turned out at Halifax to see them defeat Wakefield. From that point, rugby fever gripped the county. The following season 12,000 people shoehorned themselves into the same ground to see Wakefield defeat Kirkstall in the final. Crowds increased year upon year. Across the Pennines in Lancashire rugby dominated the winter sporting scene. Not only did spectators flock to the new competition, but thousands of young men were also inspired to play the game.

Dicky Lockwood was one of those young men. Born into a working-class family near Wakefield in November 1867, he had played with local teams as a boy where his talent was quickly recognised. In 1884 he was invited to play for Dewsbury, just a few days short of his 17th birthday. In those days Dewsbury were one of the game's leading sides, led by local factory owner and future RFU president Mark Newsome.

Even at this early age Lockwood was well on his way to becoming the complete rugby player. He was brilliant in attack, deadly in the tackle and precise in his kicking, with a knack of being in the right place at the right time. Despite his short stature he combined both lightning speed and punishing strength. Less than two years after his first appearance for Dewsbury he was selected for the first of his 46 appearances for the Yorkshire county side. Shortly after his 19th birthday, in January 1887, he achieved his ultimate ambition when he made his England debut against Wales at Llanelli. He went on to equal E. T. Gurdon's record of 14 England caps and in 1894 captained England to one of their greatest victories when they routed Wales using Wales' own four three-quarter system for the first time.

Dicky's pre-eminence symbolised the growing influence of players from the north of England within English rugby. In 1889 the RFU began a new county championship tournament. In its first eight seasons, it was won seven times by Yorkshire and once by Lancashire. And by the early 1890s England were increasingly reliant on northern players. The 1892 England side, which did the 'Grand Slam' to win the Home Nations Championship (as the forerunner of today's Six Nations was called) for the first time since 1884, never had less than eight northerners in the team, and the team that defeated Scotland in the final match of that season's championship had ten.

This created a problem. As one writer of the time put it, the leaders of the RFU had 'learned the game with their Latin grammar'. But now rugby was being dominated by players from very different backgrounds. These were men whose schooling had ended before they were teenagers, who had been taught the lessons of life in a factory, down a mine or on the docks, and who had learned to play rugby on back streets, wasteland and public parks.

At first, the newcomers were welcomed by the leaders of the RFU as an opportunity to pass on the moral lessons of rugby, but it rapidly became clear that working-class players had a sporting philosophy of their own. First and foremost was an expectation of reward for results. The first rumours of payments to players in rugby emerged in the late 1870s. The first paid player for whom records survive was C. E. 'Teddy' Bartram, a dazzling three-quarter, who in 1881 was appointed assistant secretary of Wakefield Trinity for an annual salary of £52, although his duties were negligible – the provision of such a sinecure being a common way for amateur county cricketers to be paid for playing while retaining their amateur status.

It wasn't just payments to players that concerned the RFU leadership. Working-class crowds jeered and booed opposing players and match officials, a custom that many rugby traditionalists found deeply offensive. Perhaps worst of all, working-class teams soon began to display a mastery of rugby which meant they often triumphed over their supposed social superiors. This was not the way the game was supposed to be.

By 1886 this frustration had turned to alarm. Thanks to soccer, the leaders of the RFU had seen the future and they did not like it. In early 1885 the Football Association legalised professionalism and within a matter of 18 months professional teams from working-class industrial cities were dominating the game, pushing aside clubs like the Old Etonians and the Royal Engineers that had ruled the FA Cup since its inception in 1871. The problem – and a solution – was spelt out with characteristic bluntness by Arthur Budd, a solicitor turned doctor who became president of the RFU:

> Only six months after the legitimisation of the bastard [of professionalism] we see two professional teams left to fight out the final [FA] cup tie. To what does this all end? Why this – gentlemen who play football once a week as a pastime will find themselves no match for men who give up their whole time and abilities to it. How should they? One by one, as they find themselves outclassed, they will desert the game and leave the field to professionals ... The Rugby Union committee finding themselves face to face with the hydra have determined to throttle it before he is big enough to throttle them. ... No mercy but iron rigour will be dealt out.[4]

For Victorian middle-class men like Budd, the word 'professional' invariably meant 'working-class', and so to curb the threat of working-class players and avoid the fate of soccer, the leaders of the RFU decided to outlaw payments to players. By banning payments and other incentives, they hoped to stem the flood of working-class players into the game.

In October 1886 the annual general meeting of the RFU voted to ban all forms of payment to players, whether in cash or kind. Rugby was now an amateur sport. All accusations of players receiving, asking for or being offered payments would be investigated and, if found guilty, the accused would be suspended or expelled from the game. Yorkshire's Harry Garnett, who became RFU president in 1889, captured the mood of rugby's leaders: 'If working men desired to play [rugby] football, they should pay for it themselves, as they would have to do with any other pastime.'[5]

And that was to lead to Dicky Lockwood standing trial to save his career.

Rugby's Witchfinder General

In 1889 Lockwood transferred from Dewsbury to Heckmondwike. His new club, based in a small town south of Bradford, had recruited a roster of star players, including two other England internationals, many of whom also found jobs in the town's textile factories. Rumours abounded that Lockwood was also being illegally paid by the club. The leaders of rugby in Yorkshire launched an investigation into the transfer and Dicky was called before the Yorkshire Rugby Union committee to answer the charge that he was secretly a professional.

The prosecution was conducted by the Rev. Frank Marshall. Born in West Bromwich and educated at Cambridge, he had moved to Huddersfield in 1878 to take up the post of headmaster of the local Almondbury Grammar School. Self-important and extravagantly bearded, he soon became president of the Yorkshire Rugby Union. For him, rugby was a way of instilling Muscular Christian morality into the young men who played it.[6]

The decisive trial took place in September 1889 and lasted three days. It proved to be a battle of wits that resembled a classic chess match. There were no legal representatives; each man spoke for himself. The

Cambridge-educated clergymen, author of textbooks on Shakespeare, Sir Walter Scott, Euclid and the Bible, came face-to-face with a factory labourer from the mining village of Crigglestone.

It was not as easy as Marshall imagined. Slowly, it became apparent that he had no conclusive evidence and that his questioning was merely designed to browbeat Dicky into a confession. When he ended his cross-examination, it was clear that Marshall's case had no substance and Dicky was cleared of the charge of professionalism.

Within minutes of the decision, telegraph operators relayed the news to every rugby-playing town and village in Yorkshire. In Heckmondwike hundreds of supporters gathered in the town's market place in anticipation of the decision. When the telegram was read out to the crowd, the news 'was received with an outburst of cheering, the gathering in all respects resembling those witnessed at an exciting political election'. This was about more than a popular player; this was a victory over the establishment.[7]

Other players were not so lucky. Wakefield Trinity's Teddy Bartram was banned for life at the twilight of an illustrious career for receiving a non-repayable 'loan' from the club. George Broadbent of Holbeck was investigated for allegedly receiving wedding presents from his club. Clubs also felt the whip of amateur discipline. Heckmondwike, Leeds Parish Church, Leeds St John's, Wakefield Trinity, Cleckheaton and Brighouse Rangers were all suspended for months for breaching the amateur code. Across in Lancashire, Werneth, a town near Oldham, found themselves suspended for four months for providing a job in an ironworks for England international Abe Ashworth.

This constant turmoil undermined the credibility of rugby. Accusations of professionalism could mean that a club could no longer be certain that their star players could play in the next match. Worse, an accused team itself could no longer be sure that it would play its next match, and even those sides with a clear conscience could suddenly find themselves without a game if their opponents were accused of professionalism. For clubs that had invested thousands in grounds, grandstands and facilities, such arbitrary and unexpected interruptions to their cashflow could not be tolerated.

The pitiless pursuit of professionalism also caused rugby to fall behind soccer. As one concerned rugby fan wrote to his local newspaper in 1890, 'the association game is slowly but surely taking our best men, as it is only likely that they will play where they can be paid'.[8] When Heckmondwike were suspended in 1889, their England international three-quarter John Sutcliffe decided to switch to soccer and signed for Bolton Wanderers. He eventually became one of only three men to be capped for England in both codes.

As the 1890s began, rugby was wracked by civil war over the question of amateurism. On one side were those clubs in the north of England whose players and spectators were predominantly from the industrial working classes. On the other was the leadership of the RFU, supported by clubs who shared their belief that rugby was a game for young men who shared the values of the public schools. The territory they fought over was the moral high ground of whether it was better to play the game for no reward, or to allow players to benefit from their rugby talents.

This clash of cultures could not last. Something had to be done to rescue rugby from itself.

Mr Miller makes his mark

Of course there were similar tensions wherever rugby was played by different classes. In the south-west of England rumours abounded of under-the-counter payments to players. Gloucester and Torquay were both found guilty of breaches of the amateur regulations in the 1890s. In the Midlands, Leicester, Coventry and Northampton had long been suspected of paying players and offering jobs to players they wished to recruit. Leicester were investigated for professionalism in 1896 and its local league structure was awash with allegations of players receiving gifts and remuneration.[9] In South Wales, 'boot money' payments to players was an open secret.

The situation in the north of England was different. The sheer number of rugby clubs in Yorkshire and Lancashire posed a threat to the RFU, which feared that the two counties could eventually outvote the supporters of amateurism. There was real substance to this fear. In 1895, the RFU had 416 adult clubs in membership, with Yorkshire and Lancashire accounting for almost 48 per cent. There were also many other clubs in both counties which were not members of the RFU. If the northerners organised themselves, the leaders of the RFU feared they would be ousted by men who favoured broken-time payments and the game would abandon the values that it had inherited from Rugby School.

James Miller was the man who put himself at the head of the north's reform movement. A science teacher, he was also devoted to rugby, representing Yorkshire five times before becoming a dynamic and far-sighted administrator of the game.

In 1891 he proposed that players who lost wages because they took time off from work to play rugby should be compensated by what were known as 'broken-time' payments. Rugby, he told a meeting in the spring of 1891, 'is no longer the pastime of the public schools and the leisured classes alone; it has become the sport of the masses – of the wage-earning classes in our great manufacturing centres, … It is unfair to expect working men to break time to play football without their being remunerated.'[10] Broken-time payments, he hoped, were the sensible middle ground between amateur zealotry and untrammelled professionalism.

Miller's ideas for reforming rugby didn't stop with relaxing its amateur rules. In the same year, he also called for rugby to move to 13-a-side. By reducing the number of players on the field, he argued that the fast and free-flowing four three-quarters system of the Welsh that Dicky

Lockwood had introduced to the Yorkshire team would reach its full potential. And, he argued, making the game more spectacular would also help to counter the threat of soccer.

There was only one problem. The leadership of the RFU had no desire to change the way the game was played. Many, like Arthur Budd, disliked the four three-quarter system anyway, and they had no intention of compromising on amateurism. Ultimately, the leaders of the RFU would prefer to see the game split rather than compromise over the question of amateurism. As the England cricketer and Cambridge rugger blue Frank Mitchell argued, if the working-class player 'cannot play the game for the game itself, he can have no true interest in it, and it were better that he left us'.[11]

The decisive battle of the civil war took place in September 1893 at the RFU's annual general meeting at the Westminster Palace Hotel in London. The two opposing sides marshalled their supporters like armies mobilising for victory. *Pastime*, the weekly magazine edited by N. L. Jackson of Corinthians FC, devoted its front page to the simple headline 'All Hands', calling on all supporters of amateurism to make sure that their club sent a delegate to the meeting. In Yorkshire, a special train of 12 coaches was chartered for delegates, who paid ten shillings for the day trip and were picked up at 11 towns on the way.

When James Miller strode to the podium to propose the motion that 'players be allowed compensation for bona-fide loss of time' the atmosphere crackled with anticipation. Everyone knew that this was the most decisive moment in the game's short history. There was no room for compromise, no turning back for either side. By the end of the meeting, the fate of rugby would be sealed.

Times had changed, argued Miller. Why, he asked, should not these men be recompensed for the loss of wages they suffered through playing rugby? He highlighted the case of Bramley's England international forward Harry Bradshaw. Bradshaw had played in England's victory over Ireland at Lansdowne Road earlier that year. Although his travel and hotel expenses had been paid, he still had to take three days' unpaid leave from his job in a textile factory in Leeds. Miller's message was simple: 'why should not the working man be able to play the game on level terms with the gentleman?'[12]

The opposition's major speaker was Newcastle businessman William Cail. He argued that to legalise payments to players would lead to them being bought and sold like cattle, as was the case in soccer. When the Rev. Frank Marshall took the floor to speak, he point blank told the delegates from the north that if they wanted to pay players they should leave and form their own rugby union, a view repeated by RFU secretary Rowland Hill.

The mood of the meeting was not one of compromise. The amateurs had mobilised their supporters and took advantage of the RFU's numerous school and college clubs to boost their voting bloc. When it was announced that the proposal to allow broken-time payments had lost by 282 votes to 136, there was little surprise but much anger. The gloves were off. It was no longer a case of *if* rugby was going to split, but *when*.

Endgame

Barely three months after the momentous 1893 meeting Dicky Lockwood led England on to the field against Wales for their opening match of the 1894 Home Nations Championship. The Welsh had run away with the championship in 1893, defeating the three other nations to win what had become known as the Triple Crown by employing their revolutionary four three-quarters system, and most observers expected them to do the same again. But things turned out to be very different.

As captain, Lockwood persuaded England to adopt the Welsh four three-quarters system for the first time. Alongside him in the line was Halifax flyer Fred Firth and West Hartlepool sensation Sammy Morfitt.

The forwards boasted Yorkshire powerhouses Harry Bradshaw, Jack Toothill, Harry Speed and Tom Broadley. The combination of speed, power and brains blew the Welsh apart. Morfitt, in his first England match, scored the opening try. Bradshaw then barrelled his way over the line before Firth twice slashed through the Welsh defence to set up tries for Lockwood and the Geordie scrum-half Billy Taylor.

By the time Newport's Fred Parfitt scored a consolation try near the end of the match the English players were already celebrating their 24-3 victory, the highest score by England since the very first Anglo-Welsh game in 1881. It was the crowning moment of Dicky's career. He completely overshadowed Welsh captain Arthur Gould 'with merciless persistency, and in all his long career Lockwood has never played with greater judgement or effect,' wrote one newspaper.[13]

It was perhaps also England's greatest ever victory, but it also marked the end of an era. By the time the sides met again on English soil, Lockwood, Firth, Toothill and Bradshaw had been banned for life by the RFU, with Morfitt, Speed and Broadley sharing the same fate shortly after. The national side would win only three of their next 15 matches with Wales. But unlike most sporting setbacks and slumps, the collapse in England's fortunes had little to do with events on the field and everything to do with happenings off it.

The defeat of the broken-time proposal had put both camps on a war footing. In August 1894 the stand-off finally erupted into open warfare. The Lancashire Rugby Union charged Leigh with paying two of its Welsh players. Found guilty, they were suspended for ten weeks, placed at the bottom of the championship table and forbidden from charging admission to any matches rearranged due to the suspension. Three weeks later, Salford suffered the same treatment. In November Wigan, too, suffered an identical fate. Swinton, Tyldesley, Broughton Rangers and Rochdale Hornets then found themselves under investigation. The season had been reduced to farce, crippling clubs financially and causing supporters to despair.

In summer 1895 the RFU provocatively announced that from September all clubs and players accused of professionalism would be assumed guilty until proven innocent. Knowing that they were about to be picked off one-by-one, the leading northern clubs made their move. With clubs travelling from as far away as Widnes in the west and Hull in the east, they decided to meet at Huddersfield's George Hotel on the evening of Thursday, 29 August.

On the stroke of 6.30 p.m. officials from Batley, Bradford, Brighouse Rangers, Broughton Rangers, Halifax, Huddersfield, Hull, Hunslet, Leeds, Leigh, Liversedge, Manningham, Oldham, Rochdale Hornets, St Helens, Tyldesley, Wakefield Trinity, Warrington, Widnes and Wigan voted to 'form a Northern Rugby Football Union, and pledged themselves to push forward, without delay, its establishment on the principle of payment for bona-fide broken-time only'. Rugby would never be the same.

The following Saturday, the new league of the Northern Union kicked off, featuring 22 of the best teams in the north. By the end of the decade they would be joined by almost every rugby club in Cumbria, Lancashire and Yorkshire.

Life would never be the same for Dicky Lockwood and James Miller. To no one's surprise, immediately after the split Lockwood joined the rebels and transferred to Wakefield Trinity, where he captained the side and at last had the opportunity to be openly and honestly paid for his rugby talents.

In 1897, however, he was declared bankrupt when the pub he managed ran into financial difficulties; he was forced to sell all his household furniture and take up manual work once more. In 1900 he returned to play for Dewsbury, eventually retiring in 1903. Just 12 years later he died after a second operation for cancer, one day short of his 48th birthday. The Little Maestro became the forgotten genius of English rugby union, his feats forgotten, his reputation ignored.

The same fate befell James Miller, although for different reasons. After his broken-time proposal was defeated in 1893, his reforming zeal faded. He opposed the 1895 split and in the years that followed became one of the most vociferous supporters of pure amateurism. After many years on the Yorkshire Rugby Union committee he was elected treasurer in 1922. It was to be his downfall. Unbeknownst to his colleagues he embezzled over £1,000 from them over the next four years. Justice eventually caught up with him and in 1927 he was sentenced to six months' imprisonment for theft. His life had been shaped and then shattered by the question of money.

The same was also true of rugby.

PART II

TOWARDS FIVE NATIONS

Rugby was not, and could not be, confined to England. The Scots could claim a rugby heritage almost as venerable as that south of the border. In Ireland the game would acquire a unique status across communities and, eventually, a border. And for the Welsh, rugby would become as much a part of the national culture as the National Eisteddfod, Augustus John and Dylan Thomas.

Like no other sport, rugby both encouraged national rivalries yet brought the nations of the British Isles closer together. International matches became an arena where patriotism was played out but politics put aside.

And when France was invited to become part of this British club in 1910, it brought with it new ways of approaching the game and older, deeper and more historic rivalries. Rugby was no longer the sole property of the Anglo-Saxon and Celt.

5

SCOTLAND: 'RUGBY FOOTBALL: THE REAL GAME OF THE TWO COUNTRIES'

They say Edinburgh is at its most magnificent in the spring. Fine, bright and freshened by a pleasant easterly wind, Monday, 27 March 1871 justified its reputation, as if to welcome the historic event that the city would soon witness.

For it would be here, at around three o'clock that afternoon, that Scotland would play England for the very first time, and international rugby was born.

As with most of the key developments in rugby history, the origins of the match were not straightforward. In fact, the real impetus came not from within rugby circles, but from soccer. In March 1870 England played Scotland for the first time in an unofficial soccer international at the Kennington Oval in London. It resulted in a 1-1 draw but was deemed such a success that another match was played in November of the same year. This time Scotland were beaten 1-0. More importantly, it led to a wave of complaints about the match by Scottish adherents of the rugby code.

It wasn't difficult for them to find things to criticise. The Scotland soccer team in the first match had fielded only one Scottish-born player. The side in the second had just three. Charles Nepean, who turned out for the Scots in the second match, was deemed eligible for selection on the grounds that his cousin had married a Scot. Not only was the soccer side accused of being unrepresentative by the rugby men, they also denied that soccer was an authentic Scottish sport. H. H. Almond dismissed the 11-a-side game as 'a modification of the parent code'. Backing him up, *Bell's Life* declared, incorrectly as it turned out, that 'Scotland does not own a single club patronising the dribbling code'.[1] But what really rankled with the Scots was that the soccer team could not defeat the English. As the great Scottish forward R. W. 'Bulldog' Irvine would later say, rugby's supporters felt that it fell to them to 'defend the honour of Scotland'.[2]

So, in the second week of December 1870, the captains of the five leading Scottish rugby clubs issued a challenge to 'any team selected from the whole of England, to play us a match, twenty-a-side, Rugby rules, either in Glasgow or Edinburgh, on any day during the present season'.[3] They argued that soccer rules could not be deemed a true test of the footballing prowess of the Scots because so few clubs played the game north of the border. The challenge ended with a promise of a 'hearty welcome and a first-rate match'.

There was a positive response from Blackheath secretary Ben Burns, who, although living in London, had been born in Perth and educated at Edinburgh Academy, and the date of the match was set for the last Monday in March. England were to be captained by Blackheath's Frederick Stokes, a young London solicitor who had been educated at Rugby School. Frank Moncreiff, an accountant in Edinburgh who was the son of the Lord Advocate of Scotland, would have the honour of being the Scots' first ever national captain.

As the big day approached, the England players travelled up from London, Manchester and Liverpool and arrived in Edinburgh on the Sunday morning before the match. They spent the afternoon taking in the air at Arthur's Seat and Calton Hill, before turning their thoughts to Monday's challenge. Despite the fact that the England 20 had been selected from ten different clubs, it doesn't appear to have occurred to anyone that a training session before the match might have been useful. Indeed, the morning of the game was spent having photographs taken at Ross and Pringle's in Edinburgh's George Street.

In contrast, the Scots left nothing to chance. They had held two trial matches to decide on their line-up. They also insisted that, unlike the recent England versus Scotland soccer internationals, players had to be born in the country they represented. Even so, England fielded the same Ben Burns from Blackheath – a last-minute replacement for Oxford University's Frank Isherwood who failed to travel up to Edinburgh – and the Scots selected Northumberland's Tom Marshall. Yet no one could claim that, even with these anomalies, the teams were not representative.

As with the English side, the Scots players were drawn entirely from the privately educated professional middle classes. Between them, the two sides fielded seven solicitors and half a dozen bankers and stockbrokers. One player, Scotland's Alfred Clunies-Ross, was the scion of the ruling family of the Cocos Islands.[4] On the day of the match, the high social tone of the occasion was emphasised by the fact that the man collecting the one shilling admission money from the enthusiastic crowd was John MacDonald, the future Lord Kingsburgh, Lord Justice Clerk of Scotland.

He had his work cut out. Estimates of the crowd in the press ranged from four to eight thousand. Well-dressed spectators from Glasgow poured out of trains and made their way from Princes Street to the ground at Raeburn Place, home of the Edinburgh Academicals rugby and cricket teams. Nor was the crowd restricted to men. 'Many a fair lassie's brown eyes sparkled with enthusiasm as she foretold the triumph of the thistle,' reported *Bell's Life*.[5] The crowd was packed on all sides, while many spectators watched from the hill. A crackle of anticipation was in the air.

At 3.30 p.m. the teams appeared and the honour of kicking off the first ever international fell to the Scottish captain. England, wearing white shirts with a red rose, played with 13 forwards, three half-backs, three full-backs and just one three-quarter. The Scots, starting a tradition of forward play that would last for the next century, dispensed with the three-quarter and played with 14 forwards. As well as an extra man in the pack, the Scottish forwards were also heavier than England's, with an average weight of 12 stones, three pounds each. They were also much more skilled at dribbling the ball on the ground, something that would be a feature of Scottish play for the next 60 years, but was also, noted *Bell's Life*, a 'feature of the game rarely seen round London'.

This advantage in the forwards paid dividends when, after a scoreless first half, Angus Buchanan, a forward from Edinburgh's Royal High School Former Pupils, scored a pushover try, much to the chagrin of the English players who felt that the ball had not been grounded. England responded when Clapham Rovers' Reginald Birkett went over for a try in the corner but almost on full-time the Scots made sure of victory with a try from one of their three half-backs, William Cross, who, had there been a man of the match, would undoubtedly have been named it for his 'brilliant all-round game'.[6] After 100 minutes of battle – each half lasted 50 minutes, as it would not be until 1926 that 80 minutes became the standard length of a match – the honours had fallen to the Scots.[7]

As would be the case for the entire subsequent history of Anglo-Scottish internationals, the losers attributed their misfortune to the perfidiousness of the match officials. Future RFU president Arthur Guillemard blamed the narrow pitch – it was only 55 yards wide rather than the standard 70 yards used in England – for England's defeat. But most importantly, he claimed that both of Scotland's tries should not have been allowed because of illegal build-up play.[8] The ubiquitous H. H. Almond, the Scots' appointed umpire, overruled English protests, despite admitting he was unsighted for the first try. Nor did he take kindly to English players appealing to him to change his mind.[9] It would not be the last time that a match official ruled against the side making the most noise.

Almond made one other crucial decision in the match. Midway through the game, according to Irvine, some of the players on both sides asked to be allowed to hack. The two captains, Scotland's Honourable Francis Moncrieff and England's Frederick Stokes, 'both looked as if they ought to say no and would rather like to say yes', but Almond stood firm, telling the players that he would walk off the field if they started to hack.[10] If he had been less decisive and allowed hacking in an international match, the course of rugby history may have been different.

The following day the match ball was decorated with ribbons and displayed in Johnnie Bowton's confectionary shop in Hamilton Place, just around the corner from Raeburn Place. It symbolised the role that the match had played in propelling rugby into Scottish culture, lifting it 'from a parochial to a national, or, it might justifiably be claimed, to a universal position'.[11]

The importance of rugby, and especially international rugby, to the Scottish middle classes symbolised the complex relationship between the Scots and the English in the mid-Victorian era. On one hand, Scotland seemed to be moving towards assimilation with the south. The Scotch [sic] Education Department, established a year after that first rugby international, was based in London. Numerous members of the Scottish ruling elite were educated at English public schools and universities, and many went on to pursue military careers with English regiments. There were even calls for Scotland's unique legal system to be brought into line with England's to foster greater economic integration.[12]

Yet on the other hand, the sense of Scottish national identity and distinctiveness did not diminish. Despite the encroachments of Westminster, Scottish politics remained largely in the hands of the Scots. Even the sentimental and clichéd popular art and literature featuring a never-ending stream of highland stags and kilted lairds reflected a Scottishness that may have been nostalgic for a mythical past, but was still fiercely Scottish. Most importantly, despite the apparent integration into English culture and politics, Scottish businessmen, politicians and administrators saw themselves as equal partners of the English in the creation of the British Empire. This alliance was sealed by the extraordinary wealth that accrued to them from Britain's global dominance. Britain, its culture, its politics and its successes, were as much the creation of the Scots as of the English.

This was precisely how the rugby-loving professional and administrative classes of Glasgow and Edinburgh saw their relationship with English rugby. Looking back on the first rugby internationals from the 1920s, R. J. Phillips described how, 'fifty years ago racial difference between the countries was more pronounced ... Scottish patriotism was a very real and live thing'.[13] The Scots believed themselves to be equal partners in the development and protection of the game.

Rugby had a similar lineage on both sides of the border. As in England, the impetus for the development of Scottish rugby had come from elite private schools. Edinburgh Academy (founded in 1824), Loretto (1827), Merchiston Castle (1833) and Glasgow Academy (1845) not only educated young Scots for the challenges of a burgeoning economy and an expanding empire, but were also cradles of rugby. Edinburgh High School had played a type of traditional football as early 1810 and a 'football' club had been formed at Edinburgh University in December 1824. The university club's rules were typically vague, although hacking and tripping were banned.[14] Like other clubs of the time, the university side was short-lived, lasting just eight years. But it was the game played at Edinburgh Academy that provided the groundwork for rugby.

The boys appear to have played some kind of football game since the creation of the school in 1824. By the 1840s its matches bore more than a passing resemblance to those played at Rugby School. One old boy recalled that 'the most cruel hacking with iron-toed and -heeled boots was allowed and suffered in what was called a "muddle" – the modern maul'.[15] In the mid-1850s, allegedly inspired by Francis Crombie, a pupil who had moved there from Durham School, a version of Rugby

School rules was adopted. Francis became school captain and his elder brother Alexander played a central role in establishing Edinburgh Academical Football Club in 1857. Spurred by the evangelical zeal of the 'Accies', as they would become known and, as in England, the mania for Muscular Christianity rugby matches began to take place regularly between elite Scottish schools.

In 1858, the first of what would become an annual match between the school and Merchiston took place. By 1870, there were ten senior clubs regularly playing rugby football in Scotland. Foremost among them were the former pupils sides, Edinburgh Academicals, Glasgow Academicals, Merchistonians and Royal High School Former Pupils (FPs), the universities of Edinburgh, Glasgow and St Andrews, plus Edinburgh Wanderers, Roland's Rooms (a fencing and gymnasium club in Edinburgh), and West of Scotland, as well as another six clubs that played irregular fixtures. Eight schools had taken up the game as part of their curriculum.[16]

As might be expected, Scottish rugby did not lack for confidence. In a number of ways it actually led the English. In 1867, four years before the formation of the RFU and the creation of a common rule book for English rugby clubs, the Accies decided to push for a unified set of rules for all Scottish sides. The aim, as with the Football Association in England, was to overcome difficulties that arose when two clubs with different rules or interpretations faced each other. Promoted by H. H. Almond, the unified rules were agreed and printed in a green-covered booklet, *The Laws of Football as Played by the Principal Clubs of Scotland*, in the spring of 1868.

Although no copy of the *Green Book*, as it was known, seems to have survived, it may well be that the first international match was played according to its rules. This would account for the disquiet of the English side about the game. For example, the narrow pitch seems to have been the norm. The ball had to be thrown into the line-out at the point that it crossed the touchline, unlike in England at the time where it was taken from wherever the thrower-in picked the ball up.[17] The Scots also called their half-backs 'quarter-backs', a tradition that would be continued in American football.

Some of the Scots' innovations, such as the position of the line-out throw, were later incorporated into the rules of the RFU. Edinburgh clubs had even discussed counting tries as part of the scoring system in the 1860s, something that was only included in the RFU's rules in 1875. Most significantly, in December 1871, the Scots were also involved in one of the first senior matches to be played 15-a-side, when the touring West of Scotland defeated the North of Ireland club by a goal to nil in Belfast.[18] This was more than five years before the official end of 20-a-side matches.

Given the dynamism and independent-mindedness of Scottish rugby, it should not be surprising that some of its leaders came to regret that when the Scottish Football Union (as the Scottish Rugby Union was called until 1924) was formed in March 1873 it simply accepted the RFU's rulebook. As the wily H. H. Almond pointed out, this not only restricted the ability of the Scots to implement their own ideas about the game, but also inadvertently gave the English the sole right to arbitrate on controversies about the rules of rugby. This would become a running sore in subsequent decades.

The next Scotland versus England match was played in London in February 1872 when England regained their honour with a two goals to one victory at the Kennington Oval. It was a match notable for a Scottish player having his kit torn in a tackle and being forced to wear a mackintosh to cover his embarrassment as he ran to the pavilion for a new pair of shorts.[19] When the two sides met again in 1873 it would be in Glasgow, one of only two matches that England would ever play in that city. It was not a pretty sight. Played on a mudheap in heavy rain at Hamilton Crescent cricket ground, it was held by some as being the match responsible for the subsequent popularity of soccer in the city, such was the dire quality of the play.

The match also established the tradition of drunken antics that would become euphemistically known as 'high jinks' when an unnamed English forward was found drunkenly driving a mail cart to the railway station in the wee hours of the morning after the match. Fortunately his teammates persuaded him to leave the cart and go back to the hotel before the police arrived.[20]

With the exception of an 1882 victory in Manchester, the Scots found themselves playing second fiddle to the English throughout the 1880s. But by the end of the decade, there was little fraternal feeling between rugby's two founding nations. The lightning rod for the tension was the 1884 international at Blackheath's Rectory Field. It was a dull game in bitterly cold weather that would have been quickly forgotten were it not for a controversial England try scored by Richard Kindersley. The Scots claimed that one of their players had knocked the ball backwards with his hands – which constituted a knock-on according to the rules then in force in Scotland – and therefore a scrum should have been awarded to England. At this time there was no advantage rule in force and after arguing with the two captains for ten minutes the umpires decided that the try should stand. Wilf Bolton duly converted to give England a hollow victory.

Bitter controversy gripped the game for the next year, causing the 1885 Calcutta Cup match to be cancelled amid a mountain of acrimonious correspondence between the English and the Scottish unions. The English claimed, with some justification, that if Kindersley's try were disallowed Scotland would benefit from the fact that it had broken the rules. The Scots insisted on the letter of the law being enforced and argued that the issue be judged by a neutral nation. They were supported by the Welsh and Irish rugby unions and the three proposed establishing an International Rugby Football Board (IB) to be the ultimate authority on the rules of the game.[21]

The RFU was not prepared to allow such an overt challenge to its authority. It would not agree to equal representation on any international governing body. It pointed out that the English game had three times as many member clubs as Ireland, Scotland and Wales combined. The RFU seemed to exacerbate the situation in 1886 when they unilaterally introduced a points system for deciding matches, with three points for a goal and one for a try. This was not accepted by Ireland, Scotland or Wales, who preferred the old system of deciding matches by goals, or tries if no goals were scored.

Stalemate ensued and England did not play any home internationals in 1888 or 1889. In late 1889, fearing the impact on the standing of the sport of yet another England-less Home International series, the antagonists agreed to appoint arbitrators to reach a binding decision. When they reported back in April 1890, the arbitrators agreed that the IB should be solely responsible for the rules of the game but also found in favour England's demands for control of the IB. Of its 12 members, six would be from England, with two each from the other nations. Rule changes could only be made with a 75 per cent majority, ensuring that England stayed in control.[22]

By the time the settlement had been agreed in 1890, the game in Scotland was no longer played solely by privately educated middle-class young men from Edinburgh and Glasgow. As in the north of England and South Wales, the game had begun to permeate the working class. In Scotland this was not the industrial proletariat of the expanding cities – factory workers, miners and shipyard workers would come to prefer soccer – but workers in the small textile towns and villages around the River Tweed on the western border of Scotland and England.

As in West Yorkshire, woollen cloth was the region's most important product. Galashiels specialised in tweed, Hawick in hosiery and knitwear, and Melrose in linen, ensuring a local rivalry that would fuel the emergence of rugby clubs in the 1870s and 1880s. Hawick rugby club had been formed in 1873, followed by Gala (1875), Kelso (1876), Melrose (1877) and, lagging somewhat, Jed-Forest (1885). The Waverley railway line between Edinburgh and Hawick had opened in 1849, directly linking Galashiels, Melrose and Hawick. This would be the arterial link that allowed Borders rugby to flourish. Rugby in the Borders was passionate and intense, a game for all the classes that brought together the local businessman and the factory hand. It had a popular culture that was almost a world away from the elite atmosphere of the Edinburgh and Glasgow clubs.

Indeed, these two worlds rarely met. No Borders player was selected for Scotland before Gala's Adam Dalgleish made his debut in the Scottish pack against Wales in 1890, an achievement that remained rare until after the First World War. Such was the estrangement between the two worlds of Scottish rugby that in 1901 the Borders clubs began their own league in direct violation of the game's opposition to league competitions. Still in existence today as the world's oldest league in rugby union, it aroused the suspicious of the Scottish rugby establishment in Edinburgh. 'Among the mill-hands who play for Hawick, Jed-Forest, Galashiels and Melrose, the evil [of professionalism] might here and there crop up,' wrote the journalist E. H. D. Sewell, but the league was not seen as a threat and allowed to continue. In deference to the amateur sensibilities of rugby union's leadership, however, the league champions did not receive a trophy.[23]

Perhaps the most marked difference between the clubs in Edinburgh and the Borders was in the region's love of the 'short game', or seven-a-side rugby. Originating in Melrose in Scotland in April 1883, the idea appears to have been suggested by local butcher and rugby player Ned Haig as a way of raising money for the club. The competition took place on 28 April 1883 as part of the Melrose Sports carnival. The appeal of seven-a-side was sealed by the home side's defeat of deadly rivals Gala in the final, after which the tournament became an annual affair. Although many of the Borders clubs started their own sevens' contests, it wasn't until the 1920s that 'limited player' rugby began to become popular across rugby union, most notably with the start of the Middlesex Sevens in 1926 by the exiled Scotsman Dr J. A. Russell-Cargill.

The popularity of sevens once again distinguished the Borders from Scottish rugby's elite, and it also underlined how much Borders rugby had in common with the game in the north of England. The first type of 'short form' rugby began in September 1879 with a six-a-side tournament in Huddersfield. Played under regular rugby rules in ten-minute halves, Huddersfield's six overran Leeds 23-0 in the final. Other six-a-side tournaments were played over the next three or four years across the region. As in Melrose, six-a-sides were played with the aim of raising money for the club or, more often, for local hospital charities. By the mid-1880s nine-a-sides had replaced sixes, attracting large crowds and raising thousands of pounds. But unlike in the Borders, suspicions about professionalism – winning teams were usually presented with valuable gifts – were not ignored by the authorities. In August 1890, the Yorkshire Rugby Union suspended eight teams for playing in a summer six-a-side tournament. The following month the Lancashire Rugby Union outlawed games of less than 15 players, leaving short-form rugby confined to Scotland for the next 30 years.

The cultural similarity between the textile towns of the Borders and the rugby regions of the north of England also led to a steady trickle of Scottish players who 'went south' after 1895 to take advantage of the payments available for their skills in the rugby league of the new Northern Union. These ranged from Melrose's Jim Moffat, who scored a try for Oldham in the 1899 Northern Union Challenge Cup final, to Hawick's Dave Valentine, who went to Huddersfield in 1948 and became the first man to lift the Rugby League World Cup when he captained Great Britain to unexpected victory over France in the final in Paris in 1954.

But as the 19th century drew to a close the world that Borders rugby and its working-class players occupied rarely concerned the leadership of the Scottish game. Scotland stood alongside England as the upholders of what it saw as the principles of rugby. Men like H. H. Almond and James Aikman Smith, who would be secretary of the Scottish Rugby

Union from 1890 to 1931, were even more committed to the amateur values and moral purpose of rugby than their counterparts in the south. Scottish teams played the game in their own unique manner, a style dominated by forwards dribbling the ball ahead of them, challenging opponents to throw themselves down in the face of a forward rush. 'Feet, Scotland, Feet' was the cry from the enormous crowds that assembled for internationals in Edinburgh. By the time of the 30th anniversary of the first ever international Scotland stood second to England as the most successful rugby nation. On 9 March 1901, the national side imperiously dismissed England at Blackheath 18-3, scoring four tries and in the process securing the Triple Crown and carrying off the Home Nations Championship for the fifth time. Despite the rise of soccer in the land of the thistle, rugby would still claim to be the real game of the Scottish nation.

6

IRELAND: A NATIONAL IDENTITY

Blood. Few rugby matches are played without it, and in many more the presence of blood is a badge of honour, a symbol of commitment and a tribute to courage.

For one young Dublin rugby player in 1868, the sight of blood was not only an indication of the intensity of the game but also pointed to his future. Tall, robust and flame-haired, the bustling forward was a fixture in the Trinity College, Dublin, side that won all of its 27 matches that year. A multi-talented athlete and rower, he would win accolades on the rugby pitch, the athletics field and in the gymnasium. His rugger fame was such that, 20 years after he had ceased to be a student, his deeds were remembered in the first serious history of the game, the Rev. Frank Marshall's *Football. The Rugby Union Game* of 1892.

But unlike more than 170 medical doctors who would become famous for their exploits in Irish international rugby, Bram Stoker's relationship with blood off the field would be literary rather than medical. For in his youth, there was no more ardent a rugby enthusiast than the creator of Count Dracula.[1]

This should come as no surprise. Trinity College, Dublin, was the cradle of rugby in Ireland. For athletically minded young Protestant Irishmen like Stoker, who graduated three years before Catholics were admitted to the college in 1873, Trinity was not only a seat of learning but a source of almost limitless sporting opportunities.

In 1854, Trinity students from Rugby and Cheltenham schools had founded what appears to be Ireland's first club of any type of football. For its first six years of existence, members were content to play matches between themselves, such as 'Freshmen versus the Rest' and 'English-educated versus Irish-educated'. And when it did play its first match against external opposition, the Wanderers team that it faced was a club of Trinity graduates.[2]

The early rules under which Trinity played were somewhat unclear.[3] That first match against the Wanderers stretched over two days and it wasn't until 1868 that the club appears to have adopted a formal set of rules. These were based on those of Blackheath rugby club – hacking was banned, for instance – and anticipated the rules that would be adopted by the Rugby Football Union when it was founded in 1871.

As luck would have it, the Trinity rules were noticed by Dublin sports shop owner John Lawrence, who two years earlier had begun publishing an annual *Handbook of Cricket in Ireland*, an Irish version of *Wisden Cricketers' Almanack*, and he published them in his 1868 edition. Given the importance of cricket to the schools and colleges of Protestant, and to a lesser extent Catholic, Ireland the inclusion of Trinity's rugby rules in the *Handbook* offered a ready-made solution for those schools, colleges and cricket clubs looking to take up a winter sport, and rugby began to spread among the private schools of the island.[4]

In the north of Ireland similar events were taking place. In the same year that Trinity codified their rules, old boys of Rugby and Cheltenham schools living in Belfast emulated the evangelism of their fellow former pupils in Dublin and formed the North of Ireland Football Club (NIFC). As in the south, rugby took hold in the north's elite schools and colleges, highlighted by the January 1869 clash between the NIFC and Queen's College at Ormeau Park that took three consecutive Saturdays to decide the victor.[5] By December 1871 rugby in the north was strong enough for the NIFC to host Glasgow's West of Scotland club, which the visitors won by a single goal. As well as being the first fixture between teams from Ireland and Scotland, the match was notable for being played 15-a-side, a formation favoured by the NIFC, five years before the commonly used 20-a-side was finally abandoned by rugby. In 1873 the first Anglo-Irish match was played when Trinity's College Park hosted a team from Liverpool.[6]

These growing international links and the increasing number of clubs led not unnaturally to discussions about forming a national governing body for the sport in Ireland. On 10 December 1874, in response to an appeal from Trinity, five Dublin clubs – Trinity itself, Wanderers, Engineers, Bray and Lansdowne – and three from Ulster – Portora, Dungannon and Monaghan – met to form the Irish Football Union (IFU). Its aim was spelt out by its first president, W. C. Neville: 'to make the game more popular in Ireland, it is proposed to establish an annual international match … interprovincial matches, and matches North versus South.'[7]

A month after this new body had voted itself into existence, clubs in Belfast formed their own Northern Football Union of Ireland (NFUI). The reasons for the northern clubs going their own way are unclear but may well have been due to their resentment of Dublin's dominance of rugby affairs. The two organisations remained separate until February 1879 when a compromise was reached and they merged to form the Irish Rugby Football Union (IRFU). In the meantime, the disagreements between Belfast's NFUI and the Dublin's IFU were put on hold and the two bodies agreed to select a joint side for the Ireland team to play against England at The Oval in London on 15 February 1875.

The arrival of the men in green

The match was scheduled for a 2.30 kick-off on a Monday afternoon. When the two teams arrived at the ground 'the Oval presented the appearance of an extensive quagmire'. No one was in any doubt that the match would be, in the words of the reporter from *Bell's Life*, 'a mudlark on a large scale'.[8]

This was not the only problem facing Ireland. The match was played under 20-a-side rules, which presented an immediate problem to the Irish who were used to playing 15-a-side. Of their 20 players, all but six came from either Trinity or the NIFC. The potential advantages of players from the same clubs knowing each other's play was, however, undermined by the late withdrawal of several prominent players from the side, including two of Trinity's best backs, Smith and Robinson, and three players from the north. These changes meant that it was not until the morning of the match that the Irish finally decided that George Stack would captain the side. In contrast, England had a settled, experienced side that had earned its spurs through its annual encounters with the equally battle-hardened Scots.

As for the match itself, only the most optimistic Irishman expected anything but a drubbing. Even the fact that Ireland's green and white hooped shirts were made of heavy wool, rather than cotton, put them at a disadvantage in the wet mud. The kick-off was caught by England's William Milton, who would go on to play a crucial role in the development of South African rugby, and he promptly booted the ball back deep into Irish territory. Under immediate pressure from the English forwards, the Irish touched the ball down behind their own goal-line. Ulsterman R. D. Walkington took the drop kick out from under his own goalposts but the ball barely scraped to the 25-yard line.

It was to set the tone for the rest of the afternoon. The Irish were forced to touch the ball down behind their goal-line another 14 times. The English won easily, although the final score of two goals and a try to nil flattered the visitors. H. O. Moore, the rugby correspondent of *The Field*, lamented the performance of the Ireland team and suggested that he could find 20 Irishmen living in London who could put up a better display than than the official side.[9]

Nevertheless, the fact that the Irish could play an international match with England gave a tremendous boost to rugby's public profile. And in Ireland, a country where national identity was continuously being discussed, debated and contested, that meant that rugby was becoming more than just a game played by schools and universities; it was emerging as a sport of national importance.

Rugby's new status was given further impetus in December of 1875 when the England side crossed the Irish Sea to play the first international match on home soil. It took place at Leinster Cricket Ground in the south Dublin suburb of Rathmines. England once more prevailed, this time by a goal and a try to nil, but the Irish acquitted themselves well. The most memorable action of the match saw their half-back A. P. Cronyn race 70 yards to the very edge of the English goal-line stripped to the waist. The Irish had learned their lesson from The Oval and swapped their woollen shirts for cotton ones, but these proved to be as flimsy as the original shirts had been heavy: Cronyn had his ripped from his back by a would-be tackler on his own 25-yard line. Undeterred, he weaved between the English 20 until England full-back A. P. Pearson managed to tackle him inches before he could make history and score Ireland's first ever international try.

Not until 1881 could Ireland finally hold its own on the international stage. In front of the largest crowd yet seen for any type of football match in Belfast, the Irish battered the visiting Scots' line all afternoon yet were constantly foiled by both fate and the men in blue. With just five minutes left, the Scots were forced to drop out from their own goal-line. The ball ended up in touch but Ireland's Barney Hughes made a quick throw-in. The ball went through two pairs of Irish hands before ending up with Trinity winger J. C. Bagot, whose snapped drop kick sailed between the uprights and into the history books. Ireland had won at last. 'Men, women, and children embraced each other indiscriminately,' recalled journalist J. J. MacCarthy. 'The spell of sorrow was broken.'[10]

A whole island game

The strides made by the national side, not to mention the sheer excitement of many of even its losing matches, spurred the game onwards and upwards. The first inter-provincial match was staged in November 1875 when Ulster triumphed over Leinster, and in March 1878 Munster played its first match as a province. At a club level, the game spread beyond the the two major cities and made inroads in the south of the island. A club had been formed in Cork in 1870 and in the same year Midleton College FC had been formed to the east of the city. In March 1875 Rathkeale, a club in County Limerick, became the first from the province of Munster to affiliate to the IFU. A year later a club was established in Limerick and it took its place in the IFU in 1877. Knock-out competitions known as Senior Cups, frowned upon by the RFU in England, were none the less started in Leinster (1882), Ulster (1885) and Munster (1886). Eventually, the clamour for rugby would also reach the far west and the Connacht RFU was established in 1885, although it was to be another 11 years before it too could boast its own Senior Cup.[11]

Rugby also developed a tight hold on the private schools. As in England, Irish educationalists modelled their schools on the Muscular Christian traditions of *Tom Brown's Schooldays* and so naturally rugby took its place at the heart of school life. In 1876 the Ulster Schools' Cup tournament began. It was won by Armagh's Royal School, founded in 1608 during the plantation of Ulster by British settlers, who defeated the Royal Belfast Academical Institution, which had been created for the sons of Belfast merchant and professional classes in the early 19th century.

It was the start of an illustrious history. Royal went on to win the cup seven times in the first decade of its existence but the Institute would win it outright 29 times at the time of writing. Similar school traditions were established across the island. In 1887 the Leinster Schools Senior Cup began, and would become as integral to middle-class Dublin's social life as it was to its sporting world. Blackrock College won the title in its first year, the first of its 67 victories. In Munster, a schools' challenge cup had been set up at the same time.

As Blackrock's domination of Leinster schools' rugby highlighted, rugby was as important to elite Roman Catholic schools as it was to their Protestant counterparts. Formal bans on Catholics serving in the civil service and the judiciary had been removed in 1829 and this led to schools and colleges being created for middle-class Catholics. Outside of Ulster, these would provide the backbone for Irish schools' tournaments. Yet despite doctrinal differences, the importance of rugby to Catholic and Protestant schools was exactly the same. The physicality of the game was not always appreciated by those boys for whom it was supposed to build character. As a young boy James Joyce was sent to Clongowes Wood College, a Jesuit School in County Kildare where rugby vied for importance with the Catechism. He did not appreciate it, as his fictional alter ego Stephen Dedalus described:

> after every charge and thud of the footballers the greasy leather orb flew like a heavy bird through the grey light. He kept on the fringe of his line, out of sight of his prefect, out of the reach of the rude feet, feigning to run now and then. He felt his body small and weak amid the throng of players and his eyes were weak and watery.[12]

As would be the case around the world, for every boy who enjoyed throwing himself into the tackle there was at least one other for whom, like Joyce, it would evoke either dread, boredom or both.

By the late 1880s rugby's popularity had begun to extend beyond its heartland constituency of elite schools and the middle classes. In particular, the game began to make headway among the working classes of Cork, Limerick and the towns and villages of Munster. The clubs that had begun the game in the province were generally founded by men with a connection to Trinity College or an English public school. But the Roman Catholic Church's toleration of Sunday recreation – in contrast to the Sabbatarian instincts of the Protestant churches across the British Isles – meant that there were greater opportunities for working men to play rugby. For shop workers and agricultural labourers Saturday remained a working day. Only Sunday was free. Limerick and Cork both saw the emergence of 'Sunday clubs', rugby teams comprising a majority of working-class players. Sunday cup competitions, in contrast to the elite Senior Cups that were played exclusively on Saturdays, were organised in both cities and attracted thousands of working-class spectators.

The symbol of the changing nature of rugby in Munster was Limerick's Garryowen FC. The club was founded in 1884 by Protestant businessman W. L. Stokes, local baker and Labour politician Tom Prendergast, and ships' rigger and future Home Rule MP Mike Joyce. Its first captain was post office clerk and future Irish international Jack O'Sullivan.[13] The club's ability to recruit talented players regardless of background or social status undoubtedly contributed significantly to its success. From the start of the Munster Senior Cup in 1886 to the end of the century, the club lifted the trophy on ten occasions and only failed to appear in the final once.

Although the club would give its name to the towering kick that would be known as the 'up and under' in England and the 'bomb' in Australia, its true innovation was to bring together players, officials and supporters of different religions, political outlooks and social backgrounds. This was a new phenomenon in Irish rugby. By eschewing narrow class or religious interests, Garryowen had more in common with clubs in the north of England and South Wales such as Wigan or Llanelli, which united wide sections of local society in pursuit of sporting civic pride and turned rugby into a mass spectator sport. Indeed, by 1900, rugby in Munster was played, watched and enjoyed by people of all classes and religions, something that could not be said of the rest of Ireland.

This was partly due to the policies of the IRFU. In 1882 there had been discussions about starting a national knock-out tournament for Irish rugby clubs. The success of soccer's FA Cup in England had demonstrated the impetus that a cup competition could give to a sport. But, like their counterparts in the English RFU, the Irish rugby authorities rejected the idea, and so passed up on the opportunity to make rugby Ireland's truly national sport.[14] Its timing could not have been worse.

Different Irelands, different codes

Unlike the reluctant leaders of Irish rugby, the Irish Football Association (IFA) had started its own national knock-out cup for Irish soccer clubs in 1881. Soccer in Ireland at that time barely existed at all. *R. M Peter's Irish Football Annual* for 1880 listed just four soccer clubs in the entire country, in contrast to 88 rugby teams. The IFA itself had only been formed in 1880 but it had an evangelical zeal for promoting the round-ball game that soon put it on a par with rugby.

In February 1882 the first Irish national soccer side took the field against England. The match ended in a disastrous 13-0 loss, but soccer could now boast international competition on a par with that of rugby. Nine years after its formation, the IFA had grown from a mere four clubs to 124. Rugby could no longer claim to be Ireland's only national sport.[15]

If rugby was losing out numerically to soccer, it now also faced a challenge from a sport that questioned rugby's very right to be considered Irish at all. In November 1884 Michael Cusack, an ex-teacher at

Blackrock College and former keen rugby player, led the formation of the Gaelic Athletic Association, dedicated to the promotion of games and sports that it believed were specifically Irish. 'We tell the Irish people to take the management of their games into their own hands, to encourage and promote every form of athletics which is peculiarly Irish, and to remove with one sweep everything foreign,' he wrote.[16]

Initially, the GAA seemed to present little threat either to rugby or soccer. Its focus was on athletics and its most important team sport was hurling. But Cusack and his supporters had captured the mood of the 'Gaelic Revival' in late Victorian Ireland. Gaelic football took its place alongside renewed interest in the Irish language, the flowering of Irish literature and the revitalisation of nationalist politics. There was just one problem with the GAA's revival of native Irish football. There was no such thing.

Of course, many different forms of football had been played in Ireland over the centuries, just as elsewhere in Britain and the rest of the world. *Caid*, a form of folk football that was played both over fields and in smaller areas, was claimed by Cusack and his supporters to be the direct ancestor of their version of football. In reality it had no more in common with the GAA's version of football than with any other code. Not only that, but many Irish rugby enthusiasts have countered by arguing that *Caid* was actually the original form of rugby. Indeed, Father Liam Ferris even went so far as to argue that as William Webb Ellis had spent time as a child in Tipperary, *Caid* must have been his inspiration when he supposedly picked up the ball and ran with it in 1823.[17]

Early attempts by the GAA to develop a distinct set of Irish rules floundered. Scoring methods and team size were unclear. Some clubs simply saw the GAA's version of football as a form of rugby. A number even switched freely between the two sports. Cork's Nil Desperandum FC, winners of the GAA county title in 1889, began as a rugby club and switched back and forth before finally sticking with the Gaelic game. Laune Rovers in Kerry and Tipperary's Arravale Rovers followed similar paths.[18] It wasn't until the late 1880s that a distinct form of Gaelic rules began to emerge, and even then many of the game's innovations bore more than a passing resemblance to those of Australian Rules football.

But it was as much what it did off the field as on it that allowed Gaelic football to challenge rugby. Not only did the GAA present itself as the upholders of the culture of Catholic Ireland, it also portrayed rugby as an alien sport. Rule 27 of its constitution banned members from playing or even watching 'foreign' sports. Although 'the ban' was imposed with varying degrees of success, it effectively meant that once a player had chosen Gaelic or rugby football, it was very difficult to change.

The GAA also organised itself on the basis of the local parishes across Ireland, ensuring that the majority of the population, which still lived and worked in the countryside, had a local team that it could support. And the fact that GAA sports were played on Sundays, the one free day that was common to virtually everyone, gave them the widest possible appeal. Outside of Munster, where the oval ball game extended across all classes, Irish rugby was seen, without too much exaggeration, as the sport of the privileged middle classes.

One game, two nations

The narrow base of support for rugby in Ireland may have contributed to the limited success of the national side. Although the profile of the international game continued to grow, it rarely brought glory. In its first decade of competition, Ireland won just four matches. In 1893, the side won no matches and scored no points. And then, suddenly, water turned to wine.

Eighteen ninety-four saw the side's first Triple Crown triumph as they swept aside their rival nations. Another winless season followed but in 1896 the championship was again lifted, only a 0-0 draw with Scotland at Lansdowne Road depriving them of another Triple Crown.

Three years later, the Triple Crown returned as Ireland swept all before it, conceding just a single penalty goal. But it would be almost 50 years before a Jack Kyle-inspired side would repeat the feat.

The distance that had developed between rugby and the majority of Catholic Irish sports' fans by the 1900s was highlighted in a famous story told by Bethel Solomons, Ireland's first Jewish rugby international. Fearing he would be late for Ireland's 1909 home match against England, he hailed a cab in the centre of Dublin. He told the cabbie that he wanted to go to Lansdowne Road. 'It's for the Ireland rugby international,' explained Solomons. 'Ireland?' snorted the driver dismissively, 'it's nothing but fourteen Prods and a Jew.'[19] This was certainly unfair to Solomons, who was not only a proud Jewish Irishman, but also to the other 14 players, Protestants or not. But in a country like Ireland, sport and politics were entangled even more than usual.

In the spring of 1912 British prime minister Herbert Asquith introduced a Home Rule bill to bring a degree of self-government to Ireland. The following year, rugby in Northern Ireland ground to a virtual halt as swathes of players joined Edward Carson's Ulster Volunteer Force, a paramilitary group committed to resisting Home Rule. Military training in defence of the union with Britain took precedence over rugby and many rugby pitches became drill grounds for the UVF.[20] When war finally did come, it was not civil war but world war. Momentarily, unionist and nationalist Ireland found common cause in the patriotic fever of war against Germany. In Dublin around 200 players joined the IRFU's specially created Volunteer Corps. But even in the midst of world war, rugby could not escape the conflict that would rip Ireland apart.

On 24 April 1916 the Volunteer Corps marched back to Dublin following a day of drill practice. Led by IRFU president Frank Browning, who had been capped by Ireland at both rugby and cricket, they entered the city carrying flags and beating drums. They did not know that this Easter Monday had been chosen by the republican Irish Volunteers and the Irish Citizen Army as the day to stage an armed insurrection that would go down in history as the Easter Rising. As the Volunteer Corps approached the Grand Canal they were fired upon by the republican forces, who assumed they were government reinforcements. Browning and three others were killed, and three more seriously wounded.

Blood had acquired an altogether more serious and deadly meaning for rugby in Ireland.

7

WALES: THE DRAGON'S EMBRACE

Rhys Gabe was one of the finest three-quarters ever to lace a boot for Wales. Almost six feet tall and weighing just shy of 13 stones, he was bigger than most backs of the early 1900s, yet possessed of a speed and elegance unusual for man of his size and strength. He played 24 times for Wales between 1901 and 1908, scoring 11 tries – a remarkable ratio in an era when tries were hard to come by – and starred in the pioneering 1904 British Isles tour to Australia and New Zealand, playing in all four 'Test' matches, as internationals between the nations of the British Empire were known.

History remembers Gabe above all for his pivotal role in the most famous, and perhaps most important, match ever played by Wales. Playing outside captain Gwyn Nicholls, he provided the last, crucial pass in a flowing Welsh movement that resulted in his winger Teddy Morgan bursting down the touchline to score the only try of the historic 1905 match against the touring New Zealand All Blacks.[1] Even more crucially, it was Gabe who made the last-gasp try-saving tackle on All Blacks' centre Bob Deans – the 'Goliath of the Backs' – just millimetres from the Welsh line, thus ensuring the New Zealanders' only defeat of their historic tour.

Rhys Gabe was also a symbol of the age. Like many in the Welsh team that tamed the All Blacks, he came from humble origins. Wales was rapidly becoming a modern industrial nation and Gabe was one of many young working-class and lower middle-class boys who benefited from the social mobility that the Welsh educational system offered. He had attended Llanelli Intermediate School and gone on to train in London to be a teacher. A gifted all-round athlete, good enough to play county cricket, he represented his teacher training college at water polo and regretted not being able to develop his talents as a cyclist. He returned home to teach in Cardiff and established himself as one of the brightest stars in Wales' all-conquering team of the 1900s.

In 1903 he found himself at a dinner sitting next to the doyen of Scottish referees, Crawford Finlay. Finlay, like many in English and Scottish rugby at the time, was concerned that the game's social tenor was threatened by its popularity among the working classes. He wondered aloud to Gabe why the Welsh selected 'miners, steelworkers and policemen for their international teams' and suggested that such types should play rugby league.[2]

For someone like Gabe, who had played alongside men from the industrial working class his entire career, such an attitude was incomprehensible. The success of the Welsh side was based on its ability to combine players from all social backgrounds, from barrister to boilermaker. A third of all those who made their debuts for Wales in the 1900s were manual workers, a proportion of players far in excess of that of their rivals in England, Ireland or Scotland. Welsh rugby prided itself on what it called its 'democratic spirit'.

Sadly, history does not record Gabe's response to Findlay's unalloyed snobbery, but we do know that when Findlay refereed the Wales versus England game the following year, he penalised the Welsh 11 times in the first half alone and, with the scores locked at 14-14 with just a minute to go, disallowed a Teddy Morgan try due to an alleged forward pass from … Rhys Gabe.

From private recreation to public obsession

Welsh rugby did not begin with such inclusive intentions. Just as in Ireland and Scotland, the game had been brought to Wales as part of the expansion of elite education in the mid-19th century. In particular, rugby entered Wales through the gates of St David's College in Lampeter. Founded in 1822 to train young Welshmen for the ministry, the college received its royal charter in 1828, making it the oldest university in Britain outside Oxford, Cambridge and the Scottish universities. In 1850 the Rev. Rowland Williams was appointed vice-principal and, having been a devotee of sport during his time at Cambridge University, immediately introduced sport and particularly the Rugby School game into the curriculum.

From Lampeter, the game slowly extended its reach to other Welsh schools and colleges. Llandovery College began playing different types of football shortly after it opened in 1848 and started to play regularly against the Lampeter students from the 1850s. Monmouth and Cowbridge schools followed suit and took up Rugby School rules in the 1870s. Christ College, Brecon, one of the oldest schools in Wales, had been transformed by the mid-Victorian educational boom and threw itself into the enthusiasm for games, embracing rugby rules in 1875.

The young men educated at rugby playing private schools in Wales and in England provided the impetus for the formation of the adult clubs that would provide the backbone of Welsh rugby. Old Llandoverians and Old Monmouthians were prominent in the founding of Neath (in 1871) and Newport (1874) respectively. Cardiff (1875) was established by old boys of local private schools. The first captain of Llanelli (1875) was an Old Rugbeian.

In the circumstances of its birth, Welsh rugby was therefore no different from its Scottish and Irish cousins, but the world into which it was born could not have offered a greater contrast. South Wales was a society in ferment, bursting with the sheer force of sudden industrialisation. Fuelled by a seemingly inexhaustible supply of coal, the region grew like a baby colossus. Between 1880 and 1910 around 300,000 workers from England flocked to South Wales to find jobs in the coal, iron and steel industries. In the 1851 Census Cardiff's population was a mere 20,000. Over the next two generations, it grew to 182,000 people in 1911. The Rhondda Valley, the powerhouse of Welsh coal production, went from barely 2,000 people in 1851 to being home to over 152,000 in 1911. The engine of industrialisation drove the whole of Welsh society at breakneck speed into modernity, and rugby was at its forefront.

The catalyst for rugby putting itself at the heart of the industrial and cultural revolution that was sweeping Wales was, as so often, soccer. Looking for a way to raise its profile, in 1877 the Football Association of Wales began its national knock-out tournament, the Welsh Cup. In response, the South Wales Football Club – Welsh rugby's governing body at the time – bought a 50 guinea trophy and invited rugby clubs to take part in the South Wales Challenge Cup.

Eighteen clubs entered, each paying two guineas to take part, and on 2 March 1878 Newport lined up against Swansea in the first final. Two thousand spectators, the biggest crowd yet seen at a rugby match in Wales, gathered at Bridgend to watch the contest. In a thrilling game, Newport bested Swansea by a single goal to nil and returned home to a huge welcoming crowd, a civic reception and a special banquet.[3]

They repeated their success the following year when they defeated Cardiff, one game in an unbeaten run that lasted for five seasons. The cup cemented their position as the country's leading team and, more importantly, the tournament put rugby at the centre of South Wales' popular culture. By the time that the Welsh Football (later Rugby) Union was formed in 1881 rugby was no longer merely a game, it was a mass spectator sport, a commercial leisure pursuit and a source of civic pride and local rivalry.

Towns, villages and even streets that had been jolted into life by the Welsh industrial revolution found in rugby a way to make their presence felt and unite the locality. By 1890 there were more than 220 teams playing rugby in Cardiff alone.[4] For tens of thousands of immigrants, rugby was their route to Welshness and belonging in their new country. The popularity of the South Wales Challenge Cup transformed rugby from a game for the elite of Welsh society to the common interest of almost all classes and sections of the population. 'The fact is,' noted the *South Wales Daily News* in 1879, the public 'have grown to look upon the matter [of the cup] as one where the credit of the town is at stake.'[5]

Just like the Yorkshire Cup in the north of England, the South Wales Cup attracted massive crowds and inspired the formation of hundreds of rugby clubs. In the coalfields and docklands, young men formed teams with as much enthusiasm as those who had learned the game between Greek and Latin lessons. Teams like Blaina Ironsides and Bute Dock Rangers took their place alongside Llandovery College Old Boys and Old Monmouthians FC.[6] The intense local rivalry also meant that elite teams began to open their doors to talented working-class players who could give them an edge in their battles for local supremacy. By 1886, Llanelli, founded by young men educated at Rugby School and Oxford, won the South Wales Cup with a team that included ten manual workers.[7] Welsh rugby had become a game for all the classes.

In this dynamic and vibrant environment, where scientific discovery underpinned industrial development and the thirst for the spectacular was unquenchable, rugby reflected the forces of change at work in society. The South Wales Cup was one example of the initiative and freshness of thought in the game. Newport arranged cross-border fixtures with English clubs to boost their attendances. They also arranged the first sporting contest in Wales to take place under floodlights when in 1878 they played Cardiff on a wintry evening. But the most important innovation took place on the field of play itself.

In 1884 English-born Frank Hancock, heir to a Cardiff brewing and banking family, was called into the Cardiff team as a replacement three-quarter for their match at Cheltenham College. He had a stunning game, scoring two tries, but for the next match with Gloucester, Cardiff's regular three-quarters were all fully fit. This presented the Cardiff committee with a selection dilemma. At this point in the evolution of rugby, teams still played with just three three-quarters and nine forwards. But Hancock's outstanding form meant that he could not be dropped from the side.

The Cardiff selection committee decided to zig when it should have zagged and opted to play with four three-quarters and just eight forwards. It was such a success that Cardiff continued with the revolutionary formation for the rest of the season. By 1885 almost every team in Wales was using it, none more triumphantly than Cardiff themselves, who won 26 out of 27 matches that season, scoring 131 tries while conceding just four.

Outside Wales, conventional thinking asserted that rugby was a game primarily for forwards and that the withdrawal of one man from the scrum would mean that a side would never win the ball. And anyway, the critics said, if the new system was so good, why were the Welsh so bad when it came to international rugby? They had a point.

Wales played their first international in 1881 against England. It was nothing short of disastrous. Thirteen tries were scored by the English and it could have easily been more. Fortunately another year elapsed before Wales' next international, which resulted in a first victory over an even weaker Irish side at Lansdowne Road. It was to be seven years before a victory was achieved against the Scots. England took even longer. Eventually, in 1890, playing England in the mutually unfamiliar surroundings of Dewsbury's Crown Flatt ground, Wales finally emerged victorious from battle with their greatest rivals. Dewsbury's own William 'Buller' Stadden, one of the first Welsh players to 'go north' and play for a team in Yorkshire, took advantage of slack

England play, threw a short line-out ball to himself and crashed over for the winning try.

A major factor in Welsh dominance at Dewsbury was the crisp passing and precise combinations of their four three-quarters. They bamboozled the three English three-quarters, outflanking and turning them inside out time and time again. Despite the close score, this was a convincing win that silenced many of the scoffers. By 1892 a number of the more tactically progressive English clubs started to embrace the new system, including Blackheath, Oldham and Stadden's Dewsbury. In England's annual North versus South match that year both sides fielded four three-quarters. And as we have seen, Yorkshire, and later England, captain Dicky Lockwood introduced it into his county championship team and eventually into the England side itself. Soon sides using three three-quarters would be as obsolete as 20-a-side teams. But it was the following year that Welsh tactical innovation and sheer talent irresistibly came together to make history.

Led by Arthur Gould, a genius of a three-quarter who had no peer as the greatest Welsh player of his era, Wales overcame England by a solitary point in a see-sawing match in Cardiff. It was only the second time they had beaten the English and the first time they had won on native soil. Buoyed with self-confidence, Gould's men then journeyed north to Edinburgh to beat off the Scots by 9-0 before returning home to shut out Ireland by a solitary try to nil at Llanelli. Joy was unrestrained – at long last, Wales had won the Triple Crown. The dragon could now look the other rugby-playing nations in the eye.

Going north

Welsh rugby had risen to such heights thanks to the inclusive, cross-class composition of its teams. Wales did not have the networks of private schools and universities that provided the English, Irish and Scottish sides with a constant stream of young middle-class men keen to play and excel at rugby. As a small country – according to the 1901 Census, its population was barely two million, less than half that of Ireland and Scotland – Wales had to embrace rugby talent from all sections of society. But this brought problems. Men used to working five and a half days a week in a mine or a steel furnace believed that hard work deserved financial reward, off and on the pitch.

Although agreeing with the RFU's imposition of amateurism on the game in 1886, the leaders of Welsh rugby had a much more pragmatic approach to paying players than the zealots in the English RFU. Former Welsh international three-quarter Bill McCutcheon began his career with Swansea in the mid-1880s and later suggested that payments of one form or another were being made to players for as long as he had been playing. One, five, ten and even twenty pound notes would mysteriously appear in a player's boots after a match, so-called 'boot money'. Occasionally the Welsh Rugby Union would undertake routine house-cleaning and shine a light into its darker corners – in 1901 Treherbert were accused of offering Pontypridd's Dawson £1 a week and in 1907 allegations were made that players were commonly paid between a sovereign and six shillings per match – but as long as discretion remained the better part of the deal, English-style witch-hunts and purges were avoided.[8]

In the north of England, clubs were richer, crowds bigger and the rewards more lucrative. From the early 1880s the more ambitious Welsh players had started to look north. There was a natural bond between South Wales and the north of England. Both were dominated by heavy industry – coal mining defined the economies of the two regions – and in each rugby was a mass spectator sport. Just as the Welsh had invented the four three-quarter system, Yorkshire sides had similarly introduced tactical innovations such as defined positions for forwards, 'wing-forward' play and passing moves from the scrum. A bond quickly formed between the two regions where rugby was industrial, inclusive and innovative.

The link was cemented on and off the field. For example, in 1884 Wakefield Trinity, Batley, Dewsbury and Hull visited Cardiff, Llanelli, Neath and Newport. Short tours by clubs, especially at Christmas and Easter, became highlights of the season for players and supporters alike. Touring sides from the north would be met with outpourings of civic celebration, as Llanelli forward Elias Jones remembered:

> Hull were especially popular visitors, and I remember that the horses were taken out of the brake in which they were to travel and the brake dragged to the Thomas Arms by the people who had gathered to welcome them. It was a remarkable sight, for many had secured cotton waste from the works and lit this to form a torchlight procession. Arriving at the Thomas Arms, there were scenes of great enthusiasm, and the Hull captain had to make a speech from the balcony.[9]

Slowly but surely rugby migrants began to tread a path northwards from the Valleys to the Pennines and its hinterlands. The first player recorded as having 'gone north' seems to have been Llanelli's international full-back Harry Bowen, who signed for Dewsbury in 1884 but returned home after just a handful of games. The following year Newport's international James Bridie signed for Manningham in Bradford. But the first Welsh player to make a real impact in the north was Cardiff and Wales half-back 'Buller' Stadden who, along with teammate Angus Stuart, went to Dewsbury in September 1886.

Stadden claimed the two had made the move because of unemployment in Cardiff and 'having made a few friends during Dewsbury's tour of the Principality, they naturally steered for Yorkshire and got employment and a place in the Dewsbury team'.[10] They had been lucky enough to find jobs with woollen spinners Newsome, Sons & Spedding. It was, of course, sheer coincidence that Mark Newsome, one of the sons in the company title, was also the president and former captain of Dewsbury rugby club …

Across the Pennines in Lancashire similar moves took place. Oldham set the pace by signing Bill McCutcheon in 1888, swiftly followed by his fellow international Dai Gwyn. Perhaps the most famous Welsh signings before the 1895 split were the mercurial brothers David and Evan James, who transferred from Swansea to Manchester's Broughton Rangers in 1892 for a reputed signing-on fee of £250, in flagrant violation of the RFU's amateur regulations. Some Welsh players would even advertise openly in northern newspapers: 'General Clerk requires a situation, knowledge of French; highest references; wing-three-quarter Welsh team', read one such advertisement in the *Yorkshire Post*.[11]

The great migration north did not go unopposed in Wales. In 1899 the *Western Mail* reported that a Wigan scout had been thrown into a river at Penarth to discourage his activities. Welsh clubs also responded in kind to the northern threat by offering star players inflated expenses and attractive jobs. For some, the social networks of the leading Welsh clubs offered greater opportunities for social mobility, one benefit the northern clubs could not match.

Working-class players' desire to be paid, and the ability of clubs in Yorkshire and Lancashire to pay them, ultimately forced the Welsh Rugby Union to surreptitiously condone payments, in one form or another, to players. Sooner or later, it was inevitable that they would clash head-on with the RFU in England.

Arthur Gould and future of Welsh rugby

When the crisis finally came it broke over the head of the player who, more than any other individual, was the symbol of Welsh rugby's rise to glory. Born in 1864, Arthur Gould made his debut for Newport as a teenager and led its all-conquering side of the early 1890s. Talented and charismatic, Gould seemed to embody the very soul of Welsh rugby. He was already a household name in the Valleys before he captained Wales to the Triple Crown in 1893; but the unprecedented success of the Welsh team catapulted him to national celebrity status. To criticise Arthur Gould was to criticise Wales itself.

In 1897, after Gould had led Wales to their third victory over England on his home ground at Newport, the *South Wales Argus* and the *South Wales Daily News* began a campaign to give him a national testimonial. Money poured in from across Wales and its diaspora. In 1897 the Welsh Rugby Union presented Gould with the deeds to his house, which had been purchased with the testimonial's funds. The RFU immediately declared this act of generosity to be a violation of the amateur regulations. In February 1897 the International Board rubber-stamped the RFU's position. In protest, the Welsh withdrew from the board. It seemed that it was now only a matter of time before a formal split occurred.

But the condition of rugby caused both sides to hesitate. Less than two years earlier English rugby had split over broken-time payments. A break with Wales now would weaken international rugby, strengthen the new Northern Union and deal a potentially lethal blow to the prestige to the RFU. Confronted with a stark choice of enforcing its amateur rules or maintaining its authority, the RFU chose the latter.

So, at its annual meeting in September 1897, the RFU declared that, although Gould was guilty of professionalism by accepting the deeds to his house, 'exceptional circumstances' meant that he would not be banned from rugby. RFU secretary Rowland Hill admitted that the decision 'was a question of expediency'. F. E .Smith, the future cabinet minister Lord Birkenhead, openly admitted in *The Times* that the decision was made to 'prevent the great accession of strength to the Northern Union which would have followed had the Welsh Union been driven into their arms'.[12]

The 'Gould compromise' would define the relationship between Welsh rugby and the RFU for the next century. Provided a certain decorum was maintained, the RFU would not look too closely at Welsh affairs, and Welsh clubs would continue to make boot-money payments to working-class players. As long as the Welsh clubs pretended not to play their players, the RFU would pretend to believe them. The WRU's refusal to enforce the rules of amateurism with the same zealotry as the RFU was the crucial factor in keeping the game unified across the classes and avoiding a repeat of the 1895 Northern Union split. Rugby was thus maintained as the national game of Wales.

The dragon rampant

If the RFU's willingness to compromise helped the Welsh game domestically, it was the Englishmen's unwillingness to compromise with the northern clubs that most benefited Welsh rugby internationally. By driving out the supporters of broken-time in the north, the RFU weakened English rugby and its national side so grievously that they simply ceased to be competitive.

England did not win a single match against Wales between 1899 and 1909. Their only respite was a 14-14 draw with England at Leicester in 1904, the same match in which Crawford Finlay overruled Teddy Morgan's last-minute match-winner because of the alleged forward pass from Rhys Gabe. The amputation of the northern clubs in 1895 had devastated the English game, clearing the way for Wales to dominate international rugby for a generation.

This remarkable run of Welsh success cemented rugby's place at the heart of Welsh popular culture and national identity. It could not have happened at a more propitious time. Wales in the 1900s was consolidating a new national identity, unifying its greatly expanded population around symbols of the past and present. Cardiff was granted the status of a city in 1905, the same year in which David Lloyd George, Wales' most charismatic politician, was appointed President of the Board of Trade, the first Welshman to hold such a high office for over 200 years. In 1907 the National Library of Wales and National Museum of Wales were founded. The 1900s was the decade in which Wales became a modern nation.

The Welsh national revival was not separatist and nor did it seek independence. It wanted parity with England as an equal member of the British Empire. And no cultural force demonstrated this better than rugby. On the rugby pitch the Welsh were not merely the equal of England, they were clearly superior. Between 1899 and 1909 Wales won five Triple Crowns, with another in 1911 thrown in for good measure. The vitality and vigour of the Welsh nation could be measured out in tries, goals and international championships.

Nowhere was the unity of rugby and Welsh national identity demonstrated so powerfully and thrillingly than at Cardiff Arms Park on 16 December 1905. It was here that Wales lined up against the unbeaten All Blacks. It was New Zealand's 28th match of the tour, in which they had scored 801 points and conceded a mere 22. England, Ireland and Scotland had all been summarily despatched, with only the Scots managing even to score against them. But Wales had carried off their third Triple Crown earlier in the year and were full of confidence that they could contain the storm from the land of the long white cloud.

It was an epic clash. Thirty special trains steamed into the Welsh capital, disgorging thousands of home supporters eager to be part of the greatest spectacle the nation had ever seen. An hour before kick-off the gates were closed as 50,000 shoehorned themselves into Cardiff Arms Park, and untold numbers were left outside of the ground. The atmosphere crackled with anticipation.

The two sides came out for the fray and, as the All Blacks finished their haka, Wales' Teddy Morgan and his side began to sing 'Hen Wlad Fy Nhadau' (Land of My Fathers), which was lustily taken up by tens of thousands of spectators. The Welsh side had planned this as a way of bringing the crowd into the game and gain an early psychological advantage over the New Zealanders. Inadvertently, they had also begun the tradition of singing national anthems before internationals.

The game began with brutal intensity. Rucks, mauls and scrums were contested as if the fate of the world depended on them. The Welsh sought to nullify New Zealand tactics by keeping the game tight and dominating it through their forwards. Full-back Bert Winfield's kicking constantly pinned the All Blacks in their own half, forcing them into set-piece confrontations and restricting their ability to run the ball.

Stealing a leaf from the visitors' book, Newport's Cliff Pritchard was employed as a wing-forward – or 'flying man' in the words of *The Times*' reporter – allowing the Welsh to nullify the impact of New Zealand captain and wing-forward Dave Gallaher. The wily Welsh forwards also waited for the New Zealand pack to form and then seized the loose head. This made it difficult for their opponents to win the scrum, depriving them of so much possession that some journalists wondered if they had stopped contesting for the ball.

When Teddy Morgan crossed for a try on the half-hour mark, the tables seemed to be turning. Lacking key players such as winger George Smith, forward Bill Cunningham and, most importantly, five-eighth (as the fly-half was referred to Down Under) Billy Stead, the All Blacks struggled to maintain their rhythm and structure. They were not helped by the unsympathetic Scottish referee John Dallas, a last-minute compromise after both sides had rejected each other's choice, who appeared to share a widespread British distaste for the All Blacks' scrum tactics.

With less than ten minutes remaining, Wales had one hand on the unofficial world championship of rugby union. Then the All Blacks broke through the Welsh defence and from just outside the Welsh 25-yard line, Bob Deans – great-uncle of future All Black player and Wallabies coach Robbie Deans – raced away for what seemed a certain try. Confident he would score and seeking to make the conversion easier he changed direction to run towards the goalposts.

It was a fateful decision. It gave Rhys Gabe a split second to launch himself at Deans just as he lunged for the line. It was no try. Deans, according to referee Dallas, had been stopped a fraction short of the line. No one in black believed that Deans had not scored. Some in red could not be certain either. But neither disbelief nor doubt could change the decision. When Dallas finally blew for no-side (full time), Wales had defeated the mightiest rugby nation in the British Empire.

No one could now argue that rugby was not the national game of Wales, a symbol of its resurgence and force for the unity of all its population. From the seeds that were sown in the elite schools and colleges, in little more than 30 years the game had blossomed into the flower of the nation. In Wales, the nation and rugby were one and indivisible.

8
FRANCE: THE BARON, THE RED VIRGIN AND RUGBY'S BELLE ÉPOQUE

Paris's Château de Bagatelle and its grounds were born in the spirit of sporting competition. Situated in Bois de Boulogne, perhaps France's most famous public park, it was built in just 63 days after Marie-Antoinette wagered her brother-in-law, the Comte d'Artois, that he could not build a new chateau in under three months. In later years, the magnificent grounds that surrounded the building would become one of the Bois de Boulogne's most popular attractions. It was here in March 1892 that French rugby held its first championship final.

The two sides that contested that inaugural final were the most prestigious in Paris – and therefore in all France. Racing Club de France had been founded in 1882 as a multi-sports athletic club. Stade Français was marginally the younger club, formed a year later. For those Parisians who had begun to take an interest in the new game that had been imported from over the Channel, it was a keenly anticipated contest.

Both teams approached the match with different tactics. Stade were the more traditional side, playing with nine forwards and just six backs, as was still common in England. In contrast, Racing fielded just eight forwards and used the extra player as a second full-back, a formation used regularly by Yorkshire clubs, which they hoped would add defensive strength at the back and an extra option when attacking.

When the game kicked off in front of 2,000 spectators it was Racing that dominated the early stages, attacking with 'great vivacity' according to the official match report. Stade's defence held them at bay, not least thanks to the last-ditch tackling of Guernsey-born winger Pierre Dobrée.

Then, just before half-time, Stade turned the tables when Louis Dedet capitalised on a mistake by Racing's Alexandre Sienkiewicz and scored the historic first ever championship final try. Racing's gamble of playing two full-backs and eight forwards looked to have backfired. Dobrée, a student at the Sorbonne who had also attended Cambridge, converted, adding two points to the one awarded for the try, and Stade went in at half-time leading 3-0.

Racing used the break to make some tactical changes and came out determined to seize the initiative. Eventually, the pressure told and with ten minutes to go Racing forward Adolphe de Pallissaux managed to force his way over for a try in the corner. Gaspar González de Candamo y Rivero, one of the two sons of the Peruvian ambassador to the United Kingdom in the team and nephew of the president of Peru, stepped up to level the scores with a conversion from the touchline. The ball sailed between the posts and the teams were locked together at 3-3.

As full-time approached, Racing's forwards once more pushed Stade back. Eventually star fly-half Frantz Reichel forced his way over the goal-line but the weight of Stade defenders meant that he was unable to ground the ball. A 'maul in goal' developed as Reichel continued to struggle to get the ball down but eventually the referee blew his whistle to end the play and awarded Racing a 'tenu en but' worth one point.

At last their pressure had taken Racing into the lead. They could not have been luckier – later that year the ambiguous rule that had given them the point was abolished by the RFU and play would have been restarted with a scrum. But that day, the referee's interpretation of the law gave them the decisive advantage.

But was it? With just two minutes left, a Racing forward was penalised on the halfway line. Dobrée stepped up to attempt the penalty goal. With hearts in mouths, Racing players and supporters could do nothing but watch as Stade had one last opportunity to take the championship. Dobrée's kick had the power, the distance ... but not the accuracy. It sailed past the right upright and the referee blew for no-side. Racing were the champions of France. As the teams congratulated each other and the crowd streamed on to the pitch, cheers rang out, 'Vive le Racing Club! Vive le Stade!' and Racing held aloft the championship shield, the *Bouclier de Brennus*.

This was not just a match. It was a major social occasion for many of the French elite. A glance at the backgrounds of each of the two sides' players highlighted the social tenor of the game. As well as two nephews of the president of Peru, the Candamo brothers, four other players shared the aristocratic prefix 'de' before their surname. Ferdinand Wiet was in the French diplomatic service specialising in the Middle East, Félix Herbet was a merchant, Paul Dedet a senior official in the Ministry of Commerce and Edouard Bourcier Saint-Chaffray became a diplomat in Laos and Vietnam. Four other players, including Stade captain Courtney Heywood, were Britons living in Paris in business or government service.[1] But the most socially prestigious, and the man who would leave the greatest legacy to history, was none other than the referee: Pierre de Frédy, Baron de Coubertin.

Coubertin and the battle for rugby

Coubertin is remembered today as the founder of the modern Olympic Games, but he also has a crucial place in the birth of rugby in France. Born in 1863 to an aristocratic family whose forebears had survived the French Revolution, as a teenager he had been one of the legions of readers captivated by *Tom Brown's Schooldays*. He came to idolise Rugby School headmaster Thomas Arnold and made his first visit to the school in 1883.

He returned in 1886 and two years later published *L'Education en Angleterre*, which explained Arnold's educational principles to a French readership and argued for British sports to be included in the French school curriculum. Although he was almost religiously devoted to all British sports, rugby held a particular place in his heart. No other sport, he believed, possessed the 'combination and the drama' of rugby.[2]

Rugby and soccer had originally been taken to France by English expatriates in the 1870s. F. F. Langstaff, a South Western Railways manager, formed the dual-code Le Havre club in 1872 while directing the construction of rail network in northern France. The Bordeaux Athletic club was formed by British textile and wine merchants five years later in 1877. But France was not even the first continental nation to take up rugby.

Germany and Holland both began playing the game before the French. In Germany, a rugby club had been formed at Heidelberg College as early as 1870. In 1878 DFV Hannover was formed, and remains Germany's oldest rugby club. Two years later two rugby teams in Frankfurt, Germania and Franconia, merged to create FC 1880 Frankfurt, still playing the game today. The first football club of any kind to be established in Holland was the rugby-playing Koninklijke Royal Haarlemsche Football Club founded in 1879 in Haarlem.[3]

Yet it was only in France that rugby became a dominant sport and a vital part of national culture. In Germany, Holland and the rest of Europe soccer became the national sport. How did rugby, which considered itself the very embodiment of Anglo-Saxon manhood, become as important to France as it was to England? The founders of rugby were none too complimentary about the French. In 1861 one of Rugby's school magazines wrote that without hacking the sport would be nothing more than a 'pretty little skirmish in the Champs Elysées', while one of the clergymen founders of Wakefield Trinity declared that 'one Englishman [is] equal to five Frenchmen'.[4]

For an explanation of Gallic passion for the oval ball, we must turn to politics. Less than a month after the foundation of the RFU, France suffered a humiliating military defeat. On 17 February 1871 the Prussian army marched through Paris to mark the French government's surrender in the Franco-Prussian War. Germany was now the dominant power in continental Europe. France was eclipsed. But worse was to follow. As the government in Paris collapsed, the Parisian working class rose up, seized power and established the revolutionary Paris Commune. By the end of May the French army had regained control of the city and drowned the uprising in blood. At least 6,000 people were killed in the repression that followed.

For men like Pierre de Coubertin and the French elite, defeat by the Prussians and the revolt of the workers was traumatic, a profound shock to the system. They were desperate to restore France's international prestige and national glory. Some looked to the east for answers. In Germany, gymnastics was the most popular sport, usually allied to nationalist politics. Their French admirers set up hundreds of similar gymnastics clubs, many of which had openly patriotic and militaristic names like 'Revenge', 'Alarm' and 'Sentinel'.[5]

But Coubertin and many others like him looked westwards to learn from Britain and its empire. For the Baron and his supporters, Britain's rise to global dominance was underpinned by the importance of sport to national culture. On his second visit to England Coubertin visited Rugby School and, standing in the school chapel, 'dreamed that I saw before me the cornerstone of the British Empire'.[6] This belief that sport could restore France to its former glory led to Coubertin enthusiastically promoting rugby as a game for the French and especially for the French education system.

Rugby was slowly adopted by prestigious French *lycées* (high schools) that shared Coubertin's call for a French renaissance by emulating the British. It was pupils of Paris's Condorcet and Monge schools that formed Racing Club in 1882. Likewise, Stade Français was an initiative of old boys of Saint-Louis and other schools on the Left Bank of the Seine. By the end of the 1880s rugby had become an essential part of the curriculum of Paris's elite high schools.

The clamour for British sports continued to grow throughout La Belle Époque, as the period 1871–1914 would be known, and in 1887 Racing Club secretary Georges de Saint-Clair, an aristocrat who had been educated in England, set up the Union des Sociétés Françaises de Course à Pied (Union of French Athletic Clubs) in conjunction with Stade Français to promote British sports in France.

Perhaps piqued by Saint-Clair stealing a march on him, five months later Coubertin formed his own Comité pour la Propagation des Exercises Physiques (Committee for the Promotion of Physical Exercise), supported by former French prime minister Jules Simon and Dominican educator Father Henri Didon, the man who in 1891 coined the phrase 'Faster, Higher, Stronger' that would later become the motto of the Olympic Games. The following year the two organisations merged to form the Union des Sociétés Françaises de Sports Athlétiques (USFSA), presided over by Coubertin.

One of the USFSA's first acts was to organise that inaugural rugby championship between Racing and Stade Français in 1892. For those who suspected that the playing of rugby was somehow unpatriotic for a Frenchmen, the USFSA designed the *Bouclier de Brennus* championship shield to leave no doubt. It prominently bore the inscription 'Ludus Pro Patria' – 'the game for the Fatherland'. Rugby was on its way to becoming as French as it was British.

L'Ovalie versus the capital

Although that first championship final was contested by two Parisian teams, the popularity of rugby had already begun to expand beyond the capital. Bordeaux, the capital of the French wine industry and historic regional adversary of Paris, had begun to play rugby in the early 1880s, thanks to a combination of expatriate English wine merchants and French *lycée* teachers and students.

British sports were introduced into Bordeaux schools thanks to the efforts of doctor and sports enthusiast Philippe Tissié. In 1888 Tissié founded La Ligue Girondine d'Education Physique, dedicated to promoting the health benefits of sport in schools. Initially he encouraged a game called *barette*, a form of touch rugby that appeared to be related to ancient French football games such as *la soule*, but students soon hankered after the more physical modern version of rugby. Filled with enthusiasm for the game, in 1889 Tissié-inspired local *lycéens* founded the first adult club outside of Paris, Stade Bordelais. Others quickly followed and in 1893 Tissié's Ligue merged with Coubertin's USFSA, strengthening rugby's position as the region's up and coming sport.

From Bordeaux, rugby flowed into the villages and towns of south-west France. Agen, Marmande, Tonneins, Montauban, Colomiers and Saint-Gaudens all succumbed. Toulouse, at the southern end of the Garonne river, lacked the British connections of Bordeaux, but the game was established there by local students. Indeed, of the 13 Toulousain rugby clubs established by 1912 eight were high school or university sides.[7] Beyond the Garonne valley, Bordelais enthusiasts for the game founded clubs in Bergerac, Oloron and numerous other places in the Aquitaine region. Further afield, in 1892 Nantes followed suit with Stade Nantais and in 1893 Lyon students from the local Lycée Ampère formed FC de Lyon.[8]

But it was the south-west that quickly became a fortress of rugby. *L'Ovalie* – the Oval Land – as it would become known, stretched from Bordeaux in the north down to Biarritz in the Basque Country at the Spanish border, and right across the foot of the Pyrenees to Perpignan on the Mediterranean coast. Although rugby clubs eventually stretched across almost the whole of southern France to Toulon and beyond, it was the south-west that would become the beating heart of the game.

Rugby spread so rapidly across the region thanks to an extraordinarily propitious set of circumstances. The late 19th century was a process of intense centralisation and nation-building for France. The coming of roads, railways and the telegraph brought to an end the unofficial autonomy of France's regions, especially in the south. Educational reforms reinforced this sense of growing national unity, especially by standardising the teaching of the French language.

This drive for national revival made communications with Paris easier, helping knowledge of rugby to radiate out to provinces, but it also intensified provincial opposition to the capital. As in the north of England, regional resentment of the capital and all of its works helped to foster a deep sense of injustice in *l'Ovalie*, and those emotions were expressed through rugby.

These feelings came to a head on 30 April 1899 at Le Bouscat, a suburb of Bordeaux. For the first time ever, a team from outside Paris took its place in the French championship final. In front of 3,000 spectators, Stade Bordelais came face to face with Stade Français, the mightiest team in France, which had played in all eight of the previous finals, winning six. *Les Bordelais* had advanced to the final by defeating Stade Toulousain, earning them the right to be seen as the representatives of the provinces in the battle against the haughty metropolitans.

In a further echo of English rugby's north–south divide, Stade Bordelais's forwards were assigned positions in the scrum, a tactic pioneered by Yorkshire side Thornes in 1883, whereas Français followed the traditional practice of 'first-up, first-down' with the scrum being formed by whichever forwards got there first. Powered by a combination of this tactical innovation and emotional crowd support, Bordelais emerged from the fray 5-3 winners and the new holders of the *Bouclier de Brennus*. The provincials had finally defeated the metropolitans and, Bordelais or not, the entire south-west celebrated.

The triumphant Stade Bordelais side was a microcosm of rugby in the city. British expatriates were represented by centre-three-quarter

Campbell Cartwright, scrum-half Arthur Harding and, off the field, club president and local shipbroker James Shearer. The rest were the sons of the local bourgeoisie who had learned the game at school, and would become the future businessmen, administrators and politicians of the region. Their triumph would earn them a place in rugby history and local folklore.

They reached the final again the following year, but found themselves overwhelmed 37-3 by a Racing Club determined not to let the honour of Paris fall in the manner that their rivals had done the previous year. But the size of the defeat did not matter for those in the south-west who saw rugby as a proxy war against the nation's capital. Stade Bordelais made their third successive final appearance in 1901 – and this time they repeated their famous victory 3-0 over Stade Français.

But as if to confirm the arrogance of the capital, Stade Français protested against the result, claiming that three of the Bordelais players were not qualified to play in the match. Earlier that year Stade Bordelais had merged with Bordeaux University Club and the Parisians claimed that three former university players had not been members of the merged club for the required three months. The USFSA agreed with their fellow Parisians and ordered the teams to replay the final in Paris. Outraged at this arrogance, Stade Bordelais refused to replay – and the USFSA declared Stade Français champions.

The decision inflamed local opinion and united the whole of the south-west against the capital. Rugby had become a topic of conversation far beyond sports lovers. It had become a symbol of historic injustice and thwarted ambition. The game was now part of the cultural and political fabric of the region, and this was reinforced every time the championship final was played in the 1900s.

In 1903 Stade Toulousain made their first appearance in the final, going down 16-8 to Stade Français. The next five finals saw the enmity between Stade Bordelais and Stade Français replayed every year, with *les Bordelais* winning four of the five. Indeed, although it could not be known at the time, Stade Français's 1908 win would be the last time a Parisian team would win the *Bouclier* for over fifty years – and *les Français* would not lift the shield again until 1998.

The 1909 final confirmed that the axis of power in French rugby had shifted south, and particularly to the Garonne valley. For the first time two sides from the south-west met to decide the championship. Stade Bordelais played Stade Toulousain at Toulouse's Stade des Ponts Jumeaux in front of 15,000 spectators, the largest crowd ever to watch the final. The significance of the occasion was not lost on the local press; *Le journal des sports* famously proclaimed that the match would avenge 'all the provinces for the great injustices they have too long endured and for the unjustified humiliations that Paris believes it can inflict'.[9]

The final became a festival of south-western solidarity. Toulouse supporters welcomed their visitors with 'Vive Bordeaux', who responded in kind. But there was little fraternity on the pitch. Under a baking sun Stade Bordelais forwards exerted their dominance and exploited their superiority in dribbling the ball. After a single try in the first half, they ran away in the second, scoring another four tries and cantering home 17-0.

The next five finals before the outbreak of the First World War redrew the rugby map. The championship itself had grown into a competition that had 16 qualifying groups and subsidiary competitions for second XVs and second division clubs. In 1910 FC Lyon defeated Stade Bordelais to take the *Bouclier* to the Rhône valley in an upset so surprising that many of those waiting in Bordeaux for their heroes to return thought the result was a hoax.

There was no mistake the following season when Stade won all 22 matches to recapture the title, a feat repeated in 1912 by Stade Toulousain, earning the team the nickname of *la Vierge Rouge*, the Red Virgin, because of the spotless record of the men in red. It was Stade Toulousain's first championship, the significance of which was only apparent in the 1920s when it became clear that the epicentre of French rugby had shifted to Toulouse and that Bordeaux, the birthplace of *l'Ovalie*, was no longer the powerhouse it was in the 1900s. The *Bouclier* of 1911 was to be its last.

The tide of rugby continued to flow southwards towards the towns and villages bordering the Pyrenees. In 1913 the shield made its first visit to the Basque Country when Aviron Bayonnais, a rowing club that had only begun to play rugby in 1904, destroyed Paris's University Sporting Club de France 31-8. The following year the title crossed from the Atlantic coast to the Mediterranean when it was won by the French Catalans of Perpignan with a single-point victory over the unheralded Stadoceste Tarbais from the foot of the Pyrenees.

As the intensity of rugby increased, so, too, did the numbers watching it. Championship final crowds grew to unheard of levels: 12,000 crammed into Stade Bordelais' Le Bouscat ground to see them lift their seventh championship, 15,000 were at Toulouse to see them defeat Racing Club. Paris's Stade Colombes hosted 20,000 to see Aviron hand a rugby lesson to the local university students.

Such vast crowds brought large amounts of money into the game. Unlike the upper-class Anglophiles of Parisian rugby, the rest of France had a rather ambiguous attitude to Anglo-Saxon amateurism. The great 19th-century French novelist Stendhal had once remarked that 'who says amateur says dunce' and this was certainly the actual, if not the written, attitude of clubs in *l'Ovalie* to payments to players.[10] Intense competition between local towns and villages became the focus for rugby, eclipsing even the rivalry with Paris, and success could only be won with the very best players. The parallels between the game in south-west France and northern England did not go unnoticed. An enthusiastic Frenchman pointed out in a letter to the Northern Union in 1912 that French clubs made broken-time payments to players, leading him to suggest that a rugby league match should be played across the Channel.[11]

And, as was the case in Yorkshire, Wales provided a fertile source of rugby expertise for French clubs. Welshman James Crockwell was instrumental in bringing the free-running game to Pau's Section Paloise club in 1907. In 1909 the great Welsh and British Isles international fly-half Percy Bush unexpectedly became British consul at Nantes, coincidentally at the same time that former Bordeaux captain and businessman Pierre Laporte was establishing a senior club in the city.[12] Stade Bordelais themselves became embroiled in controversy when their Welsh coach, William Priest, openly tried to recruit players from Wales and Scotland. So blatant was Priest – he had openly advertised for players in Scottish newspapers – that the USFSA was forced to investigate.

Led by the redoubtable Cyril Rutherford, a Scot who played for Racing in Paris and who would became the first secretary of the French Rugby Federation after the First World War, the commission of enquiry found the club guilty and Priest was dismissed. He sued for wrongful dismissal and was reinstated. Nor did it deter *les Bordelais*, who in 1912 signed 'Billy Bordeaux', otherwise known as William Morgan, brother of Teddy Morgan who had scored the Welsh try that beat the 1905 All Blacks.[13]

Perhaps the most famous and influential Welshman playing in France at this time was Aviron Bayonnais' Harry Owen Roe. A three-quarter from Penarth, in 1912 he broke Aviron's try-scoring record and was also a noted drop-goal expert. But it was as the club's player-coach that he made the most impact as architect of the 'la manière Bayonnaise', the style of play in which 'tous les joeurs sont des trois-quarts' ('all players are three-quarters'). The phrase was made famous by Aviron captain Fernand Forgues and his brothers who had written a book, *La Manière Bayonnaise en Football Rugby*, but it was Roe who put it into practice, coaching his side to such a level of technical brilliance in 1913 that Perigueux were swept away 38-0 in the championship quarter-final and Stade Bordelais shut out 9-0 in the semi-final before the unfortunate Parisian students were put to the sword in front of their home crowd. The magic of Basque rugby owed much to its own Welsh wizard.

The men over *la Manche*

As rugby grew increasingly important for French local pride, it also became a symbol of French national pride. Rugby was a game with Anglophilia at its heart, and its French supporters were keen to encourage contacts across the Channel. Just a month after the first championship final in 1892, Stade Français hosted a visiting Rosslyn Park side. Underlining the close Anglo-French relations of the founders of French rugby, the match was arranged thanks to the Urwick brothers, one of whom played for the London side and the other was a secretary of Stade Français.

The following February a combined Stade/Racing team led by Frantz Reichel crossed the Channel to play two matches in London, losing to the Civil Service club and Park House FC on consecutive days.[14] Racing Club visited Oxford in February 1894 where, watched by Pierre de Coubertin, they went down 27-6 to the university. The status and confidence of Parisian rugby was boosted in March 1894 when Stade narrowly defeated visiting Rosslyn Park and Civil Service sides. 'The Frenchmen have made immense strides in the game,' wrote a member of the Civil Service side. 'They showed great dash and speed, while their tackling was extremely robust.'[15]

Buoyed by their victories, Stade then ambitiously invited Bradford side Manningham over in December 1894. But unlike the previous English visitors to Paris, Manningham were one of the strongest clubs in England – indeed, 18 months later they would be the inaugural champions of the Northern Union. Accompanied by more than 120 supporters, they travelled overnight from Bradford and arrived in Paris the following morning at 5.38. At the Vélodrome de Courbevoie later that day they brushed aside Stade by 27-0. Two days later they returned home, arriving back in Bradford early on the Friday morning, and fought out a hard-earned 3-3 draw with Batley on the Saturday afternoon.[16]

Stade's defeat did little to halt the progress of French rugby. The subsequent controversy about Manningham's amateur status – they were a predominantly working-class team and supporters of the RFU believed that they had paid their players – taught the Parisians the importance of upholding a strictly amateur ethos. Subsequent invitations were only made to those above reproach, notably Oxford and Cambridge universities who became popular visitors.

Given Coubertin's love of rugby, it was only natural that when Paris hosted the 1900 Olympic Games rugby would be part of the programme. The early Olympics were ramshackle affairs and the Paris Games were staged as part of the 1900 Exposition Universelle. Just three nations competed in the rugby tournament but only the French attempted to select a representative side. The German team was actually Frankfurt 1880 FC and Britain was represented by a scratch side of largely Birmingham-based players who called themselves 'Moseley Wanderers', not to be confused with Moseley FC, the city's leading side. Of the Wanderers' players, only Arthur Darby had played international rugby, having turned out the previous year in England's defeat by Ireland at Lansdowne Road.

In contrast, the French side comprised the best that Racing and Stade Français had to offer, including the inestimable Frantz Reichel. The squad also included Constantin Henriquez de Zubiera, Stade's Haitian three-quarter, who became the first black athlete to compete in the Olympics, and Cornelius Roosevelt, whose father was the cousin of US president Teddy Roosevelt and would later become a Hollywood film-maker. Four of the side were also members of the silver medal-winning French tug-of-war team.

Unsurprisingly, they defeated the Germans 27-17 and then easily overcame the Wanderers. The English side couldn't get back across the

Channel to play the Germans so the French were awarded the gold medal and the silver was shared between the two visiting teams. With a mere two games played, it was not an auspicious start to rugby's Olympic career.

Not until 1906 did France get its next taste of international rugby. There could not have been a greater contrast. This time their opponents would be the touring All Blacks, fresh from their British tour that had seen them lay waste to all bar one of their luckless opponents.

The game took place on New Year's Day 1906 on a frozen pitch in a cold drizzle, but it was a match that warmed each and every French rugby supporter. Ten thousand people gathered to watch the All Blacks cross for two tries in the first three minutes. An embarrassing capitulation seemed on the cards. But then, as the play swung back and forth, France took a leaf out of the tourists' book and a flowing movement saw forward Noël Cessieux crash over the New Zealand line to make 8-3. 'Up went a great shout,' reported the New Zealand *Press*. 'Le Brave! Cessieux, Cessieux! Un essai, un essai! Beautifully dressed Parisiennes waved their umbrellas and added their pretty voices to the tumult. Dignified and substantial-looking Frenchmen were looking more excited than if they had won £50,000 in a lottery.'[17]

The All Blacks stepped up a gear and scored two more tries to go in at half-time 18-3 up, but more was to come for the French. No sooner had the second half begun than Georges Jérôme touched down for a converted second try, but 18-8 was as good as it got for the French and the New Zealanders once again pulled away, scoring another six tries to make the final score 38-8. But for the French, this was as good as a victory. Eight points equalled the most scored against the All Blacks on their tour. It was the greatest day in French rugby history and the harbinger of future glory, as the London *Daily Telegraph*'s reporter exclaimed breathlessly:

I came back from the game in a delirious crowd of young Frenchmen. They dreamed of the day when [Rugby] football shall become a national game in this country. ... One had only to see and hear the delight of all young boys, and elderly boys as well, when France scored a try, then actually a second try, and converted it, to understand what strides athletics have made in France within the last few years.[18]

They would make equally giant strides over the next few years.

PART III

MAKING A RUGBY WORLD

In the 19th-century world of the British Empire and beyond, sport was one of the innumerable cultural links that bound Britain and the English-speaking nations together – and rugby quickly emerged as the leading winter sport of the Empire.

In New Zealand, the game became embedded deep in the national culture. In South Africa, it grew to be a passion that overcame the enmity between the Afrikaner and the English-speaking communities.

Elsewhere, rugby evolved in new and different ways. In Australia, it fractured into league and union, while its southern states began with rugby rules but developed a unique new game. And in Canada and the United States, rugby provided the starting point for two entirely different sports.

But whatever the code, rugby's influence was such that the shape of winter sport in most of the English-speaking world of the 19th century was most definitely oval …

9

NEW ZEALAND: ALL BLACKS IN THE LAND OF THE LONG WHITE CLOUD

At first glance it might seem inevitable that New Zealand would become a rugby superpower. After all, in *Tom Brown at Oxford*, the sequel to *Tom Brown's Schooldays*, Tom's best friend Harry East, the boy who introduced him to the game of rugby, emigrated to New Zealand to help conquer a new frontier for the British Empire.

Published in 1861, the book did not repeat the success of its predecessor. But if its leaden prose failed to seize the imagination, it did capture something of the mid-Victorian passion for imperial expansion. British settlers first arrived in New Zealand in the early 1800s but Aotearoa, or the Land of the Long White Cloud, as the indigenous Maori called it, only became part of the British Empire in 1840 with the signing of the Treaty of Waitangi. As British authority over the two islands was consolidated, not least through the confiscation of millions of acres of Maori land, the newly arrived immigrants set about creating a 'Britain of the South', a microcosm of the British culture and society they had left behind 14,000 miles away.[1] And few things were more important to them than sport.

By the 1860s, as in the rest of the English-speaking world, many different versions of football games were being played across the two islands of the colony. The first recorded football match in New Zealand took place in December 1854 at Christchurch on the South Island to celebrate four years of British settlement'.[2] Interest in the game grew to such an extent that New Zealand's first organised football club was formed in Christchurch in 1863. The club apparently played a 22 a-side version of football as played at Radley School, Berkshire, in England.[3]

Rugby was barely played in these early years. The Radley version of football – a dribbling-type game that resembled soccer – was popular and Australian Rules football was also played, in large part due to Melbourne being the major shipping link to New Zealand. In the 1860s a gold rush took place in Otago on the South Island, and attracted prospectors and workers in their thousands from the earlier gold rush in Victoria, many of whom played the Australian game. When it was founded in 1868, Nelson FC, the first club in New Zealand to play rugby rules, initially played both soccer and Australian Rules.

Rugby was a latecomer to the New Zealand sporting scene. The first recorded match did not take place until May 1870, when Nelson played Nelson College in an 18-a-side match under Rugby School rules. Nelson had taken up rugby rules at the urging of one of its members, Charles Monro, the son of the speaker of the New Zealand parliament who had been educated in England at Christ College in north London. The school was modelled on Arnold's Rugby and many of its pupils left with a missionary zeal for their game. Monro was one of them, and he not only persuaded Nelson to play Tom Brown's game, he also set up and coached a team in Wellington and then refereed the first game of rugby to be played on New Zealand's North Island in September 1870. The following year, Wellington's first organised rugby club was formed.

A similar tale of rugby evangelism accounts for the emergence of the game in Dunedin, the capital of Otago. At around the same time that Monro was refereeing the first match on the North Island, Old Rugbeian George Sale was appointed professor of classics at the newly founded Otago University. A year after his arrival Otago hosted its first rugby match when the university played a team of pupils and former pupils of

Otago High School.[4] The following year Sale was elected president of the new Dunedin FC. Despite such apparent progress, the club abandoned rugby for a period in 1875 when it played both Australian and soccer rules.

As George Sale's experience in Dunedin showed, even a determined commitment to rugby was not enough to ensure that it would become the nation's or even a town's leading sport. It had to find a deeper social significance, and not just for those who played and watched. To become established in the hearts and minds of thousands if not millions of people, rugby had to be more than a recreation for a few. It had to find a role in society as a whole.

Fortunately for the game, in 1876, following a bitter power struggle, New Zealand's national parliament abolished the autonomous provincial governments. Without their own governments, provinces such as Auckland, Canterbury and Otago lost a vital outlet for the expression of local pride. Into this vacuum stepped rugby, which provided a sporting arena for provincial rivalries as fierce and intense as anything politics could offer.

Rugby also gained from one of the major reforms that the national parliament introduced following the abolition of the regional governments. New Zealand's first railways had been built by each province using different sized tracks. Parliament was determined to prevent this becoming the norm, as it had in Australia, and from 1876 began building a national rail system with a standardised gauge. Alongside the railways, the telegraph, newspapers and steamship travel also developed rapidly, and rugby was ideally placed to take advantage of New Zealand's communications revolution.

Inter-provincial rugby matches could now be facilitated. Results could be telegraphed across the two islands in an instant. Although not yet strong everywhere, rugby became established in the major provincial centres, such as Auckland in 1873 and Waikato and Taranaki the following year. As railways and telegraph wires criss-crossed the colony, rugby became a common cultural denominator – and it was also a vital link with Britain.

When an Auckland representative rugby team set sail on a tour of provincial capitals in September 1875 it stimulated a sense of national identity by bringing the provinces closer together while at the same time promoting those very same regional rivalries. Three thousand people came to see the visitors in Christchurch and a similar number watched the tourists on a Wednesday afternoon in Dunedin. The tour became much more than a sporting occasion. Wherever Auckland played, it was treated as a civic festival, with businesses closing to allow the game to be watched and civic receptions organised for the teams. Local pride and provincial self-esteem were at stake. In order to ensure that honour was upheld, the strongest teams had to be fielded. And that meant maximum proficiency at rugby.

Within three years, rugby was the dominant winter sport in New Zealand. Rugby clubs began to spring up across the two islands. Helped by easier travel and communication and inspired by a civic athleticism, every town had a team. In July 1879 the first provincial rugby union was established in Canterbury, providing a regional structure for clubs and a selection panel to choose the strongest possible group of players for the provincial team.

Its lead was followed by Otago (1881) and Auckland (1883) and by 1893 18 provincial unions had been formed across New Zealand's two islands. According to some estimates, by the time the New Zealand RFU was formed in 1892 there were around 700 sides playing rugby across the colony.[5] In the space of a single generation, from 1870 to 1890, rugby had become the undisputed national sport of New Zealand.

Native New Zealanders

It was not just on the domestic front that rugby in New Zealand started to acquire national importance. Unlike its rival football codes, rugby could provide regular competition with colonial rivals across the Tasman Sea in Australia. In 1882, a representative team from New South Wales (NSW) toured New Zealand. Although the NSW side was more experienced, it lost three of its seven matches to Auckland (twice) and Otago. The tour was such a success that NSW quickly issued an invitation for a New Zealand team to visit Australia in 1884.

The 1884 tourists to Australia altered the balance of rugby power between the two nations for ever. New Zealanders saw that the 1882 NSW team relied on passing the ball through the hands rather than dribbling it along the ground. By 1884 New Zealand rugby had embraced this modern style of playing, improved on it, and shocked NSW rugby when, in the first game of the tour, they ran in ten tries to defeat a representative side representing western Sydney's Cumberland district by an astonishing 33-0.

Playing in dark blue shirts embroidered with a golden fern on the chest, they went through the eight-match tour undefeated and won all three games against the NSW representative team. 'They gave an exhibition of football such as has never been witnessed in Australia before,' recorded the *Sydney Telegraph* after New South Wales had been wiped out 28-2 in the second 'Test' match.[6] Thousands flocked to see the tourists. Trans-Tasman rugby rivalry had been well and truly ignited.

The tour also highlighted the commercial potential of rugby and hinted that rugby tours could emulate international cricket as profitable entertainment. The 1884 tour was organised and underwritten by a Dunedin businessman, Samuel Sleigh, who had been given a free hand by the New Zealand provincial rugby unions.[7] When Sleigh visited England in 1886 he met the RFU but they showed no interest in touring Down Under, saying that it would be 'left to either New Zealand or Australia to take the initiative in establishing international matches'.[8]

Sleigh did not capitalise on this opportunity but Thomas Eyton, an Essex-born businessman from Paihia, near the tip of New Zealand's North Island, stepped in. Eyton had been in England for the 1887 jubilee of Queen Victoria and had seen the large crowds that watched rugby matches. He also thought that English standards of play were not that much higher than those in New Zealand. He decided to organise a tour of New Zealand rugby players to Britain.

To maximise the tour's appeal, Eyton wanted it to be composed entirely of Maori players, not because he was sympathetic towards indigenous rugby, but simply because he believed it would be more profitable. In late Victorian Britain, racially stereotyped travelling shows of African, Australian aboriginal, Maori and Native Americans were immensely popular with audiences. Billed as curiosities of the Empire, such shows would attract spectators through lurid promotions of primitive behaviour and feats unknown to 'civilisation'. In 1868 the first Australian cricket team to visit England was composed of Aboriginal players, who performed boomerang, spear-throwing and dance exhibitions alongside their not inconsiderable cricketing skills. This was Eyton's model for a successful Maori rugby tour.

He was not alone in his vision. Back in New Zealand, Auckland forward Joe Warbrick had had exactly the same idea. But Warbrick had one advantage over Eyton: he was Maori. Warbrick had been one of the stars of the triumphant 1884 tour. A fast, strong full-back or three-quarter with a penchant for dropped goals, he was described by Samuel Sleigh as 'a player without a vestige of funk'. Born in 1862 to a Maori mother and a Pakeha (European) father, he became a boarder at the elite St Stephen's Native School in southern Auckland. Alongside Otago's similarly prodigious Jack Taiaroa, whose father was a Maori MP and who had been educated at the rugby nursery of Otago High School, Warbrick was one of the first Maori to play for New Zealand. Well known and well liked across the game, his popularity gave him the authority needed to lead a tour to Britain. He lacked just one thing: the money to finance a team.

He linked up with Eyton and James Scott, a Gisborne pub landlord, who raised £2,000 to finance the tour. By the beginning of April all the arrangements had been made and 26 players had been selected by Warbrick.[9] To Eyton's disappointment they were not all Maori. In fact, according to historian Greg Ryan, only five players had two Maori parents. Another 14 had Pakeha fathers and Maori mothers but five had no Maori lineage at all, and two of those were not even born in New Zealand. The team became known officially as the New Zealand Native Football Team, a subtle but suitably imprecise shift of emphasis.[10]

Warbrick had been forced to add non-Maori players to the side in order to ensure it was competitive. The reality was that there weren't enough Maori playing top-flight rugby at this time. Players like Warbrick, and his three brothers who toured with him, were exceptional. Their mixed-race ancestry had allowed them to go to high-status schools where they imbibed the rugby game. But outside this small elite, Maori at this time appear to have taken little interest in the game. Not only was the Maori population in decline in the second half of the 19th century, it was also largely rural based. As Greg Ryan has also shown, contrary to mythology, New Zealand rugby was always a largely urban game. And the bitter legacy of the mid-century wars with the colonists led many Maori to reject British culture and its sports.[11]

It took the Native team six weeks to reach England. They eventually landed at Tilbury Docks, London's newest and most important port, on 27 September 1888. Six days later they stepped out on to the pitch at Richmond to make history. They were the first representative side from outside Britain ever to play in England. And they became the first ever New Zealand side to perform a haka and to wear what became the iconic black jersey and black shorts, with a fern leaf incorporated on their shirt badge. They easily defeated a weak Surrey side and over the course of the next week defeated the stronger counties of Kent and Northamptonshire.

Much to the surprise of their hosts, far from being curiosities from the ends of the Empire the Native team were formidable opponents. They played a further 22 matches over the next two months, winning 16, drawing two and losing just seven. Four of those losses were to the northern powerhouses of Hull, Wakefield, Halifax and Swinton but among their many victims was the Ireland national team, which they swept aside five tries to two. Shortly after, the British satirical magazine *Punch* bemoaned:

> By Jove, this is a rum age;
> when a New Zealand team
> Licks Bull at goal and scrummage.[12]

The tour proceeded with brutal pace. On the first half of the tour, the tourists played 36 matches in just 87 days. In the second half, the pace increased to 38 in 86 days. Injuries came thick and fast, and the team began to show signs of fatigue and demoralisation. But such was their popularity in the north of England – the 'acme of English football', according to the *Otago Times* – that a number of crack northern sides, Brighouse Rangers, Halifax, Hull, Widnes and the champion county side Yorkshire, organised second matches with the tourists.[13] Thomas Eyton praised the northern sporting press for their support, saying that they 'became almost members of the Maori brotherhood'.[14]

By the time the match against England came around in February, the Native team had been so successful that, in the words of one reporter, 'there were not a few supporters of our winter game who looked with some anxiety towards the trial of strength between the Mother Country and the Maoris'.[15] But complaints about the supposed roughness of the Native team's play and suggestions that the tour itself verged on professionalism had become increasingly common in the south of England.

Fearful of an embarrassing upset, the England selectors named a strong side, featuring eight players from the north, including Dicky Lockwood. It paid off. The English struck first, as Morley's Harry Bedford scored two tries thanks to shoddy handling by the full-back Billy Warbrick behind his own line.[16] But the New Zealanders were disgruntled, claiming that Warbrick had actually touched the ball down on both occasions before Bedford could put his hands on it.

Worse was to follow. Just after the start of the second half, England's centre three-quarter (and future England cricket captain) Andrew Stoddart attempted to break through the defence but was grabbed by Tom Ellison, who explained later that: 'by a quick wiggle, however, he escaped but left a portion of his knickers in my possession. He dashed along and the crowd roared; then suddenly discovering what was the matter, he stopped [and] threw the ball down.'[17]

Doing the decent thing, the New Zealanders stopped play and formed a circle around Stoddart to preserve his modesty. Believing that the ball was dead, they waited for referee, and RFU secretary, Rowland Hill to order a scrum to restart play. He did not, and Frank Evershed, a handy forward and scion of the Evershed brewing family, promptly picked up the ball and ran in to score a try. Incensed at the blatant breach of the gentlemanly code they thought the English upheld, George Williams, Dick Taiaroa and George Wynyard walked off the field in disgust. Eventually they were persuaded to return but the spirit had gone out of the match and England won by four tries to nil.

When the time came to return home, there was no farewell, official or otherwise, from the RFU. The antipathy was mutual. Joe Warbrick believed that when the tourists lost they were tolerated but 'as soon as they commenced to win they were hooted and the papers were full of the weakness of the home side and the rough play of the visitors'. His experiences led him to believe that 'as a place of amusement England is, I should say, the rich man's paradise and the poor man's Hades'.[18]

The tour finally ended in Auckland on 24 August 1889, 14 months and 107 matches after it had begun. The side had won 78 of those matches, lost 23 and drawn six. They had also played nine matches of Australian Rules when they stopped off in Melbourne on the way home, of which they managed to win three, and apparently two games of soccer in the Newcastle region of Australia. For sheer numbers of games played, it was the greatest rugby tour ever.

From a playing perspective, the tour had been a huge success, raising the profile of rugby in Britain in the face of intense competition from soccer, which had launched the Football League in the same season as the New Zealand visit. But it had also highlighted deep fissures within the game. The New Zealanders were widely suspected of being professionals, and by the definition of the RFU they probably were. The RFU's imposition of strict amateur regulations on the game in 1886 outlawed all forms of payment to players. Although Warbrick and Eyton denied that the team was anything other than amateur, the financial records of the tour were never revealed.

The RFU's unrelenting opposition to any sign of professionalism caused New Zealand rugby to look over its shoulder continuously for fear of offending the Mother Country. The Otago union withdrew its competition trophy in the 1890s in case it transgressed the amateur regulations and New Zealand RFU was initially unsure what to do with the Ranfurly Shield donated to it by the Governor of New Zealand in 1902, it being well known that the RFU was opposed to cup competitions.[19] And the perennial suspicion that touring sides could not adhere to the amateur code meant that it would be another five years before another touring side left New Zealand.

All-conquering All Blacks

In 1893, nine years since they had destroyed the cream of Australian rugby, the New Zealanders returned to Sydney. This time it was an official tour, organised by the newly formed New Zealand Rugby Football Union. Established in Wellington in 1892, the new governing body brought together the provincial rugby unions in a national organisation, although it wasn't until 1895 that all unions finally affiliated. And at its first meeting, at the urging of one of the heroes of the 1888 Native team, Tom Ellison, delegates voted to adopt the black shirt with a silver fern as the national team colours.

Captained by Ellison, the 1893 tourists once again swept through Queensland and New South Wales, winning nine of their ten games. But they also suffered their first ever defeat on Australian soil when New South Wales caught them napping and ran out 25-3 winners at the Sydney Cricket Ground. Over 50,000 attended the matches against NSW, once again highlighting the growing popularity of rugby and its commercial potential. The following year New South Wales made their first tour across the Tasman Sea since their pioneering visit of 1882. It wasn't until their seventh game that they managed a win but they did manage to overcome an unofficial New Zealand XV by 8-6. As the cycle of reciprocal tours emerged, public interest exploded.

The New Zealanders returned to Australia in 1897, and their three matches against New South Wales attracted a total of 72,000 spectators. When 27,000 fans turned up for the third and decisive match, the Sydney sports weekly *The Referee* proclaimed that 'no greater public interest has ever clung to any other rugby contest played in the Southern Hemisphere'. Despite another victory by the visitors public interest in rugby continued to expand. And so did respect for the all-conquering New Zealand team: 'might we advise them to seek fresh foes on English, Irish and Scotch fields?' suggested *The Referee* after they had run in six tries in the last 15 minutes of the last match against NSW.[20] It was advice that the New Zealanders were to take on board with a vengeance.

An official tour of Britain had first been mooted at the formation of the NZRFU in 1892. It was raised once again by Tom Ellison in 1898 but no serious progress was made until the NZRFU's 1902 annual general meeting when a delegate from Canterbury proposed that a tour take place in 1903. After extensive discussions and planning delays, the tour was scheduled for the British 1905–06 season.

Enthusiasm increased exponentially with the arrival in 1904 of David Bedell-Sivright's British touring team. Unlike earlier British tours to South Africa that were selected on players' availability rather than form, the 1904 tourists boasted a strong back line, including Welsh maestros such as Rhys Gabe, Teddy Morgan, Percy Bush and Tommy Vile, and powerful forwards such as Blair Swannell, 'Boxer' Harding and Bedell-Sivright himself. They were unbeaten on the Australian leg of the tour, taking the Test series 3-0, but found the opposition much stiffer once they crossed the Tasman Sea.

The British narrowly won the first two matches, although not without controversy. Each side accused the other of cheating. The British objected to New Zealand's scrummaging tactics, which involved a seven-man formation consisting of two front-row forwards to hook the ball out of the scrum, three second-rowers and two back-rowers – known as a 2-3-2 scrum – plus a 'wing-forward' who would feed the ball into the scrum and shield the scrum-half at the back of the scrum as the ball came out. For their part, the New Zealanders were shocked at the physicality of the British players. The play of Bedell-Sivright, about whom it was claimed that 'his conception of football was one of trained violence', caused much ill feeling, as did the widespread belief that the British side too easily resorted to gamesmanship when it suited them.[21]

When the two teams played their first ever Test match in front of a capacity 20,000 crowd at Wellington in August 1904, expectations and tension were running high. Despite the reputation of the British forwards, the New Zealand pack dominated the game, allowing winger Duncan MacGregor to cross for two tries to steer the home side to a 9-3 win. 'Every young New Zealander today will feel an inch taller because of the victory that was won at Wellington by the football champions of the colony,' exclaimed the *New Zealand Herald* proudly.[22] As if to underline the superiority of the colonists' rugby, the tourists could manage nothing better than a draw in their remaining three matches, which culminated in a humiliating 13-0 loss to Auckland.

Anticipation for the 1905 tour of Britain could not have been higher. The first 17 tourists were named at the end of February 1905, three more in March, two of whom later withdrew, and the final seven in June. Contrary to popular belief that the success of New Zealand rugby was due to the predominance of farmers in its teams and the strenuous outdoor life led by a rural population, only three of the 27 tourists were farmers. Fifteen were blue-collar industrial workers, three more worked in transportation and six were from the white-collar professions.[23] This was a side that represented the modern, urban world.

They finally arrived at Plymouth on board the SS *Rimutaka* on 8 September 1905. No one in Britain or New Zealand had the slightest inkling of the tsunami that was about to engulf rugby. It started in Newton Abbot, Devon, on 16 September. Within three minutes of the opening match of the tour against the county side, the All Black five-eighth Jimmy Hunter ran in for the opening try of the tour. Seventy-seven minutes later, the All Blacks had scored a further 11 tries to win by an amazing 55-4. Their opponents, who next year would win the English county championship, could manage only a single dropped goal in the final minutes of the match.

To demonstrate this was no fluke, the tourists then scored another 11 tries in a 41-0 rout of Cornwall. Two days later they laid waste to Bristol in another 41-0 victory, although this time they were restricted to a mere nine tries. Northampton and Leicester kept the margin of defeat down to 32 and 28 points respectively but it wasn't until their seventh match, against the reigning county champions Durham, that the All Blacks finally conceded a try in a relatively narrow 16-3 win.

But New Zealand tries kept on coming. Fifteen were racked up against a combined Hartlepool side, nine against Northumberland, 13 against Oxford University. The All Blacks were not only vastly more skilled and tactically sophisticated than their English opponents, but they also approached the game with a very different attitude. Their focus was on running, passing and scoring tries. Unbelievably for a touring rugby union side, they would leave Britain having scored more than twice as many tries as goals: 205 tries to 102 goals, only two of which were drop goals. Nowhere was their different philosophy more apparent than in their attitude to penalties. Instead of the accepted British practice of kicking for goal when awarded a penalty, the New Zealanders invariably ran the ball at penalties. Indeed, they scored a mere four penalty goals on the entire tour.[24]

It would be two months before the All Blacks were seriously challenged. On a freezing, foggy day in Edinburgh, Scotland pushed the tourists to the limit and led 7-6 at half-time. Playing with three half-backs and only three three-quarters, Scottish tactics were to keep the ball tight in the forwards and restrict the All Blacks' running game. According to *The Times*, the Scots' backs never passed the ball and rarely ran with it, preferring to hoof the ball into touch to set up their forwards.[25] With under ten minutes to go, a historic victory seemed in sight when, camped on the New Zealand line, the Scottish forwards worked the ball out to Lewis MacLeod who set himself for a drop goal. It was on target but fell agonisingly below the crossbar. From the drop-out the All Blacks launched an attack that swept across the pitch for George Smith to touch down in the right corner. Three minutes from time, Bill Cunningham sealed the issue by gathering and scoring after a chip kick over the head of Scottish full-back John Scoular. As narrow 12-7 winners, however, the All Blacks no longer looked quite so invincible.

Neither Ireland nor England, their next international opponents, got anywhere near them. Both lost 15-0, with England conceding five tries on a quagmire of a pitch, with four going to Duncan MacGregor. This litany of abject failure against the New Zealanders was ascribed fashionably by some to the growing 'degeneracy' – physical and otherwise – of the British, but the more perspicacious commentators pointed out the simple fact that not only was English rugby divided in two but also that soccer accounted for a significant proportion of Britain's best athletes. In New Zealand, rugby union had no competitor for the athletic cream of the nation's youth.

This was proved in December when the tourists went to Wales. At that time, there were no professional soccer or rugby league clubs in South Wales and rugby union ruled supreme. With the pick of the most talented players and fuelled by intense local competition, Welsh clubs were strong enough to test the All Blacks in a way that, Scotland excepted, they had not experienced on tour. Newport, Cardiff and Swansea tested the All Blacks to the very limit, losing by three-, two- and one-point margins respectively. Most notably, Swansea prevented the tourists from scoring a try for the first time, losing narrowly 4-3 thanks to a lucky drop goal from Billy Wallace.

The New Zealanders' biggest test came against Wales itself. As we now know, the fate of the match pivoted on a Bob Deans' disallowed try, and the Welsh held on to a victory that cemented rugby union as Wales' national sport. But for the New Zealanders the disallowed try was the solitary flaw that denied them the perfect tour, a setback that they would forever seek to avenge.

Despite the loss, the All Blacks returned home national heroes. The tour had made rugby the single most important cultural symbol of the New Zealand nation. The All Blacks became the embodiment of the strength and vitality that New Zealanders believed their nation possessed. In the decades that followed, the deeds of the 1905 tourists became part of the national mythology.

For the world of rugby, the All Black tour was the equivalent of another epochal event of 1905, the naval battle of Tsushima, when the might of Tsarist Russia's fleet was humiliated by the Japanese navy. The old order had been defeated, a new power had arisen and a revolution was in the air.

10

SOUTH AFRICA: FROM GOG'S GAME TO SPRINGBOKS

When Sommie Morkel ran out into the pouring rain in front of 40,000 English rugby fans on a cold Saturday afternoon at Crystal Palace in December 1906, it was not the first time he had found himself surrounded by the British.

Six years earlier, the tough forward had faced a similar yet far more deadly situation. On the evening of 10 March 1900, he and 1,500 other Afrikaners had assembled at Driefontein in a final effort to block the way of British forces as they swept across from Kimberley to take Bloemfontein, the capital of the Orange Free State, just 40 miles away. Despite being outnumbered and outgunned, Morkel and his fellow *burghers* held the British off until late in the evening, killing 82 and wounding 342.

As darkness fell the British, supported by Australian and Canadian cavalry, began to assert their superiority and the Free State line collapsed. Many of the Afrikaners disappeared into the night but a determined 22, Morkel among them, fought on until they had no choice but to surrender. Now clear to advance, the British forces marched into Bloemfontein three days later and it seemed that the Second Anglo-Boer War, known simply as the Boer War in Britain, was reaching its final stages.[1]

It was not. The Afrikaners responded to the fall of their towns with a gruelling campaign of guerrilla warfare. The British replied by forcing the civilians into concentration camps and inflicting a scorched earth

126

policy across Afrikaner land. The killing would continue mercilessly for another two years.

For Sommie Morkel the war was over. Within a few weeks, he was en route to a British prisoner-of-war camp on the island of St Helena in the middle of the Atlantic Ocean, where some 5,000 Afrikaners would spend the rest of the war squeezed into two camps, Deadwood and Broadbottom. In all, 24,000 POWs would be incarcerated here and in similar camps in Bermuda, Ceylon and India.

Over 1,200 miles from the war, Morkel and his fellow prisoners had to find some way to pass the next two years. Morkel for one suggested playing rugby. Soon a tournament developed in the Deadwood camp and challenge matches were being played against Broadbottom. This was no ordinary kick about. The Deadwood side fielded three current internationals as well as future Springbok Morkel. The Afrikaners' commitment to rugby was intensified by the fact that their British guards would only play soccer. For the first time, rugby had become a symbol of Afrikanerdom.[2]

So when Sommie Morkel lined up against England on that winter's afternoon in London, he could be forgiven for thinking that he was about to play with men who, just a few short years ago, could have been shooting at him or jailing him. Men like Billy Miller, Fred 'Uncle' Dobbin and John Raaf had all fought for Queen and Country in that long and arduous South African war. Now, here they were ready to give their all in pursuit of an oval ball.

And to make matters even more tense, Miller, Dobbin and Raaf were playing for the same team as Morkel. Despite being on opposite sides in a war that had led to the deaths of 17 per cent of the Afrikaner population, they were now all Springboks.

Gog's game and beyond

South African rugby union was forged on a partnership between English speakers who prided themselves on their Britishness and Afrikaners who were resolute in their rejection of Britishness. Coming just four years after the end of what is known today as the Second Boer War, the 1906 Springbok tour was organised specifically to create a sense of national unity between the two distinct white communities of southern Africa.

The tour captain was an Afrikaner, Paul Roos, the vice-captain the English-speaking Harold 'Paddy' Carolin. The team had been chosen to ensure parity between the two communities. 'The tour has united us,' Roos told his players before they embarked for Britain. 'South Africa was one, and all differences had been forgotten. ... We now understand each other better, and if that is going to be one of the results of our tour, we shall be more than satisfied.'[3]

It was a remarkable achievement so soon after the end of the war. It was even more notable because rugby had been brought to South Africa only a generation earlier by the largely expatriate British community that settled in the Cape Colony following its acquisition by Britain in 1814. There was little interest in taking the game to Afrikaners, and the Afrikaners had even less interest in playing it.

The first organised football-type games in South Africa appear to have taken place at Cape Town's Diocesan College, which had been established in 1849. In later years the school would become known as 'Bishops', one of the nation's most important rugby nurseries, but it did not begin by playing rugby. In 1861 a new principal arrived from England. Canon George Ogilvie had been educated at Winchester College and was a firm believer in the educational value of football for his boys. Like most young footballers educated at a public school, he possessed supreme self-confidence and was convinced of two things. Firstly, his old school's code of rules was currently the best way to play football. And, secondly, he could improve on them.

The boys at Bishops therefore played a version of the Winchester College football game. The original form of the game was played with a round ball but the scrum, known as a hot, was a central feature of the play. Scoring consisted of goals, conversions and behinds, a feature still found today in Australian Rules football. The game was constrained by a small pitch, due to the location of the school, but teams were usually 15-a-side. It is not clear which elements of the original game were retained by Ogilvie, nor what new features he introduced, but his version of football – known as 'Gog's Game' after his nickname – became the leading form of the game in Cape Town for the next decade.[4]

Although a one-off 18-a-side match of indeterminate rules had been played between teams of 'Home-Born' and 'Colonial-Born' players some 500 miles east in Port Elizabeth in May 1862, it was Cape Town that became the cradle of sport in South Africa.[5] In August 1862 Cape Town's first adult match took place when a Civil Service team took on a Military team of officers drawn largely from the 11th Regiment based there.

The game was kicked off by the Civil Service's Adrian van der Byl, who was widely recognised as one of the best footballers on the field. In many ways van der Byl's personal story anticipated that of South African rugby. Born in the Cape to an English mother and an Afrikaner father, he was educated in England at Marlborough College. Looked after by his elder brother, the Liberal MP Philip van der Byl, he moved to Edinburgh in 1855 and attended Merchiston School in Edinburgh, where in 1858 he captained the school in what was probably the first ever inter-schools match, against Edinburgh's Royal High School, and then again later in the year against Edinburgh Academy, the world's oldest continuous rugby match.

The press was quick to link the game with the principles of Muscular Christianity: the match displayed 'strength and science worthy of *Tom Brown's Schooldays*,' wrote the *Cape Argus*.[6] Among the hundreds of fascinated spectators at both matches was Canon Ogilvie and his schoolboys. Ogilvie challenged the two sides to create a combined team to play a team from his school under Gog's Game rules. Despite the fact they were playing a team of adults, Bishops emerged victorious from the challenge match the following week. The kindling had been lit, and enthusiasm for football, albeit of Gog's unique brand, spread across the elites of Cape Town and the wider Cape Colony itself. Although for its initial decade the game was mainly played by schools and army regiments, by 1875 adult clubs began to be formed to play the game.

The growth of the game was both spurred by and a consequence of the rapid political changes that were taking place in South Africa. By 1858 a combination of incessant war and famine had forced the Xhosa peoples of South Africa to abandon their independence, allowing large-scale immigration into their former lands by British settlers. In the following decade the English-speaking population grew rapidly, bringing with it a love of sport and, crucially, the wealth with which to play and enjoy it. In the late 1860s the discovery of huge diamonds near what would become the town of Kimberley started a mass 'diamond rush' that brought thousands of prospectors flooding into South Africa.

Clubs like Hamilton's, Green Point, Gardens and the Country Club were formed by members of the professional and merchant classes and became part of the cultural and social fabric of life in the Cape. The year 1875 saw the creation of a football club at Stellenbosch, an Afrikaans-speaking town a little over 30 miles from Cape Town. It was to be the first incursion of rugby into the Afrikaans world.

The game was still played according to Gog's rules of the early 1860s, although these had been amended in 1873 by a local committee led by John James Graham. But across the British Empire, rugby was becoming part of the international cultural network that linked the English-speaking middle classes of the world. In 1877 the first English cricket tour to Australia had taken place and highlighted how, in an age of rapid sea travel and telegraphic communication, sport was becoming increasingly important to the British Empire. So, keen to assert their essential Britishness, not least against their Afrikaner neighbours, voices were heard in the Cape calling for the adoption of what many saw as the most British of games: rugby.

In 1876 the Western Province club had split over the question of adopting rugby rules, with the anti-rugby faction leaving to set up Villager's football club, which would later become a bedrock of rugby in the Western Cape. Although the adoption of rugby was initially viewed as a failure, the fact that it was the most popular code in the Mother Country carried substantial weight in the Cape community. One of the most prominent spokesmen for this view was Frederick St Leger, the editor of the militantly British *Cape Times*, who used his columns to encourage greater cultural links with 'Home'.

This appetite for change found its champion in England rugby international and talented organiser William Milton, who arrived in Cape Town in late 1877. A strong runner and talented kicker, Milton had played as a 19-year-old in England's defeats of Scotland in 1874 and Ireland in 1875. He was also a splendid cricketer and would captain South Africa in its second ever Test match against the touring England side in 1889. In later life he would be Cecil Rhodes' right-hand man and become the 'Administrator' of Southern Rhodesia. On arrival in the Cape, Milton immediately joined the Western Province cricket club and, soon after, Villagers football club.[7] He soon became the secretary of the club and within months had established himself as a powerful figure in local sports administration.

Less than a year after his arrival, he had arranged for Villagers and Hamilton's, the two leading club sides, to play an exhibition match under rugby rules. He then persuaded John James Graham, the man who had codified the local football rules in 1873, that rugby was a better game and the province should switch its allegiance. At the annual general meeting of Villagers in May 1879, Graham and Milton proposed that the club should adopt rugby rules. Their motion was carried unanimously. It was, Milton would say later, 'the real beginning of the rugby union game in the Cape'.[8]

A national game?

The 1879 season saw almost every club in the Western Cape playing rugby. One of the last teams to hold out against the code was Bishops, who, perhaps in memory of Canon Ogilvie, carried on playing their old game until they ran out of opponents. Rugby began to spread across the Cape and, in 1883, a Western Province Rugby Football Union was founded as the governing body of the game in the region. As if to demonstrate their loyalty to the Mother Country, the new organisation applied for membership of the RFU.

Rugby's expansion was not simply down to the enthusiasm of its supporters. Southern Africa underwent convulsive changes from the late 1870s that enabled rugby to flourish. The defeat of the Zulu nation by the British Army in 1879 consolidated British rule in Natal and led to the growth of schools that played rugby in the south-eastern province. A short war between the British Army and Afrikaners in the Transvaal during 1880–81 led to an increase in British nationalist feeling and the number of troops stationed in South Africa. The former increased the desire for symbols of Britishness while the latter brought rugby balls and players. And in 1886 gold was discovered in Witwatersrand. Prospectors poured into the Transvaal, creating the boomtown of Johannesburg in the process and transforming the economy of South Africa.

As economics and immigration pulled the South African regions together, rugby began to play a unifying national role. In 1883 the first knock-out cup competition began, the Western Province Grand Challenge Cup. As in many other parts of the world, the tournament was the catalyst for rugby to expand beyond its enthusiasts and become part of the everyday life of local society. The first winners were Hamilton's, whose inaugural champion team included four Versfeld brothers, one of whom, Loftus, would become a central figure in the South African game – and would eventually have one of the most famous stadiums in the rugby world named after him. In the first decade of the cup, Hamilton's won it a further five times and Villagers three times.

The game's growing prominence was further enhanced in 1884 when a team from Kimberley, where the discovery of diamonds had transformed farmland into a burgeoning city in less than a decade, toured the Western Cape. Rugby had been taken to Kimberley by British Army regiments and teachers. The social tenor of the game can be gauged from the fact that Kimberley's Pirates rugby club had been named after the Gilbert and Sullivan operetta *The Pirates of Penzance* had been staged in the city. Three thousand people watched the Kimberley tourists play Villagers, an almost unprecedented crowd for a sporting event in South Africa.[9]

The next few years witnessed an explosion of interest in the game across English-speaking South Africa. The Griqualand West (home province of Kimberley) RFU was formed in 1886, followed by the Eastern Province RFU in 1888 and the Transvaal, where clubs such as Johannesburg's Wanderers and Pirates had been formed in the late 1880s by English speakers, in 1889.

It was these three provinces that would join Western Province in competing for the inaugural provincial championship – that later become known as the Currie Cup – in 1889. That same year the South African Rugby Board (SARB) was created. In 1890 the newly formed Rugby Union of Natal, an area previously dominated by soccer, was presented with a knock-out competition trophy by local diamond magnate Sir Thomas Murray. The success of the Murray Cup would eventually lead to rugby eclipsing soccer in the region. Rugby was now a force throughout South Africa.

It was also a sport enjoyed by all races. Under the apartheid regime, it became commonplace for white rugby players and commentators to claim that black and 'coloured' people were not interested in the game. 'It's not in their culture,' claimed Springbok hooker Uli Schmidt typically, albeit years later, in 1994, when asked why there were so few black players.[10] But rugby was a vital part of black and coloured culture in the 19th century. When Kimberley played in Cape Town on its groundbreaking 1884 tour, the crowd reflected the multi-racial nature of South Africa:

> Men of every shade and colour and position could be seen. The Malay [as Muslims were incorrectly called by the English-speaking press] and the Negro were there, as well as the elite of Cape Town society; and the varied and bright costumes of the ladies, set off as they were by the large white canvas enclosure and marquee, made quite a pretty sight.[11]

It wasn't just as spectators either. Excluded from membership of white clubs and governing bodies, in 1886 the Western Province Coloured Rugby Football Union (WPCRFU) was founded by four non-white clubs. In 1898 the WPCRFU started the tremendously popular Fernwood Cup tournament. In that same year black African clubs formed a City and Suburban Rugby Union. In the Eastern Cape rugby had been played by Africans as early as 1878 when it had been introduced into Port Elizabeth's Anglican school for Africans, the 'Kaffir' Institution. The city's first African club was Union RFC, founded in 1887. Port Elizabeth's Coloured Rugby Union was founded in 1892. In Kimberley, the Griqualand West Colonial RFU became one of the first non-racial sports organisations in South Africa. It was founded in 1894 by Isaiah (Bud) Mbelle, the first African to pass the Cape Civil Service entrance exam, and had enough African and Muslim teams that there were soon enough sides to run three divisions.[12]

Bud Mbelle was the driving force behind the creation of the South African Coloured Rugby Football Board in 1897, the direct counterpart of the exclusively white SARB. He persuaded Cecil Rhodes to provide the funds for a trophy for a national non-racial provincial tournament based on the structure of the Currie Cup. The Rhodes Cup was a magnificent piece of silverware that reportedly cost more than the (gold) Currie Cup. Its first winners in 1898 were, as was so often the case on the rugby field, Western Province.

The reality of racial oppression and poverty meant that matches were often difficult to organise and facilities far below those provided for the white population. Segregation and poverty made travel to and from games extremely difficult, yet despite often appalling conditions, the enthusiasm for rugby continued to burn brightly into the 20th century.

If there was one group in South Africa for whom rugby was not a significant part of its culture in the Victorian era it was the Afrikaners. Some Afrikaans speakers had been involved in the game, most notably at Stellenbosch where a team had existed from 1875 and the forerunner of what became Stellenbosch University had begun to educate the sons of the Afrikaner middle classes in the values of rugby from the 1880s.[13] But the Afrikaner population of the Transvaal and Orange Free State was a largely rural, farming community for whom organised games had little appeal. As the British Army discovered to their cost, target shooting rather than team sports was among the Afrikaners' most popular pastimes. When rugby clubs were established in Pretoria, Johannesburg and other Afrikaner towns, they were largely the creation of English speakers.[14]

It should come as no surprise to find that people who had been in constant conflict, armed disputes and at war with Britain over the previous century would not have any interest in playing its sports. The real mystery is how and why Afrikaner indifference to rugby would turn into a deep passion in the space of a generation or two.

Two nations, one team

It was men like Bill Maclagan who helped transform Afrikaner sporting culture. Educated at Edinburgh Academy, Maclagan made his debut for

Scotland as 19-year-old in 1878 while playing for Edinburgh Academicals. A fantastic defender at full-back or in the three-quarters – 'Bulldog' Irvine once said that he 'would rather fall into the hands of any back in the three kingdoms than into those of W. E. Maclagan' – he captained Scotland in the notorious 1884 Calcutta Cup match, when the dispute over the English try led to the formation of the International Board and England's withdrawal from the Four Nations.[15] He moved to London to become a stockbroker in 1880 and captained London Scottish until he retired in 1891. In all he wore the blue shirt 25 times over 13 years, a record for his era.

There was a last hurrah for Maclagan. In 1889 C. Aubrey Smith's England cricket team had toured South Africa to public acclaim. Although Smith's side won their matches easily, the tour was a financial success and a triumph for the imperial cultural bond. Inspired by its cricketing cousins, the South Africans approached the RFU about the possibility of a rugby tour in 1891. Suspicious that tours could lead to professionalism, the RFU insisted that there had to be 'nothing of a money-making speculation in the undertaking' and that it had to be entirely under its control.[16]

They were relieved when Cecil Rhodes, indisputably the richest and most powerful man in South Africa, guaranteed to underwrite the tour. Moreover, the RFU's selection committee picked only players they could trust, which largely meant that they had been privately educated. At the head of the team they placed the unimpeachable amateur and resolutely respectable Bill Maclagan.

So when Maclagan and his men boarded the RMS *Dunottar Castle* in Southampton in June 1891 their mission was to play good rugby, uphold the honour of the RFU and strengthen the ties of the British Empire. Appropriately for such a historic tour, the *Dunottar* was also making her maiden voyage. The ship was a symbol of the changing world that was making international rugby possible. Her state-of-the-art technology enabled her to cut the length of the voyage to Cape Town from 42 to just 17 days.

This was not her only contribution to rugby history. The *Dunottar* was owned by the Castle Shipping Line of Sir Donald Currie, a keen supporter of sports of all kinds. He sailed down to the Cape with the team and presented them with a gold trophy that he asked be awarded to the best South African side they encountered on the tour. It would then become a championship trophy to be competed for by the South African provinces. Henceforth to be known as the Currie Cup, it was to become one of the most famous trophies of the rugby world.

The tour was a triumph. Although the side was selected only from English and Scottish players and was not at all representative of even these countries' best players, the tourists won all their 20 matches as well as the plaudits of all who saw them. The South Africans even had the advantage that their captain for the first test, Herbert Castens, refereed the third and final Test match in Cape Town.

For Bill Maclagan it was a personal triumph. At the age of 33 he played in all but one of the games, was the third highest try scorer and had helped to rescue international rugby from the suspicions of professionalism and commercialism that the RFU feared so much.

The tour was as much a success for the South Africans on and off the field. Although none of their sides managed to win a match, a number had restricted Maclagan's men to a single score, including Griqualand West, to whom the Currie Cup was presented. 'I have little doubt that in the future a representative South African team will be found well to hold its own with the best of British teams,' commented RFU secretary Rowland Hill. He was not to know that it would be 78 years before his own England side would again defeat 'a representative South African side'.[17]

The tour also demonstrated that rugby was not only a strong link with 'Home' as most English-speaking South Africans regarded Britain, but was also an arena to play out international rivalry. This was one of its advantages over soccer, which in areas such as Natal was still more popular than rugby. Although soccer clubs from Britain did make the voyage to southern Africa, none had the prestige of rugby or cricket tours. Rugby was now the foremost winter sport of the Empire.

Maclagan's tourists also raised the profile of rugby among Afrikaners. As part of their diplomatic duties, a delegation from the side met Paul Kruger, the prime minister of the Transvaal-based independent South African Republic, and the symbol of Afrikaner resistance to British rule.[18] On the pitch, Stellenbosch had restricted the British to a 2-0 victory in the last match of the tour, the tourists' lowest score and narrowest winning margin of the tour. The South African team for the final Test included the unmistakably Afrikaner Japie Louw and the brothers Hasie and Oupa Versfeld. There could be no doubt that Afrikaners, used to challenging the British in politics and military affairs, could now also do the same on the rugby field.

That feeling was reinforced five years later, when a British team returned. That touring side was no better than the 1891 team – eight of the side never won national caps – although, instead of Scots and Englishmen, the 1896 side comprised English and Irish players. This time five of the 21 matches were held in Johannesburg in the Transvaal, which just eight months earlier had been the target of the Jameson Raid, a botched British attempt to provoke an uprising against the Afrikaner government in the Transvaal.

The symbolism of a South African side confronting the British in unconquered Johannesburg, despite the majority of the team being English speakers, could not fail to resonate across the region. But it was in Cape Town two weeks later that the future of South African rugby was glimpsed. Led by a forward pack containing Paul De Waal, Herman van Broekhuizen, Pieter Dormehl and Charlie van Renen, the South Africans outplayed the British to take the fourth Test match 5-0. At a time when British–Afrikaner relations were on the brink of open war, it was a victory with significance that would stretch far beyond the playing fields of the Cape.

Three years later, war did indeed break out.

From POWs to Springboks

The Second Anglo-Boer War broke out in October 1899 – the first was the brief confrontation of 1880–81 – and rugby went into almost complete hibernation. By the time the war finally ended in May 1902 with the signing of the Treaty of Vereeniging, between 20,000 and 28,000 Afrikaner women and children had died in British concentration camps, together with probably 20,000 black men, women and children (of whom no accurate records were kept) and around 27,000 soldiers of both sides. The Transvaal and the Orange Free State lost their independence and became territories of the British Empire. Ultimately, they would take their place as parts of the Union of South Africa when it constituted in 1910. For the Afrikaner population, the war left a legacy of distrust, suspicion and hostility to all things British

There was one exception to this. Koot Reynecke was from the Orange Free State. He was captured as a teenager and, just as Sommie Morkel had been imprisoned in St Helena, sent to a prisoner-of-war camp in Ceylon. There he learned to play rugby and when peace was declared he went to Stellenbosch to become one of its outstanding forwards. In 1910 he earned his Springbok cap against Tommy Smythe's touring British side. Without his experience as a POW, where the enthusiasm and experience of privately educated young men helped the game find its feet, he might never have picked up a rugby ball.[19]

This grounding in the camps helped to give rugby a distinctively Afrikaner appeal, as a symbol of Afrikaner resistance and self-sufficiency. When men like Morkel and Reynecke returned home, rugby was part of the story they told about how they survived and kept their spirits high. It was no coincidence that it was in 1902 that the first adult club was formed in Bloemfontein, the capital of the Orange Free State.[20]

As the British government began the process of uniting white South Africa after the war, the growing importance of rugby to Afrikaners meant that rugby's role in the informal diplomacy of the British Empire became even more important. This was also to the liking of the RFU. Rowland Hill said that rugby tours had 'great Imperial importance in binding together the Mother Country with the Overseas Dominions', and less than a year after the end of the war it announced that a British team would tour South Africa.[21]

Led by another Scotsman, Mark Morrison of Edinburgh's Royal High School Former Pupils, the tourists comprised English, Scots, Irish and a solitary Welshman, Reg Skrimshire. Skrimshire would eventually move to South Africa himself and play for Western Province. Like its predecessors, no attempt was made to select the best British players. Seven of the 21 tourists never played for their countries, and even Skrimshire had not played in an international for four years. In fact, with the exception of Morrison and his fellow Scottish forward David Bedell-Sivright, who would lead the 1904 British tour to Australia and New Zealand, perhaps the only player with a lasting legacy was Louis Grieg, who later became an adviser to the Royal Family and a supporter of Oswald Mosley.

Within days of their arrival, the team suffered a shock to the system, losing the first three matches of the tour. They won their next five on the Cape but then moved inland and lost to Kimberley twice and, most symbolically, twice to a Transvaal side featuring Sommie Morkel in the forward pack. They stayed in Johannesburg for the first Test, where they drew 10-10. A fortnight later they could only manage a 0-0 draw in the second Test at Kimberley. With the series tied, the deciding final Test, and last match of the tour, was played at Newlands Stadium in Cape Town one week later.

It was the home side that emerged victorious, thanks to two tries and a conversion. The British team failed to register even a point. It was the first time that the South Africans had won a Test series – and they would not lose another at home for 55 years. It was also the first time that the team had worn the now famous green shirt. Up until the last Test, South Africa had traditionally played in white, but perhaps sensing that they were about to make history, it was suddenly decided to change to a more distinctive colour. Captain Barry Heatlie suggested the green of the Old Diocesans club and the tradition was born.

The decisive victory to take the series meant that rugby had achieved something that South African cricket had failed to do in four previous England cricket tours – it wouldn't be until 1906 that the South Africans would defeat England on the cricket pitch. So in the course of 80 minutes, rugby had become a symbol of South African national pride. For English speakers, it was an example of the intense rivalry with the Mother Country. For the Afrikaans speakers, it was a way of teaching the arrogant British a lesson. Both communities now had something that united them.

This made rugby a precious commodity in South African politics, and its place at the heart of the creation of the new Union of South Africa was cemented by the South African team's historic first overseas tour of Britain in 1906. The side comprised an equal number of English and Afrikaans speakers and was led by Paul Roos, a commanding Afrikaner forward who had learned his rugby at Stellenbosch; his vice-captain was Harold 'Paddy' Carolin, an English-speaker who had been educated at Bishops. Between them, they embodied both traditions of South African rugby.[22]

When Roos and his men landed at Southampton in September 1906 anticipation was high. This was partly because of the shock that the All Blacks had given British rugby the previous year, but it was also due to the fact that there had already been three tours to South Africa and there was a degree of familiarity with its players. 'Relentless tackling, good following-up and a capacity for effective dribbling in the loose' was how *The Times* described the strengths of the South African pack, also noting that the backs were very speedy. Their flying three-quarter, Japie Krige, even reminded its correspondent of Dicky Lockwood. But, he opined, while they might defeat the majority of club sides, he did not expect them to triumph over the 'national fifteens'.[23]

Before they even took to the field, however, they made a decision that was to shape the future not only of rugby but of their country. Aware that the British press would inevitably give the team a nickname Roos, Carolin and the tour manager Cecil Carden decided to come up with one first. Roos suggested 'Springbokken', after the name of the small antelope embroidered on the green team shirt, and another tradition was born.[24]

They eventually made their British debut at Northampton, where a massive crowd saw them romp home 37-0 against an East Midlands representative side. Over the course of the seven weeks they despatched all of their opponents with conspicuous ease, running in 354 points to a paltry 21. Only Glamorgan offered a serious challenge, restricting the margin of victory to a mere 6-3 in front of 40,000 at Cardiff Arms Park. Although the physiques of the Springboks were commented upon, as were those of all visiting southern hemisphere tourists, a key factor in the success of the side was their tactical innovation.

Their forwards packed down in a 3-4-1 formation – three in the front row, four in the second and a single back-row forward. Paddy Carolin appears to have been responsible for introducing the tactic to the tourists but, as usual in South African rugby, there is an unresolved debate as to whether it originated with the Villagers team or at Stellenbosch. The 3-4-1 formation meant that the scrum could be wheeled around more easily to attack, and that the two flankers in the second row and the back-rower (who would become known as the number eight in modern rugby) could quickly detach themselves to attack or to snuff out opposing moves from the base of the scrum. It was the beginning of the modern scrum. English tactics, still based on solid pushing, were no match for it.

It might have been the case that the Springboks' canter through English rugby encouraged complacency. Missing an injured Roos, the tourists were overwhelmed by the Scottish forwards led by David Bedell-Sivright, who, along with Scottish captain Louis Greig, had an insight into the South African style of play, having toured there in 1903. Foreknowledge proved to be the key to the 6-0 Scottish victory, which was sealed by tries to each of Scotland's wingers, Ken McLeod and Alexander Purves.

The Springboks did not allow themselves to be caught napping again. A week later they ran in four tries to defeat Ireland 15-12 and the week after that pulled off their most remarkable victory with an 11-0 win over a Wales team that comprised the core of the side that had conquered the All Blacks just a year earlier. In the circumstances, England's 3-3 draw in the pouring rain at Crystal Palace was the highpoint of English rugby in the new century.

But even this could be taken as a moral victory for the South Africans. The England winger who scored the equalising try was Freddie Brooks, who lived in Rhodesia, then considered by many as part of South Africa. Paddy Carolin wanted to select him for the Springbok tour but a five-year residential qualification had been introduced by the selection committee. Brooks had come to England at Carolin's request with the aim of calling him into the team as a replacement for an injured player. He played a few games for Bedford to keep fit and then suddenly found himself named in the England team to face the side that he had intended to play for.[25]

The Springboks made their last appearance against Cardiff at the Arms Park. Desperate to restore Welsh pride after what had been seen as a humiliating defeat in the international match, Cardiff put on a show of classic Welsh back play with each of their four three-quarters running in tries to take down the tourists by the handsome margin of 17-0. The claim of the Welsh to a place in rugby's emerging world elite was still strong.

The Cardiff result aside – after all, it was the tourists' final match in Britain and injuries had taken their toll – the tour was a triumph for the Springboks. They had come to what many in their party regarded as the Mother Country, and certainly what all felt to be the home of rugby, and returned with just two defeats from 28 matches. Moreover, they had endeared themselves to their British hosts in a way that the All Blacks had not. 'The clean character of the South Africans' game has won for them a higher reputation all through the country than that which the New Zealanders secured,' said the *Guardian*. 'They have no system of tricks for execution when the referee was not close at hand, and the penalties against them for infringing the rules have been surprisingly few in number.'[26] It came as no surprise to find the RFU keen to invite them back and they returned in 1912, more than a decade before the New Zealanders or Australians received a similar invitation.

But the most striking impact of the tour was felt when they returned home to South Africa. The tourists, exclaimed veteran politician and journalist J. H. Hofmeyr, 'had made Dutch and English almost one, and had taken a great step in the direction of racial unity, whilst they – the poor, petty statesmen and politicians – had been trying to do the same thing in the past in vain'.[27]

There was little domestically that English speakers and Afrikaners could agree upon, but when it came to uniting against the outside world no other sport, nor indeed any other cultural activity, offered the same opportunity as rugby. The Springbok, the emblem that had been quickly adopted in a hotel meeting room by Roos, Carolin and Carden, would become the national symbol of white South Africa, not just of its sports teams but of its national airline and many other institutions.

And thanks to the experiences of men like Sommie Morkel, rugby itself had come to be one of the most important of all South African institutions.

11

AUSTRALIA: WALLAROOS AND KANGAROOS

It took 252 days for the 11 ships of the 'First Fleet' to reach Botany Bay from Great Britain in January 1788. En route, they suffered chronic infestation and water-rationing, encountered raging seas and freak storms, and witnessed the deaths of 48 of their number and the births of 20 babies.[1] Their arrival marked the beginning of modern white Australia.

One hundred years later, in April 1888, the 'first fleet' of touring rugby players arrived on Australian soil, having taken just 42 days to complete the journey. In stark contrast to their predecessors, the rugby tourists' ship, the *Kaikoura*, was equipped with electric lights, a smokers' lounge, a piano and a library.[2] Sea-sickness and occasional rough weather were the only threats to their wellbeing. Their arrival would ensure that rugby became Australia's pre-eminent international winter sport.

Of the 22 tourists who made the trip, 14 were from the north of England and played for clubs that after 1895 would become rugby league clubs. Three came from the small industrial town of Hawick in the Scottish Borders, one each from Edinburgh and Cambridge universities, one was described as an unattached gentleman and one came from Douglas in the Isle of Man. The final tourist was Andrew Stoddart, the future England cricket and rugby captain who also played his rugby for Blackheath.

The side offered an insight into where the strength of British rugby lay in the late 1880s. At their head stood Bob Seddon. Born in Salford, he captained Broughton Rangers before moving to Swinton. Seddon was a warehouseman whose rugby talent had seen him rise to the highest levels of the game. Now he had reached the pinnacle of rugby: he was captain of the first British touring team to Australia and New Zealand.

Seddon had earned his position: a skilful forward of some brilliance, he possessed all the qualities of a natural leader. Shrewd, smart and brave, he was able to stay calm in a crisis. 'I don't think I was born to be drowned,' he wrote home after the *Kaikoura* had encountered especially stormy seas en route and he had almost been swept overboard.[3] Sadly, he was to be proved wrong.

As the team made its way across the big cities and country towns of Australia and New Zealand, Seddon was their spokesman, leader and inspiration. But, while spending an afternoon rowing on the Hunter River in Maitland, New South Wales, his boat overturned and he was unable to free his feet from the boat's stirrups. And there, alone and trapped by a simple, everyday mistake, Bob Seddon drowned. He would never know the extent of his importance to the game that he graced.[4]

The clash of the codes

In the century that separated the arrival of the two pioneering groups, three million people, mainly from Britain but also from Europe and the Far East, had flocked to *Terra Australis*. Initially a penal colony and then a magnet for those seeking to make their fortunes in the mid-century gold rushes, Australia became a land for those British immigrants who wanted to build a 'New Britannia', a better version of what most of them called the 'Mother Country'. The same would be said about their attitude to rugby.

Nineteenth-century Australia was nothing if not British. Until 1901, when it became a unified nation, it was a continent of independent colonies linked only by geography and a shared sense of Britishness. One historian has even remarked that it was a 'suburb of Britain'.[5] Australians ate British food, read British newspapers and played British sports. The first recorded cricket match took place in 1803 in Sydney, athletics meetings were staged as early as 1810 and by the 1830s horse racing was taking place regularly throughout New South Wales, the first colony to be established by British settlers in 1788. And, just as in Britain, *Tom Brown's Schooldays* became both an Australian bestseller and a guide to the moral importance of games.

It was no surprise when, in July 1858, Tom Wills, a young Australian who had been educated at Rugby School, placed an advertisement in the weekly *Bell's Life in Victoria* (itself based on London's *Bell's Life*) calling for the formation of a 'foot-ball club' to help keep cricketers fit during the winter. Less than a year later, in May 1859, he chaired a meeting of the Melbourne Football Club in the city's Parade Hotel that drew up the first set of rules for 'foot-ball' in Australia. The rugby version of football had been established Down Under.

Or had it? Although Wills had been a keen player of rugby at school, he believed that improvements could be made to the game's rules. Some of his fellow committee members thought that even more radical changes were needed. So, although the Melbourne game began as a version of rugby, it quickly evolved into something quite different.

First to go was the offside rule. Melbourne FC saw nothing wrong with players standing yards in front of the ball-carrier waiting for him to kick it to them. And because the quickest way to get the ball to a downfield player was a long, high kick, the ability to jump above opposing players to catch the ball on the full – known as a 'mark' – became a vital skill.

The Melburnians also didn't like players being allowed to run with the ball in their hands, so they insisted that the player had to bounce the ball every five or six yards when running with it. And, for reasons that have never been clear, passing the ball from the hands was frowned upon. Instead, the ball had to be held in one hand and punched with the other to a teammate.

There were other differences, too. The crossbar was removed from the goalposts and the shape of the pitch shifted from rectangular to oval. Very quickly, the new game was seen as a uniquely Australian version of football, one that reflected Australia's special character. Tom Wills, it was later claimed, had told the 1859 meeting that 'we shall have a game of our own'.

As with so much in the history of sport, this was simply another case of inventing a 'tradition'. All of the elements of Melbourne game could be found in the versions of football played at the same time in the English-speaking world. The mark was a feature of RFU and Football Association rules. Sheffield football rules originally did not have an offside rule. Bouncing the ball while running was a rule that could be found in the types of football played by some private schools, such as Bramham College in Yorkshire, not to mention across the Atlantic Ocean at Princeton University, whose rules of football also shared the Melbourne penchant for punching the ball instead of passing it.[6]

But if the rules of Melbourne football were not as distinctive as its supporters believed, the game was unique in one very important way: it was the first type of football to become a mass spectator sport anywhere in the world. Melbourne was part of Victoria, the colony to the south of NSW that had been founded in 1851. In the same year it became a colony, gold was discovered in Victoria and Melbourne's population grew from 23,000 to 268,000 in just 30 years.[7] As the gold rush brought people flooding into the city, their appetite for amusement and recreation was voracious. As early as the 1860s, when rugby and soccer in England were still largely pastimes for the privately educated, thousands of people were going to 'Victorian Rules' (later known as Australian Rules) football matches in Melbourne. Football fever was first diagnosed Down Under.

In contrast, the original version of rugby in Australia was very much the sickly cousin of Australian sport. Rugby was the leading winter sport in Sydney but still very much the preserve of the elite. The first recorded game of any type of football in Australia took place in 1829 when the *Sydney Monitor* reported that soldiers at Sydney Barracks had been playing football, a game that the newspaper for some reason felt compelled to point out was 'much played in Leicestershire'.[8] But little else was heard of the game for the next 35 years.

It wasn't until the middle of 1865 that the first rugby clubs were started in Sydney. In 1859 and 1863 Sydney's Albert Cricket Club had published Rugby School's rules in its handbook, and members of the club led the way in founding Sydney Football Club on 30 May 1865. They played a team from the Australian Cricket Club in July and then against Sydney University, destined to become one the central powers of Australian rugby, in August.

Frustrated by their lack of opponents, in June the following year Sydney FC decided to switch to Victorian Rules and hoped to arrange matches with Melbourne clubs. Sydney University's team had to content itself with matches against the Military and Civil Cricket Club. But by 1869 no rugby, nor football of any sort, seems to have been played in Sydney, apart from a couple of matches between the university and the crew of the visiting HMS *Rosario*. The game appeared to be all but dead.

It was a man called Monty Arnold who administered the kiss of life to the ailing sport. Monty and his brother Richard (who had attended Rugby School) were the sons of William Arnold, later speaker of the New South Wales' parliament, and both were passionate about rugby. In 1870 they helped to found the Wallaroo Football Club, named after an indigenous animal closely related, as the name suggests, to the wallaby and the kangaroo.

As might be expected, Wallaroo players were drawn from young men who had attended Sydney's elite schools. The formation of the club coincided with a number of these schools taking up rugby. Newington

College, Sydney Grammar and King's School, Parramatta, were among those that played early inter-school matches and which would over subsequent decades become pillars of Sydney's 'Great Public Schools' (GPS) rugby.

The Wallaroos also appear to have been the first side in Australia to switch from the traditional 20-a-side rugby to 15-a-side when they played the Volunteer Artillery's 10th Battery in 1871. As early as 1870 Sydney's *Town and Country Journal* had complained about the number of 'mauls and scrimmages' in the game, an early indication of an Antipodean preference for open, running rugby. By 1873, 15-a-side had become the norm in Sydney.[9]

The following year, the Wallaroos called a meeting of clubs around Sydney to decide on a common set of rules and establish a governing body for the game. Supported primarily by Sydney University and the city's elite schools, ten clubs came together and in June 1874 announced the formation of the Southern Rugby Football Union, rugby's first governing body to be formed outside England and Scotland. The fact that they chose to be the 'Southern' RFU was an indication that they saw themselves as the southern hemisphere branch of the English RFU.

Progress was slow. By May 1877 only three other clubs had joined the original ten members of the SRFU. Crowds were sparse and the game was still the preserve of the privately educated. In contrast, Victorian Rules football in Melbourne was booming. Thousands of people from all classes attended matches, dozens of clubs had been formed and the code was spreading to Tasmania and South Australia. Not surprisingly, many in Sydney looked enviously at the vitality and excitement of the rival code to their south.

In 1877 the dissatisfaction with the state of rugby felt by many in Sydney was matched by the growing desire of Melburnians to expand their game. Carlton FC, arguably Melbourne's leading Victorian Rules club, agreed to play two matches against Waratahs FC, Sydney's most vocal critic of rugby's rules. The first match between the two sides was played under rugby rules. The second used the Victorian version of football rules. Unsurprisingly, each club won the match played under its own code, but the interest in Victorian Rules led the SRFU to discuss switching codes. However, loyalty to rugby's British links and a shared suspicion of the southern upstart meant that the Sydney clubs narrowly rejected the proposal. Shocked into action by this threat to its very existence, rugby in Sydney shook off its torpor and began to grow.

A similar story can be told of rugby in Queensland, the colony immediately to the north of NSW. A football club had been formed in Brisbane, the state capital, in 1866 that had played a loose form of Victorian Rules. It was another decade before two more teams were set up. They opted for rugby and Brisbane FC switched to rugby rules to enable matches with the newcomers. But isolated from other rugby teams – Sydney was more than 450 miles away – the Brisbane clubs only tinkered with the rules and by 1880 were back playing the Victorian game.[10]

The turning point came in 1882 when, in an attempt to develop links between Queensland and NSW, the captain of Brisbane FC, Pring Roberts, wrote to the Wallaroo club in Sydney suggesting a game between the two sides. Many in Brisbane also wanted to play against the Victorian Rules clubs in Sydney, but the SRFU made the Queenslanders an offer they couldn't refuse. If the visitors only played rugby, the SRFU would pay all the costs of the tour.[11]

From that moment, rugby in Queensland never looked back. Four thousand spectators watched them lose to NSW at the Sydney Cricket Ground but the visitors then shocked the Sydney sporting scene by winning their next two matches, the last against the Wallaroos themselves. The Queenslanders invited NSW to Brisbane in 1883 and triumphed over their rivals by a single point. The match also happened to be the first time in the southern hemisphere that a whistle had been used by a referee, Sydney's Monty Arnold.[12]

A few months later Queensland clubs formed a Northern Rugby Football Union to be rugby's governing body in their colony. Regular inter-state matches followed and victory over NSW in Sydney for the first time in 1886 further boosted rugby's fortunes. By 1889, 25 clubs were playing the game. Rugby's status as Queensland's number one football code had been sealed.

Triumph of the tourists

As the growth of the game in Queensland demonstrated, nothing stimulated interest in rugby as much as matches against touring teams. Rivalries between the Australian colonies could be played out on the rugby field. But the early and rapid development of Victorian Rules in Melbourne actually hampered its ability to gain support in NSW and Queensland. Melbourne teams were so good there was no chance that any team from outside Victoria could defeat them, which made the game rather pointless as a way of celebrating colonial pride for anyone other than the Victorians.

Once they had realised the popularity of tours, rugby administrators in NSW were quick to capitalise on this. In 1882 they despatched a team to New Zealand to become the first ever rugby tourists to the 'Shaky Isles', so-called because of the earthquake activity. Captained by Sydney University's Edward Raper, the tourists were as much ambassadors for Australia as they were rugby evangelists. The tour ended equitably with NSW winning four matches and the New Zealanders triumphing in three. Another rugby rivalry had been established.

Inter-colonial matches between NSW, Queensland and New Zealand became major public events and rugby quickly became the dominant winter sport in Australia's eastern states. The size of crowds now watching the battles between NSW and Queensland had not gone unnoticed by sports promoters and in 1887 the cricketing entrepreneurs Alfred Shaw and Arthur Shrewsbury started to investigate the possibility of organising a tour of British rugby players to Australia and New Zealand.

It was to be a strictly money-making venture. The team would play rugby in New South Wales and Victorian Rules in Victoria, thus maximising their appeal to Australian sports fans. When Shaw and Shrewsbury approached RFU secretary Rowland Hill for official backing, he refused to 'support or approve' the tour but would not forbid players from taking part. He also warned 'players must not be compensated for loss of time'.[13] This was to be a strictly unofficial tour.

Although Shaw and Shrewsbury would have preferred the RFU's backing, its firm insistence on amateurism also served their business interests. 'If the rugby union can get players to come out without paying them anything, all the better for us,' noted Shrewsbury.[14] But there was no doubt that each British tourist was being paid to play. W. H. Thomas of Cambridge University was paid £90. Andrew Stoddart, who was appointed captain after Seddon's tragic death, had been 'bound' to the tour by an advance payment of £50. The most unfortunate player was Halifax forward Jack Clowes, who naively admitted to an RFU inquiry before the tour that he had been given a £15 advance by the organisers. The RFU promptly declared him a professional, but he had already set sail for Australia and could not play in any rugby games on tour. He can perhaps be seen as the symbolic convict on the trip to Australia.[15]

The team arrived in New Zealand for the first leg of the tour on 23 April 1888. Over the course of the next month they won six out of nine matches, drawing with Wellington and losing to the powerful Auckland and Taranaki sides. The New Zealanders were taken aback by the way in which the tourists heeled the ball out of the scrum and the speed with which they passed the ball among the backs. These were lessons they would take to heart and which would eventually become hallmarks of New Zealand rugby.

The tourists then went back across the Tasman Sea to Sydney to embark on the first half of the NSW leg of the tour, winning four matches and drawing one. Three days after a 10-10 draw with a King's School 'Past and Present' side they took to the field in the Melbourne suburb of Carlton to play their first ever game of Victorian Rules football. It was not a success. Carlton FC, one of the biggest names in the Victorian game, run amok, scoring 14 goals to the tourists' three. As to be expected from a team of talented athletes, however, the more the tourists played Victorian Rules the better they became. They eventually won seven of their 19 matches in the unfamiliar code.[16]

Reinvigorated by their non-rugby interlude, the tourists then went through NSW, Queensland and a second leg in New Zealand without losing a match. They returned home in November, having won 27 of their 35 rugby matches. But their impact could not be measured simply by a win-loss ledger. As they wound their way down Australia's eastern seaboard, they attracted bigger crowds than had ever been seen before for rugby matches.

The tourists had established rugby as the game of NSW, Victorian Rules was the sport of choice of Victoria, and henceforth never the twain would meet. The tour also had a deeper cultural impact. As the Australian press noted, the majority of the British tourists, including their captain, were men from the industrial working classes in the north of England. Rugby in Sydney and Brisbane had traditionally been the preserve of the upper and middle classes, but the tourists demonstrated that it was equally a game for those who earned their living with their hands. To compete successfully against overseas visitors, wrote *The Referee*, 'I should like to see ... the working-man element introduced into our clubs'.[17]

This could not have come at a more propitious time. Australia was in the midst of an industrial boom. Sydney and Brisbane both doubled their populations in the 1880s. Legislation to reduce the standard working day in Australia now meant that manual workers had leisure time to fill – and few activities could match the excitement and involvement provided by rugby. The game rapidly became popular in the industrial heartlands of NSW and Queensland. And, just as in England's northern counties, the coming of the working-class player to the game brought new and intractable problems.

The great rugby rebellion

Although it deferred to the RFU for leadership and inspiration, Australian rugby had never fully shared that body's outlook on the game. Rugby players and supporters Down Under preferred an open, passing game rather than the heavy scrummaging of the English. Cup and league competitions, frowned upon by the RFU as harbingers of professionalism and dirty play, were commonplace. And amateurism in Australian sport was less rigid than in England.

Despite the growth in the number of clubs in Sydney, the sport was still dominated by upper-class gentlemen's clubs like the Wallaroos and Sydney University. Such clubs were based on social networks and had no ties to local communities. In contrast, more and more clubs began to be formed to represent local, and especially working-class, areas such as Balmain, Newtown and South Sydney.

Just as had happened in northern England, rumours soon began to circulate that the best working-class players were being paid to play for certain clubs. In early 1898 the New South Wales RFU investigated claims that NSW players Billy Howe and George Outram had received payments to play in the previous season's series with Queensland. Yet calls for NSW's working-class players to be properly compensated for travel and other expenses could be read regularly in the Sydney sporting press. The clash between rugby's past and its emerging future was symbolically highlighted in 1898 when the Wallaroos played the recently formed Sydney FC, composed of working-class Sydneysiders. In a vicious, spiteful and bloody match, Sydney FC emerged victorious by 15-5. The writing was on the wall.

The rigorous amateurism favoured by the RFU and the NSWRU seemed unfair to the average Australian. More to the point, it seemed downright hypocritical. The British tours of 1899 and 1904, and New Zealand's numerous visits, brought money pouring into rugby's coffers thanks to the huge attendances that touring sides attracted: for example, 34,000 saw the first Test match between Australia and Great Britain at the Sydney Cricket Ground in 1904. Major club matches in the early 1900s could also pull in crowds of up to 20,000. Yet none of that cash found its way to players – indeed, they often found themselves out of pocket because of the distances they had to travel and the (unpaid) time they had to take off work to play.

Things came to a head at the start of the 1907 season when rugby authorities decided to discontinue the official medical insurance scheme for injured players, despite income from matches almost trebling between 1902 and 1906. This meant players had to arrange their own insurance. At the same meeting the Metropolitan Rugby Union, which ran the club game in Sydney, voted to increase its secretary's salary to £250, roughly twice a manual worker's average wage.[18]

In July the All Blacks played NSW at the Sydney Cricket Ground. Fifty-two thousand spectators, an Australian record, saw the visitors triumph 11-3, but while the game brought more than £2,500 into rugby union coffers, dockworker Alec Burdon, one of rugby's star forwards, was left unable to work after damaging his arm and shoulder a few weeks earlier. The ending of rugby's insurance meant that he received no money while injured.

Players' resentment at their treatment at the hands of the rugby union hierarchy now reached boiling point. Blair Swannell, a tourist to Australia with the 1899 and 1904 British sides now living in Sydney, warned that 'the players will take the matter into their own hands, and go from one extreme to another, electing to office officials pledged to what every lover of Rugby football should strive to prevent – professionalism'.[19] His prediction was about to be proved correct.

In 1906 the Auckland City team visited Sydney. In the side were four members of the triumphant 1905 All Black tourists to Britain, including George Smith and Charlie Seeling. There is strong evidence that Smith met with disgruntled Sydney rugby players and discussed the possibility of starting a Northern Union rugby league competition. Smith's athletics and rugby careers had taken him to England and he was well aware of the success of the Northern Union in England. He may even have secretly met English NU officials.[20]

While this was going on, Victor Trumper, arguably Australia's greatest batsman before the arrival of Don Bradman, and Labour Party politician Harry Hoyle were also actively seeking to channel players' discontentment towards a new deal for Sydney rugby. Regular meetings began to be held at Trumper's sports shop in Sydney's Market Street. Shortly after the Northern Union had accepted Albert Baskerville's proposal for a professional New Zealand team to tour Britain to play rugby league, Glebe forward Peter Moir turned up to one of Trumper's meeting with a telegram from George Smith, by now one of Baskerville's closest collaborators. It asked if the group would be prepared to organise a team to play the New Zealand team in Sydney on its way to the UK. They agreed unanimously, aware that the next steps they took would be momentous ones.

In late June a Sydney newspaper warned that Baskerville's side – known as the Professional All Blacks – could include Australian players. By the start of August the trickle of rumours of a breakaway rugby league had become a torrent and Sydney held its breath for the arrival of the rugby rebels. On 8 August 1907, 50 people, including representatives of eight clubs and five first-grade team captains, met in the centre of Sydney at Bateman's Crystal Hotel on George Street.

Chaired by Harry Hoyle, the meeting voted to set up the New South Wales Rugby Football League (NSWRFL) and organise a committee to select a team to play against Baskerville's team. Four days later, 'Dally' Messenger, the Eastern Suburbs three-quarter and the biggest name in Australian rugby, announced that he was joining the NSWRFL. He was just one of 138 players who had signed up with the new organisation.

Shortly after, the Professional All Blacks arrived in Sydney. Dubbed the 'All Golds' by their opponents in the press in reference to their allegedly mercenary instincts – although the team's profits would be divided between the players, as happened on Australian cricket tours – they drew 20,000 to the first of three matches against NSW on 17 August. The series was played under rugby union rules as the Northern Union rule books had yet to arrive. A week later, Messenger announced he would be joining Baskerville's men as a guest player on their British tour. In mid-September, the rugby union authorities banned all those players who had turned out against the All Golds, once more highlighting the unfairness of the old game. Rugby league was up and running, and the NSWRFL was confident of its success.

As the tumultuous season ended, frenzied activity continued behind the scenes. In January 1908, rugby league clubs were founded in all of the major districts of Sydney. The first to be formed on 9 January was Glebe, at the heart of working-class Sydney. 'The league was formed because it was believed that the set of conditions controlling the [rugby] football unions were not suitable for the democracy and social conditions of the Australian people,' Harry Hoyle told the meeting.[21] Nine clubs were admitted to the first NSWRFL premiership which kicked off on 20 April.

The previous month in Brisbane, the Queensland Rugby Association had been founded and immediately affiliated with the NSWRFL. Bolstered by the tremendous success of the All Golds tour of Britain, the Northern Union agreed to an Australian side touring for the 1908–09 season. In May the inaugural rugby league Test match was played between Australia and New Zealand. For the first time, the Australian players wore a kangaroo on their jerseys. Henceforth, 'the Kangaroos' would be the name by which the national rugby league would be known.

Now the warehousemen, wharfies and manual workers of NSW and Queensland had a 'game of their own'. Australian rugby had come a long way since the days of the Wallaroos.

12

FROM RUGBY TO GRIDIRON:
THE UNITED STATES AND
CANADA

'I thought they were dead,' said American three-quarter Norm Cleaveland of American fans who had been attacked by French spectators. 'We were sure that it was only a matter of time before they got their hands on us.' It is unusual for a rugby team to be frightened. Even rarer for one to be scared of a rugby crowd. And quite unknown in an Olympic final.[1]

But that was the situation facing the United States team in the second half of the final of the 1924 Olympic rugby final in Paris. As the Americans turned the screw on their French opponents, extending their 3-0 half-time lead, the 40,000 crowd grew angrier and angrier at the prospect of the gold medal crossing the Atlantic.

Fighting broke out between French and American supporters in the stands of the Stade Colombes. Punches were exchanged between players on the pitch. Injured spectators were passed down on to the running track that circled the ground. Americans were taken to the US dressing room for emergency treatment.

When Welsh referee Albert Freethy finally blew for no-side, the Americans had unexpectedly triumphed 17-3 over a French side captained by the great Adolphe Jauréguy. It was their second Olympic rugby gold medal, and not even a violently hostile crowd invasion when Freethy's final whistle sounded could take that glory away from them.

It was a completely unexpected victory. France played in the Five Nations, had defeated Scotland and Ireland in full internationals and had a vibrant club competition. The US team, by its own admission, comprised half American footballers and half 'old rugby players'. Some said that they were 20-1 underdogs. The result was arguably the biggest shock ever in world rugby.

It could not be said that the events off the field were unexpected. Only three teams had entered the Olympic rugby tournament in 1924 – though that was one better than the 1920 competition – and the crowd had been viscerally hostile to the Americans when they earlier defeated Romania 37-0. The French Olympic Committee publicly appealed for good crowd behaviour in the days leading up to the final.

Controversy had dogged the Americans since their arrival in France. Their pugnacious manager Sam Goodman had argued with the French about referees, photography rights and payment of expenses. His side had been locked out of training grounds and had their valuables stolen from dressing rooms. These Americans in Paris were most definitely not made to feel at home, nor did they want to be.

The irony was that they were only there because the French had invited them. At the 1920 Antwerp Olympics in Belgium, the Americans had also surprisingly defeated the French in the final 8-0. In September 1923 the French Olympic Committee invited the Americans back to the 1924 Games, which were to be held in Paris. It is possible that they had revenge in mind. More likely is that they relished the prospect of huge public interest and large crowds.

There was only one problem. Rugby was barely played at all in America, except for a small pocket of northern California. The side that won Olympic gold in 1920 had disbanded when they arrived home, so the handful of Californian rugby enthusiasts had to advertise for players to take part in try-outs. Around 80 hopefuls took part in a series of matches and trials before a 23-man squad was finally chosen. Six had played in 1920 and 15 came from the universities of California, Santa Clara and Stanford.

Even in a three-team tournament that interested no one else in the rugby world, the United States' win was an almost unbelievable achievement. It would seem to be the perfect launch pad for the spread of the game across North America, raising the profile of rugby and inspiring thousands to take it up. But neither the gold medal of 1920 nor that of 1924 caused the faintest murmur of interest across the Atlantic. The sporting press barely raised an eyebrow.

The reason was simple. Rugby in the USA had had its chance, had blown it and was now as good as dead.

How British rugby became American football

Rugby came to America as part of the great passion for British games that conquered the English-speaking world in the 1860s and 1870s. Advances in communications and huge waves of immigration sent enthusiasm for sport across the oceans.

In the two decades between the founding of the Rugby Football Union in 1871 and 1890, when 25,000 people watched an American football match between the universities of Princeton and Yale on Thanksgiving Day, more than 1.7 million British people crossed the Atlantic to make a new home in the United States. Another 409,000 went north to Canada.

The Atlantic Ocean seemed to be shrinking, too. In 1866 Britain and America were linked for the first time by a commercial transatlantic telegraph cable. Rapid advances in technology, such as ocean-going steamships, railways, and printing meant that rugby was not just limited to the British Isles but could be reported, discussed and played across continents.[2]

Just as in Britain and Australia, *Tom Brown's Schooldays* was a bestseller in North America: it became a model for educationalists and sportsmen alike. Americans and Canadians began to see sport as an important way of passing on moral values and physical education to boys and young men. In 1872 the *New York World* even reproduced the book's description of a rugby match as part of its coverage of the inaugural Yale-Columbia football game.[3]

There were also increasing concerns about the lack of physical fitness among white-collar workers in the professions such as law, medicine and finance. The average New York citizen was wealthier than the average Londoner, noted the *New York Times*, but the position was reversed when it came to health. 'This difference between ourselves and our transatlantic kinsmen in respect of physical development is to be found in the greater prevalence through England of a taste for all manner of manly and athletic exercises.'[4]

Despite seizing independence from the British only a hundred years earlier, many members of America's WASP (White Anglo-Saxon Protestant) elite still felt a deep connection to British culture. In the first serious history of American football, its author Parke H. Davis waxed lyrically about the 'many places in England [which are] so endeared to Americans by the ties of sentiment that we feel an ownership therein ... Where is the football man from the field, side line, or stand who does not feel that he is an inheritor in the glories of Old Bigside at Rugby?'[5]

So naturally when American universities started to play football they looked to Britain for guidance. After fitful attempts to play soccer-type games or develop local sets of rules, the 1870s saw the major universities on America's East Coast – Harvard, Yale, Princeton and Columbia – adopt the rugby version of the game.

But as happened wherever rugby was played at this time, argument raged about how the game should be played and how the rules could be changed to make it more attractive to play and watch. And Americans, like Australian rugby players in Melbourne in the 1860s and northern English players in the 1890s, would develop rather different ideas from those of the RFU. This meant that by 1900 they would be playing an entirely different game – American football.

Just like the legend of William Webb Ellis, American football developed its own 'creation myth'. In the same way that the Webb Ellis story painted a picture of a sport that owed everything to the public schools who supplied the RFU with its leaders, so American football's tale emphasised how uniquely American its game was.

The story revolved around Walter Camp, a genuine Connecticut Yankee born into a prosperous New England family. He went to Yale in 1875 and became the starting half-back for the university rugby team. But, so the story goes, he was dissatisfied with the rules of the game, considering them too vague and based on old British traditions that were inappropriate for the 'New World'.

Filled with American 'can do' spirit, he set about reforming rugby to make it more acceptable to his countrymen's desire for clarity and certainty. In particular he thought the scrum was distinctly un-American, writing in 1886:

English players form solid masses of men in a scrummage and engage in a desperate kicking and pushing match until the ball pops out unexpect-edly somewhere, leaving the struggling mass ignorant of its whereabouts, still kicking blindly where they think the ball may be.[6]

To alleviate this problem, in 1880 he proposed that the scrum should be abolished and in its place the two sets of forwards should line up opposite each other. He invented the 'snap', when the 'centre-forward' hands the ball back to the quarterback, to make the game less chaotic. Eventually the forward pass was introduced.

Thanks to Camp, so his supporters claimed, American football quickly became a sport that reflected the vibrant, competitive society of the modern United States, in contrast to the conservative old world of Britain. The new American form of rugby certainly caught on in the colleges and universities of the USA. By the end of the decade spectators were attending college football matches in their thousands to watch educational and sporting giants like Harvard, Yale and Princeton do battle.

But this standard tale of how Walter Camp invented American football is its own scrum of fact, fiction and supposition. The story is not that straightforward. Indeed, the first and most glaring problem is that, when it came to playing rugby without a scrum, the Canadians got there first.

In October 1875, a full five years before Walter Camp proposed abolishing the scrum in America, the first Canadian rugby enthusiasts had proposed precisely the same thing at a 'Football Convention'. Nine clubs met to discuss the rules of the game in Toronto and decided to adopt the rules of the RFU. But three clubs voted against. These clubs essentially wanted to play rugby without the scrum, which was of course unthinkable to those who had been brought up with the game in Britain. But eventually the reformers, led by McGill and Toronto universities, won the argument, and rugby in Canada began its evolution towards gridiron-style Canadian football.

What's more, when Columbia, Harvard, Princeton and Yale students met in November 1876 to found the Intercollegiate Football Association (IFA) and agree a common set of rules, they also adopted the RFU rule book but unlike the Canadians left the scrum rules untouched.[7]

Still, arguments about the rules raged between the various universities, with the big debate being about the number of players in a team. The first IFA meeting voted for 15-a-side but Walter Camp's Yale wanted 11-a-side. They had played 11-a-side teams ever since 1873 when a team of footballers from Eton College visited from England. Yale unexpectedly won the match which was played under a hybrid set of rules, despite Eton rules being nearer to soccer than rugby.

The Yale men's surprising success convinced them that 11 men were all that was needed to play the game. They did attempt to compromise in 1877 when they suggested to Harvard that they play a 13-a-side game but they were rebuffed and so continued to push strongly for 11-a-side.[8] Eventually, in October 1880, the other universities agreed to Camp and Yale's proposal and American football officially became 11-a-side.[9]

This move to 11 players fundamentally changed the way the Americans played rugby. With just six or seven forwards, instead of the normal nine or ten found in a 15-a-side team at that time, a traditional rugby scrum was impossible. As we have seen, in rugby at this time the aim of the forwards was not to heel the ball backwards but to dribble it forward through the thicket of legs and boots of the opposing pack. Opponents could line up several columns deep, preventing headway from being made for considerable periods.

However, with fewer opposing forwards, kicking the ball forward resulted in it quickly emerging out on the opponents' side, giving them use of the ball to set up their own attack. Conventional scrummaging was completely counter-productive. Yale and the other teams playing 11-a-side rugby therefore began to line their forwards up in a single line, which became known as the 'open formation', so that they could heel the ball behind them to their backs as quickly as possible.

At the same time that teams were reduced to 11, the 'snapback' – where the ball was passed backwards to the quarterback (itself a Scottish rugby term for the scrum-half) – was introduced. Two years later, in 1882, the 'downs' rule was introduced, which gave a team three 'downs' to get the ball five yards upfield or hand it over to the other team. This was later increased to four downs and ten yards.

True disciples of the Walter Camp myth believe these changes were uniquely American. But similar changes would also take place in Canadian rugby and in rugby league. Even blocking, which allowed players without the ball to be tackled, was not unknown in the early days of rugby and was a tactic used by Blackheath and at Rugby School itself.[10] There was nothing specifically American about the way Walter Camp changed rugby. Even as late as December 1893 the *New York Times* could still call the American game 'rugby'.[11]

What did make the game uniquely American was not one of Walter Camp's innovations at all. It was the legalisation of the forward pass in 1906. Introduced to open up football and reduce its defensive brutality, this rule change more than any other gave American football its distinctive character. Camp, by this time dubbed 'the father of American football', remained agnostic on this fundamental change that marked the definitive passage of the game from rugby to American football.

American rugby's second chance

By the 1890s American football had become the major winter sport spectacle in the United States. It drew enormous crowds, often bigger than those for baseball, and commanded vast coverage in the press. It had become the concern not only of university presidents, for whom the game raised huge amounts of money, but of the president of the United States himself, Teddy Roosevelt. Its importance to the education and entertainment of the citizens of the United States meant that it was now a truly American sport.

The original game of rugby was hardly played at all. Where it was, it was a game for expatriate Britons. In 1882 the 'British Foot-Ball Club' was formed in New York to play rugby under RFU rules. The new club even met Camp to try to persuade him to abandon his rule changes, to no avail.[12]

But other than for those with a nostalgic yearning for the game of their youth, rugby had little purpose for an America basking in its 'Gilded Age'. Amateur sport was so dominated by universities and schools that there was no room for the traditions of the rugby club. And Americans had little use for the British network that rugby offered to countries of the Empire. Only the most generous could describe the game as anything but comatose.

And then, in 1905, American football sailed into the greatest storm it had yet encountered. Ever since the 1890s there had been concerns about the violence and brutality of the game. These worries came to a head in the 1905 season, when 18 deaths and 150 serious injuries were sustained in matches.[13] Such was the outcry that Teddy Roosevelt – who was quoted as saying that *Tom Brown's Schooldays* was one of two books everyone should read – met representatives of Harvard, Yale and Columbia university football teams to encourage them to change the rules of the game to reduce its dangers.[14] As a consequence, the following year the forward pass was introduced into the game.

But on the West Coast of America, disillusionment with the violence and commercialism of the American game was not so easily dislodged. Rugby had first been played at the University of California in 1882 but had been replaced by American football in 1886 as that code swept through US colleges. Now, two decades later in January 1906, the universities of California and Stanford announced that they were abandoning football altogether and taking up rugby union.

The decision to switch back could not have been taken at a better time. The triumphant All Black tourists were on their way back home from Britain and France, returning across North America, and they were keen to fly the flag in the USA for rugby in general and for New Zealand in particular.

Arrangements were hastily made and in early February 1906 the All Blacks arrived in northern California to play two exhibition matches against a British Columbia side from Canada. Despite being on tour for over six months, the tourists unsurprisingly romped home in both games, at Berkeley by 43-6 and then in San Francisco by 65-6. Despite the one-sided nature of the games, the press were effusive in their praise: 'the superiority of rugby to our own amended game was demonstrated even more forcibly at the very interesting contest of last Saturday,' declared the *San Francisco Chronicle*.[15]

The experiment was interrupted two months later when the San Francisco earthquake reduced much of the city to rubble. But support for rugby grew and California and Stanford were joined by the universities of the Pacific, Nevada and Santa Clara, plus numerous northern Californian high schools and San Francisco's elite Olympic athletic club. On the East Coast, where the All Blacks had played an unofficial match against a pick-up New York team when they arrived in the US, an Eastern Rugby Union had been founded in April by three clubs. There was even talk of an American universities rugby tour of New Zealand. Rugby was back.[16]

The game's international significance was enhanced by a changing world situation. Japan's defeat of Russia in their 1904–05 war meant that the Pacific Ocean had suddenly become a region of intense diplomatic interest. The Anglo-Japanese Alliance had been signed in 1902, causing consternation to the newly federated Australian government, whose 'White Australia' policy was based on racist fears of Asian domination. The Australians sought to counter fears that the British might abandon them to the Japanese by developing links with the United States.[17]

For its part, Teddy Roosevelt's government wanted to demonstrate that despite Japanese success America was the dominant naval power in the Pacific. So in late 1907 it despatched a fleet of 16 battleships on a goodwill tour of the region, calling at major ports on both sides of the ocean. In August 1908 it visited Auckland, Sydney and Melbourne. It did not go unnoticed in these cities that their guests had chosen to call this mighty display of sea power the 'Great White Fleet'.

As part of this Australian–American courtship the 1908–09 Wallabies played three games in California on their way back from their tour of Britain in February 1909. The Australians won all three matches, but the margins were sufficiently narrow to suggest that West Coast rugby was improving rapidly. To give even greater hope to American rugby enthusiasts the 'Big Game,' the annual showdown between Stanford and California, showed no signs of diminishing in importance as northern California's most prestigious sporting event, despite the switch from gridiron to rugby.

Filled with hope for rugby, that summer an American Universities team of students from California, Stanford and Nevada made a 16-game tour of Australia and New Zealand, the first overseas visit by a US representative rugby team. Despite only winning three and drawing two matches, the students were never outclassed, and the tour was considered a success by all concerned. When they returned home in August the San Francisco *Sunday Call* was sufficiently impressed to ask in a headline: 'Will California Produce Rugby's World Champs?'[18]

Further justification for this optimism was seen in 1912 when the West Coast hosted an Australian touring side. They were known as the Waratahs, rather than the Wallabies, despite the fact that six of the tourists came from Queensland rather than New South Wales, the state that had traditionally borne the Waratah nickname. They played 11 matches and lost by a point to both California and Stanford, although they played the former three times and the latter twice. Most significantly, they narrowly defeated the USA national side in its first ever international by a mere 12-8.

But under the surface, all was not well. The Australians disliked the American approach to the game, feeling that the Californian tackling was too physical and that US players were apt to take advantage of the rules. Coming just four years after the split with rugby league in Australia, the tourists were determined to uphold the amateur ethos – and the American approach smacked too much of the professional attitudes that the gentlemen from Down Under had so recently rejected.

For their part, the Americans were becoming frustrated with what they saw as the domination of rugby by forward play. In 1913, California suggested that teams should be reduced to 14-a-side by the abolition of one of the forwards. From his vantage point as the 'Father of American football', Walter Camp mischievously informed the sporting public that the Californians weren't even playing the best type of rugby.[19] 'The Northern Union game, especially in Lancashire and Yorkshire, would be a revelation to many of those who have merely seen the more mediocre play,' he argued. 'The men who form these teams are of excellent physique, strong and powerful, putting up a hard, vigorous game with tackling that is earnest enough to be severe.'[20]

Matters came to a head with the 1913 All Blacks tour of California. Any hopes that American rugby ascendency would continue its upwards trajectory were brutally extinguished by the New Zealanders. In 13 unbeaten games they scored 508 points while conceding just two penalty goals, including a 51-3 demolition of the US national team at Berkeley.

Only two sides kept the tourists below the 30-point mark. American rugby was humiliated. Instead of promoting the game, the tour demonstrated that, far from being potential 'World Champs', America was no more than a second-rate rugby nation. That was not a message American sports fans wanted to hear.

To make things worse, the University of California fell out with Stanford over the selection of the national team. In the midst of this confusion and demoralisation, voices were heard calling for a return to American football. As college football continued to grow in importance in the US, many in California felt isolated from the intense intercollegiate and increasingly nationwide rivalries of the sport.

Played by a handful of local universities and now offering no prospect of international prestige, rugby's appeal ebbed away. In 1915 California pulled the plug and declared that it was going to return to American football: 'from now on it will be the American game for Americans, and, best of all, for California,' declared the *Daily Californian*.[21] Stanford carried on until 1919 before accepting the inevitable. Rugby's second chance in America was all but gone.

Canada: rugby versus 'rugby'

Unlike America, Canada was a faithful and loyal member of the British Empire. Like Australia, New Zealand and South Africa, she enjoyed the status of a 'white dominion' of the Empire. As might be expected from an outpost of Britain, various types of informal football had been played in Canada since the late 1780s. British soldiers, sailors and traders played the game initially, but the first 'foot-ball' club that appears to have been formed in Canada was in French-speaking Montreal in July 1865.[22]

As in the rest of the English-speaking world, 'football' clubs began to be formed in the mid-19th century, the first being the Hamilton Tigers in Ontario in 1869. But the driving force behind rugby in Canada was Montreal's McGill University. In 1874 it had challenged Harvard University to a two-game series. Harvard played its own brand of football rules at the time but the second game was played under rugby rules. The success and enjoyment of the game caused the Harvard men to abandon their own rules and embrace rugby.

At the time rugby was arguably the most influential sport in Canada. It also had an important impact on the early rules of ice hockey. According to Canadian historian Michel Vigneault, the first set of ice hockey rules drawn up by the 'father' of the sport, James Creighton, forbade the puck from being passed forward and specified that when it went out of bounds it had to be brought back into play with a type of line-out.

Most of the players involved in the first recorded game of indoor ice hockey in Montreal in 1875 were rugby players from McGill University, the cradle of Canadian football. Although these borrowings from rugby gradually faded from the game, ice hockey's prominence today as Canada's undisputed national sport owes not a little to its unrelenting physicality and strong sense of local identity, qualities that make it a close cousin of rugby in spirit if not in technicalities.[23]

But, as in America, the official rules of rugby were not as readily appreciated by rugby players themselves. A 'Football Association of Canada' had been formed in 1872 to draw up an agreed set of rules for Canadian clubs to follow. Nominally the RFU's rules were followed, but this did not stop clubs trying to improve on them.

As we have already seen, the scrum quickly became a bone of contention. At the 1875 Toronto 'Football Convention', critics attacked the scrum for being, in the words of the McGill delegate, 'monotonous, uninteresting and dangerous' and explained that in Ontario some clubs simply refused to take part in scrums. 'The majority of disinterested spectators will probably conclude that it is a far more interesting and more scientific practice for members of a team to kick or play into each others' hands, than for both sides to engage in a melee where no advantage results from precision, agility or experience,' he argued.[24] It was this difference over the philosophy of rugby that led to the emergence of what became known as Canadian football.

The new style of playing caught on quickly, not least because it offered the opportunity for university sides to play their Ivy League counterparts across the border in the USA. When the Canadian Rugby Football Union was founded in 1884, it adopted its own set of rules that did away with scrums and brought the ball back into play after a tackle by the ball being heeled back to a quarterback. As in America, rugby played under the rules of the RFU almost disappeared.

Despite Canada's huge distances, rugby teams in its western provinces followed the eastern clubs and adopted the new rules. Winnipeg RFC, 1,500 miles away in Manitoba, later to become famous as the Winnipeg Blue Bombers, were one of the founders of the Manitoba Rugby League in 1888. By the mid-1880s, when most Canadians used the word 'rugby' they meant Canadian football, the governing body of which was known, confusingly, as the Canadian Rugby Union.

The one place where rugby retained its traditional meaning was in Canada's furthest western province of British Columbia. The game had been played in British Columbia from the 1870s when a team was formed in Victoria, the capital of the province situated at the tip of Vancouver Island. Ten years later in 1887 a team was formed in Vancouver itself and there was sufficient interest in the game for the British Columbia Rugby Union to be established in 1889.

In 1895 the McKechnie Cup was inaugurated, to be competed for by the three leading provincial sides.[25] A combination of sheer distance from the changes taking place in Toronto and Montreal, alongside an ingrained sense of Britishness, meant that rugby remained the leading code of football in the west. Indeed, it was not until the 1920s that a governing body for Canadian football was formed in the province – confusingly titled the British Columbia Rugby Football Union.

Unlike the southern hemisphere rugby-playing nations, Canadian rugby suffered dearly from its isolation from the rest of the rugby world. Tours between Britain, Australia, New Zealand and South Africa took place regularly in the 1890s and 1900s, but Canada was not part of the imperial rugby network. It barely registered on British rugby's radar. The Rev. Frank Marshall's comprehensive history of the game, *Football: The Rugby Union Game*, did not once mention Canada.

In an attempt to bring Canada into rugby's imperial network, in 1899 Ireland made a tour of Canada's eastern states. It was Ireland's first ever international tour and the first rugby tour to Canada. The tourists arrived in Nova Scotia, where rugby retained some support, and surprisingly lost 5-0 to Halifax. They then moved on to Quebec and Ontario and played eight matches against sides that were essentially Canadian football teams. In some they even agreed to amend rugby rules to make it easier for the Canadians to compete.

Despite the often ad hoc nature of these matches, the Irish were sufficiently impressive to inspire the formation of a handful of rugby clubs committed to amateur principles. But by this time, Canadian football was not only the dominant code it was also becoming a completely different one, played by teams of 14, with no scrums and its own scoring system. In 1921 it reduced the size of teams to 12 and in 1929 legalised the forward pass. 'British' rugby was a very poor cousin.

For those few in Britain who knew how weak Canadian rugby was, it came as something of a surprise at the start of December 1902 to hear that the 'All-Canada' rugby team had set sail for its tour of Britain.[26] Largely comprised of players from British Columbia, the tourists won the first of its 23 tour matches with an 11-8 victory over Ulster.

They managed another eight wins, including a memorable 8-0 triumph over Bristol but played no internationals nor against any English counties. To say it was a low-key tour would be an overstatement. It passed with almost no press coverage and not much more spectator interest. Nor did it do much to encourage interest in Canada.

In fact, Canadian rugby appeared to be rather reticent about promoting itself at all. In 1906 it committed an extraordinary act of self-sacrifice. Instead of welcoming the 1905–06 All Blacks to British Columbia on their journey home from Britain, it sent the British Columbia representative side down to San Francisco to play the New Zealanders in order to capitalise on the split in American football.

To further the US link, the Canadians established the J. Cooper Keith Trophy, in which the winner of the Stanford–California 'Big Game' would play the top British Columbia side for the unofficial title of West Coast champions.[27]

Three years later the 1908–09 Wallabies did make it up to Canada on their way home from Britain, comfortably defeating Vancouver and Victoria. In 1912 the Wallabies returned once more for the first full-scale tour of the American West Coast by an international side. Reflecting diplomatic interests, 13 of the 16 matches were played in the United States.

By the time the tourists had completed the American leg and ventured north to play the Canadians they were suffering the after-effects of generous Californian hospitality. 'We were never in bed. That was the trouble. I've never had such a time in my life,' confessed winger Bob Adamson.[28] The Canadians, more experienced in rugby than the former American football players to their south, proceeded to win all three matches against the Australians. Rugby looked set for a Canadian rebirth.

The optimism that these victories engendered in Canadian rugby was short-lived. The following year, the All Blacks toured North America. After rampaging through California, they racked up 102 points to nil in their three games against Vancouver and Victoria, the latter having the dubious privilege of playing the tourists twice in the space of four days.

The scale of the defeats did rugby no good in its on-going battle with Canadian football and it continued to be a marginal sport in Canadian life. Outside of Nova Scotia, where it retained some support across all classes, the game remained confined to those sections of the Empire-loyal Canadian middle classes for whom it was a cultural bond with the British Mother Country.

So, isolated on the sporting Galapagos of the North American continent, rugby evolved into something new and unique, leaving its progenitor weak and underdeveloped. In doing so, new myths, legends and rivalries emerged, yet the essence of rugby – speed, skill, physicality and indomitable spirit – remained in its American and Canadian versions. Even with two Olympic gold medals, rugby would struggle to break into the mainstream. It would take a new era of globalisation to end North American rugby's not so splendid isolation.

PART IV

GOLDEN YEARS AMIDST THE GATHERING STORM

Rugby was now part of the fabric of the daily lives of millions of people around the world. It had become the sport of the elite professional and the manual labourer, stiff upper-lipped Englishmen and wild colonial boys. Each made the game their own, played in their own way and with their own traditions and culture, and nowhere was this more true than in England where it appeared to be played by men from mutually incomprehensible worlds.

And for both rugby union and rugby league, the years before the First World War were an indisputable golden age, filled with great players and unforgettable matches, which set the template for both games for the rest of the century.

In August 1914, however, that glorious epoch came to an end. Rugby, and the lives of the men who played and watched it, would never be the same again.

13

HAROLD WAGSTAFF AND THE PHANTOMS OF BASKERVILLE

It was a game that almost did not take place, one that the teams' managers and players did not want, yet it became one of the greatest rugby matches ever played.

On 4 July 1914, exactly one month before the outbreak of the First World War, the British rugby league team was reduced to nine fit men yet still held off the might of Australia at the Sydney Cricket Ground to win 14-6 and lift the rugby league Ashes.

With no substitutes allowed, injured men played until they could no longer carry on. Forwards played in the backs. And Douglas Clark, perhaps one of the toughest men to play rugby and a world champion wrestler, sobbed at the side of the pitch when his injuries finally wore him down.

For rugby league, the match became a synonym for unquenchable bravery and determination, the very embodiment of the spirit of the game. The Sydney press dubbed the game the Rorke's Drift Test, comparing the players' bravery with the British Army's rearguard action against an overwhelming Zulu army in South Africa in 1879.

The game almost never happened. The tourists arrived in Australia at the end of May with the first Test scheduled for 20 June, but the popularity of the tour led to the match being put back to 27 June. Yet no one had thought to rearrange the second Test match that was scheduled for 29 June. Amazingly, two Test matches were to be played within 48 hours of each other.

Furthermore, the third Test match still had to be played on 4 July, just five days later. Faced with an exhausted squad and a spate of injuries to star players, the two co-managers of the British tourists, St Helens' Joe Houghton and Huddersfield's John Clifford, asked the Australian authorities to postpone the final Test until August and play it in Aussie Rules-mad Melbourne.

Ted Larkin, the New South Wales Rugby League secretary responsible for the tour arrangements, refused to rearrange the match. When the British managers told him they would not play, he telegrammed the Northern Union (NU) to protest. Back in England, the NU officials received Larkin's telegram with sympathy. The return telegram from Joe Platt, the NU secretary, which arrived at lunchtime the day before the match was due to take place, was unequivocal. 'We confidently anticipate that the best traditions of Northern Union football will be upheld by you. We hope that you will expend every atom of energy and skill you possess to secure victory; failing which, we hope you will lose like sportsmen.'[1]

Despite this instruction, Joe Houghton still disagreed with the decision to go ahead and left it to his co-manager John Clifford to rally the players behind the decision.

'You are playing a game of football this afternoon, but more than that you are playing for England, and more even than that, you are playing for right versus wrong. You will win because you have to win. Don't forget that message from home. England expects every one of you to do his duty.'

Two decades later, tour captain Harold Wagstaff remembered how moved his team were by Clifford: 'I was impressed and thrilled as never before or since by a speech.' The players left the meeting in determined silence.[2]

When they finally emerged on to the Sydney Cricket Ground pitch on the afternoon of 4 July, there were five changes from the side announced 48 hours earlier. First-choice players Gwyn Thomas, Johnny Rogers, Bert Jenkins and Fred Longstaff were all injured. Even Alf Wood, Thomas's replacement at full-back, was playing with a badly broken nose.

Britain's slim chance of victory soon slipped close to zero. Immediately after Australia kicked off, Halifax winger Frank Williams injured his knee and spent the rest of the first half hobbling around the pitch, before going off for good early in the second half.

Powerhouse prop Douglas Clark then broke his thumb. He struggled on but he, too, was forced to go off in the second half after he fell awkwardly under Arthur Holloway's tackle and dislocated his shoulder. When he realised his match was over, he wept tears of frustration.

But the greater experience of the NU side told. Despite having only 11 fit players, they dominated play and led 9-0 at half-time, thanks to a try from Leeds' Willie Davies and three goals from Oldham's Alf Wood.

In the second half, the Australians tried to take advantage of the 11-man British side. Free-running South Sydney forward Billy Cann was moved out of the pack and into the backs. Australia were now playing with eight backs and five forwards against England's seven backs and four forwards.

'It hardly seemed possible that England could withstand such force of numbers,' wrote the *Sydney Morning Herald*, 'but so desperately stubborn was the defence that Australia was frustrated at every move.'[3] With 20 minutes to go, it could only be a matter of time before the British team cracked.

Just as they seemed about to buckle, Wagstaff slashed through the Australian defence and passed to Chick Johnson, the Widnes forward who had taken Williams' place on the right wing. Johnson cut back inside and was left with only Howard Hallett, the Australian full-back, to beat.

Faced with the chance to seal the match, Johnson's old-style forward instincts took over and, to the surprise of Hallett, he dropped the ball to his foot, dribbled it past the full-back and grubbered over the line to score. Wood converted the try to make it 14-0.

It was still not over. A few minutes later Oldham's Billy Hall was taken off with concussion and Australia finally began to click. Wally Messenger and Sid Deane both touched down for unconverted tries. Then the tourists also lost stand-off Stuart Prosser after a heavy blow winded him. The British were down to nine men.

The whistle could not come soon enough, and, when it did, it was Wagstaff's men who had won the Ashes with an immortal 14-6 victory.

It was undoubtedly the greatest match in rugby league's short, 19-year history – and with it the future of the game in both hemispheres was assured.

The Northern Union men

Press and the players were united in attributing the British success to one man: captain Harold Wagstaff. Sydney journalist J. C. Davis wrote, 'Wagstaff, always a great player, that day became the ubiquitous, and the king of the game ... Wagstaff the Great.' Australian captain Sid Deane, later to play for Oldham and Hull, recalled that 'Wagstaff was not only brilliant in attack and wonderful in defence but his leadership was a most important factor in the team's success'. Douglas Clark wrote simply, 'Harold was the man'.[4]

Born in 1891 in Holmfirth, Yorkshire, Wagstaff first played for his local amateur side, Underbank Rangers, at 14. The next season, in September 1906, he scored the club's first try under the NU's new 13-a-side rules. Two months later he signed for Huddersfield aged 15 years and 175 days, then the youngest ever professional player. Two years later he made his debut for the Yorkshire county side. Shortly after, aged 17, he made his England debut against the pioneer 1908 Kangaroo tourists. At just 19, he was appointed captain of Huddersfield, a post he was to hold for the next 15 years. At 22, he became captain of the national side.

Wagstaff's performance and character in that third Test match surprised no one who was familiar with rugby league. Indeed, Wagstaff had almost come to symbolise the new game. From his quintessentially northern surname that emphasised the flat vowel sounds of Yorkshire – and naturally he was 'Arold, not Harold – to his championing of his sport, he seemed to embody the very spirit of the game. 'I am a Northern Union man all the way through,' he declared in the first line of his autobiography, 'and I was suckled in the Northern Union game.'[5]

He was the leading representative of a new generation of players who had grown up with the Northern Union and had never played rugby union. In fact, it was not until that 1914 tour of Australia that he even saw a union match. It was emblematic that he had scored one of the first tries under the new 13-a-side rules that the NU introduced in June 1906, rules that marked the final break with the union code on and off the field.

As well as reducing teams to 13 by removing two forwards, the 1906 rules introduced the play-the-ball, whereby the tackled player stood up and heeled the ball back to a player standing behind him. Although the rule seemed a radical departure from traditional rugby union – and to some more akin to American football – in fact it was an attempt to return to the very earliest rules of rugby, which allowed the tackled player to hold the ball until his forwards gathered around him, whereupon he would place it on the ground, shout 'Down' and the scrum would begin.

These two rule changes transformed rugby league into a fast, exciting spectacle. In the first fortnight of the new season more than 800 points were scored and the *Athletic News*, the most influential of the northern sports weeklies in Britain, declared in a headline that the new rules were 'completely vindicated'.[6]

Underneath, the 1906 rule changes reflected a different philosophy of how rugby should be played. Rugby in the north of England, as well as in most of South Wales, Australia and New Zealand, was viewed as a handling and passing game, in which the scoring of tries was the most important feature. So the first major rule change enacted by the NU after the split was to make tries the most valuable way of scoring by reducing the number of points for all goals to two, while a try earned three points. In contrast, in 1891 the RFU had raised the value of the drop goal to four points, making it the most valuable scoring method.

At the same time that goals were reduced in value, the NU also abolished the line-out. Northern rugby saw it as both useless and dangerous, giving rise to endless penalties and excuses for fighting. It was initially replaced by a 'punt-out' when the ball went into touch but that proved to be even more chaotic than the line-out, so it was replaced with a scrum. Although this was more orderly, it exacerbated the problem of the profusion of scrums in the game – a Halifax versus Hunslet match in 1902 saw 110 scrums and this was by no means exceptional. The 1906 rules solved the problem at a stroke, putting the focus on handling and running with the ball. The modern sport of rugby league had been born.

It was just in time, because rugby everywhere was under intense pressure from soccer, and especially in the north of England. In 1903 the Football League had made the first breach in the West Yorkshire rugby stronghold when Manningham, the inaugural rugby league champions, switched to soccer and reinvented themselves as Bradford City. In 1904 the leadership of Holbeck NU side, which played at Elland Road, disbanded the club and founded Leeds City, the forerunner of Leeds United. In rugby heartlands across the north, professional soccer began to challenge the oval ball. The radical rule changes of 1906 finally created a dam against the rising soccer tide.

North versus south

Ten years after the split the NU probably had more adult clubs under its wing than the RFU. It had undoubtedly been helped by the fanatical amateurism of the RFU in its pursuit of the professional bogeyman. In September 1895 the RFU's first general meeting after the split reiterated its opposition to all forms of payments and passed new regulations that contained 27 clauses and a further 12 sub-clauses. All members of NU clubs, whether paid or not, were classed as professionals. Transgression of the rules was met by a life ban from rugby union.

Eventually, as had happened in Wales, expediency triumphed over principle and the northern breach in the game was stopped at Leicester. The club had been the most important in the midlands for 20 years and, like the clubs in the north, operated on a commercial basis that placed winning above all else. The Tigers had first been investigated for professionalism in 1896 and its local league structure was awash with allegations of players receiving gifts and remuneration. In August 1893 Manningham forward Ernest Redman moved from Bradford to play at Welford Road, a move that happily coincided with his being appointed the landlord of a local Leicester pub.[7]

The whispers about the Tigers' somewhat semi-detached relationship with amateurism turned into a roar by 1907 and the RFU set up a commission to investigate not just Leicester but Northampton and Coventry, too. It found unaudited accounts, expenses being paid without receipts, 'unnecessary refreshments' for players and four former Northern Union players on the books. Yet despite players being told to repay money to their clubs, the report declared Leicester not guilty. Shocked by the decision, Charles Crane became the first and only RFU president ever to resign. Rowland Hill argued against expelling Leicester because it 'would be to practically break up the union'.[8]

As Hill realised, Leicester's expulsion would inevitably mean that they joined the Northern Union. The other midlands' clubs would fall like dominoes. But the RFU's blind eye to Leicester had closed any vision the NU had of becoming a national game. Apart from short-lived clubs in Coventry and the south-west in the years immediately before the First World War, the Northern Union was unable to attract any more clubs from the RFU.

In many ways it didn't matter to the NU. Its leaders and most of its supporters were content to be exactly what their organisation said it was: the *Northern* Rugby Football Union. The north was for them the true England, open, meritocratic and competitive, the centre of trade, industry and of serious, professional sport. As the historian A. J. P. Taylor remarked about his Victorian Manchester grandfather, for them 'London was the enemy; it represented everything he disapproved of and which he supposed, perhaps wrongly, that Manchester had defeated'.[9]

Their attitude was summed up in the phrase that emerged soon after the split, 'T'best in t'Northern Union'. It referred to anything that was of the highest quality, implying that if it was the best in the Northern Union, it was the best in Britain regardless of what the southern-based establishment believed. It was a reminder of how rugby had become part of the symbolism of northern life, reflecting the region's widespread and heartfelt sense of Us against Them.

The first heroes of rugby league – as the game officially became known in 1922 – were men who were born, lived and worked in the close-knit northern communities that they represented. One outstanding example was Hunslet's Albert Goldthorpe. He made his debut as a 16-year-old prodigy in 1888 and played for the club for 22 seasons before he finally retired in 1911. His feats as a three-quarter in union and then as a half-back in rugby league, most notably captaining Hunslet to the rugby league Grand Slam of 'All Four Cups' in 1908, earned him the title of 'Ahr Albert'.

His contribution to his community did not stop when he left the rugby pitch. He organised benefit matches to raise funds for striking workers and in 1904 the local schoolboy rugby tournament was named in honour of him. When the triumphant 1908 side paraded their trophies through the packed streets of Hunslet, the horse-drawn charabanc carrying the players was decorated with banners proclaiming 'Three Cheers for Albert'.

If rugby league had deep roots in its local communities, it also had an international impulse. Just a year after the rule changes that had transformed northern rugby, the game was established in New Zealand and Australia. The success of Baskerville's All Golds and the subsequent Kangaroo tourists was crucial in giving the NU a sense of international importance. In 1910 Salford's Jim Lomas led the first British rugby league touring team to Australia and New Zealand, helping to consolidate the sport in those countries and establish a cycle of reciprocal tours that set a template for the rest of the century.

The greatest of all the teams of that first golden era came from the town that had given birth to the game: Harold Wagstaff's Huddersfield. Dubbed the 'Team of All the Talents', the side combined native northern talent, such as iron-man forward Douglas Clark and scything winger Stan Moorhouse, Welsh imports like pocket-rocket scrum-half Johnny Rogers and goal-kicking forward Ben Gronow, and Antipodean stars including Edgar Wrigley, the youngest ever All Black, and Australian winger Albert Rosenfeld, who played in the first ever rugby league match in Sydney. In the four years up to 1915 Huddersfield finished top of the championship table every season, won the Challenge Cup twice, the Yorkshire Cup three times and emulated Hunslet's grand slam 'All Four Cups' in 1915.

Huddersfield played the game in a fast, open style that made maximum use of the opportunities provided by the new rules, developing new tactics that moved the game far beyond the lumbering set pieces of the past. In 1912, the team's sweeping back play and irresistible forward momentum enabled Rosenfeld to score an unbelievable 78 tries in the season, a record that no one thought could be beaten. Yet two years later, the side found yet another gear and Rosenfeld touched down for 80 tries, a mark unlikely ever to be threatened.

By the end of the Edwardian era, the Northern Union had not merely preserved the deep community roots that rugby had set down in the great boom of the 1870s and 1880s, it had also reinvigorated the sport through innovation and expansion. A sense of the thrill that rugby league now engendered was captured by a London journalist who ventured north to report on the 1910 Challenge Cup final for the *Daily Graphic*:

> The spirit of Rugby is not dead, nor does it sleep. The true spirit of Rugby is as alive as ever in England, and the ancient glamour of a glorious old sport has not yet departed from the hearts of the people. A journey to Huddersfield on Saturday, where Hull and Leeds fought out a gallant struggle for the much coveted honour of the Northern Union Cup, would have been sufficient to convince any reasonable person of this fact ... It was a thrilling and delightful spectacle.[10]

Baskerville's phantoms

The Northern Union's rugby revolution may have been confined geographically to the north of England but it unleashed forces across the rugby world. When the tremors of the northern rebellion met the shockwaves caused by the 1905 All Blacks' tour to Europe the subsequent turbulence led to an entirely unexpected consequence: the expansion of rugby league to Australia and New Zealand.

The incredible success of the All Blacks masked the fact that the tour had brought to boiling point the pressures that had been building up in New Zealand rugby over the past decade. When the team arrived back home at Auckland in March 1906 it was announced that the tour had made a profit of almost £9,000. Yet the players, now lauded as national heroes of a young and virile New Zealand, had received only three shillings per day expenses.

The months spent in England had also revealed to many of the tourists that 'working-men' rugby players did not simply have to grin and bear the situation. They had seen at first hand that the Northern Union paid players and that it was possible for them to benefit from their rugby talent. What was more, the principles of the Northern Union game, even before its decisive rule changes of 1906, matched the open rugby philosophy of much of New Zealand rugby.

As in all revolutions, a catalyst was needed to light the tinder. According to a 1928 account George Smith, the All Black winger, met with the Northern Union while on the 1905 tour. He had also had the opportunity to study the NU during his 1902 trip to Britain to compete in an athletics' meeting. Moreover, George Stephenson, a native of Otago and a theatre entrepreneur, had played for Manningham both before and after 1895, providing a direct link to the new rugby. There is also evidence that Smith stopped off in Sydney on his way home from the All Blacks tour to discuss the situation in Antipodean rugby and the Northern Union with his Australian rugby contacts.[11]

Certainly the All Blacks' return home in 1906 must have been quickly followed by discussions about switching to the Northern Union, because barely 12 months later, in March 1907, Canterbury postal clerk Albert Baskerville announced that a professional All Black side would tour England later that year to play NU clubs. Baskerville was a well-known player in New Zealand but was perhaps better recognised as the author of *Modern Rugby Football*, a book that promoted open rugby and decried the sport's unthinking adherence to tradition. He was the public face of a grass roots movement of disgruntled New Zealand players.

As soon as Baskerville made the announcement, he was declared *persona non grata* and banned from all rugby grounds by the New Zealand Rugby Union. The NZRU then demanded that every player selected for that year's North versus South Island match sign a declaration that they were amateurs and would assist the NZRU to identify tourists and stop the tour taking place.

In England, Cecil Wray Palliser, the Agent General of New Zealand in the UK and the NZRU's delegate to the RFU, called Baskerville's tour 'some kind of sensation to save the Northern Union' which he portrayed as under threat from 'the renewal of the spirit of real Rugby'. 'It is a phantom side', he stated, a description that was gleefully seized upon by Baskerville's supporters.[12]

But the grievances of New Zealand's players ran deep and the local press reported that Baskerville 'has met with even more success than he anticipated'.[13] Duncan MacGregor, the railwayman who scored four tries against England in the 1905 international, was one of the first to refuse to sign the NZRU's ultimatum. Baskerville claimed to have received requests to join the tour from 160 players, including 18 of the 1905 All Blacks. Of his 28-strong party, nine were All Blacks, including four from the 1905 tour, and 11 other players had won regional representative honours.[14]

The 'phantom side' arrived in Leeds on the evening of 1 October and were overwhelmed by the crowd that had gathered to greet them at the railway station. Just like the celebrating crowds that welcomed home victorious cup-winning sides, the tourists found themselves at the centre of an outpouring of local pride and jubilation:

> Wright, the New Zealand captain, called for 'three cheers for the people of Leeds', which were followed by the stirring Maori war-cry and further cheering. The players were escorted to the Grand Central Hotel by the Hunslet charabanc and the Northern Union officials in carriages, together with the still cheering crowd. The crush was so dense in Boar Lane and Briggate as to cause the stoppage of traffic.[15]

After a few days acclimatising to the new sport – amazingly, the tourists had never seen, let alone played, a rugby league match – they took to the field and were unbeaten in their first eight matches, before losing to Wigan in front of 30,000 spectators. Initially, they used classic New Zealand wing-forward tactics and arranged their backs using two five-eighths and three three-quarters, but found that the well-drilled NU defences easily snuffed them out.

When the tourists arrived back home in June 1908, ten months after the tour had started, they had won the three-match Test series against the Northern Union representative side, been watched by over 300,000 people and made a profit of over £5,500 that the players distributed among themselves. New Zealand rugby union had been thrown into turmoil as rugby league quickly grew in popularity.

By 1914 Auckland had 39 rugby league teams, equalling the number of union clubs, Canterbury had 16, approximately a third of the total union clubs, while Wellington's nine was dwarfed by 58 union sides.[16] The new game quickly began to make headway among New Zealand Maori, and in May 1908, even before the tourists returned home, a Maori team led by the great three-quarter Opai Asher had crossed the Tasman Sea to play a series of matches against Australian rugby league teams, the first tour since the 1888 pioneers to be based on the Maori community.

The NZRU's response was predictable. Provincial unions in Taranaki, Wellington, South Canterbury, Otago, Southland and Auckland expelled dozens of players.[17] But behind this draconian approach, the leadership of New Zealand rugby union was divided. There was a significant body of opinion that felt for a long time that the NZ game was too much in thrall to the RFU. The Canterbury and Otago rugby unions proposed reforming the rules along the lines of the Northern Union, even suggesting that if the game did not change the NZRU should split from the RFU and form its own breakaway union with Australia. Nimble-footedness by NZ administrators and RFU promises of international consultation headed off the immediate threat but the debate would continue until the outbreak of war in 1914.

The hopes of the rugby league pioneers were not completely fulfilled and the fears of the rugby union loyalists were not totally confirmed. League recruited strongly in New Zealand's industrial working-class areas such as Auckland's docks and the west coast's mines, but union commanded the schools, the professions and the majority of players. In many ways, rugby in New Zealand came to resemble that of England, the two versions of the game occupying almost mutually exclusive social groups and cultural values. To be a 'leaguie' in New Zealand was to be an outsider, someone who was prepared to swim against the tide.

But tragically, Albert Baskerville, the man who brought the 13-a-side game to New Zealand, did not live to see it established in his homeland. As his tourists arrived in Brisbane in May 1908 for the last leg of their arduous tour, he complained of a chill. Undeterred, he still planned to play in the match against Queensland. The day after the Queensland match he was diagnosed with influenza.

Within three days he had developed pneumonia and was admitted to hospital. Late in the afternoon of Wednesday, 20 May the team visited the hospital after defeating a Brisbane representative side 43-10. They found Baskerville in a coma. At six o'clock, surrounded by the men whose lives he had transformed and who through him had themselves transformed rugby, he died. He was just 25 years old.[18]

Kangaroos versus Wallabies

One of those men whose life had been changed by Baskerville's tour was Herbert Henry 'Dally' Messenger, the touring side's sole Australian. He had not gone on tour to make up the numbers. Dally was the greatest star in Australian rugby. As a rugby union stand-off half for the Eastern Suburbs club in Sydney, he came to prominence thanks to his uncanny ability to read a game and prodigious kicking feats. He was well known for kicking goals from inside his own half and, allegedly, even from his own 25-yard line. Baskerville's capturing of Messenger as a tourist, which was only agreed to when Messenger's mother gave her seal of approval, not only gave the tour instant credibility among Australian rugby fans, but also unlocked the door for many other Sydney players to ally themselves with the new rugby.

When he finally returned from the tour, the first Australian rugby league season was well under way. Nine clubs started the inaugural New South Wales Rugby League season and the competition went head-to-head with Sydney's Metropolitan Rugby Union. Neither organisation could establish dominance over the other and the attention of the general public was drawn more to representative state and national matches. As the season ended, the battle for supremacy switched to Britain when both the league and the union announced that they would be sending teams to tour the Mother Country in the 1908–09 British season.

The league tourists arrived at Tilbury in September 1908 with a silver-grey kangaroo in tow. The English newspapers initially dubbed the union side the 'Rabbits', but the players apparently objected to being named after what most Australians viewed as an imported pest, and the nickname 'Wallabies' was adopted. Neither tour was a spectacular success. The Wallabies lost to Llanelli, Cardiff, Swansea and Wales, as well as the Midland Counties in England, a defeat which made them the first modern touring side to lose to an English team. Worse, controversy dogged the tourists. Accusations of professionalism and ungentlemanly tactics were never far from the surface. Scotland and Ireland refused to play them.

Three Wallabies were sent off during the tour, including Syd Middleton in the prestigious match with Oxford University. The snootier sections of the British press saw the side as a reflection of the moral failings of the Australian nation. Scottish rugby writer Hamish Stuart wrote that the Wallabies 'are sublimely unconscious of their delinquency and are sincerely surprised when accused of unfair practice'.[19] The Australians for their part were surprised at their treatment. The tour manager James McMahon complained that 'as visitors to the Mother Country, as representatives of part of the British nation, [the players] could not understand and were certainly not prepared for such hostility as was shown them by a section of the press'.[20] To cap it all, the tour made a loss of £1,500. It was almost 40 years before another full Australian touring side would return.

The one success that the Wallabies did have was one that only later became important. They won the 1908 Olympic gold medal for rugby by brushing aside Cornwall, the only other team in the tournament, 32-3. The RFU and the other British rugby unions refused to enter national teams so the Cornish side represented Great Britain by virtue of being that year's English county champions. It was not an auspicious event. 'The match was played more or less to bare benches on a dark afternoon in a Scotch mist,' reported *The Times*. 'The footballs were kept in a perpetual state of greasiness by their frequent finding of the swimming bath which ran along one of the touchlines.'[21]

But the Kangaroos were little more successful than their union cousins. It did not help that the industrial heartland of rugby league was undergoing one of the worst economic slumps in a generation.[22] The tour was a victim of its own ambition – lasting six months and taking in 45 matches, of which the Kangaroos won just 17 – and made a loss of £418. James Giltinan, the tour manager and promoter, found he had been declared bankrupt when he returned home.

But when the two touring teams arrived back in Australia, the tide began to turn in favour of league. Despite the relative lack of success of the two touring sides, the fact that Australia could send two sides to tour Britain at the same time pointed to the extraordinary strength and popularity of the game Down Under. So Bill Flegg, an influential official of Eastern Suburbs rugby league club, hatched a plot to have the two teams play each other under rugby league rules.

The only problem was that financial failure of the Kangaroo tour meant that there was little money to attract the Wallabies. So the NSW Rugby League approached Sydney businessman James Joynton Smith, whose interests in hotels, newspapers and racecourses seemed to make him the ideal person to underwrite the cost of signing the Wallabies. Fourteen Wallabies, including the captain Chris McKivat, eventually signed up – indeed, as many pointed out at the time, the Wallabies split along class lines, the defectors all being from working-class occupations.

Eighteen thousand people turned up to see what the Sydney press had labelled 'the match of the century' and they were not disappointed. The game flowed from end to end and the Wallabies coped admirably with the new rules, taking an 18-16 lead in with them at half-time. At 26-26 with seconds remaining, it was the magical Messenger who rescued the day for the Kangaroos with a deft pass that allowed Newtown left winger Frank Cheadle to race through and score in the corner. The conversion failed but the Kangaroos had snatched a 29-26 victory. The Wallabies won the next two matches but the Kangaroos won the fourth and final match to tie the series. The four-match series under rugby league rules had captured the imagination of Sydney's sporting public and the balance tilted decisively to league.

Over the course of the next two seasons, rugby league began to pull away from union. Not only were crowds bigger at league games but the union authorities retreated from ideas about reforming rugby and gradually became more exclusive. But most importantly, rugby league had an international dimension that Australian rugby union did not. Regular tours to and from Britain gave league a meaning for the vast majority of Australians who still thought of themselves as British. Jim Lomas's 1910 Northern Union tourists attracted large crowds wherever they played. For the opening match of the tour the visitors were led out by a lion, thus becoming the first side to be known as the Lions.[23] The following year the New Zealand league team toured Australia and in 1911 the Kangaroos returned to Britain, led by the former Wallaby McKivat. This time the Kangaroos were successful on and off the field, winning 28 of their 35 matches but, most importantly, taking the rugby league Ashes back home with them. Financially, the tour was so profitable that each player took back a bonus of £178.

By the time Harold Wagstaff's British Lions reached Australian shores in May 1914, rugby league was the major football code of Australia's most populous states, New South Wales and Queensland. And, just as in England and New Zealand, it had come to represent not simply a different way of playing rugby, but also a different view of life from that of the majority of people who led the union game. The manager of the 1914 Lions, John Houghton, reflected this when he told a Sydney newspaper that the tourists wanted to 'propagate their game of [rugby league] football because they believed it was the people's game'.[24]

This was even more apparent in Australia than in Britain, where the links between league and the labour movement were obvious. Harry Hoyle, the first president of the NSWRL, was a prominent railway workers' union activist and an Australian Labour Party election candidate. Ted Larkin, the league's first full-time secretary, was an elected Labour Party MP. Future Labour prime minister Billy Hughes was the patron of Glebe, while North Sydney's patron was Teddy Clark, the first president of the cabman's union. In Queensland, the central figure in the split from rugby union was Jack Fihelly, the future deputy leader of the Queensland Labour Party and prominent Irish nationalist.

In rugby league such men found a game in their own image. Uniquely for sports teams of the time, the British tourists were captained and led by working-class men like Lomas and Wagstaff – manual workers from the industrial heartlands of Britain – just as the Australian players and spectators were. For ordinary Australians, the new rugby presented an image of Australia the way they hoped it would be: working class, democratic and meritocratic. As Horrie Miller, Ted Larkin's replacement as NSWRL secretary would later write, rugby league:

is a game for every class and all classes to play. It is not a caste game. Any game which brings together, on the field of sport, men and boys of every type, must be a nation-builder … it is essential that every class in a community should understand and appreciate the worth of every other class.[25]

It was a philosophy that would serve the rugby league in Australia and the rest of the world for the next century.

14

BRITISH RUGBY BEFORE 1914: STOOP TO CONQUER

The date was 15 January 1910. The west London suburb had never seen anything like it. As if drawn to an irresistible vortex, thousands surged through its leafy lanes and past its handsome terraced houses.

On trains from Waterloo, trams from Shepherd's Bush and buses from across the metropolis they came, heads up, elbows jostling and walking briskly, anxious to get out of the insistent drizzle and to arrive in time for the 2.45 p.m. kick-off. And when the continuous, snaking crowd reached Whitton Road they saw the new stadium.

Twickenham.

They had come to see England take on Wales in the second match of that year's Five Nations. They had also come to see the new national stadium of English rugby. Almost three years in its planning and building, Twickenham was yet another consequence of the success of the 1905 All Blacks' tour. Both the New Zealand and the following season's South African matches had attracted 40,000 crowds, but there was no rugby ground big enough to cope with such numbers and the RFU had reluctantly staged them at Crystal Palace.

The idea for the stadium came from William Cail, a hard-headed Newcastle businessman who was the RFU's treasurer for 31 years until his death in 1925. Responsibility for the project fell to William 'Billy' Williams, an RFU committee man and the referee who had come to public attention when he penalised the 1905 All Blacks 12 consecutive times for offside in their tour match against Surrey. Williams found a ten and a quarter acre site just north of Twickenham railway station and in 1907 the RFU acquired it for £5,572. The land had previously been a market garden – thus it acquired the nickname of 'Billy Williams' Cabbage Patch'.

When building was finished, the stadium, comprising two covered stands 340 feet long with 3,000 seats each on the east and west sides of the ground, a south terrace for 7,000 standing and a mound on the north end that held a similar number, stood as a symbol of the RFU's self-confidence and a statement of the health of rugby union after the turmoil of the 1890s and early 1900s. The threat from the north had been resisted and the south-east was once more the undisputed centre of the game. If, as J. G. Ballard later described it, Twickenham was the Maginot Line of the British class system, the new stadium was its citadel.

The journey to see that first international match on a damp Saturday in January was something of a pilgrimage for many of the 20,000 or so spectators. It wasn't the first match at the new ground – regular tenants Harlequins had kicked off the season there with a 14-10 victory over Richmond on 2 October 1909 – but it was its baptism as a national stadium, a fact underlined by the presence of noted rugger man the Prince of Wales, who in just over three months' time would ascend the British throne as George V.

Since the start of the 20th century England had played primarily at Blackheath and Richmond, but also occasionally at Leicester, Gloucester and Bristol, but now no longer would the national side play at undersized or inadequate grounds. Like Scotland's Inverleith and Wales' Cardiff Arms Park, English rugby now had a home of its own. This was the start of a new era.

Traffic congestion and the crowd's unfamiliarity with the new stadium led to the start of the match being delayed by 15 minutes. When the two sides finally came out on to the field the ball was handed to Bridgend captain Ben Gronow to kick off. Gronow was a prodigious goal-kicking forward who later that year would quit his stonemason's job in the Valleys to join Harold Wagstaff's Huddersfield rugby league team, but today he had the honour of commencing Twickenham's inaugural international. He dug his heel in to make a divot in the middle of the halfway line, placed the ball, retreated a few steps and then sent the ball sailing past the England 25-yard line, where it was caught on the full by England captain and fly-half Adrian Stoop.

Of all the thousands of events, decisions and tactical variations that took place over the 80 minutes of a rugby match, the most predictable moment was the kick-off. The ball would be fielded by the receiving team, and then kicked into touch in order to gain territorial position and set up the opening line-out. At this point, battle would commence. Short of the receiver knocking on or his kick not finding touch, there was an almost universally accepted inevitability that all matches began in this way.

But Adrian Stoop was neither a man who valued predictability nor one who bowed before inevitability. For him, the new age that the match heralded was about much more than the stadium. It was also the start of the new way that England played the game.

So, as the Welsh forwards ran towards Stoop in expectation of the ball flying back over their heads into touch, he simply ignored convention and ran back up the field with the ball in hand. As the first surprised Welsh defender approached him, Stoop passed the ball to his left and the ball moved rapidly across his three-quarter line. Stunned, the Welsh raced to get back to cover the move.

When the ball reached England's Ronnie Poulton on the left wing, the Harlequins' winger made a perfect cross-field kick towards the posts. A quick scramble for the ball followed before it was passed back out along the three-quarter line to Frederick Chapman on the right wing, who squeezed in for a try in the right-hand corner. Just 75 seconds into the match, it was 3-0 to England.

The Welsh, and the crowd, were stunned. For the past decade, England had played a predictable forward-dominated game, in which kicking for position and goals was their main, and usually only, strategy. Now here they were unleashing a devastating back-line movement of which the All Blacks would have been proud.

Chapman's try was unconverted but the lead was stretched to six a few minutes later when he slotted over a penalty goal. The shocked Welsh team finally gained its composure and Tom Evans scored a try from close range to get the Dragon back into the game. But just as half-time approached England scored again.

Scrum-half D. R. 'Dai' Gent, a Gloucester man despite his Welsh nickname, worked the ball from a loose scrum and passed it out to Bert Solomon, the Cornish centre making his debut, who cut through the centre of the Welsh defence, threw a dummy that completely bamboozled Welsh full-back Jack Bancroft, and waltzed in under the posts. Chapman converted and England led 11-3 at half-time. Well-organised defence from England restricted Wales to a solitary Reggie Gibbs try in the second half and the match ended in an 11-6 victory to the side playing at their new home. It was Wales' first defeat in three years. Most significantly, it was England's first win over Wales since 1898.

With the exception of a 0-0 draw with Ireland later in the tournament, England romped through the championship, lifting the title as the only unbeaten side. It was the first time that they had won a full championship since 1892. This was indeed a new era.

The road to Twickenham

It had been a long road back for English rugby union. In the aftermath of the 1895 split, the game shrank dramatically. In the decade that followed, the RFU was reduced from 416 adult clubs to just 155. England also ceased to be a serious force at international level. In the five seasons after the split, England won just four, and drew two, out of

15 matches. Between 1900 and 1910, they won a mere 11 matches, with four of those against the international neophytes of France. In 1905 their only international points of the entire season came from a solitary try scored by Sydney Coopper.

Yet, the weaker English rugby grew, the stronger the game became in other countries. The fact that the Welsh David could regularly slay the English Goliath gave rugby a huge national significance for Wales at a time when the modern Welsh nation was being forged. Much the same could be said about the game in New Zealand and South Africa. If the All Blacks had returned from their 1905 British tour with a string of defeats by strong English sides and the national team, their symbolic value to the young New Zealand nation would have been much reduced.

The weakness of English rugby was especially important to South Africa. Rugby's ability to bring together English and Afrikaans speakers so soon after the end of the Anglo-Boer War was because the game provided an arena in which South Africans together could defeat the British. Defeat at the hands of a stronger England might have reduced rugby's importance to the status of the South African cricket team, for whom failure against England was a common occurrence.

The paradox of England's weakness being a source of strength to other nations meant that the 1900s was the decisive decade for international rugby. Not only did it allow the game to become embedded in the national psyche of Wales, New Zealand and South Africa, it also allowed the flowering of the greatest generation of players that the game had yet seen.

The symbol of Welsh success was Gwyn Nicholls, the Welsh 'Prince of Three-Quarters'. Nicholls was a classical centre whose aim was to make space for his winger and then provide the perfectly timed pass to put him in the clear. But he was also a notable tactician, who masterminded the 1905 triumph over the All Blacks. His goal was to create a team of 'fifteen chess masters … each knowing instinctively not only the best thing to be done, but that all the other fellows know it also and are falling, or have fallen, into their places accordingly.'[1]

Nicholls' brilliance was enhanced by his equally eminent fellow three-quarters, Rhys Gabe in the centre and Teddy Morgan and Willie Llewellyn on the wings, arguably the greatest Welsh attacking force until the immortal sides of the 1960s and 1970s. But the linchpin was scrum-half Dicky Owen, the heart of the side, who pumped the ball from the forwards out to backs poised for attack. The diminutive Owen – he was no taller than five feet five inches – helped to create the modern scrum-half role, shifting the position from being interchangeable with the outside-half to one which commanded the area of the scrum.

A steelworker by trade, Owen would fire out passes from the base of the scrum like bullets, putting his three-quarters in motion almost as soon as the ball was out of the scrum. By the time he retired from international rugby in 1912, he had played in six Welsh championship-winning sides, carried off three Grand Slams and been victorious over every international side bar the Springboks.

If Wales were the unofficial world champions, Scotland were not far behind. They had won four championships in the same decade, defeated the 1906 Springboks 6-0 and pushed the All Blacks further than any side other than the Welsh. Their Achilles heel was an inability to beat the Welsh, recording just three victories over them between 1900 and 1920, and none of those was in Wales. It was not the only difficulty under which they laboured.

The Scottish Football Union, as Scottish rugby's governing body was then called, was the most zealous defender of absolute amateurism conceivable. Compared to the strict and particular amateurism that prevailed north of the border, the RFU were backsliding compromisers. To the Scots, the 1905 All Blacks' expenses payments of three shillings a day marked them as professionals.[2] When they discovered that the 1908 Wallabies would also receive three shillings a day, the Scots refused to play them. Offended at the RFU's refusal to ban the tourists' payments, the Scots then announced that they would not play against England in 1909.

After much negotiation, the RFU and the Scots eventually agreed that three shillings a day was permissible but players had to provide receipts before being given any money. Faces saved on both sides of the border, the 1909 Calcutta Cup took place on schedule and the Scots scored what they believed to be a double victory in an 18-8 win at Blackheath.[3]

At heart, the Scots did not believe it was possible to make international tours and remain true to amateur principles. The problems presented by tours were highlighted by the 1908 Anglo-Welsh tour to New Zealand and Australia. To no one's surprise, Ireland and Scotland refused to supply any players. In March 1908 the Scots even suspended one of their own players, Tom Wilson, merely for accepting a place on the tour because he would receive three shillings per day in expenses. To remove any suspicion of professionalism, the Welsh players chosen to tour were all drawn from the well-to-do sections of society who could afford to pay their own touring expenses, much to the chagrin of the Welsh rugby authorities.

Despite such careful social selection, the tour was a disaster, not least because one member of the touring party was revealed by the New Zealand press to be former Swinton rugby league player Frederick Jackson. Despite a reasonable record against provincial sides and a 3-3 draw in the second Test at Wellington, the tourists crashed to defeats of 32-3 in the first Test at Dunedin and 29-0 in the final Test at Auckland. The Australian authorities, locked in mortal combat with the newly formed rugby league, could not even manage to organise a Test match against the tourists.

The British officials also alienated their hosts by their high-handed behaviour. When tour manager George Harnett returned home he suggested that in future the RFU 'should keep in touch with the South African players, who besides being amateur to the core, are genuine sportsmen who play clean and honestly'.[4] A British team did not return to the Antipodes for another 22 years.

As Harnett had stated, South Africa was another matter. It was common for the 1906 Springboks to be compared favourably with the previous year's visit of the All Blacks. 'Men who have played against both sides confess that for the sheer pleasure of sport the South African matches have been unequalled,' said the *Guardian*.[5] The relative ease with which people could travel to South Africa meant that there was significant cross-fertilisation on and off the field. As early as 1903 South African Jimmy Macdonald had played on the left wing for Scotland and was joined in 1905 by fellow countryman Harold McCowat. South African-born James Davey, Rupert Williamson and Reg Hands would also turn out for England between 1908 and 1910.

It was therefore only natural that a British side visited South Africa for the fourth time in 1910, losing the Test series 2-1 but enjoying a controversy-free tour, and the Springboks were invited back to Britain in 1912. As usual, the tourists struggled against Welsh club sides, losing to Newport and Swansea and getting the better of Cardiff and Llanelli by single point each. But they swept the board against the national sides, not conceding a point apart from a typically astonishing Ronald Poulton try for England.

Despite the regular and often brutal dismemberment of British teams by the South Africans there existed a bond between them and British rugby that was deeper and more profound than the often suspicious relationship that England and the other home nations had with New Zealand and Australia. Yet, as the century progressed, it was a bond that would become increasingly problematic.

Stoop to conquer

Like many of the South Africans against whom England played, the architect of England's transformation into a power in world rugby was himself of Dutch extraction: Adrian Stoop. A descendant of a wealthy Dutch family, for his 21st birthday his father gave him a marble mine on the Turkish island of Marmara, which provided him with a more than comfortable income for the rest of his life. Educated at Rugby School and Oxford, he made his debut for Harlequins in 1901 while still at Rugby and left an indelible mark on the game, as a player, tactician and, later, administrator.[6]

Not a man to suffer fools gladly, Stoop came into the game when English rugby had hit rock bottom. The 1895 split had not only drained a huge reservoir of talent from the England side, but the purging of all opposition and the suppression of criticism had caused the English game to slip into a torpor of conservatism. In contrast, Wales had never stopped innovating and Scottish tactical nous ran far ahead of their Sassenach cousins. 'The English fifteen,' complained the *Daily Mail*, 'rushed bull-like into the fray with no set plan of campaign. It was as though we were engaged in modern warfare having armed our soldiers with weapons of the Crimean period. We fairly courted defeat.'[7]

Stoop's frustration at the state of English rugby might have remained just that, but his career began to blossom at precisely the time that the 1905 All Blacks had thrown the rugby world into turmoil – his first international match was England's 1905 game with Scotland – giving him the perfect circumstances in which to put his ideas into practice.

Many of these ideas he shared with the All Blacks. One was a shared disdain for the reflex kick for touch. Another was the belief that all players, backs and forwards, should be able to pass the ball and back up the ball-carrier. And, perhaps most controversially for English rugby, he felt that specialist expertise should be developed for each position. In Stoop's system each player had precise responsibilities, tactics were prepared for each stage of the game and moves were planned and practised constantly. 'It is only when the mechanical details make no demand on the brain that the brain is free to devote itself to the game,' he argued.[8]

This was especially true for his own position of half-back, where he insisted on one half-back being the scrum-half, taking charge of feeding the scrum and distributing the ball, and the other being the outside, or fly-half, who would act as the link between the scrum and the three-quarters. Although this was commonplace in New Zealand, Welsh and Northern Union rugby, the amateur ethos in England resisted too much specialisation by players.

Stoop was able to push through his reforms at Harlequins partly because his status meant no one could accuse him of being sympathetic to professionalism. He had chosen to play for Quins because they were less stuffy and conservative than Blackheath or Richmond, then the two leading London sides. In 1905 he was appointed club secretary and the following year he became team captain. As secretary he began to seek out talented players for the club, rather than leaving selection to chance or social connection, and as captain he welded his charges together with tactical aplomb.

Under his leadership, Harlequins assembled a devastating array of back-line talent. Centres John Birkett, Douglas Lambert and younger brother Frederick 'Freek' Stoop, scrum-half Herbert Sibree and, most famously, three-quarter Ronnie Poulton, set new standards for English back play, thrilling crowds and devastating opposing defences alike. Quins became the most successful and the most attractive club side in England.

The year 1910 was the one in which Stoop's Harlequins generation came to maturity and transferred their club success to the international stage. In the final five seasons before the outbreak of the First World War England began to reap spectacularly the rewards of the Stoop system. Although the man himself made his last international appearance in 1912, his legacy remained. The 1910 championship was followed by a shared championship with Ireland in 1912 and then two consecutive Grand Slams were won in 1913 and 1914 under the leadership of Poulton, the prodigiously talented three-quarter who was Stoop's natural successor.

Stoop had conquered. The ponderous, forward-based tactics that had defined English rugby union for the long years after 1895 were gone. Stoop and Poulton, the two old boys of Rugby School, resurrected the image of the dashing public school three-quarter who could score tries at will. The success of Stoop's Harlequins and his England side demonstrated to many that, in the words of the rugby correspondent of *The Sportsman*, 'the English selectors have lamentably erred for years past in ransacking the industrial centres for working-men players when they had the English [public] schools so full of genius in Rugger'.[9] He had returned the game to its roots.

The road to 1914

The end of the decade was the highest point in rugby's first wave of globalisation. New Zealand, South Africa and Australia had all visited the British Isles. Touring teams from Britain had been sent to the three southern hemisphere countries. There had even been a tour to Argentina in 1910 by an England side led by John Raphael, the first Jewish player to be capped by England, that also included three Scotsmen.

One final addition to rugby union's new world order was made in 1910. France were finally admitted to what had traditionally been called the Home Championship, transforming it into the Five Nations Championship. Their heroic two-try loss to the All Blacks in Paris on New Year's Day 1906 persuaded the RFU that the French were now capable of playing internationals against top-tier sides, and a couple of months later the Parc des Princes welcomed England. In 1908 matches with Wales began and the following year Ireland hosted the newcomers at Lansdowne Road. France were beaten comfortably in each but did enough to suggest they would be competitive in the Five Nations.

As it turned out, it didn't take long for France to record their first victory, against Scotland in the opening match of the 1911 Five Nations. Despite playing a substantial part of the match with only 14 players – Stade

Français winger Charles Vareilles simply did not show up and replacement André Francquenelle missed his train and arrived after the match had started – the French outscored the Scots by four tries to one and then hung on in the dying minutes to scrape home 16-15. It would be their only international win until 1920.

The final match of the 1914 Five Nations Championship brought the fledging French side face-to-face with a resurgent England at the height of its power. The English had already wrapped up the Triple Crown in a 16-15 thriller with Scotland at Inverleith so the match against France at Paris's Stade Colombes on 13 April had an air of inevitability about it.

Things did not look so simple five minutes after kick-off when Toulouse forward Jean-Louis Capmau finished off a flowing handling move by touching down to give France an improbable lead. Midway through the half England clicked into gear and right-winger Cyril Lowe scooted in for his sixth try of the tournament. But the French were not subdued. Bristol full-back William Johnston spilled a high ball from Besset and André evaded Lowe's attempted tackle to score in the left corner. France were back in the lead.

England had been notoriously slow starters throughout the 1914 campaign and it required the intervention of the captain, Ronald Poulton Palmer, to drag them back into contention. Poulton Palmer – who had changed his name to Palmer earlier in the year in order to acquire an inheritance from his uncle, G. W. Palmer, the Huntley and Palmer biscuit magnate – had succeeded Stoop as England captain. Although business had taken him away from Harlequins to Liverpool, his effortless corkscrew runs and imperceptible changes of pace continued to express the essence of Stoop's system. He scored two quick converted tries down the left and England went in at half-time with a fortunate 13-8 lead.

The story was very different in the second half, when England cut loose and raced away from the French. Lowe completed a hat-trick for a total of eight tournament tries in the season – still a record today – while his captain went one better and scored four. France managed to get back to 24-13 when Fernand Forgues surged through a gap to put Marcel-Frédéric Lubin-Lebrère in for a try. But as the French tired the English backs turned the screw and three more tries took the final score to 39-13. It was a match that would live long in the collective memory of rugby.

But this would not be for the reasons that were apparent on that fine Monday afternoon in Paris.

15

A GREATER GAME? RUGBY AND THE FIRST WORLD WAR

On Wednesday, 7 February 1917, Darb Hickey finally arrived on the Somme.

It had been five months since he'd left his home in the Sydney district of Glebe to join his fellow recruits to the 56th (New South Wales) Battalion of the Australian Imperial Force. With more than 2,000 other patriotic Australian men he boarded the troopship SS *Ceramic* at Sydney docks and set sail for England on 7 October 1916.

He had signed up to fight in Europe in May 1916, but he was no ordinary volunteer. Born John Joseph Hickey, he was known as 'Darb' not just to friends and family but to thousands of Australian rugby fans. A big centre-three-quarter who was as skilful as he was strong, Hickey had been a pioneer tourist with the 1908 Wallabies before switching to rugby league and starring for Australia in the 1910 series against the touring British Lions.

It was Hickey who had incensed the English RFU on the 1908 tour when it was revealed that he had actually signed to play in the fledgling Sydney rugby league competition in 1907 – and had even had his photograph taken in the New South Wales league line-up to play Baskerville's New Zealand league side – before changing his mind and sticking with union. On the Wallabies' return Down Under, he had switched back to league and become a star with the Glebe club before the outbreak of war. Like thousands of other Australian rugby players of both codes, he had now decided to join the cause of the Mother Country against Germany. Less than four weeks after his arrival on the Western Front, Hickey was invalided back to England with severe frostbite. When he returned to France he resumed his duties as a driver and took part in the 56th Battalion's battles at Bullecourt in France and then at Villers Bretonneux, Peronne and St Quentin Canal in Belgium.[1]

He was in Belgium when the war ended and could count himself one of the lucky ones to survive. Of the 331,814 Australians who had fought in the war, 61,859 – almost one in five – were killed. Over 150,000 were wounded. In Hickey's battalion alone 1,630 men were wounded and 529 never returned home.

He finally arrived back in Glebe on 20 July 1919 and was formally discharged from the army in September. Hickey was a proud man who had worked his way up from being a labourer to owning his own butcher's shop, where he displayed the caps, medals and trophies from a glittering rugby career. But customers and visitors who came to talk rugby with him would never see the campaign medals, nor any other memorabilia from his soldiering days. Wishing to forget everything about the war, he threw them into the waters of Sydney Harbour.

Ready for war

Rugby had always prided itself on being more than a sport. Ever since it began at Rugby School, it believed its role was to train young men to be leaders of the British Empire at home and abroad, in war as in peace. Indeed, the link between rugby and military duty was one of the underlying themes of *Tom Brown's Schooldays*, most famously when Tom describes the face of the School House team captain before a match as 'full of pluck and hope, the sort of look I hope to see in my general when I go out to fight'.[2]

English- and Afrikaans-speaking players had already played prominent roles in the Anglo-South African War of 1899–1902. Many other players fought on the British side, most famously the 1905 All Blacks' captain Dave Gallaher, along with New Zealand league pioneers Bumper Wright and Dan Fraser, as well as Australian players such as future Kangaroos forward Dan Frawley and 1904 international Frank Nicholson. Blair Swannell, the Englishman who had toured Australasia with the 1904 British side and then become the only Englishman to play for Australia in 1908, rose to the rank of lieutenant during his service in South Africa.

Rugby's links with the armed forces ran deep. Many British rugby union clubs such as Harlequins, Blackheath and London Scottish had close links with the Territorial Army. A significant number of privately educated players joined the Officer Training Corps at school or university. Both Adrian Stoop and Ronald Poulton Palmer were keen Territorial officers. Poulton had joined the OTC in his first year at Oxford in 1908 and declared himself to be 'frightfully keen on soldiering'. Across the Irish Sea, the vast majority of Ulster's Protestant players had joined Edward Carson's Ulster Volunteer Force to repel the threat of Irish Home Rule and Irish international Albert Stewart would become a UVF company commander.

When war was finally declared in the summer of 1914, it was as if, in the words of one keen rugby fan, 'the game for which they had been preparing for so many years' had begun.[3] Within hours of war being declared on 4 August, the RFU found itself inundated with requests for guidance from members. Initially C. J. B. Marriott, the RFU's secretary, told clubs that it would be 'advisable' to carry on playing but so many players voted with their feet and flocked to join the colours that it soon became clear that season would have to be abandoned. On 4 September the RFU formally cancelled all matches, and called upon all players aged between 19 and 35 to enlist. It also proposed the formation of a rugby players' battalion.

However, after consultation with the War Office, Marriott told the clubs 'it is not feasible to form a separate battalion of Rugby men', but that 'various commanding officers … will gladly accept for their Regiments a company (about 120) of Rugby men who could be enlisted together'. He then asked volunteers to send their particulars directly to him.[4] In fact, the prospect of a national battalion had already been scuppered by the rush to join local regiments.

Following the RFU's lead, the Welsh Rugby Union called upon its players to join up as quickly as possible. 'Welshmen have the reputation for not being wanting either in pluck or patriotism,' it declared. 'We therefore appeal with confidence to all Welsh rugby football players, untrammelled by imperative domestic ties, not to allow any selfish reason to prevent them from answering the urgent call of their King and Country.'[5] In Dublin, Irish RFU president Frank Browning persuaded the 7th Dublin Royal Fusiliers to set up a 'Pals' Battalion of rugby players, which went on to fight in Gallipoli and Salonika. In France, too, the young men of the professional and business classes who led the game flocked to join up.

At club level the scene at Harlequins' annual general meeting was typical. Most members turned up in khaki, having already volunteered, and £500 was donated to national war funds. Ronald Poulton Palmer wrote to his parents just after the declaration of war that 'Germany has to be smashed, i.e. I mean the military party, and everybody realises, and everybody is volunteering. And those who are best trained are most wanted, and so I should be a skunk to hold back.'[6]

In Scotland, 638 players joined up in the first two months of the war. Hugh Harper, the secretary of the West of Scotland club, wrote to his members to tell them that 'as so many members owing to the war are not available for football, the committee have decided that all fixtures for the coming season be cancelled', and urged the remaining ones to 'promptly offer their services to some branch of His Majesty's Forces'.[7]

Elsewhere, clubs and officials devoted considerable energy to recruiting volunteers. Leicester secretary Tom Crumbie used his club's Welford Road ground as an enlistment centre and recruited 3,500 local men for the forces. Most notable among their number was Edgar Mobbs, the former dashing three-quarter for Northampton and England. He immediately volunteered for the army but was told that, at 32, he was too old to be an officer. Undeterred, he enlisted as a private and set about raising his own corps in Northamptonshire. He recruited 250 men in just three days who became the 7th (Service) Battalion of the Northamptonshire Regiment.

The Northern Union was no less enthusiastic about the war effort, its secretary Joseph Platt declaring it 'the bounden duty of every player as well as every football enthusiast of suitable age and capacity to give his best service to the nation'.[8] More than 1,418 NU players signed up in the first nine months of the war, despite many being industrial workers engaged in war work. Following the guidance of the War Office, the NU continued with the 1914–15 season – indeed, soccer and horse racing continued much as normal until well into 1915 – but this did little to deter players from enlisting. Every club lost men to the army. Runcorn shed almost all of its playing staff as 23 players volunteered. Swinton and Broughton Rangers both offered their grounds to the armed forces and Wigan reserved one stand for free admission to men who had signed up. In April 1915 all competitions were suspended until the end of the war.[9]

The pattern was repeated in Australian and New Zealand rugby. In April 1915 the New South Wales Rugby Union suspended its club competitions for the duration of the war and threw themselves into the recruitment campaign. H. Y. Braddon, the president of the NSW Rugby Union, was also the chairman of the Sportsman's Recruiting Committee in Sydney. Half of those who joined its Sportsman's Battalion were rugby union players. In Sydney, the Manly rugby union club declared that it would do its all 'to prepare the members for active service when they came of military age'. The NSW Rugby Union even set up its own drill and rifle clubs 'for the purpose of providing military training for members before joining the armed forces'.[10]

As in Britain, the Australian rugby league authorities decided that league competitions should continue while at the same time encouraging players and supporters to join the army. 'It is their duty to respond to the Empire's call by enlisting, and if that not be practicable, by actively participating in training, in drill and rifle shooting,' the NSW Rugby League told its followers in 1914. By the end of 1915, 800 players had enlisted.[11] But the fact that rugby league's competitions continued while rugby union tournaments ceased during the war led to widespread accusations that league was unpatriotic, fuelling the deep hostility that already existed between the codes.

Even today, the charge is repeated and used as an explanation for league's eclipse of union in Australia. In fact, rugby union club matches did not stop during the war but continued as friendly matches in NSW and Queensland.[12] And in reality, the league game had been drawing far bigger crowds since at least 1910, when *The Referee* had warned that the 'union game is not regaining its popularity. Matches which formerly attracted from 13,000 to 25,000 people now coax from 1,000 to 2,500 … the schism has hit the old game hard. Some of the controllers of rugby union football may not yet be able to thoroughly realise this. Nevertheless they are now facing a problem which in time may swell from a small hill to a towering mountain.'[13] The die had already been cast in favour of league well before the advent of war.

A greater game?

Far from rugby union stopping during the war in Britain, it became an important feature of military and civilian life. League, in contrast, lacked the support of the armed forces and was played only sporadically. Regular matches involving international rugby union sides began in London before the end of 1914 when the Public Schools and Universities Battalion beat a Canadian military side in front of 3,000 spectators at

Richmond. On New Year's Day 1915, 20,000 spectators turned out at Leicester to see the Canadians play.[14] In August 1915, Northampton staged a tournament for English and Scottish military sides that drew over 8,000 spectators.

By 1916 London had become the centre of an international military rugby circuit. The huge influx of troops from Australia, New Zealand and South Africa greatly expanded the pool of players available to military rugby union sides. Matches became more frequent, of a much higher quality and attracted large crowds. In February 1917 it was announced that a 'New Zealand Trench Team', comprising Kiwis fighting on the Western Front, would be playing matches in London and that ticket applications for their matches were being taken. Such a naked appeal to spectators in the midst of war seemed to have raised eyebrows and the team's visit was quietly cancelled.[15]

In France the presence of armed forces was also felt on the rugby field. In November 1916, Stade Français played and won against a British military side comprising players from across the Empire. The same year a French military side played an American ambulance unit. At the start of 1917 American expatriate journalist and sports administrator Allan Muhr, who had played for France against the All Blacks in 1906, organised an invitational Paris side, Lutétia, to play against military sides. Among its numbers was French international forward and wartime fighter ace Maurice Boyau. In January they defeated an ANZAC team and an Australian ambulance side. Matches were regularly organised between French and other army sides of the Allies. These were great crowd pullers and they also showed how far French rugby had advanced, thanks to a 15-14 win over a British artillery side featuring five England internationals and a narrow 5-3 loss to a New Zealand side in front of 20,000 in February 1918.[16]

The growth of military rugby in England from 1916 also owed much to the influx of Northern Union stars into the army following the introduction of conscription. By October 1916 rugby union matches featuring Northern Union players were so common that the RFU was forced to make a public announcement that:

> Northern Union players can only play with Rugby Union players in bona-fide naval and military teams. Rugby Union teams can play against naval and military teams in which there are Northern Union players. Munitions workers cannot be regarded as naval and military players. These rulings only obtain during the war.[17]

For the first time since 1895 union and league players could officially play alongside each other. A number of rugby-supporting commanding officers made full use of the new dispensation. The most famous was Major R. V. Stanley, Oxford University's representative on the RFU Committee, whose Grove Park Army Service Corps (Motor Transport) team in south London included Huddersfield's international stars Harold Wagstaff, Douglas Clark, Ben Gronow and Albert Rosenfeld. Not surprisingly, they won all but one of their 26 matches, including those against Australian and New Zealand military teams, scoring 1,110 points while conceding just 41.

Their only reversal was a 6-3 defeat by the United Services, thanks to a last-minute try by Scottish international Roland Gordon, who 18 months later would be killed in France. The United Services team was as star-studded as the Grove Park side, featuring eight rugby union internationals plus Wigan's Billy Seddon and Leeds' Willie Davies. Davies was also the captain of the Devonport Royal Navy depot team that featured nine NU players, including future England league captain Jonty Parkin and Harold Buck, rugby league's first £1,000 transfer player. Although sporting restrictions were lifted during wartime matches, social etiquette remained. Wagstaff addressed his wing-three-quarter partner, Harlequins' Lieutenant Nixon, as 'Sir' and Nixon reciprocated by calling his centre 'Wagstaff', even in the middle of a match when they were discussing tactics.

Rugby was also played informally in combat zones. Jack Robinson, Rochdale's international Northern Union winger, took part in a match during the Battle of Neuve-Chapelle in March 1915, later suffering serious shrapnel wounds. Despite his injuries his enthusiasm for rugby remained undimmed. 'Our boys out yonder will have their game of football under all sorts of conditions,' he said. 'It comes as a tonic and a relaxation from trench duty and I cannot understand anybody in England ever questioning the advisability of the game'. The Gordons played the Queen's Own Cameron Highlanders before the Battle of Loos in September of 1915. The day before the Battle of the Somme commenced the commanding officer of the 13th Battalion of the Rifle Brigade broke his collarbone in a match between Officers and Other Ranks.

Ronald Poulton Palmer played his final game of rugby in Belgium in 1915 when he captained the South Midland Division (Forty-Eighth) versus the Fourth Division. The poet and novelist Robert Graves played full-back for the First Battalion of the Royal Welch Fusiliers in a match in France.[18] Henri Amand, the inaugural captain of France for the 1906 match against the All Blacks and a future president of the French Rugby Federation, vividly remembered his last match at the front in 1915: 'We got changed in our trench. I played alongside Géo André [the French international winger and Olympic athlete], but the game was soon interrupted. The Germans put up an air-burst shell over the pitch and nobody wanted to hang around after that.'[19]

However, unlike soccer, organised rugby competitions in the field were not common. One rare exception was a battle cruiser competition staged in 1917, won by HMS *Lion*, the flagship of Vice Admiral William Pakenham. Things were different for Australian and New Zealand soldiers, whose love of rugby of any code far outstripped soccer, and formal and informal competitions took place across the various theatres of war. Troops played league and union in Cairo before departing for Gallipoli in the spring of 1915. One typical example was on the Western

Front, when a rugby league tournament was held in the latter stages of the war by the Australian Imperial Forces. It was convincingly won by the Mudlarks, the team of 4th Machine Gun Company of the AIF's Fourth Brigade.[20]

For most British troops, however, rugby came in a very distant second to soccer in popularity. The war diary of Huddersfield's Douglas Clark for 1917 describes his exploits in a number of soccer matches while he served in France but only one game of rugby. His friend and team-mate Harold Wagstaff had no alternative but to play soccer while stationed in Egypt since no rugby at all was played.[21] Except for soldiers from rugby-playing regions in northern England, South Wales or the Scottish Borders, rugby was generally viewed as a game for officers. Paul Jones, the former captain of the Dulwich College first XV, wrote home from France in October 1915 that 'the Tommies – the English ones, at least – think soccer the only game, so one must cut one's cloth to one's opportunities'.[22] This was a division that would have significant consequences once the war had ended.

No longer a game

Rugby also believed that it could make a unique contribution to the war effort. 'Rugby football above all games,' wrote Lord Jellicoe, Admiral and First Sea Lord during the war, 'develops the qualities which go to make good fighting men. It teaches unselfishness, *esprit de corps*, quickness of decision, and keeps fit those engaged in it.'[23]

Others seemed to believe that war was an extension of the game itself, *The Spectator* going so far as to describe the horrors of trench warfare as 'being not unlike the scrum in Rugby football'.[24] Even after the war had ended Major General Sir C. H. Harrington ascribed the Allies' victory to 'those loyal and unselfish three-quarter backs, Sir Douglas Haig, General Pershing and the King of the Belgians, and those grand attacking forwards, our respective army commanders'.[25]

Such claims were patently silly. All sports, from cricket to polo, claimed that they were uniquely suited for military training and service, and for many rugby players the reality of war quickly came into conflict with any notions about the game being preparation for combat. Leicester forward Bill Dalby wrote home at the end of 1914 and described an attack on his trench. 'On one occasion all but one German [attacking the trench] turned and fled, and he came on shouting, "Me no done for," but he was a second later. It is nice to read of these things, but not so nice to be in it. We had this sort of thing for four nights and lost half the men in that time.'[26] Devon county player and long-serving RFU committee member Ted Butcher, one of a handful of survivors in Edgar Mobbs' Brigade of the Northamptonshire Regiment, suffered from nightmares for the rest of his life.[27]

For some players, years of preparing for military service at school and university meant that they were as keen for battle as they were for rugger. Billie Nevill, a rugby player at Dover College who helped organise the famous East Surrey Regiment's attack on German lines at the Somme that was led by an officer kicking a football into no-man's-land, wrote to his parents that 'war is the greatest fun imaginable'.[28] Eleven months before he was killed in action, Paul Jones, the former captain of Dulwich College XV, wrote that 'in my heart and soul I have always longed for the rough and tumble of war as for a football match'.[29]

Regardless of their varying degrees of enthusiasm for warfare, the vast majority of rugby players who served in the war would eventually find themselves confronted with the reality of combat. The toll of death and injury quickly became harrowing. At club level alone, over the course of the war Bristol lost 300 members. Forty-five of the 60 players in London Scottish's four pre-war XVs were killed. Richmond lost 73 members, Rosslyn Park 72, Liverpool 57 and Hartlepool 33. Of the Old Merchant Taylors' 1914 first team 13 were killed and two permanently disabled; these are just some of the more prominent examples. In the Northern Union, Leeds lost 15 of 51 players who served, Widnes lost

13, Hull 12 and Swinton 9. In 1919 the *Athletic News* tried to compile a list of NU players who had not returned home. It traced 760 players, of which 103 had lost their lives.[30] In Australia, the NSWRU announced in April 1916 that 109 of its registered players had already been killed in action. The Eastern Suburbs club in Sydney reported, of its 82 members who 'went to the help of the Motherland, twenty have made the supreme sacrifice'.[31] There are many others, including German players, of whom we know nothing.

Thanks to their prominence, we do know a lot about international players who were killed during the war. In the southern hemisphere, nine Australian rugby union internationals and four league internationals never returned home. Thirteen New Zealand internationals lost their lives, including Dave Gallaher, the captain of the 1905 All Blacks, along with another six league internationals. Five Springboks were killed. Four British league internationals and ten Irish union internationals were sacrificed. For the rest of northern hemisphere rugby the toll was unremittingly grim: 13 Welsh, 24 French, 27 English and 30 Scottish internationals were killed.

The first rugby international to be killed in action seems to have been the great Stade Toulousain half-back Alfred Mayssonnié. The little general of the all-conquering *Vierge Rouge* side, 'Maysso' was reported missing during the Battle of the Marne on 6 September 1914 and later declared dead. The first British soldier reported as killed in action was Scotsman Ronnie Simson. A career soldier in the Royal Field Artillery who scored a try on his debut for the defeated Scotland side in the 1911 Calcutta Cup, he was hit by enemy shellfire during the First Battle of the Aisne and died on 14 September 1914. He was just 24 years old.

Two days later his fellow Scot, Dr James Huggan, who as a winger had scored against England in the last Calcutta Cup match before the war, was blown up while attending to wounded German soldiers. He was the first to die of the 11 players in that 1914 Calcutta Cup match who would not return from the war. The following day, former England forward Captain Charles Wilson was killed, again during the Battle of the Aisne.

The first Australian to die was Ted Larkin, the Labour Party MP and secretary of the NSW Rugby League, at Gallipoli on 25 April 1915, the same day as Blair Swannell. They were two of four Australian internationals who fell at Gallipoli. Four months later Albert Downing became the first All Black victim of the war when he too was killed at Gallipoli. The Dardanelles also claimed the lives of David Bedell-Sivright, captain of the 1904 British touring team to Australia and New Zealand, Scottish international winger William Church, and Billy Nanson, who had won two caps for England at rugby union before joining Oldham rugby league club.

Many more players met their end in the trenches of the Western Front. England and Gloucester forward Harry Berry was one of 262 men in the 1st Battalion Gloucestershire Regiment killed in a single day when they went over the top at the Battle of Aubers Ridge in May 1915. That same month Basil Maclear was killed near Ypres, the first Irish international to lose his life and one of 647 out of 668 men in his battalion to die in a German assault on their trenches. Former Richmond captain Harry Alexander was killed just 13 days after he arrived at the front in October 1915. Ronald Poulton Palmer was killed by a sniper's bullet only five weeks into his first tour of duty. England internationals John King and Noel Slocock were killed on the same day in August 1916 on the Somme, two of more than a million casualties of that battle. Four All Blacks – James Baird, James MacNeece, George Sellars and Reginald Taylor – were among the 3,660 New Zealand troops killed in the attack on Messines Ridge in June 1917. Eighteen French internationals were killed in combat in France, including four airmen, among them Stade Bordelais forward Maurice Boyau, who was shot down in September 1918.

In total, 130 rugby union internationals and untold thousands of non-internationals perished in the First World War, but did the deaths of so many players really substantiate the claim of a headmaster writing to *The Times* early in 1919, that rugby 'proved itself to be unequalled by any other game as a school of true manhood and leadership'?[32]

About ten million combatants died in the war, and the number of elite sportsmen among them was but a fraction. Comparison with other sports are both odious and meaningless. Neither the Football Association nor the Northern Union kept comprehensive lists of their players' war records.[33] There is also something distasteful in citing the deaths of hundreds of young men to claim the superiority of one sport over another. In the years immediately after the war and in subsequent decades of the next century, many in rugby union would be quick to point to the sacrifice of the war as evidence of the sport's greater moral purpose.

Just months after the Armistice, Bob Oakes, a future RFU president, shared similar sentiments. 'We now know how splendidly the Rugby footballer, in common with every British soldier, fought – aye, and how magnificently he died!'[34] Such views contrasted sharply with the symbolic images of soccer during the war. The memory of informal games between British and German troops in no-man's-land during the impromptu truces of Christmas 1914 gave soccer an image of peace and international brotherhood counterposed to rugby union's militarism.

Oakes' sentiments were not shared by every rugby player who served. Darb Hickey was not alone in the disgust that led him to throw his service medals away. His fellow dual code international, New Zealander Phonse Carroll, declared himself a conscientious objector and refused to fight. Dr John MacCallum, the fearsome forward who captained the Scotland team that pushed the 1905 touring All Blacks to the limit, declined to serve in the British Army and also became a conscientious objector, in 1916.[35]

As these men understood, like millions of others who may or may not have played or watched rugby, sport was not war and war was most definitely not sport.

PART V

CHALLENGE AND CHANGE IN THE INTERWAR YEARS

After the turbulent decades before the First World War, rugby emerged from the war stronger than ever. For rugby union's followers around the world, its war record self-evidently demonstrated the moral force of the game, and it consolidated its grip on its traditional constituencies.

Even in the midst of economic depression, rugby league also deepened its roots in its working-class communities and extended its appeal to France, where it would eventually find itself engaged in a life and death struggle.

And a new rivalry emerged, as South Africa played New Zealand for the first time, locking both countries into a battle for supremacy of the rugby world that would shape the future of the game ...

16

ALL BLACKS VERSUS SPRINGBOKS: BATTLE FOR THE WORLD

Ranji Wilson was a star. 'One of the greatest forwards in the world,' declared the London *Daily Mail*. 'Wonderful,' exclaimed *The Times*, after he dominated another game for the New Zealand Services team in 1919.[1] Born in Christchurch to an English mother and a West Indian father, Ranji won ten caps for the All Blacks before the war, becoming as famous for his skills with the ball in hand as he was for tight work in the forwards. He was so versatile that he had even played on the wing with distinction for the NZ Services.

Now, just a few months after the end of the war, he was starring in the nearest thing to a world cup that rugby union would have until 1987: the 1919 Inter-Services Tournament for the King's Cup.

The huge popularity of inter-services rugby in the last two years of the First World War, coupled with the hundreds of thousands of players from across the British Empire who were waiting to be demobilised, led to calls for a major international tournament to be staged once peace had been declared. In the spring of 1919, apparently at the request of the War Office in London, a 16-match competition was organised featuring representative sides from the services of the rugby-playing nations of the British Empire.[2]

The tournament had an explicitly political aim, as *The Times* explained. 'It is a most practical means of continuing and strengthening the bonds of interest between us and our relations scattered over the world. War has brought all parts of the Empire closer ... and the strongest of [ties] is the common interest in British games.'[3] To underline this, the British combined services side was officially known as the 'Mother Country'.

Alongside the Mother Country and the RAF, who had decided to participate under their own name, Australia, New Zealand, South Africa and Canada competed in a league table over two months with matches being staged in front of massive crowds at Swansea, Portsmouth, Leicester, Newport, Edinburgh, Gloucester, Bradford and Twickenham. Almost half the New Zealand side were full internationals and everything suggested that they would finish unbeaten at the top of the table. That was until their last match when Australia, who had earlier lost to the Mother Country and the RAF, pulled off a memorable performance and outscored the New Zealanders by two tries to one, eventually scraping home 6-5.

Three days later the Mother Country triumphed over South Africa, leaving them tied with the Kiwis at the top of the table. A play-off was hastily arranged four days later on a Wednesday afternoon at Twickenham. There, in a tight game, the New Zealand forwards led by Ranji Wilson came out on top to defeat the Mother Country 9-3, in front of an audience which included the New Zealand prime minister William Massey, in Europe for the talks on the Versailles Treaty. Although etiquette forbade the words to be uttered, no one could now doubt that New Zealand were indeed rugby union's world champions.

Three days later, after a 20-3 win over the French Services team, they were presented with the King's Cup by the King of England himself, George V. International rugby union was back, and the success of the inter-services tournament confirmed once more that it was truly the winter game of the British Empire.

The King's Cup was also the first time that New Zealand had met South Africa in the international rugby arena. Although New Zealanders had played English-speaking South Africans in friendly matches during the Anglo-Boer War, national representative sides had yet to face each other. Half-hearted attempts had been made to invite the 1905 All Blacks to stop off in South Africa on their way home and the New Zealanders invited the Springboks before the war but costs had proved prohibitive for the South Africans.[4]

Despite the fact that the New Zealand services side comfortably overcame the South Africans 14-5 in the King's Cup, two days after the match the South African Rugby Board (SARB) cabled William Schreiner, the former prime minister of the Cape Colony and past president of SARB who was now the South African High Commissioner in London, asking him to approach the New Zealanders and Australians to tour the country on their way back home.

The New Zealanders agreed and their 29-strong touring party arrived in South Africa on 17 July to much acclaim. Over the next six weeks they played 15 matches, winning 11, drawing one but losing to Griqualand West, Western Province and a Combined Cape Town/Stellenbosch University side. As the tour progressed, it was clear that a deep rivalry had been ignited, as the mayor of Cape Town recognised when he told a civic reception that 'when South Africa and New Zealand meet in an international game, it will be the greatest day in the history of rugby football'.[5]

There was just one difference between the New Zealand team that had thrilled British crowds to win the King's Cup and that which left such a legacy in South Africa. Ranji Wilson, 'perhaps the greatest player in the Service team' according to the *Natal Witness*, was not one of the tourists.[6]

Two weeks before the New Zealand squad was due to sail for Cape Town, the SARB executive had met and voted 8-6 to send a confidential telegram to London. 'If visitors include Maoris tour would be wrecked and immense harm politically and otherwise would follow. Please explain position fully and try arrange exclusion.'[7] Ranji, who had captained the New Zealanders in a number of matches in Britain, was told that he could not tour because of the colour of his skin. Parekura Tureia, the Maori five-eighth who had been described as 'a player likely to win a game all by himself', was also passed over for selection.[8]

Rugby union's greatest international rivalry, its most intense contest and the very expression of South African and New Zealand manhood, was founded on the exclusion of those whose skins were not white. It would be a scar that would define the game for the rest of the century.

The world championship of rugby

The success of the white New Zealanders in South Africa meant that the NZRU began to make preparations for a reciprocal tour almost as soon as the Services' side returned home late in 1919. Less than two years later, in July 1921, the Springboks arrived, having warmed up with a short tour of Australia, where they had won all five of their matches, including whitewashing New South Wales in a three-match series in Sydney.

As the Australians noticed, South African rugby owed more to the British game than did that of New Zealand. The power of the Springbok game lay in the play of the forwards both in the loose and in the scrum. The ball was kept tight and opposition mistakes seized upon and turned to maximum advantage. The difference in the two nations' style was exemplified in the scrum. Although they had used a 3-4-1 scrum formation on their 1906 tour of Britain, the South Africans still largely favoured the traditional 3-2-3 formation. In contrast, the All Blacks' 2-3-2 scrum had two men in the front row designated as hookers with the aim of raking the ball out as quickly as possible so that the scrum-half could launch his backs into attack. The eighth forward, the rover, never actually packed down but would feed the scrum and then stand his ground to protect the scrum-half from opposing forwards. This was, of course, the 'wing-forward' play that had so frustrated the British during the 1905 All Blacks' tour.

The two systems were tested to destruction in front of 20,000 people at the first Test at Dunedin. The first half saw a much heavier South African pack dominate possession, creating momentum and space for their backs. Starved of the ball, the All Blacks found it difficult to get off the back foot and when Attie van Heerden scored in the right corner from the blind side of the scrum half-time saw the visitors leading 5-0.

With the Springboks now kicking into the sun in the second half, the New Zealanders started peppering them with short, high kicks. The Springboks proved equal to the challenge until a lucky bounce took the ball into the arms of Wanganui forward Moke Belliss who touched down for a converted try that tied the scores.

The All Blacks then took the lead following a Springbok kick that was gathered by right-winger Jack Steel on the halfway line, who then beat three defenders to touch down between the posts. Percy Storey clinched the victory with a try on the left wing just before full-time. The All Blacks had triumphed 13-5 in the epic match that everyone had hoped for.

The two sides reassembled for the second Test in Auckland a fortnight later and once again there was nothing in it. Billy Sendin crossed first for a Springbok try but the All Blacks clawed their way back and lock-forward Andrew McLean forced his way over from close range and the teams went into half-time locked up at five points each.

The South African forwards' strength and short passing gradually wore down the New Zealanders. As full-time approached the Springbok forwards once more forced the All Blacks into a defensive scrum near their own line. The ball came out on the New Zealand side but Jack Steel's relieving kick went straight down the throat of veteran South African full-back Gerhard Morkel standing a few yards in from touch. As the All Black forwards raced to close him down, he launched a drop kick that sailed clear over the bar for four points. Nine-five ahead, the Springboks held their grip on the match until no-side was whistled. The Test series was tied.

In the three weeks that passed before the third and deciding match, the Test series grew in importance from a sporting contest to one for the very soul of the New Zealand nation. 'When a nation ceases to be interested in the career of her representatives in sport, it spells not only the decay of sport but the decadence of the nation,' explained the *Evening Post*. 'We simply cannot afford to lose the third Test.'[9]

Only Wales and Australia had ever defeated the All Blacks in 24 Test matches since the start of the century. The taste of defeat was rare and unpleasant. But the rivalry with South Africa went deeper. Both were young nations and, in an age when the British Empire was the dominant world power, both measured their value as nations by their relationship to the Mother Country. To become the world champions of rugby union – however unofficial that title would be – was a way in which South Africa and New Zealand could stake a claim to be a major power in the Empire.

That link between sport and politics came raging to the surface the week before the final Test. The Springboks narrowly defeated a Maori representative team 9-8 at Napier in a rough and undisciplined game. Two days later, the Napier *Daily Telegraph* published a telegram from Charles Blackett, the *Johannesburg Star* reporter accompanying the tourists, which described the game as 'the most unfortunate match ever played. ... the spectacle of thousands of Europeans frantically cheering on a band of coloured men to defeat members of their own race was too much for the Springboks, who were frankly disgusted.'[10]

Blackett also alleged that the tourists only agreed to play the Maori after pressure from the tour manager Harold Bennett. Bennett denied the accusation and apologised to his hosts but the damage had been done. New Zealand's belief that its race relations were harmonious was piqued, and the third Test became an even greater trial of the merits of the two nations.

Indeed, the determination to be victorious led the New Zealand selectors to take the unprecedented, and according to the rules of the game completely illegal, step of calling former New Zealand rugby league captain Karl Ifwersen into the side at five-eighth. Ifwersen had been capped for the Kiwis in 1913 and then captained them in 1919. In early 1921 the Auckland Rugby Union persuaded him to switch to union and he captained the provincial side against the Springboks. Now he ran out in front of 35,000 spectators at Wellington eager to see history being made.

The game itself was a disappointment. Heavy rain meant that the muddy ground was covered in standing water and the match quickly became a war of attrition. The All Blacks occasionally managed to break through the Springboks line but were unable to outfox Gerhard Morkel at full-back, whose experience and positional sense snuffed out each probe. It ended 0-0.

If it was a frustrating outcome for both sides, it could not have been a better result to keep the flame of rivalry burning vigorously between the two countries. The struggle to be world champions had become more than a game; it was now a quest.

'To Win the World's Title'

It would be seven years before the two sides met again, when the All Blacks made their first tour to South Africa in 1928. Meanwhile, the gap between New Zealand and South Africa and the rest of the rugby union world continued to grow.

In 1924, the All Blacks made their second visit to Britain, going one better than in 1905 by winning all of their 32 matches to earn the sobriquet 'The Invincibles'. Even Wales proved no match, and were despatched 19-0 at Swansea. The only side to threaten them was

Wavell Wakefield's England, whose brutal approach to the game led to New Zealand forward Cyril Brownlie becoming the first player ever to be sent off in an international match less than ten minutes after the kick-off.

Earlier in 1924, a fifth British Isles team (they would not be known as the Lions until after the Second World War) had toured South Africa. Captained by England forward Ronald Cove-Smith, the side could not claim to be the best of the British game. Alongside superb players like Wales' Rowe Harding, Scotland's New Zealand-born winger Ian Smith and England forward Tom Voyce, the squad also contained players whose international careers could be diplomatically described as brief. With the exception of a 3-3 draw in the third Test at Port Elizabeth, the Springboks swept the tourists aside, comfortably winning the other three Test matches.

The game had gone from strength to strength in South Africa, especially among Afrikaans speakers. Fierce local competitions and the growing importance of the provincial Currie Cup, together with the international profile that the game offered meant that rugby had become a means of making a mark on the world. Whereas once the game had been the preserve of elite private schools, now it began to take a hold across the educational system. The decade saw the number of schools playing in the Transvaal rise from nothing to 30 playing for the A. G. Robertson Cup. Western Province had 100 school teams playing the game, Johannesburg 85. Perhaps most symbolically, the Afrikaans Boys' High School in Pretoria took up the game in 1920 and soon *Die Witbulle*, as the school's first team was known, became the dominating force in the region.[11]

In New Zealand, the intensity of the game had continued to increase. Despite a dominant Hawke's Bay side, eight different teams won the Ranfurly Shield, known to all as the 'Log o' Wood', between 1921 and 1928. It had been presented for the first time in 1902 by the Earl of Ranfurly, the Governor of New Zealand, and competed for on a challenge basis, the trophy being passed on to whichever side defeated the current holders. The shield became the new symbol of the inter-provincial and local rivalries that had spurred the development of rugby in the 19th century, and the fact that it was won through challenge matches meant that, if all the elements were aligned on any given day, any team could have a chance of glory, whether it was little Manawhenua or mighty Wellington. And, as part of this growth, Maori participation also increased. The Hawke's Bay that held on to the Ranfurly Shield for so long had a large number of Maori players and three of the biggest stars of the 1924 Invincibles were Maori: the immortal George Nepia, half-back Jimmy Mill and five-eighth Lui Paewai.

Anticipation in both countries of the All Black tour of South Africa in 1928 could not have been higher, but for the New Zealand selectors the quest to become world champions was subordinated to the racial policies of the South African Rugby Board. In June 1927, the New Zealand Rugby Union told its provinces confidentially that no Maori players would be selected for the South African tour. George Nepia, the world's greatest full-back, and Jimmy Mill, who had been instrumental in the 1924 tourists' wins over England and Wales, were left at home, and aspiring Maori players were ignored. Outside the Maori community, there was little protest.

Despite the All Blacks winning six of their eight opening tour matches before the first Test, most critics predicted a Springbok win. But as their form improved and the rugby began to flow, hopes were raised back in New Zealand, 'To Win The World's Title', the *New Zealand Truth* proclaimed on the eve of the first Test in Durban. But despite a tight first half when only a Bennie Osler drop goal separated the sides, the Springbok pack stormed over the New Zealanders in the second half to win 17-0. It was the biggest defeat ever suffered by the All Blacks.

Three weeks later battle was rejoined at Ellis Park in Johannesburg. After being pushed off the ball and starved of possession in the first Test, this time the All Blacks radically changed their approach to scrummaging and abandoned their 2-3-2 formation in favour of the Springboks' 3-4-1 technique. Although 3-4-1 had been used on their 1906 British tour, it was only in the mid-1920s, thanks to Stellenbosch University coach A. F. 'Oubass' Markötter, that it became the common method of forming a scrum.[12] The tactical shift paid off and New Zealand squeaked home with a drop goal and a penalty to two penalties.

Thus forearmed, the South African pack switched up a gear for the third Test and ground the All Blacks down. But unlike the claustrophobic defensive sieges of the first two Tests, this time the play flowed back and forth with five tries being scored. With a minute to go, the Springboks were hanging on to an 11-6 lead when a final back-line movement by the All Blacks set their left-winger Bert Grenside into the clear. But as he dived for the corner two Springboks threw themselves at him and pushed him into touch. South Africa now held the upper hand with one Test to go.

They did not take that advantage. The fourth Test went 13-5 to the All Blacks, not least due to the tourists adopting the Springboks' tactics of playing a tight game in the forwards. The overwhelming emotion in New Zealand was one of relief, but the frustration felt by the South Africans in not clinching the series was tempered by the fact that they were clearly the better side. In their eyes, there was no doubt that they were the unofficial world champions.

Hemispheric pressure

The gap between British rugby and the southern hemisphere nations was about far more than the standard of play. The New Zealanders had always viewed the sport primarily as a handling and running game, and the arrival of rugby league in 1907 gave rise to calls for reform of the rules of the game. In Auckland, where league was strongest, the provincial union introduced a series of reforms as early as 1916, including a ban on direct kicking into touch, which became known as the 'Auckland Rules'.

Substitutes were also allowed on both sides of the Tasman Sea, something that was anathema to the RFU.

In 1919, the NZRU, supported by the New South Wales Rugby Union (then the governing body of Australian rugby union), proposed to the International Rugby Football Board (IB) a series of rule changes designed to speed up the game and relax the amateur regulations. They also called for the establishment of an Imperial Rugby Board with equal representation for the three southern hemisphere 'colonies' and the four home nations. The IB turned them down flat, but the New Zealanders and the Australians continued to lobby for a voice in international rugby affairs.

Rugby politics reflected the politics of the Empire. The 'white dominions' – Australia, Canada, New Zealand and South Africa – had been campaigning for greater equality with Britain and the 1926 Imperial Conference had issued what became known as the 'Balfour Declaration', stating that the Dominions and Britain were self-governing nations of equal status. Five years later the Statute of Westminster granted legislative equality for the Dominions. This was the type of relationship that the rugby administrators of Australia and New Zealand wanted for their sport.

But the IB proved to be less amenable than the British government. It vetoed any discussion on the amateur regulations and refused Dominion representation on the IB. As a concession, the IB agreed to 'dispensations' that allowed Australia and New Zealand to forbid direct kicking into touch from inside the 25-yard line.

These differences between Britain and the Dominions came to a head on the 1930 British tour to Australia and New Zealand. As usual, the tour was entirely organised by the RFU and managed by its former president James Baxter. Baxter had a reputation for what could euphemistically be described as 'plain speaking' and was not afraid to voice his opinions. In Auckland, a journalist asked him why he thought rugby league was so popular in the city. 'Every town must have its sewer,' he replied.[13]

On the first match of the tour, the British were dumbfounded to see the Wanganui players head back to their dressing room at the end of the first half, contravening RFU regulations which stated that players should stay on the pitch at half-time. Baxter was also disturbed to see All Black players advertising products, contrary to the RFU's rules on professionalism. But what irritated Baxter most was the New Zealand use of 'wing-forward' play and their 2-3-2 scrum. This had been an issue on both All Black tours of Britain and Baxter described the tactic as 'a menace to the game'.

Despite unexpectedly winning the first Test, when Newport's Jack Morley squeezed in at the corner in the last minute for a 6-3 win on a snow-covered Dunedin pitch, the British lost the series 3-1. When they returned home, Baxter persuaded the RFU to change the scrummage rules to outlaw New Zealand's wing-forward and the 2–3–2 formation. The 'dispensations' were also withdrawn, although they were later reinstated to assuage Antipodean anger.

Conspicuous by their absence from these controversies were the South Africans. In fact, they were loyal supporters of the British position. Springboks' manager Harold Bennett had told the New Zealand press in 1921 that 'first of all, we stand by the English Rugby Union. We have always stuck fast to it. And we hold dearly to amateurism.'[14] They did not share the New Zealanders' approach to playing the game and, with no domestic threat from rugby league, felt no reason to change the game.

Moreover, personal ties between South Africa and Britain were much stronger than those between the British and the other countries. South African players were a common sight in an England jersey during the interwar years. Frank Mellish played six times for England in the 1920s and returned home to win six more caps with the Springboks. Brian Black won ten England caps in the early 1930s. Hubert Freakes won three caps in the late 1930s. Full-back Harold 'Tuppy' Owen-Smith scored a century in cricket for South Africa against England in

1929 and then won ten England rugby caps, three as captain, between 1934 and 1937.

Even so, the visit of the third Springbok side to tour Britain in the 1931–32 season did little to deepen the friendship. The Springboks disposed of each of the home nations with brutal efficiency, thanks to their relentless scrummaging machine and the metronome kicking of fly-half and captain Bennie Osler. They played ten-men rugby with clinical precision, recycling the ball from the scrum for Osler to find touch to set up another scrum. At this time, teams could opt for a scrum or line-out after finding touch – the Springboks always took the scrum. In the first half of the Test against England, the South African pack won 23 out of 28 scrums yet such was the conservatism of their play that just one try was scored.

Significantly, their only reverse of the tour was a 30-21 defeat to a combined Leicestershire/East Midlands side when Osler didn't play. Yet despite warm and cordial relations off the field, the dour Springbok tactics left many in Britain feeling uncomfortable. Dai Gent, the pre-war England fly-half of no mean repute, complained of Osler's tactics: 'how monotonous it all was, and how terribly irritating for his centres. Frankly I found these tactics extremely tedious.'[15]

Although the 1938 British tour to South Africa proved to be more successful than many had hoped – the tourists won 16 of the 21 non-Test matches as well as a last-gasp victory in the final Test – the Springboks once again steamrolled their way to straightforward victories in the first two Tests. By this time, though, the British tour was to the South Africans merely the brandy and cigars after the main course of their triumphant 1937 tour to New Zealand.

It had been nine years since the two sides had fought out the epic drawn series in South Africa. In that time the Springboks had lost just twice, both defeats in the five-Test series against the touring Wallabies in 1933. But the All Blacks had slumped, losing the 1929 Test series 3-0 to the Wallabies, tying their 1934 series, losing to the British touring side in 1930 and then to England and Wales on the 1935 tour of Britain. Since last playing the Springboks, the All Blacks had played 19, won ten, lost eight and drawn one. This was not the form of potential world champions.

The Springboks arrived in New Zealand in July 1937 and made their way down North Island, imperiously brushing aside provincial teams on their way to the first Test at Wellington. And it was there in front of 45,000 spectators that the African juggernaut hit an All Black brick wall. Playing out of their skins, the All Blacks held back the Springbok pack despite having only 14 players in the second half after winger Donald Cobden was injured. Ronald Ward was taken out of the pack to play on the wing and the All Blacks won 13-7 using a seven-man scrum against the Springboks' eight.

New Zealand erupted in national euphoria. But the elation was not to last. Three weeks later at Christchurch another huge crowd gathered in anticipation of an All Black series win. But the *New Zealand Evening Post* summed up the story of the match in its headline: 'Overpowering influence of mighty pack'. The Springboks won the scrums by almost two to one and, despite the All Blacks leading at half-time through two tries from Taranaki wing John Sullivan, the match was wrenched from their grasp in their second half by 13 unanswered Springbok points.

The series would be decided by the final Test match to be played in Auckland. 'The test looms up before us like a huge mountain,' the press were informed by one of the tourists.[16] Fifty thousand people crammed into Eden Park – the biggest crowd ever to assemble anywhere for anything in New Zealand – to witness the Springboks make a molehill out of that mountain. They won 17-6, scoring five tries to nil. The All Blacks were starved of the ball – the South African pack won 48 of the 76 scrums – and the Springbok backs carved their opponents to pieces.

South Africa were now indisputably the best team in the world, even if etiquette prevented them from saying so. 'This is not a struggle for a world championship. It is just a friendly visit to another country to play a friendly game of rugger,' tour manager Alex de Villiers told his hosts at a farewell banquet for his team.[17] But it was a friendship that extended only so far.

On 8 November 1936, eight months before the arrival of the Springboks, the New Zealand Rugby Union announced that, unlike previous tours by Australia and the British Isles, the South African tourists would not play against a Maori representative team. Rugger may have been a friendly game but, as Ranji Wilson discovered in 1919, politics, and especially the politics of race, came first for rugby union's leaders.

17

RUGBY DE MUERTE, À TREIZE AND À LA VICHY

France in the 1920s was gripped by fashion fever. It was the age of Coco Chanel and the *femme moderne*, bobbed hair and flapper dresses. Hats, from the bell-shaped cloche to the masculine newsboy cap, were all the rage. And this insatiable demand for hats would play a part in the crisis that would tear French rugby apart in the interwar years.

In 1922, 35-year-old Jean Bourrel became the owner of the House of Tibet hat factory in Quillan, a village of some 3,000 people nestled at the foot of the Pyrenees on the banks of the River Aude. He had been the factory manager for the past decade and now at last he could put into practice his plans to capitalise on France's mania for headwear. The factory was extended, houses built for workers and production expanded rapidly. In a short time, a third of the local population was working for Bourrel. What more could a thriving village in south-west France need?

Just one thing apparently. Quillan wanted the same as every other town and village in the region. It wanted *la gloire du rugby*.

The year after Bourrel had taken over the factory, Quillan won the third division championship. It was no mean feat for a small village with few players to triumph over bigger towns in the intensely competitive third tier of the game.

But Bourrel wanted the name of the House of Tibet to be on the nation's lips and his commercial instincts told him that rugby would generate the publicity he craved. 'I am sure to have more advertising by fighting for the championship of France than by putting up posters all over the country,' he is alleged to have said.[1] He wanted the *Bouclier de Brennus* in Quillan.

Bourrel was a man used to getting what he wanted, when he wanted. There was only one thing for it. He would have to buy a team.

So, in the summer of 1926, it was announced that seven of the Perpignan team that had just finished as runners-up in the championship final had decided to take jobs in the Quillan hat industry and would consequently be turning out for the local rugby team. They were joined by Perpignan coach Gilbert Brutus. Players from Tarbes and Toulouse also announced their enthusiasm for millinery careers which, by happy coincidence, would enable them to play for *les Quillanais*. Bourrel made sure that no one would miss the connection between his business and the club by insisting that players wore his products before and after matches.

Quillan's aggressive recruitment paid off. Less than two years later the club narrowly lost 6-4 in the final to Pau, who proudly boasted that they had 13 local players, in contrast to Quillan's ten imports. But it was to be the 1929 battle for the *Bouclier* that would symbolise both the triumph of Bourrel and the deep crisis of French rugby.

The final pitted Quillan against their local rivals Lézignan. Lézignan was a town of 6,000 inhabitants whose historic antipathy to their neighbours had been deepened by Bourrel's shameless recruitment strategy. Coached by the flamboyant former international forward Jean Sébédio, the first manual labourer to be capped by France, Lézignan played a dour forward-based game.

For most of the final it looked like the wily Sébédio would win. With his side leading 8-0 midway through the second half, the Sultan, as he was nicknamed because of his First World War service in Syria, provocatively waved a wad of cash at Bourrel and the Quillan officials in the stands, mocking their attempts to buy the *Bouclier*.

He had spoken too soon. Realising that relentless forward play was getting them nowhere, Quillan coach Brutus switched his side's focus to their superior three-quarters. Three tries followed in little more than ten minutes to see them take the championship 11-8. But fighting between players and among the 20,000 spectators continued for some time after the referee's whistle. Bourrel had won, but at what cost?

Both sides were suspended by the French rugby authorities for their conduct during the final. The violence, commercialism and contempt for amateurism on display that day summed up the crisis consuming French rugby. Over the course of the next five years, its leading clubs would break away, the national side would be expelled from the Five Nations and rugby league would be established, led by the rock of the Quillan and French pack, Jean Galia.

If rugby had once been as fashionable as the hats produced by Jean Bourrel's factory, it was now in danger of becoming as *démodé* as last year's hemlines.

La marche du rugby

When rugby returned after the war, its future could not have looked brighter. From 260 clubs in 1920 the number had grown to 880 in 1923. Huge numbers of people had flocked to watch the game. In the Five Nations in 1920, France recorded its first away win with a 15-7 victory over Ireland at Lansdowne Road. The following year the French had finished second in the table with wins over Scotland and Ireland. In 1927 a solitary try to Grenoble winger Edmond Vallet had achieved the dream of all French *rugbymen*, their first victory over England. The following year Wales fell for the first time, and in 1930 France finished the championship just one win away from the Five Nations title.

The game also became further embedded in French popular culture. The 1923 championship final had been broadcast live on national radio, allowing everyone with access to a wireless to hear Stade Toulousain's second successive final victory over Aviron Bayonnais. One hundred journalists from across France had attended *les Bleus'* 1925 match against the All Blacks in Paris. The distinctive headwear of Aviron supporters, the Basque beret, was adopted by Frenchmen everywhere in the 1920s and quickly became a distinctive, if somewhat stereotyped, symbol of their nationality.

Even France's biggest musical star, Maurice Chevalier, was keen to be associated with the game. In 1924 he sang 'Marche Rugby' to celebrate the sport on the eve of the 1924 Paris Olympics, which itself staged a high-profile but small-scale rugby competition. In 1928 French captain Adolphe Jauréguy and several Toulouse players played central roles in *La Grande Passion*, a love story set against the background of rugby rivalry. In 1929 the composer Arthur Honegger even recorded a symphonic movement, *Rugby*, with the Paris Symphony orchestra.[2]

The decade was dominated by Toulouse. In 1924, *la Vierge Rouge* had completed a hat-trick of championships. Perpignan regained the title in 1925 only for it to return to Toulouse in 1926 and 1927. The success of Toulouse was not simply due to the skill and finesse of its first XV. The historian Jean-Pierre Bodis has identified 39 different sides playing in the city during the interwar years. In 1929 France's first rugby weekly, *Midi-Olympique*, was launched there. Even so, as the right-wing writer Lucien Dubech complained, rugby still occupied more space than politics in the local newspapers.

The importance of rugby to Toulouse held up a mirror to the burgeoning popularity of the game across south-west France. By the mid-1920s there were 139 clubs in the Pyrenees and 106 in the Languedoc. The game also expanded eastwards, with Lyon, Toulon and Montferrand in Clermont-Ferrand establishing themselves in the front ranks of elite clubs. But the game's grip was not simply extending across the nation; it was also reaching down into the working classes.

In Montferrand, the rugby club had been created in 1911 by Marcel Michelin, whose tyre factory dominated the city. In Carmaux, the

Olympique de Carmaux club had been founded by the local mining company. Many other clubs were formed on the same lines. Just like Bourrel's Quillan, their patrons saw their clubs as vehicles for advertising but also as a way of creating an *esprit des corps* among their employees at a time when industrial relations in France were, to say the least, fraught. Elsewhere, workers flocked to play and watch the game.

Yet, as had been the case in England in the 1880s and 1890s, this influx of players and fans who did not share the bourgeois upbringing of the leaders of the French game were viewed with concern by many. As early as 1923 the British magazine *Rugby Football* reported that there were 20 cases of alleged professionalism under investigation across the Channel.

The replayed 1925 championship final between Perpignan and Carcassonne was, declared pre-war international winger Géo André, 'a match of brutes … on the terraces there were battles; and on the pitch, there was a battle royal … played in this way, rugby is more like the ancient games of the Roman circuses'.[3]

Although André's views on the state of French rugby in the 1920s have generally been accepted, they should be taken with a pinch of salt. The complaints about the behaviour of players and supporters echoed those made about the north of England by supporters of the RFU, even down to the analogies with ancient Rome. The increasing strength of sides like Lézignan and Quillan, socially inclusive clubs based in small towns and villages, and their eclipse of the patrician teams in the major cities worried rugby's traditionalists. After 1927 Stade Toulousain did not appear in another championship final. Racing and Stade Français made one losing appearance each in the 1920s. Stade Bordelais failed to enter the record books at all.

The traditionalists' disquiet was fuelled by two-high profile deaths during matches. In March 1927 Quillan hooker Gaston Rivière died after breaking a cervical vertebra in his neck during a scrum in match against Perpignan. More shocking was the death during the 1930 championship semi-final of Agen's 18-year-old winger Michel Pradié following a tackle by Pau's international winger Fernand Taillantou. Taillantou immediately gave up rugby but a police enquiry led to him being fined and given a suspended jail sentence.

These two deaths led to the late 1920s becoming known as the era of *rugby de muerte*, rugby of death. This was a phrase coined by Dr Paul Voivenel, an influential administrator and writer on rugby who was deeply committed to elitist conceptions of amateur rugby and feared that control of the sport would slip away from the professional and business middle classes. It was in his interests to exaggerate the violence of rugby and blame it on the lower classes.

Despite bemoaning the decline of the amateur ethos, the catalyst for open revolt among the leading patrician clubs was the Fédération Française de Rugby's (FFR) decision to introduce gate-sharing of match-day proceeds among clubs. In December 1930, Bayonne, Biarritz, Bordeaux, Carcassonne, Grenoble, Limoges, Lyon, Nantes University, Pau, Perpignan, Stade Français and Toulouse resigned from the FFR and formed the Union Française de Rugby Amateur (UFRA). They were soon joined by Narbonne and Tarbes. Collectively, these clubs believed themselves to be the cream of French rugby. And now they also believed they would be its saviours.

Yet, as was so often the case under amateurism, those who were most eager to point the finger at others were not so pure themselves. The deaths of Rivière and Pradié had occurred in matches against UFRA's Pau and Perpignan – amateur sides both – and it was Perpignan vice-chairman Marcel Laborde who openly declared that 'in order to keep our players amateur we have to pay them twice as much'.[4]

There was another factor that the UFRA clubs had taken into consideration: France's impending expulsion from the Five Nations. Tensions with the British had grown in the late 1920s and matters came to a head in April 1930 when France met Wales at Paris's Stade Colombes in the last match of the 1930 Five Nations. France had already beaten

Scotland and Ireland and were one point behind tournament leaders England, who had finished their campaign on five points. A win over the Welshmen would mean an historic first championship win for the French. Fifty thousand people, France's biggest ever rugby crowd, crammed into Colombes in anticipation of an historic victory.

It was not to be. Wales emerged battered, bruised and bloodied but 11-0 winners. French supporters took exception to the refereeing of the English Mr Hellewell, who disallowed two French tries. Hellewell felt so threatened by the crowd that he waited until play moved near to the players' tunnel before whistling for no-side to allow himself and the players a swift exit from an increasingly agitated crowd.

It was the straw that broke the camel's back. In February 1931, the International Board endorsed an RFU statement that declared 'owing to the unsatisfactory condition of the game of Rugby football as played and managed in France, neither our union or clubs under its jurisdiction will be able to arrange or fulfil fixtures with France or French clubs, at home or away'. The ban would only be lifted when 'we are satisfied that the control and conduct of the game have been placed on a satisfactory basis in all essentials'.[5] The 'satisfactory basis' was a rigorous implementation of the amateur regulations and the abolition of the championship.

If the UFRA clubs had hoped that they would be granted the right to play England instead of the FFR, they had misjudged the RFU. There was, at least for the time being, no chance of compromise, despite a plea from the future Edward VII, and the UFRA clubs rejoined the FFR at the end of the 1931–32 season.[6] For the next decade, French rugby union had to be content with matches against Germany, Italy and Romania. But soon, rugby union would not be the only kind of rugby played in France.

Le 'Néo-Rugby'

By the end of the 1920s French rugby had come to resemble rugby in the north of England or Australia before the splits that led to rugby league and initially there was speculation that the FFR might open a dialogue with the British Rugby Football League (RFL). But the FFR set its face in the opposite direction and set up the Fédération Internationale de Rugby Amateur (FIRA) in January 1934.

However, in early 1933 the RFL was contacted by two journalists from the French daily sports newspaper *L'Auto*, the forerunner of *L'Equipe*, about the possibility of establishing rugby league in France. The RFL already had good contacts in France, partially through the cycling links of RFL secretary John Wilson, who rode for Britain at the 1912 Olympics and who knew Victor Breyer, the editor of the Parisian *Echo des Sports*.[7]

After months of negotiations, on 31 December 1933 the touring Australian Kangaroos met an England side on a snow-covered pitch in an exhibition match at Paris's Stade Pershing, sponsored by *Echo des Sports*. The response of the crowd was ecstatic. Kangaroo captain Dave Brown was carried shoulder high from the field by spectators and the French press expressed amazement at the skills of the players of what became known as *Rugby à Treize* (Rugby of Thirteen).

Two days later the talismanic international forward Jean Galia, who had earlier been suspended by the FFR for allegedly offering money to players to join his club at Villeneuve-sur-Lot, signed an agreement with the RFL to bring a French team to England for a short tour in the spring of 1934. French rugby league was born.

Galia's team arrived in England in March. The 17 players had 40 international rugby union caps between them and included such fixtures in the national side as Agen's flying winger Robert Samatan and Bordeaux front-rower Jean Duhau. Despite never having played league before, the side acquitted itself well, even managing to beat Hull, one of the six club sides they met on tour.

Support poured into the new rugby. Everyone agreed that it was faster, more skilful and less violent than the attritional, forward-based game that had come to characterise French rugby union. In addition, league had one great advantage that French union had lost: top-class international rugby.

For French rugby, driven by the tension between its Anglophile origins and Anglophobe instincts, there was an overriding compulsion to test itself against the British. Galia, who had played in France's first ever wins over England and Wales in rugby union, understood this perhaps better than anyone. On 15 April 1934, a week after the Ligue Française de Rugby à Treize (LFRT) was founded, France hosted England at Paris's Stade Buffalo. Twenty thousand Parisians turned out to see a star-studded England side overcome Galia's men 32-21.

Defeated but not disgraced, France, it was clear to everyone in the stadium, had a future in the new game. The following season England were held to a 15-15 draw in Paris and, even more sensationally, in Bordeaux France defeated a Welsh team containing Jim Sullivan, Gus Risman and two-times Lion Jack Morley 18-11.

The Welsh match saw the debut of the young half-back Max Rousie, the man who, after Galia, came to represent the soul of *Treizisme*. Although he had already won four French union caps, league provided the perfect stage to showcase his complete mastery of the arts of rugby. An organiser, a creator, a finisher, Rousie's decision to join Galia signalled that league was capturing the imagination of the next generation of French rugby.

By the end of its first season the LRFT had 29 clubs, 171 in its second and 434 in the 1938–39 season. The FFR banned players, officials and even grounds associated with league. Its stodgy and politically dubious internationals against Germany, Italy and Romania held little appeal for spectators. It appeared that the FFR could do little to reverse things as it saw its affiliated clubs almost halved from 891 in 1924 to 471 in 1939.[8]

The tide did indeed seem to be turning in favour of rugby league and the crowning moment came in 1939. In February, France beat England 12-9 at St Helens, the first time a French national side had won in

England. Better was to come, when 25,000 people crammed into Bordeaux's Stade Municipal at the end of the season to see France win their first ever European Championship with a 16-10 defeat of Wales.

These rapid and almost revolutionary changes in French rugby reflected similar changes taking place in France itself. The economic depression of the early 1930s had ushered in an era of acute political and social crisis. In May 1936 the Popular Front of socialist and liberal parties won the French general election and a huge strike wave convulsed the nation.

The fact that rugby league was challenging the established order of French rugby seemed to chime with the spirit of the Popular Front. And there could be no denying that the Popular Front government extended a helping hand to the rugby rebels. Léo Legrange, the socialist minister for sport, appeared as a guest of an honour at a 1936 international match. Although Galia and his fellow *Treizistes* steered clear of politics, they had become identified with the Popular Front, something that their enemies would not forget.

Rugby *à la Vichy*

The end of the 1938–39 season saw French rugby league shining at its brightest. But the shadows were gathering. On 3 September 1939 Hitler invaded Poland and France was at war. In May 1940 the German army invaded and caused a spectacular collapse of the French nation, which divided into a German-controlled occupied zone and an unoccupied zone controlled by Marshal Pétain's collaborationist government based in the spa town of Vichy in the South of France.

Under Pétain, France underwent a 'National Revolution' and pursued a policy of 'Travail, Famille, Patrie' (work, family, fatherland) that reasserted right-wing France's traditional values. One of those values was a belief in amateur sport and the Vichy regime declared its intention to outlaw professionalism.

In theory, the Vichy ban extended to all professional sports, including soccer. But the other sports continued as amateurs and only rugby league was outlawed whether amateur or professional. Vichy's minister for family and youth, Jean Ybarnégaray, was unequivocal. 'The fate of rugby league is clear. Its life is over and it will quite simply be deleted from French sport,' he declared in August 1940.[9]

Ybarnégaray commissioned a report on the state of rugby and how it should be reorganised. Paul Voivenel, the man who in the 1920s had first come up with the term *rugby de muerte*, argued that rugby had fallen victim to 'moral decadence' and that the professionalism of rugby league was a betrayal of the moral and educational principles of the game. The *Treizistes* would be compelled to rejoin the FFR.[10]

On 10 October 1940, the LFRT was summoned to the ministry's office and informed that it was expected to help 're-establish the unity of rugby'. Three days later, on a Sunday evening following the first weekend of matches of the 1940–41 season, an announcement was made on national radio by Commandant Joseph 'Jep' Pascot, the former France and Perpignan fly-half of the 1920s who was now Vichy's director of sport. He declared that, on the basis of the Voivenel report, the LFRT would be dissolved into the FFR. All rugby league's assets, players and clubs were to be transferred to rugby union.

The ultimate responsibility for the rugby league's fate lay in far more celebrated hands than those of Pascot. Jean Borotra, the 'Bounding Basque' who won five grand slam tennis titles in the 1920s, including two Wimbledon championships, had been appointed Vichy's Commissioner for General Education and Sports in July 1940. A youthful rugby player for Aviron Bayonne, Borotra oversaw Vichy sports policy until he fled the country in 1942. A fervent believer in the amateur ethos of sport, it was he who gave Pascot the authority to 'delete' rugby league. Interviewed shortly before his death in 1994, Borotra admitted his role in the ban to English historian Mike Rylance: 'Pascot couldn't have done that without my authority.'[11]

Rugby league ended immediately with Pascot's announcement, but it would be another year before the decision would be signed into law. On the morning of 19 December 1941, Pétain issued a decree that was unique in the history of world sport. He announced that *rugby à treize* had been banned by the government. Its playing was to cease, its offices closed and its assets confiscated by the government. The decree read:

> Art. 1 – The association known as Ligue Française de Rugby à Treize, whose headquarters are at 24 Drouot Street, Paris is dissolved, authorisation having been refused it.

> Art. 2 – The property of the dissolved association, under the terms of the preceding article, is transferred without modification at the National Sports Committee, which assumes all responsibility for it and which will be represented in the liquidation proceedings by its secretary-general Mr. Charles Denis, Officer of the Legion of Honour.

> Art. 3 – The Secretary of State for National Education and Youth is charged with the execution of this decree which will be published in the Official Journal.

Rugby league had become another victim of the Vichy regime's spirit of *revanchisme*, or revenge. Pétain and his supporters wanted to settle their grievances against those they believed had taken France away from its rural, patriarchal and traditional past, whether they were socialists, Jews, trade unionists, popular frontists or the merely liberal-minded. And in their long list of retribution they also included those who had rebelled against the authority of French rugby.

For men like Borotra and Voivenel, who believed deeply in the amateur, elite traditions of pre-First World War French rugby, the campaign against league was a necessity. But for Jep Pascot, it may have been something more.

Pascot had been the fly-half in the great Perpignan team that had lifted the *Bouclier de Brennus* in 1921 and 1925. Just days after his side lost the 1926 final against Toulouse, seven Perpignan players were lured away by Jean Bourrel's Quillan, thus setting in train the revolution that led to rugby league. The Perpignan club was devastated and would not recover for a decade.

For Pascot at least, Vichy's settling of scores with rugby league was not just ideological. It was personal.

18

BRITAIN'S RUSH TO RUGBY

For the keepers of rugby union's sacred flame, it was the match made in heaven. The cream of British rugby talent had assembled on a sunny afternoon at Rugby School, on 1 November 1923, to celebrate the centenary of William Webb Ellis's historic act that created Rugby football.

A combined England and Wales side was to face the cream of Scotland and Ireland. The magisterial Welsh winger Rowe Harding, the prodigiously driven Wavell Wakefield of England and his creative half-back teammates W. J. A. Davies and Cyril Kershaw were the core of a star-studded England/Wales side. The Scots/Irish side boasted Irish full-back Ernie Crawford, star Scots winger Leslie Gracie and a pack led by the redoubtable John Bannerman.

As the 2.30 p.m. kick-off approached, the match ball was carried to the centre spot by Rugby's eldest master, Mr Jiggle. The 2,000 invited spectators who crowded around the pitch on the school's Close held their breath in anticipation. They would not be disappointed.

Wearing green and blue quartered shirts, Scotland/Ireland scored first when Ireland's Henry Stephenson touched down in the corner. The reply soon followed when a midfield break from Arthur Cornish was capitalised upon by Wakefield touching down. The try was converted, and the lead was extended when Welsh winger Tom Johnson belied his nickname 'Codger' by outwitting a cover defence expecting a run and snapping a drop goal. Then Henry Stephenson burst upfield to set up a try for Scotland's Doug Davies. In seemingly no time at all it was half-time and the English/Welsh side led 9-6.

The second half started with Mr Jiggle once more presenting a ball to be kicked off. Within minutes, showing a combination as tight as the interwoven rose and three feathers on their white shirts, the England/Wales pack drove the ball down the pitch. Vainly their opponents scrambled to recover but could do little to prevent Neath's Ambrose Baker, who before the season was out would be playing rugby league for Oldham, diving over for a try. Shortly after, England fly-half Davies dropped another goal to take the score out to 16-6.

It looked all over for the Scots/Irish, but then their forwards got their second wind and piled the pressure on their previously dominant opponents. First George Stephenson scored a try, followed shortly by Bannerman touching down. Both were converted and the scores were locked at 16-16 with time running out.

As the battle raged between the two sets of forwards, Cornish once again cut through the Scots/Irish defence and Tom Voyce made his way through the resulting loose scrum to score. The conversion was successful and England/Wales led 21-16.

With seconds remaining the Scots/Irish pack made one desperate lunge for the line and Bannerman found himself with the ball just inches from the line as the no-side sounded. The players were exhausted, the crowd breathless: 'a cleaner, harder, and perhaps a faster game has never been played anywhere,' reported one spectator.[1] All who saw it agreed that there could have been no better way to mark the game's fictional centenary.

The reconsecration of the Webb Ellis myth on that bright autumn afternoon in November 1923 was not merely a celebration of rugby's invented past, it was also an affirmation of British rugby union's future.

England's rush to rugby

Rugby union across Britain emerged from the First World War with a confidence and authority unknown since the 1870s. Three months after the end of the war an unnamed headmaster wrote to *The Times*:

> the war has come and gone, and the youth of the country has passed through the furnace of trial. In the test of that experience one game at any rate has been justified triumphantly, not only as a pastime, but as an instrument of true education, and that is Rugby football. ... is it too much to hope that all schools will consider seriously the adoption of Rugby football as the winter game for all the youth of the nation.[2]

Elite schools such as Ampleforth, Rossall, City of London, Radley, Malvern and many others took up rugby as a consequence of the war. In 1919, Winchester old boy Brigadier General Godfrey Meynell, a former commanding officer on the Western Front, started a campaign to get his alma mater to play rugby. In 1926 a furious debate erupted in *The Times* over Harrow headmaster Cyril Norwood's decision to replace soccer with rugby at the school. Soccer's supporters became so concerned that they appealed to the association of public schools, the Headmasters' Conference, to stop other schools following suit. It was to no avail. The 'rush to rugby' was unstoppable and the number of English public and grammar schools affiliated to the RFU jumped from 27 in 1919 to 133 a decade later.[3]

Rugby was helped by the emergence of another great England side in the early 1920s. England won Grand Slams in 1921, 1923 and 1924, and in the first five seasons of the decade lost just three matches. Interrupted only by Scotland's dominance of the Five Nations in the mid-1920s, another Grand Slam followed in 1928.

It was another Harlequins player, William Wavell Wakefield, who was the architect of this success. In many ways his methods anticipated modern coaching techniques. At Cambridge University he scouted for players, kept detailed records of matches and players, and drilled his team in set moves and tactics. His game plans, he explained, were based on a 'deep theory underlying every move and counter-move on the field, and to learn and apply this theory successfully a man must have all his wits about him'.[4]

He also redefined back-row play. Highly mobile and aggressive, he was able to cover every inch of ground defensively and run, pass and back up like a three-quarter in attack. He expected his back-rowers to detach themselves from the scrum in an instant and be upon the opposing half-backs like wolves on newborn lambs.

Above all, rugby was to be played unforgivingly, with the aim of establishing what he called 'moral authority' over one's opponents. 'It is one of the glories of rugger that you can put your shoulder into a man with all your strength and bring him down with a crash, knowing that if you stave in a rib or two of his he will bear no grudge against you, while if he knocks your teeth out in handing you off it is merely your own fault for tackling him too high,' he wrote in his autobiography.[5]

It was his attempt to assert 'moral authority' over the 1924 All Blacks Invincibles that led to the opening minutes of the match at Twickenham resembling a street brawl. Welsh referee Albert Freethy stopped play four times and famously sent-off New Zealand's Cyril Brownlie in the first ten minutes of the match to halt the violence.

But while their forwards were more than a match for the All Blacks, England's backs lacked their opponents' cutting edge. Despite their numerical advantage, the game eventually got away from England 17-11. It had been a memorable occasion, but not entirely for the reasons everyone hoped for. 'If that is international rugby I want nothing of it,' English forward Ronnie Hillard was alleged to have said after the game. It was his first and last international match.

For the rest of the interwar years, English rugby walked a tightrope between loyalty to its amateur principles and the increasingly important imperative of winning. It was never successfully resolved. Although England won the Home Nations outright twice in the 1930s, it would not be until 1957 before another Grand Slam was won.

Hands, Scotland, hands!

The 1923 match at Rugby School was as important for the Scots as it was for the English. Just as in England, rugby was an integral part of the culture of Scotland's elite schools and universities, and these provided the wellspring for Scotland's fabulous run of success in the 1920s.

Players from Former Pupils' and Academicals' clubs in Edinburgh and Glasgow dominated the national side, leavened by students from Edinburgh and Oxford universities. Reversing the tradition of Scottish success based on forward play, the Scots sides of the 1920s played with an attacking abandon that sometimes made spectators think that they were watching a schoolboy side.

There had been a three-way tie for the first Five Nations Championship after the war, with the Scots sharing the honour with England and Wales, who then individually won the title in 1921 and 1922 respectively. The 1922 Calcutta Cup match is perhaps best remembered for being the first match at which England wore numbered shirts. King George V, a regular visitor to Twickenham, asked James Aikman Smith, the SRU secretary, why the Scots weren't wearing them. Aikman Smith allegedly snapped back, 'Sire, my players are men, not cattle'. It wasn't until 1934 that Scotland finally relented.

In fact, both countries came late to numbering. New Zealand were the first to number players on their 1897 tour of Australia, the Australians followed suit and by 1911 rugby league sides in both hemispheres were required to number players' shirts. It wouldn't be until 1966 that rugby union adopted its distinctive descending numbering system starting at 15, having previously broadly followed the league and soccer practice of ascending numbering starting at one.

Despite the innate conservatism of it leadership, rugby in Scotland experienced an expansive golden age in the interwar years. In 1923 the Scottish side took the great English side to the wire and came within a hair's breadth of a win that would bring them the Five Nations championship. Captained by three-quarter Leslie Gracie, whose try three minutes from time at Cardiff Arms Park had despatched the Welsh, the side faced England in the last Calcutta Cup match to be played at Edinburgh's Inverleith stadium.

Outside Gracie on the left wing was Eric Liddell, arguably the fastest athlete in any sport in Britain at the time, and who would be immortalised in the Oscar-winning film *Chariots of Fire*. Both he and Gracie tormented England all afternoon but, with ten minutes to go and the home side leading 6-3, the Scots lost the ball to Harry Locke, who sprinted upfield to set up a try for Tom Voyce. Luddington converted to make it 8-6 to the visitors. Despite surges from Gracie and Liddell, the championship went to England.

Two years later Scotland were ready once more to challenge for the title. By this time Gracie had retired from international rugby and Liddell was on his way back to Tianjin in China, the place of his birth and where he would resume the missionary work of his parents. If anything, the three-quarters were now even stronger. All four were Oxford blues but only one, captain Phil Macpherson, had been born in Scotland.

Outside him on the right wing was Ian Smith of Melbourne, while the left-wing three-quarters were former All Black George Aitken, who had played in the 1921 series against the Springboks, and Johnnie Wallace, a New South Welshman who had already played for Australia against the All Blacks, and who would captain the NSW Waratahs team that toured Britain in 1927. There was a precedent for the Antipodean flavour of the Scots' back-line. In 1903, their Calcutta Cup three-quarter line comprised a South African, a New Zealander and two Australians, a favourable omen given that they had won the Triple Crown that year.

Such fluid national affiliations were not unusual in rugby at this time. Apart from an 1898 International Board ruling that no player could play for two home nations, the game had no formal rules about who could be selected for a national side. The Board was asked to rule on the matter in 1921, but refused to 'take any steps towards defining international qualifications,' instead suggesting cryptically that if a player took part in a trial match for a national side, that fact should be 'worthy of the sporting considerations of several unions'. It would not be until the 1980s that the first attempt at internationally-agreed criteria for national selection was made.[6]

The Scots' 1925 campaign opened with a seven-try mauling of France, in which Wallace scored two and Smith four. Smith then scored another four tries and Wallace two more in the next match against Wales. Ireland got off lightly with only Wallace adding to his tally in a 14-8 win at Lansdowne Road. This victory meant that the Calcutta Cup match would decide the fate of the championship, the Triple Crown and, in all probability as England still had France to play, the Grand Slam.

There could be no more auspicious occasion for the Scots to win their first ever Grand Slam. The Scottish Rugby Union had chosen the 1925 Calcutta Cup game as the match that would open their new Murrayfield Stadium in Edinburgh. Even before the First World War it had become clear that Inverleith, Scotland's home since 1899 and the first stadium to be owned by one of rugby's governing bodies, was too small for the thousands who now turned out for internationals.

In 1922 the Scottish Football Union, as the Scottish rugby union would still be known until 1924, bought the polo ground at Murrayfield and set about building a modern arena capable of hosting the crowds that international rugby now attracted. The widespread anticipation caused by Scotland's brilliant form and curiosity to see the new stadium saw more than 70,000 turn up for the Five Nations decider. Murrayfield could barely cope and large sections of the crowd saw little of what was to be one of the tournament's greatest matches.

As could be expected from a Wavell Wakefield-led England side, the English pack sought to dominate the Scots forwards and suffocate their backs. Their tactics paid off and tries either side of half-time, the second by Wakefield himself, saw England take an apparently commanding 11-5 lead. It could have been more but Scots forward David MacMyn made an unexpectedly determined charge at Luddington's attempt to convert Wakefield's try and kicked the ball away.

With 25 minutes to go, Scotland's backs finally found some breathing space and Wallace scored in the corner to cut the deficit to 11-10. Momentum now swung to the Scots who battered the English line for the decisive breakthrough. With five minutes to go scrum-half Jimmy Nelson finally got clean ball from the forwards on England's 25-yard line and passed it sharply back to his fly-half Herbert Waddell whose drop kick sailed through the England posts for a 14-11 lead.

It wasn't over yet. England centre Len Corbett stumbled and fell with the line at his mercy, and as the referee reached for his whistle Tosh Holliday went desperately close with a long-range drop-goal attempt. As no-side was blown, Murrayfield exploded. The Scots had at last won a Grand Slam, a glory made all the sweeter by it being achieved against the oldest enemy.

Theirs was a rivalry that would define British rugby in the interwar years. Only the Scots and the English would win a Grand Slam or a Triple Crown in the 1920s and 1930s. In the 1930s Scotland and England both won the Triple Crown twice, with Wales and Ireland picking up a single championship each, although neither went through the season unbeaten.

In 1938 the Scots sealed their Triple Crown with a thrilling, see-sawing 21-16 victory at Twickenham in which England managed to pull level three times, despite being outscored five tries to one. It was the first rugby international to be televised and no one who watched in the stadium or at home could have imagined the impact that the medium would eventually have on the game.

The unparalleled success of the largely privately educated Scottish team – they would win only two more Triple Crowns in the rest of the 20th century – demonstrated the extent to which rugby union in the British Isles, outside South Wales and Munster in Ireland, had rediscovered and reaffirmed its roots as a game of elite schools and universities. The essential conservatism of the game reasserted itself strongly in the interwar years.

This was as true in Ireland as it was in England and Scotland. The Irish won just one championship during the 1920s and 1930s, although they did have a half or third share in four more. Rugby had remained remarkably impervious to change in Ireland, which had seen a war of independence, a southern state engulfed by civil war and partition into two separate states in 1921. Yet Irish rugby still had a single national team and a unitary governing body representing the whole of the island. This was a unity based on Victorian concepts of Irish national identity. It wasn't until a 1932 campaign led by the largely Catholic and cross-class Munster branch of the IRFU that the Irish tricolour was flown at international matches in Dublin.

Although Catholics played the game, most notably Eamon de Valera, the first president of the Irish Free State, the game's levers of power remained largely in the hands of middle-class Unionists. Of the 16 IRFU presidents elected in the interwar years, 14 were Protestants.[7] Outside Limerick and other parts of Munster, the Catholics who played the game were generally those who had learned the game at elite Catholic schools. And, as it was to England and Scotland, exclusivity was very important to the leaders of Irish rugby. In 1927 Irish RFU president George Hamlet had worried 'it was just possible that the game might become too popular … they might get a crowd of spectators who might not be educated in the true spirit of the game'.[8]

Wooller, Wales and the All Blacks' downfall

In his history of Cambridge University, the historian Christopher Brooke observed that 'a newcomer to a Cambridge Combination Room in the 1920s was startled to find the eminent academics about him discussing their applicants almost entirely in terms of rugger'.[9] One such applicant in the early 1930s was the schoolboy rugger prodigy Wilf Wooller. Born in North Wales and educated at Rydal School, Wooller's admission into Cambridge was delayed because he failed the necessary Latin exam. Although he went on to win three blues with Cambridge, his temporary academic failure meant he became one of a select few to play international rugby while a schoolboy. After an outstanding display in the Welsh national trial match, he was picked at centre to face England at Twickenham in January 1933.

It was a mark of the reversal of rugby fortune that had overtaken Wales since the First World War that the Welsh had only defeated England on three occasions since 1920. And they had still never won at Twickenham. The team that lined up against England also reflected the way in which Welsh rugby union had also retreated back to its middle-class origins. Alongside Wooller, Wales fielded four other Oxbridge blues, two Swansea university graduates, an ex-public school boy, a magistrate's clerk and a high school teacher. A solitary miner in the pack was the only representative of the industrial workers who had made Welsh rugby so powerful before the war.

Although England took the lead with a try to fly-half and future Conservative MP Walter Elliot and went in 3-0 up at half-time, the tide turned in the second half. Welsh right wing Ronnie Boon coolly dropped a goal from inside England's 25-yard line. Then Wooller used his six foot two frame to its fullest extent to chase down Elliott over 30 yards when it looked liked the number ten was certain to score his second try. As the clock ticked down, Wooller's centre partner Claude Davey was fed good ball from a loose scrum. He drew England full-back Tom Brown and passed to Boon, who touched down to seal the game for Wales.

It was a historic win, not least because Wales would only beat England once more in the 1930s. The parlous state of the game in Wales reflected the ruinous impact of the Great Depression on all aspects of Welsh society, from its industry to its leisure pursuits. The coalfields, the engine that had driven Wales into the industrial 20th century, lost half its miners, the workforce dropping from 270,000 in 1921 to 128,000 in 1939. Long-term unemployment in some black spots in the Welsh Valleys was as high as 45 per cent throughout the 1930s. Around 500,000 people emigrated from Wales between the wars.

For rugby, so closely intertwined with the fortunes of the South Wales society that nurtured it, the impact was devastating. Some clubs were forced to close, including names such as Treherbert, Tredegar and Haverfordwest, player numbers fell, and teams struggled to find pitches, raise funds and even pay for balls. Crowds fell, too, with just 30,000 turning out to see Wales play England at Swansea in 1932.[10]

Among those half a million Welsh migrants were rugby players seeking a better future by turning to rugby league in the north of England. Names like Jim Sullivan and Gus Risman, both of whom went north from Cardiff as teenagers in the 1920s, would become legendary league figures but there were also numerous other Welsh players who made their careers and homes in league's northern heartlands. Between the two wars 392 Welsh players would switch to league.

There were also opportunities to receive money or a job in Welsh rugby union. Before going north, Dai Davies was paid a flat rate of £3 per match by Neath in the mid-1920s. Many others received similar payments. And from the late 1920s, the relatively healthier economic fortunes of some English union clubs in the south-west, such as Torquay and Weston-super-Mare, meant that it was possible for Welsh players to 'go south', and receive a job and perhaps surreptitious payments.

But the fear of being exposed was ever-present. The England full-back in that famous first ever Welsh win at Twickenham, coincidentally named Tom Brown, was banned for life by the RFU merely for meeting with rugby league club officials in 1933, despite never having seen, let alone played in, a league match. A similar fate awaited any player whose curiosity was not matched by his discretion.

This mandatory lifetime ban imposed on players who had played rugby league did untold harm to Welsh rugby. Of the 69 union internationals who switched to league in the interwar years, only 12 played at Test match level in league. Some players who went north found themselves unsuited to the different demands of the league game. But successful or not, all who played league were barred from ever playing union again. The damage caused to Welsh rugby union by the flow of players to league was another self-inflicted wound of amateurism.

However, there would be one bright spot in the unremitting gloom of the 1930s. International success had been non-existent against touring sides in the inter-war years. The 1924 All Blacks had brushed Wales aside 19-0, the 1927 New South Wales Waratahs comfortably eased away 18-8 and Osler's 1931 Springboks won a typically dour match 8-3. The glory of Welsh rugby's Edwardian golden age seemed to have disappeared alongside economic prosperity. And then, four days before Christmas 1935, everything changed.

For their British hosts, the 1935 All Blacks had lost nothing of their elan and glamour. The 1905 and 1924 tourists had left an indelible mark on the British public. The very name All Blacks had become a distinctive 'sports brand' decades before anyone had even thought up the phrase. So their arrival in England in September 1935 was greeted with almost febrile anticipation.

The New Zealanders themselves were not so confident. They had lost a series 3-0 to Australia in 1929, been unable to win a series against the Springboks and captain Jack Manchester was rumoured not to command the respect of his side as completely as previous All Black leaders. But the opening matches of the tour went according to tradition, with the visitors overcoming their first four opponents with considerable ease.

Victory, perhaps more hard-earned, was expected of them when they faced Swansea on the last Saturday of September 1935. The All Blacks would have felt even more confident when they learned that Swansea were fielding two teenagers at half-back, one of whom was still at school. It was men against boys.

But the two boys were scrum-half Haydn Tanner and fly-half W. T. H. 'Willie' Davies. Davies had just turned 19 and Tanner was still 18. Together they outwitted the All Blacks and inspired their teammates to an historic 11-3 victory. The All Whites had become only the second British team ever to defeat the touring All Blacks.

As the tour progressed, it became clear that this All Black side was not quite as invincible as its predecessors. Three matches were won by one point and, perhaps even more tellingly, the tourists kept only one clean sheet. By the time they arrived at Cardiff Arms Park just before Christmas, Wales could dare to dream that, amidst the depression facing the nation, the glory of 1905 might be possible.

The Welsh back-line that day consisted of three Cambridge University blues, two Oxford University blues, a former student of Swansea University and the boy wonder Tanner. The pack, with the exception of flanker Arthur Rees who was also a Cambridge graduate, was as representative of South Wales' industrial working class as the backs were of its professional middle classes.

The combination seemed to be paying off in a tight first half that saw New Zealand take a 3-0 lead. But Wales came out for the second half with all guns blazing. Captain Claude Davey followed up a Cliff Jones kick to touch down by the posts. Vivian Jenkins tacked on the two points and Wales were up 5-3. No sooner had the All Blacks kicked off than Wilf Wooller, who had been switched from the left wing to the centre late in the first half, took a deft pass from Jones and burst through the New Zealand defence. He kicked ahead and the ball bounced tantalising beyond his reach, but was caught by Welsh right wing Geoffrey Rees-Jones. Jenkins once again converted to make it 10-3.

Wales continued to threaten but the All Blacks refused to back down. Eventually, a weak clearance kick from Jones fell into the arms of New Zealand full-back Mike Gilbert, who stepped inside and smartly dropped a goal from 40 yards out. It was now 10-7; the All Blacks were coming back. A few minutes later Gilbert once again attempted a drop goal. It fell short but Davey and Rees-Jones made a mess of it, Nelson Ball hacked on and scored near the posts. Gilbert converted for 12-10 and Welsh hopes appeared to have been extinguished.

Worse was to come. A scrum broke up but Welsh hooker Don Tarr, who had played a pivotal role in Swansea's victory, did not get up with his teammates. A neck injury, later diagnosed as a broken neck, forced him from the field. The Welsh had to see out the last five minutes with 14 players.

It only took one man to make the decisive play and it was Wooller who once again burst through the All Blacks' defence and strode imperiously towards the try line. As he approached Gilbert, Woller chipped over the full-back's head. Yet again the ball bounced agonisingly away from his fingertips, but once more Rees-Jones was there to pick up and score in the corner. Jenkins couldn't add the two points but it didn't matter. Wales had defeated the All Blacks 13-12, their second victory in three meetings. For once, Wales could put aside all that economic depression and social despair, even if it was only for 80 minutes.

Cranmer and the prince

Two weeks later, in the final match of the tour, the All Blacks arrived at Twickenham to face England. Defeat against Wales was perhaps acceptable, given the history between the two national sides, but such an outcome could not even be considered against the English.

Yet the All Blacks had struggled against some of the better English sides. They had beaten Northumberland & Durham by a mere 10-6, Combined Services by an even slimmer 6-5 and had rescued a 10-9 win over Oxford University thanks to a touchline conversion from Mike Gilbert. The match at Oxford's Iffley Road ground had alerted them to a remarkable right-wing three-quarter who ran 75 yards to score a try from nothing. Two months later, that same winger made his debut for England against the All Blacks.

His name was Prince Alexander Obolensky and he was the son of a member of the Tsar's Imperial Horse Guard who had fled Russia after the Bolshevik Revolution. Obolensky had learned to play rugby while a pupil at Trent College in Derbyshire and then won a blue at Oxford in 1935. When the Russian prince ran out at Twickenham for the match on 4 January 1936 he was watched by an English prince, the Prince of Wales, who 16 days later would become Edward VIII.

It didn't take long for Obolensky to capture the imagination of the crowd. Halfway through the first half, his right-centre partner, Richmond's Peter Cranmer, popped up a short pass on the England 40-yard line to enable Obolensky to step inside his opposing winger and run in an arc back out towards the touchline where he glided around Mike Gilbert to score near the posts.

Not long afterwards, another sharp move by Cranmer gave the fly-half Peter Candler room to break into All Black territory on the right. As he approached the 25-yard line he passed to Obolensky, who cut back inside on a diagonal run to the left. He beat three defenders and touched down ten yards in from the left touchline for remarkable, instinctive try.

At 6-0 down at half-time, the All Blacks looked lethargic and uninspired. On the 50-minute mark, Cranmer stepped inside a couple of tired tacklers and dropped a goal to make it 10-0. It only remained to rub salt into the New Zealand wounds. Once more it was Cranmer, this time making a break on the left before passing to debutant Hal Sever on the left wing to race in from 40 yards.

At 13-0 it was the most comprehensive defeat yet administered to New Zealand in the northern hemisphere. Although the game became known to posterity as 'Obolensky's Match' – and was one of only four caps he won before his premature death in 1940 – the architect of victory was Peter Cranmer. It was he who had set up all three tries and scored the telling drop goal early in the second half.

Modest, urbane and a multi-talented sportsman who also captained Warwickshire County Cricket Club, Cranmer was the very embodiment of English rugby union's values in the interwar years. England's triumph over the All Blacks seemed to its supporters to be a vindication of the British way of rugby, with its emphasis on amateurism, sociability and not taking things too seriously.

For those who had gathered on the Close at Rugby School in 1923 to celebrate William Webb Ellis, Tom Brown and the many other myths and legends of the game, it was a confirmation of rugby union's seemingly eternal values. There could be no sweeter victory.

19

LEAGUES APART: 1919–39

It was definitely a try.

Chimpy Busch knew that he had broken the deadlock and that rugby league's Ashes would be on their way back home to Australia for the first time in almost a decade.

With only two minutes remaining in the third Test in Manchester and the scores locked at 0-0 Australia won a scrum against the feed a few yards from the England try line. Sensing that this was the Kangaroos' moment, Busch picked the ball up from the base of the scrum, ran down the blind side, shook off a couple of would-be tacklers and darted for the corner.

With one last effort from his exhausted legs, he flung himself over the England line to touch the ball down. But with Busch still in mid-air, England loose forward Fred Butters, who had chased him from the scrum, lunged across, grabbed his legs and tried to roll him into touch before the ball hit the ground. In the darkening blur of a British winter afternoon, Busch, Butters and ball hit the corner flag.

Racing up from behind, referee Bob Robinson started to signal a try – only to see touch judge Albert Webster standing motionless with his flag in the air. Busch had knocked the flag over before grounding the ball, Webster informed the referee. 'I touched down 18 inches to two feet inside the corner flag, and the touch judge was 20–30 yards down the field,' complained the Australian.[1]

According to Busch, Robinson looked at him sheepishly. 'Fair try, Australia, but I am overruled,' he confessed. His teammate Victor Armbruster recalled it differently. 'Tough luck, son,' he thought he heard Robinson tell Busch. Years later, at a safe distance from the controversy, England scrum-half and captain Jonty Parkin admitted that he too thought it was a try.

Amid the confusion, Fred Butters left the field dripping blood after tearing an ear as he made the tackle. Even in the few seconds remaining, there was no let-up in the ferocity of the match. As England desperately tried to get the ball upfield, Kangaroo full-back Frank McMillan was poleaxed in a tackle at the final whistle.

It was the first and only rugby league Test match to finish 0-0. The 35,000 spectators who packed into Manchester's Station Road Stadium on that first Saturday of 1930 had witnessed a struggle for rugby league supremacy that had them gasping at its intensity and thrilled by its skills. It was a confrontation that lived in the memories of all those who had seen it, among them a young Kenneth Wolstenholme, the future BBC soccer commentator who would utter the immortal words 'they think it's all over' at the 1966 World Cup final at Wembley, and who would recall the match in his memoirs almost 70 years later.

The 0-0 draw left the series tied at one win each. Australia had won the first Test with a seven-try exhibition of flowing football, while the second Test saw England shut down the game to eke out a dour 9-3 win. But the rugby league public, not to mention the frustrated Kangaroos, abhorred the vacuum of a tied series and so the RFL hastily arranged an unprecedented fourth Test match at Rochdale 11 days later.

Almost 17,000 spectators turned out on a chilly Wednesday afternoon to see an enthralling match. It seemed to be heading for a repeat 0-0 draw until the deadlock was finally broken after 73 minutes by a solitary unconverted try to Leeds' flying winger Stan Smith – so rugby league's Ashes remained in Britain by the thinnest of margins. And there they would remain for the next two decades.

The road to Wembley

The Manchester Test had been captain Jonty Parkin's final international match. His had been an illustrious career in which he had won 17 Test caps and been on three British tours to Australasia, captaining the side on the 1924 and 1928 tours. He was a major reason for England's domination of international rugby league.

But more than his individual brilliance and leadership qualities, Parkin embodied the essence of English rugby league. He was born just nine months before the 1895 split in the Yorkshire mining village of Sharlston, a place that would produce rugby league stars much as Detroit stamped out Ford motor cars. He signed for Wakefield Trinity in 1913 as an 18-year-old and, until the emergence of the prodigious three-quarter and fellow Sharlstonian Neil Fox in the 1950s, was indisputably the club's greatest player. He first came to national prominence playing wartime rugby union for the Devonport Royal Navy depot team. Back in his own environment after the war, he quickly became as influential in British rugby league as Harold Wagstaff had been before the war.

Streetwise, self-assured and aware of his own value, Parkin deferred to no one. The archetypal cocky scrum-half, he had an uneasy relationship with authority, on and off the pitch. Shortly after the drawn 1930 Test match, he sought to negotiate a new contract with Wakefield. They refused and put him on the transfer list at £100. Outraged that he could be bought and sold without his permission, he promptly paid the transfer fee himself and arranged to play for Hull Kingston Rovers.

Parkin and the men he played with and against were shaped by the industrial society into which they were born. Like Parkin, the overwhelming majority of rugby league players were born into mining families, worked on the docks or were manual labourers. In league's first hundred years, only five of the 617 players who appeared for the national side were privately educated. In contrast, 75 per cent of England's rugby union internationals from 1871 to 1995 attended private schools. There could be no greater marker of how far apart the two types of rugby were in England.

This was reflected in their attitudes to amateurism and professionalism. For a rugby league player professionalism was a badge of honour. It honed the rugby player's skills, increased the intensity of the game and enhanced the innovative impulses of players and coaches alike. The game became quicker, more cerebral and far more unforgiving to those who were not prepared to give their all to it. It was entertainment and it was work.

Not that anyone ever became rich playing professional rugby. Most players had full-time jobs outside the game and few could afford to live on their rugby earnings. But in the depressed decades between the wars, even such meagre sums made a big difference. For the lucky ones, a good run in the Rugby League Challenge Cup would bring bonuses on top of the £4 or £5 paid for a win in a league match, with victory in the cup final itself usually bringing a bonus of £10 per player.

As with soccer's FA Cup, the Challenge Cup became rugby league's most prestigious tournament in the interwar years. It began in 1897 with the intention of taking the excitement and rivalries of the old Yorkshire Cup and developing a rugby equivalent of soccer's FA Cup. By the 1920s the Challenge Cup final become one of the north's biggest sporting occasions, leading to calls to find a new venue to accommodate the expanding levels of interest.

More importantly, the leadership of the RFL realised that the game had to have a place in the pantheon of national sporting events. Moving the Cup final to London's recently opened Wembley Stadium, which had staged the FA Cup final since 1923, would give rugby league a national profile, rather than one restricted to the industrial north. So in May 1929 the first Rugby League Challenge Cup final was played at Wembley.

The match itself symbolised the state of rugby league in 1929. The cosmopolitan all-stars of Wigan, including five Welshmen, two

New Zealanders, a Scot but just three Lancastrians, beat a hardworking Dewsbury team, fielding just one player not born in Yorkshire, 13-2. The match was acclaimed as a great success and the crowd of 41,500 was just 331 short of the attendance record. By the late 1940s the final would be attracting crowds of over 95,000.

In the days when cars were a rarity for working-class people and long-distance rail travel expensive, the journey to and from London became as much of the ritual of the Wembley final as the match itself. Trains and buses left the finalists' towns early on the Saturday morning packed with thousands of supporters decked out in their team's colours. For most, it would be their first visit to the capital. The civic pride that had spurred the growth of rugby in Victorian times was now mobile.

The return home of the victorious team became an extended celebration of the local community. Huge crowds would gather at the railway station to greet the team, which would be welcomed by local dignitaries, and then the cup would be paraded in an open-top bus through the town. The team's journey through the town resembled a carnival parade, as the eminent sociologist Richard Hoggart recalled about the 1934 triumph of his local side: 'I remember Hunslet rugby team bringing the Cup home from Wembley years ago, coming down from the City Station into the heart of the district on top of a charabanc. They went from pub to pub in all the neighbourhood's main streets, with free drinks at every point, followed by crowds of lads prepared to risk staying out hours after their bedtime for the excitement of seeing their local champions.'[2]

It was this bond with its communities that was at the very heart of rugby league. Its clubs were part of the fabric of local life, and carried far more significance for most supporters than the national side. It was that intimate link with their locality that was probably the most important factor in ensuring the survival of rugby league clubs during the Depression. The enthusiasm and commitment of players, supporters and the wider community simply would not allow their clubs to go under.

From Woolloomooloo to Wigan

The intense localism of rugby league did not mean that it was necessarily parochial. It was a source of pride and a sign of vitality that a club could attract players from beyond their locality and country. In 1926 Wigan chairman Harry Lowe stoutly defended his club's importation policy: 'we have seven Welshmen, three South Africans, one Cumbrian, one player from the Manchester district and only one local', going on to say that without imported players, 'Wigan would become a second or third rate side'.

Welshmen like Jim Sullivan at Wigan and Gus Risman at Salford became totemic representatives of their clubs and remained household names in the game decades after their retirement. Three hundred or so other Welshmen also added a vital mix to British rugby league during the interwar years. South Africans like Attie van Heerden, the Springbok winger who scored the first ever try in a South Africa versus New Zealand international rugby union match, and George 'Tank' van Rooyen, another veteran of the 1921 Springbok tour to New Zealand, also played league for Wigan in the 1920s, a testimony to the drawing power of the sport for top-class players.

But it was players from Australia and New Zealand who added cosmopolitan glamour to the British game during the darkest years of the Depression. In June 1927, British clubs forced the removal of the long-standing restrictions on international transfers. It marked the beginning of a new golden age, providing a Saturday afternoon respite from the gloom that hung over the mining villages and mill towns of northern England. Ernest Mills and Ray Markham at Huddersfield, Vic Hey, Eric Harris and Jeff Moores at Leeds, Hector Gee at Wigan and Bill Shankland at Warrington were the most prominent of the Australians who lit up the football fields of northern England in the 1930s.

But, however much these stars delighted English spectators, their presence there brought no pleasure to Australian rugby league. It wasn't just clubs Down Under that were being deprived of their stars. Once an

Australian signed for an English club he could no longer play for his national side. By the mid-1930s the player drain to Britain had become so severe that journalists regularly worried if Australia would ever win the Ashes again.

The Kangaroos won just six of 19 Tests against England and New Zealand in the 1930s, and matters came to a head with the lacklustre performance of the 1937 Kangaroos. Disappointing crowds at tour matches underlined the importance of a competitive Australia, to both the credibility and the coffers of British rugby league. So in December 1937 the RFL reluctantly stopped all international transfers. The road from Woolloomooloo harbour to Wigan Pier had been closed.

Australia's inability to win the Ashes did little to reduce the popularity of rugby league in its strongholds of New South Wales and Queensland. Matches against the visiting English touring teams continued to attract huge crowds: 120,000 saw the 1920 three-match series in which Australia briefly recaptured the Ashes in 1920. The same number watched the 1924 series, in which a solitary Jim Sullivan conversion ten minutes from time in the second Test of 1924 had kept the Ashes in British hands. The 1928 series had been a similarly close and well-attended affair.

The 1932 Test series was watched by almost 150,000 spectators but became notorious for the second Test match, the 'Battle of Brisbane', which Australia won despite being reduced to ten men at one point because of the injuries sustained during the course of the match. After losing the first Test (once again by a Jim Sullivan conversion), anticipation was high in Brisbane that the series could be squared. Australia were 8-0 up in less than 15 minutes thanks to Ipswich teammates Gee and Wilson. At half-time it was 10-0 to the green and golds in a match that was becoming increasingly torrid and brutal.

At one point, the Australians had three men receiving medical attention off the pitch, the Australian hooker Dempsey broke his wrist and Wagga Wagga's electrifying stand-off Eric Weissel twisted his ankle.

Early in the second half, Stan Smith scored the first English try and then Wakefield's Ernest Pollard snatched a bouncing ball from under the noses of hesitant defenders to make the score 10-6 with momentum swinging rapidly away from Australia.

But just like the English in the 1914 Rorke's Drift Test, the Australians refused to concede. As time ticked away, Weissel snatched up a loose ball, slipped past the mighty Sullivan on halfway and ran into English territory on his one good ankle. Sullivan, a man whose ferocious competitive spirit was as much feared as it was admired, refused to be beaten and eventually pulled Weissel down short of the try line but the ball squirted loose, and ended up with Hector Gee who ran in to score his second at the side of the posts. Australia had tied the series with an epic performance.

Yet the series ended like every other since 1921, with Britain taking the final Test in Sydney. Once again Australia had led at half-time, only for England to sweep away with three converted tries in the second half. How different it might have been if Busch, Shankland and Victor Armbruster, three of the key players on the 1930 Kangaroo tour, had been in Sydney and Brisbane, instead of Leeds, Warrington and Rochdale.

Australia's failures were not simply due to the haemorrhaging of players to England. Just as in England, rugby league in Australia drew its strength from its intense local community links. Unlike in Britain, where the top professionals played in the top clubs in a single league, the 'tyranny of distance' in such a huge country meant that the Australian game was divided into a patchwork of local leagues and competitions. The competitons in Sydney and Brisbane vied for the status of the nation's leading league but many top players, including the brilliant Eric Weissel, spent their entire careers in what was known as country football, setting foot in the major cities only when selected for representative matches.

Although this localism might have damaged the progress of the Australian national team, it actually helped to increase rugby league's popularity at a local level. For small country towns like Boorowa or West Wyalong, over a hundred miles from each other in southern New South Wales, travel was difficult and sporadic, but to play each other in the local Maher Cup was an outlet for fierce local pride.

Similar competitions proliferated across NSW and Queensland. In the far north of the country, the Crowley Cup and its successor the Carlton Shield saw teams from north Queensland travelling 400 to 500 miles to play against each other, the extent of the journey only increasing the determination to make it worthwhile with a victory. Even in Sydney, the league's success was in large part due to the rivalry of the city's districts. As Sydney's suburbs expanded in the 1920s so, too, did rugby league. St George, destined to be one of the code's greatest clubs, joined the competition in 1921, as did Canterbury-Bankstown in 1935.

The game's audience was also broadened by the start of radio broadcasting in 1925, which brought the sport into the living rooms of people who would never have gone to a game. For much of the first decade of rugby league on the radio, listeners would have heard much about South Sydney, the side that won the NSWRL premiership in seven of the first eight years of broadcasting.

Possibly the most unexpected sign of the burgeoning appeal of the game was the formation of a rugby league club at the elite Sydney University, whose rugby union club was perhaps the very soul of that game in Australia. Founded by H. V. Evatt, who would become Australia's foreign minister, Labour Party leader and a president of the United Nations General Assembly, the university's rugby league club played in the NSW Rugby League from 1920 to 1937 as amateurs, but was never allowed to play on the university's primary playing field.

Australia's other rugby

The attitude of Australian league to its union rivals was not quite so harsh. The revival of rugby after the war led to a new wave of defections to rugby league, especially in country areas far from the metropolitan city areas. In Queensland the union game struggled to retain its support and shortly after the war played 14-a-side to counter the appeal of league's more open play. It did little to help and in 1920 the Queensland Rugby League organised two league versus union exhibition matches in Brisbane to raise funds for local rugby union.[3]

The money raised cleared the Queensland Rugby Union's debt but had the unfortunate consequence of convincing Brisbane's three leading union sides – Past Grammars, Christian Brothers and the University of Queensland – that league was the coming game. They switched to league and union was all but dead in Queensland until the late 1920s. As a consequence two of the greatest captains of the Australian national rugby union team, five-eighth Tom Lawton and scrum-half Syd Malcolm, played rugby league in the 1920s, Lawton for Queensland University and Malcolm for Ipswich.

In Sydney, rugby union consolidated its position as the game of the 'Great Public Schools' and the professional classes of NSW. For the first decade after the war, the first-grade competition was dominated by Sydney University, which won the premiership eight out of the first ten years. From 1923 the winners were presented with the Shute Shield, named after a Sydney University student, Robert Shute, who died as a result of his injuries in a friendly match in June 1922.

But the game struggled to maintain its profile when faced with the overwhelming popularity of league. Even the link with Britain, one of the proudest features of Australian rugby union, was not as strong as league's regular tours to and from the Mother Country. The controversies of the 1908 Wallabies tour had proved difficult to forget and it was not until June 1926 that another invitation to tour Britain was received from the RFU. Given the absence of organised rugby union in Queensland, the tour was made by the New South Wales Waratahs, although there were some Queenslanders, such as Tom Lawton, among the tourists.

Unlike 1908, the 1927 tour was an unalloyed success. The Waratahs played sparkling open football, losing narrowly to England's 1928 Grand Slam team and the Scottish side that would win the Five Nations in 1929. RFU president Admiral Sir Percy Royds declared that they were 'the greatest band of sportsmen that has ever visited us'.[4]

The impact of the tour provided the impetus for the renewed growth of Australian rugby union. The re-establishment of an imperial rugby union link helped to reaffirm the sport as the 'Empire game'. The game was restarted in the private and grammar schools of Queensland and universities in Brisbane and Melbourne switched from league to union. By 1929 the Queensland Rugby Union had been revived.

It was this connection, and deference, to Britain which now more than anything defined the sport, as Sydney's *Rugby News* explained in 1928:

> to the furthermost ends of the British Empire the great rugby game is played and all owe allegiance to the great controller of the game, the English Rugby Union. It is the tradition of the rugby union game that makes us stand behind that great body to which the game owes its origin. They gave us the game and we believe that its destinies can safely be left in their hands.[5]

This was the cultural cringe at its most genuflective. Nor was Australian rugby league without its deferential streak – 'We are just as British as you are,' Harry 'Jersey' Flegg, the New South Wales Rugby League president, told the 1950 British tour manager George Oldroyd – but loyalty to the British way of life was an essential component of Australian rugby union.[6] Indeed, this was how the Australian middle classes viewed themselves in general and rugby union's articulation of this was one of its biggest strengths.

The first fruits of the rebirth of Australian rugby union came the year after the Waratahs returned from Britain. Playing for the first time since 1914 as Australia, the Wallabies unexpectedly whitewashed the All Blacks, winning all three Tests in the 1929 series. In 1931 Lord Bledisloe, the Governor-General of New Zealand, presented a trophy in his name to be awarded to the winners of the series. In fact, of their first eight meetings with the All Blacks following the revival of the Wallabies, the Australians won five of them. Their 1933 tour to South Africa was less successful, with the Springboks winning the five-match Test series.

Despite its success against the All Blacks, rugby union in Australia in the interwar years would continue to play second fiddle to rugby league at home, and internationally was rarely able to escape the role of the third wheel to the All Black–Springbok rivalry.

The Kiwi connection

A similar point could be made about rugby league in New Zealand. Dwarfed by its union cousin domestically, it perpetually struggled for international parity with English and Australian giants of rugby league. The first years after the war were difficult for New Zealand league. It was slow in setting up a national infrastructure after the return of Baskerville's touring side in 1908 – the New Zealand Rugby League was not formed until 1910 – and the coming of the war hit it hard.

Rugby union in New Zealand had also taken a far more aggressive attitude to the new game. In Auckland, where league and union vied for dominance, the local rugby union authorities responded by changing their rules to make the game quicker. League was often banned at municipally owned grounds such as Christchurch's famous Lancaster Park. And the NZRU had no compunction about poaching rugby league players, a flagrant breach of its own amateur regulations, as the switch of Karl Ifwersen to the 15-a-side game in 1921 highlighted.

Even so, league still had significant support in New Zealand's industrial areas such as Auckland and the mining towns of the South Island's west coast, as well as among sections of the Maori community.

Over 35,000 people turned out in 1920 to see the Auckland representative team defeat Harold Wagstaff's touring British side 24-16, thanks to a team composed of 'beer-truck forwards and racing-car backs', as memorably described by their full-back Bill Davidson.[7]

In 1922 a Maori rugby league team undertook an eight-match tour of Australia. It won just two games, but once again the action of the league had a lasting impact on the NZRU. Concerned that Maori would be attracted to league, not least because of the Springbok tourists' anti-Maori remarks the previous year, the NZRU organised its own Maori tour of Australia and set up a Maori Advisory Board to administer the sport.

In 1926 the Maori rugby union side undertook a marathon eight-month world tour taking in Australia, Sri Lanka, England, Wales, France and Canada, losing just six games and defeating a full-strength French side 12-3 at Stade Colombes in its only international match. Little was done after that, until the New Zealand Maori Rugby League was set up in 1934, and the NZRU promptly organised another Maori tour to Australia.

By that time, league had sunk deep roots in the Maori community. In 1936 Steve Watene, later to become an MP in the New Zealand parliament, became the first Maori to captain the New Zealand Kiwis (as the national rugby league side was officially dubbed in 1938). The following year the Maori rugby league team was strong enough to record a historic 16-5 win over the touring Australians. Among the Maori players was George Nepia, the legendary full-back who had been left out of the All Blacks' 1928 tour of South Africa because of the colour of his skin.

But when it came to internationals, league could not compete with union. Although the All Golds' groundbreaking tour of Britain in 1907 had been hugely popular, league in New Zealand was essentially an amateur sport that struggled to finance extensive tours to the northern hemisphere. Even the All Blacks only undertook three European tours in the first half of the 20th century.

One attempt to solve the problem was by making the 1911 and 1921 Australian tours to Britain joint 'Australasian' tours. In 1911 four Kiwis joined the Australians – Bolla Francis, George Gillett, Frank Woodward and Charlie Savory, who would be killed at Gallipoli in 1915 – but only Francis featured in the Test side. The 1921 tourists were again officially known as Australasia but only stand-off Bert Laing was chosen from New Zealand, and he was not selected for any of the Test matches.

The New Zealand Rugby League therefore decided to bite the bullet and organise its own tour of Britain for 1926. They could not have picked a worse time to visit the industrial north of England. Coal owners had locked out miners across Britain and in May 1926 a general strike had been staged. When the Kiwis arrived, they found rugby league's heartlands in the midst of economic depression and industrial conflict.

This was brought home to them in just their second match of the tour at Leigh in the heart of the Lancashire coalfields. Unemployed fans, many of them miners who had been locked out from work for six months, refused to pay the one shilling and sixpence admission price and simply forced their way into the ground. Unsurprisingly, crowds were disappointing, and the Kiwis' standard of play no better.

The tourists were also plagued by tension between management and the players. Relations between the tour's Australian manager Ernest Mair and his senior players deteriorated to such an extent that seven players went on strike and refused to play. They left for home early and were banned from the game by the NZRL on their return. It was, in the words of historian John Coffey, the tour that died of shame.

The controversy and financial loss of the 1926 tour meant that it would be over a decade before another tour was considered. Fatefully, they chose to tour in 1939. After arriving in England on 29 August, they defeated St Helens in their opening match on 2 September. The next day war was declared. Deciding that there was no alternative but to cancel the tour, the Kiwis left for home on 14 September onboard the

SS *Rugitiki*, having spent just 17 days and played two matches on British soil at an estimated cost of between £5,000 and £6,000.

Coincidentally, the Kiwis' Australian mirror image, the Wallabies, had also decided that 1939 would be the year they would again tour Britain after a long absence. They had even less luck than the New Zealanders and did not play a single match before returning home. And thus, as the clamour of war grew, the interwar decades finished as they had begun, with rugby union strong in its traditional communities and rugby league equally as vibrant in its heartlands.

But, of course, they remained leagues apart.

20

RUGBY IN THE SECOND
WORLD WAR

For Europe, and ultimately the rest of the world, 1938 was the tipping point. Hitler declared Anschluss in Austria and incorporated his country of birth into the Third Reich. In Spain the civil war had shifted decisively in favour of Franco's nationalist forces. Government-organised 'spontaneous' demonstrations erupted in Italy demanding that France hand over Nice, Corsica and Tunisia to Mussolini. In Romania, King Carol II dismissed parliament and established his own authoritarian dictatorship. The question was no longer if there would be war, but when.

In March 1938, a crowd of 20,000 gathered in Frankfurt to watch the German national rugby union team play France. In 1934 France and Germany, supported by Italy, had established the Fédération Internationale de Rugby Amateur (FIRA) to organise rugby in Europe as an alternative to the International Rugby Football Board. Although France was the dominant power, the Germans played a central role in FIRA, so much so that German was the new organisation's official language.[1]

France had played Germany in friendly internationals every year since 1927. In just their second meeting, the Germans had pulled off a shock 17-16 win in Frankfurt. The French did not make the same mistake again and it would be another six years before Germany would score another try against them.

But from 1933 the margins of victory began to grow smaller. In 1934 France had won by a mere four points and at the 1936 final of the European tournament held in Berlin just before the Olympic Games, the French had carried off the title by a converted try. This wasn't just a story of declining French standards. The Germans lost only two matches against other countries in the 1930s and were clearly Europe's second rugby power. Now, in 1938, the margin between the two national teams had never been narrower. The match was tight and dominated by forwards. Early in the game the French conceded a penalty in their own half and the experienced German full-back, Hannover's Georg Isenberg, stepped up and slotted the ball between the posts: 3-0 to Germany.

As the game wore on, the Germans became increasingly confident. Even France's outstanding centre and captain Joseph Desclaux could not crack the German defence. The French became more desperate, unwilling to concede defeat to a nation that had been playing international rugby for barely a decade. Nothing they tried could break through the German wall of defenders. When referee Herr Krembs finally blew his whistle for no-side, the Germans were exuberant. They were now a European rugby power.

Two months later, the two sides met again in Bucharest in the deciding match of FIRA's 1938 European Championship. Both had previously defeated the hosts Romania by just three points and the decider was just as close.

At half-time another upset looked to be on the cards as the Germans led 5-3, thanks to a converted try to the German scrum-half and captain Karl Loos. But the French were determined to atone for their earlier shame and a try to Stade Bordelais' winger Robert Caunegre that was converted by Desclaux gave France an 8-5 victory and their third successive European Championship.

Barely 15 months later, Europe was at war. And once again, many of the stars of international rugby would not return to play when peace was finally restored. Eight French rugby union internationals were killed, the same number of Irish caps who died. Ten Australians, 14 Englishmen and 15 Scots lost their lives. But the country that lost the most rugby union internationals in the Second World War was the nation that had been playing the international game for the shortest time: Germany. Sixteen capped players would perish.

Rugby's European axis

It was Germany that staged the last international rugby union match before war put a stop to it all. On Sunday 5 May 1940, just five days before Hitler's forces invaded France, Belgium and the Netherlands, Italy narrowly defeated the Germans 4-0 in Stuttgart thanks to a solitary drop goal from Roma's Francesco Vinci.

Germany and Italy had been two of rugby union's biggest success stories in the 1930s, despite the fact that the IRB had little time for anyone outside the British Empire. A 1933 RFU meeting expressed the view that it 'should confine its activities to the English-speaking peoples', and in 1935 the RFU stopped accepting overseas members, preferring instead to focus its attention on 'the British Commonwealth of nations'.[2] France itself would not be accepted as a member of the IRB until 1978.

But France's expulsion from the Five Nations and the creation of FIRA galvanised the development of European rugby. Rugby, as we have seen, was first played in Germany in Heidelberg in the mid-19th century by British expatriates and was then taken up by German Anglophiles. It was also played in the early 1880s by members of DFV 1878 Hannover, the first football club of any type to be formed in Germany.

Inspired by watching British expatriates playing the game, the initiative for the Hannover club came from 15-year-old Ferdinand-Wilhelm Fricke, who attended one of the city's elite schools. The sport's popularity spread among elite German schools and in 1899 19 rugby clubs formed a German rugby union. In 1900 an annual North versus South match was played for the first time and in 1909 Hannover and Stuttgart fought out the first club championship final.

The game remained very much the preserve of the Anglophile elite of Germany and, unlike soccer, never appealed to the masses. Frick became the first chairman of the Deutsche Rugby Verband (German Rugby Federation) in 1901 but, although the Frankfurt club played in the 1900 Olympic rugby competition, it wasn't until the year of his death in 1927 that Germany played its first international match.

When Hitler came to power in 1933 rugby, like all sports, was incorporated into the Nazi Reich Federation for Physical Education. With the support of Hitler's future munitions minister Albert Speer, rugby became a small component of the Nazis' use of sport as a tool of diplomacy, hence the enthusiastic role it played within FIRA. On the eve of the Second World War the game had 52 clubs and 1,925 registered players. The German club championship would continue until 1942.

Germany's rival for the title of second power of European rugby throughout the 1930s was Italy. Rugby had been played in 1893 in Genoa by English expatriates but only emerged as a sport played by Italians in the late 1900s. Games were also regularly played by the visiting ships from the Royal Navy Mediterranean Fleet. In 1910 Racing Club de France played a Turin side and the following year the first Italian rugby club was formed by Piero Mariani as part of US Milanese, the Milan multi-sport club.

Until the late 1920s rugby remained a niche sport confined to aficionados in northern Italy. Its major role in the rugby world was as host to touring clubs from France. But in 1927 Mussolini's Fascist regime began to use sport as a vehicle for its ideology both domestically and internationally.

A 'Comitato di Propaganda' to promote and organise rugby union was set up by the regime under the leadership of Piero Mariani. It renamed itself the Federazione Italiana Rugby (FIR) the following year with 16 founding clubs based in Bologna, Milan, Naples, Padua, Rome, Turin and Udine. In 1929, after trial matches against a French side, Italy played its first international match, losing 9-0 to Spain.

As with other Italian sports, rugby was tightly integrated into the Fascist system. Mariani's successor as president of the FIR was Giorgio Vaccaro, a general in the Fascist Militia and one of Mussolini's leading sports administrators, and its longest serving president was Ettore Rossi, who would also become head of sport in Mussolini's short-lived Italian Social Republic, established after the Allies had seized control of most of Italy in 1943.

As well as its physicality, rugby union appealed to the Fascists because of its amateur philosophy, as *The Times* noted in 1929: 'the promoters of Rugby football, such as Signor Giorgio Vaccaro and Signor Turati, secretary of the Fascist Party, have realised that the game must be strictly confined, as in Great Britain, to amateurs who can be trusted to play it in the right spirit of sportsmanship'.[3]

Mussolini's press secretary and member of the Grand Fascist Council, Lando Ferretti, wrote the introduction to the regime's guide to rugby, *Il Gioco del Rugby*, published in 1928. And in 1932 Mussolini's office wrote to the RFU asking them to organise a congress of European rugby federations to create a FIFA-style federation to encourage the spread of the sport, a suggestion curtly dismissed by Twickenham as being 'neither workable nor desirable'.[4]

The Fascists gradually lost interest in rugby from the mid-1930s due to the phenomenal success of the national soccer side – which won the 1934 and 1938 World Cups – but the Italian rugby team continued to play regular internationals. However, unlike Germany, they were no match for France and would only defeat the Germans twice in their six meetings.

The Italians did not go to the 1938 European Championships, which were staged in Romania's capital Bucharest. Romania had deep cultural ties with France and it was common for the children of the

Romanian elite to be educated in Paris. In 1913 returning students established the first Romanian club, Stadiul Roman, modelled on Stade Français. Two years later, the Paris-educated Gregore Caracostea, who had played for Racing Club de France while a student, set up the Central Commission for Rugby Football.

A Romanian side played in the rugby tournament of the 1919 Inter-Allied Games held in Paris but lost heavily to France 48-5 and then 23-0 to the United States. In 1924, as we have seen, they joined France and the USA as the only sides competing in the 1924 Olympic rugby competition but once again found themselves out of their depth, losing 37-0 to the Americans and by an even more embarrassing 61-3 to the French. Nevertheless, the bronze medal was theirs by virtue of finishing third out of the three entrants.

This was perhaps the highlight of Romania's international adventures in the interwar years. The Federaţia Română de Rugby was formed in 1931, but the national side's only other successes were against lowly Czechoslovakia in 1927 and the even weaker Netherlands in 1937.

Their fortunes began to turn in the late 1930s. The game expanded beyond Bucharest in 1939 with the creation of a club in Braşov and in April 1940 the national side recorded its most significant victory when scrum-half Eugen Marculescu landed a solitary penalty to defeat Italy for the first time. Little more than six months later, Romania entered the war alongside Italy and Germany.

French manoeuvres

Despite the unsavoury nature of many of the European regimes that supported rugby in the 1930s, FIRA did more to promote the international spread of the game than the IRB. This was similar to what had happened in soccer. The English had invented association football, but it was French administrators who created FIFA and took the round-ball game to the non-English speaking world.

So it was in rugby. The French influence saw the game established in Catalonia, where it sprang to life thanks to a visiting Toulouse team in 1923. This was also the case in Czechoslovakia, thanks to the writer Ondřej Sekora taking a rugby ball and a copy of the rules of the game home with him when he returned to Brno from Paris. Former Stade Français player Jean Rey was the driving force behind the formation of the Belgian Rugby Federation in 1931. Rugby in Spain was kick-started by a visit of a French team containing the iconic fly-half Yves du Manoir.

Even those countries in which the British influence had been decisive, such as Portugal, where the Associação de Rugby de Lisboa had been founded in 1926, the Netherlands, which had established a national federation in 1932, and Sweden, where rugby began after a successful exhibition match between the crews of HMS *Dorsetshire* and HMS *Norfolk* in 1931, quickly joined FIRA.

Concern over FIRA's growing influence may well have been a factor that caused the British to invite France back into in the Five Nations. Certainly, the rapid growth and international success of French rugby league played a major part. But the exclusion of France after 1931 had also diminished the tournament and in July 1939 the British nations extended an olive branch.

But there was a condition: internationals could only be resumed if France abandoned its club championship. Delighted to be thrown a lifeline to help them against the relentless tide of rugby league, French clubs voted to abolish the championship – but had not the slightest intention of doing so. Other than the vote, not a single step was made to disband the championship.

As it turned out, Biarritz's extra-time victory over Perpignan in the 1939 championship final was the last time the *Bouclier* would be played for until 1943. The FFR suspended the competition when war broke out, although unofficial regional competitions continued despite the division of France into Nazi-Occupied and Vichy collaborationist zones.

In June 1942, six months after the government decree banning rugby league, the FFR decided that the championship could restart.

Ninety-five clubs entered, 40 in the occupied zone and the remainder in Vichy France. Eventually Aviron Bayonnais and Agen reached the final, held at the Parc des Princes in Paris. It was 0-0 until three minutes from time, when former rugby league scrum-half Jean Dubalen broke down the right, slipped the ball to Louis Bisauta who fed it to Pierre Larre who touched down just inside the right corner flag: 3-0 to Aviron and the first *Bouclier* of the war was theirs.

Dubalen was not the only rugby league player to appear in the final. Alongside him was league international Jean Dauger and hooker René Arotça, while Agen had the veteran league internationals Maurice Brunetaud and Marius Guiral, plus hooker Jean-Londaits Béhère. Vichy's ban on league had had the desired effect of revitalising rugby union.

Aviron returned to the final the following year with Dubalen and Dauger, who had now been given a job with the club that would keep him there for the rest of his career. Their opponents were a young Perpignan side that not only featured Jean Desclaux, who had switched to league in 1938, but four future league internationals, including the greatest of them all, the full-back Puig Aubert. The Perpignanais cut the Bayonnais to shreds, running in six tries to a solitary Dauger touchdown.

By the end of 1944, Aubert and his fellow *Treizistes* were back in their own game. As the Allies advanced across France, rugby league revived and was formally reconstituted in September 1944. A number of its players had been members of the Resistance. Charles Mathon and René Barnoud were active participants in the Sport-Libre movement, an underground organisation that fought against forced labour conscription and opposed the use of sport by the collaborationists.[5] François Récaborde, one of the pioneers on Jean Galia's 1934 tour to England and a founder of Pau rugby league club, was deported to Buchenwald in 1943. Galia himself used his cinema business to help Jews escape to Spain. Paul Barrière, who would become president of the French Rugby

League in 1947 at just 27, played a central role in the Maquis in the Aude region in the French rugby heartland.

On the union side, Gilbert Brutus, the coach of the Perpignan side that won the championship in 1925 and then moved to Quillan to guide them to three successive finals from 1928 to 1930, was one of the first to join the Resistance in September 1940 and died at the hands of the Gestapo in June 1944. Jacques Chaban-Delmas, who played for France in 1945 and became prime minister in 1969, was awarded the *Légion d'honneur* for his work in the Resistance.[6]

Rugby united?

France was not the only country in which rugby union found itself divided during the Second World War. In South Africa, significant sections of Afrikaner society were, if not pro-Nazi, at least ambivalent as to the outcome of the war, and rugby was split in two over the question of supporting the Allied war effort. English-speaking rugby supporters wanted to organise fund-raising matches for the Allies but many Afrikaner rugby supporters objected. They began to organise matches in aid of the *Reddingsdaadbond*, a charity for poor white Afrikaners.[7]

In the Western and Eastern Provinces, rugby split into pro- and anti-war organisations. Stellenbosch University, the powerhouse of Afrikaner rugby, resigned from the Western Province Rugby Union in 1943 in protest at the decision to raise money for the Allies. A. F. Markötter, the noted Stellenbosch coach who had popularised the 3-4-1 scrum formation, resigned from the Western Province Rugby Union claiming that its support for the Allies was politicising rugby and that it was attempting to stop Stellenbosch playing the game.

In contrast to South Africa and France, war brought a sense of unity to rugby in the rest of the English-speaking rugby world. Unlike the 1914–18 war, there was no controversy over whether sport should continue in wartime. The earlier conflict had demonstrated that sport had a positive effect on civilian and military morale. Both league and union club matches had continued during the First World War, albeit in reduced circumstances. Some clubs, such as union's London Scottish or league's Rochdale Hornets, closed for most of the war, while Blackheath and Richmond merged for the duration. County leagues were introduced by the RFL to reduce travel by clubs but the Rugby League Challenge Cup survived intact, although the final was now played over two legs in the north, rather than at Wembley.

Within weeks of war being declared in 1939, the RFU lifted its ban on rugby league players and allowed them to play rugby union while serving in the armed forces. The Welsh Rugby Union followed the RFU's lead but the Scots remained unmoved. SRU secretary Harry Simson told the press that 'his Union would not remove the ban on professionals in the Services playing for or against amateur teams'.[8]

In December 1939 a combined England/Wales side defeated Scotland/Ireland 17-3 at Richmond in aid of the Red Cross, signalling the start of a series of services-based encounters that brought together players from both codes. Nineteen forty-two saw the beginning of regular services internationals between England, Scotland and Wales, including an 8-5 Scottish win over England at Wembley Stadium in April.

As *The Times* rugby correspondent noted in 1944, the England and Wales international sides 'were ready to make use of any available rugby league talent' and consequently numerous league players turned out for the two nations in services rugby union internationals, most notably Gus Risman, who captained the Wales team twice, Roy Francis, who, despite being Welsh, was capped for England seven times, and Alan Edwards, who won six Welsh caps. Countless others turned out for a plethora of union representative teams across the armed forces.

Many rugby league players were taken aback by their experiences in the amateur code. After one match for Wales, Gus Risman claimed £4 travel expenses but 'my heart stopped when the officials told me that my expenses couldn't be right. But my heart started beating again when I was handed £8!'[9]

This intermingling of the codes reached its height in 1943 and 1944, when rugby league sides twice defeated rugby union sides under rugby union rules. In January 1943 the Northern Command Sports Board organised a union match between a Northern Command Rugby League XV and a Northern Command Rugby Union XV at Headingley. The league side overcame an 8-3 half-time deficit to win 18-11. The second game, between fully-fledged Combined Services League and Union sides, was staged at Bradford's Odsal Stadium in April 1944 and proved to be a much tighter affair but was won by the league side 15-10. The RFU reimposed its ban on league players in 1946.

Overall, the death toll of rugby players was much lower than in 1914–18. Fourteen England internationals lost their lives, including Prince Obolensky, who died in a flying accident, and the captain of England's 1913 Grand Slam side Norman Wodehouse, a vice admiral in the Royal Navy whose ship was torpedoed in July 1941. Six served in the RAF, five in the army and three in the Royal Navy. Three Welsh internationals were killed alongside the eight Irishman and 15 Scots. Fifteen Oxbridge rugby blues were killed. At club level, the absence of accurate records makes comparison difficult, but some sides suffered grievously, with Old Alleynians losing 49 members and Blackheath 24.[10]

In rugby league, Les 'Juicy' Adams, a veteran of the 1932 'Battle of Brisbane' Test match, was killed when the aircraft in which he was a gunner was shot down in the Far East in April 1945. Among many others, Leeds lost at least three players: John Dixon, John Roper and the prodigiously talented stand-off Oliver Morris, who had signed from Hunslet in the summer of 1939 for £1,500. There was a clause in his contract that the full fee was only payable if he survived the war, but he died of his wounds in Italy in September 1944.[11]

The rest of the English-speaking rugby world followed the British lead. In New Zealand, rugby of both codes continued to be played throughout the war. League players were allowed into union sides and the game's focus shifted to services' rugby. Although the Ranfurly Shield was suspended for the duration of the war, there were more inter-provincial matches and other first class matches played in most of the wartime seasons than had taken place during the entire First World War. In Australia, the NSW Rugby Union continued its club competition, with Manly and Eastern Suburbs each winning the first grade premiership twice.

Rugby league in Australia also continued. Huge crowds gathered for grand finals, not least because sport was seen as an important part of the bond with Britain. The popularity of wartime league led to it being accepted as an official military sport alongside rugby union, cricket and Australian Rules, a recognition denied British league until 1994. With the Normandy invasion of 1944, Harold Flegg declared: 'I'm sure that league men from Wigan, Rochdale, Dewsbury, Halifax, Hull, Huddersfield, Barrow and the other northern English towns will fight as relentlessly and with the same skill they display in Tests.'[12]

Between the front line and the try line

Rugby became a prominent feature of Allied sporting life in the theatres of war around the world. As early as April 1940 a strong team representing the Australian forces played a French Army side in Beirut. In front of 7,000 spectators, the Australians defeated the French 11-5, thanks to the efforts of players such as Edward 'Weary' Dunlop, Victoria's greatest ever rugby player who would become famous for his role in Japanese prisoner-of-war camps, and Basil Travers, whose Australian birth would not prevent him from winning six England caps after the war.

The Middle East would become the most important arena for rugby, partly because of the number of Dominion troops stationed there, but also because the climate was kinder to sport. In the strategic port of Alexandria in 1942, more than 40 military teams took part in a sevens tournament. International military matches featuring stars from across the rugby-playing world were common. A match between New Zealand and 'the Rest of Egypt' attracted 30,000 to Alexandria's Municipal Stadium. Five figure crowds were the norm for such 'international' games.[13]

Despite fighting on the same side, Springbok–All Black rivalry flourished and gave rise to the legend of 'The Book' for which the two sides would compete whenever they met. Each side accused the other of not knowing the rules of the game, giving rise to players taunting each other with the question 'who wrote the book?'. The fact that the book of rules was written by the English RFU with no input whatsoever from South Africa or New Zealand did nothing to diminish the intensity of the rivalry.[14]

Each national army had its own regimental and battalion tournaments, such as the Freyberg Cup for New Zealand units fighting in Italy and named after Lieutenant General Bernard Freyberg, the commander of the New Zealand Expeditionary Forces, or the Interstate Rugby League Cup played for by Australian regiments on Bougainville Island in Papua New Guinea. Wherever rugby players gathered, a game would take place.

In German prisoner-of-war camps, rugby competitions were a permanent feature of life. In Stalag IV-B in Brandenburg, an eight nations' rugby union tournament took place featuring the seven major English-speaking nations plus an 'Other Nationalities' side. At Stalag XX-A in Toruń in Poland, a Springbok side featuring the great Jewish goal-kicking prop Okey Geffin defeated a New Zealand team. Both sides played in bare feet despite the freezing Polish winter. League, too, flourished, with rugby league players in Stalag 383 in Bavaria organising two England versus Australia matches and a Lancashire versus Yorkshire game in the spring of 1943 alone.[15]

The most famous of all the military sides was undoubtedly the 1945–46 Second New Zealand Expeditionary Force team, known at the time as the Kiwis but which came to be known as the Khaki All Blacks. Conceived by General Freyberg as a way of boosting morale and raising New Zealand's profile at the end of the war, the side was selected from serving soldiers in Europe.

Captained and coached by scrum-half Charlie Saxton, the only All Black in the side, the team toured Britain, Ireland, France and Germany, playing a brand of fast, open rugby with the emphasis on handling rather than kicking. As a testimony to the wartime spirit of open rugby, the side included two rugby league players who later became All Blacks, forward Johnny Simpson and the superb full-back Bob Scott.

The side won its first 15 matches, including a 14-7 win over a Combined Services side, that included ten league players, and whitewashed Wales and the leading Welsh club sides. They remained unbeaten until three months into the tour, when they lost 11-6 to a determined Scotland. The New Zealanders went on to Paris, Toulouse and Bordeaux. Here, too, they attracted huge crowds, their open, exuberant style of play seemingly encapsulating the *joie de vivre* that came with the end of the war.

The New Zealanders also played two matches in Germany on the European leg of the tour, defeating both the Combined Services and the British Army of the Rhine. By now, however, there was no native German rugby – like culture and civilisation itself, the game had been swept away by Hitler's *Götterdämmerung*. The war was finally over, but its legacy would shape the future of rugby.

PART VI

RUGBY'S NEW HORIZONS

The years after the Second World War saw the emergence of rugby beyond its traditional centres of power with new ones appearing in Europe, leading eventually to the emergence of Italy and the expansion of the Five Nations. In the southern hemisphere, the Pacific Islands began to challenge for recognition and Argentina grew into a potential world power.

In Africa and Asia, the legacy of the empires of Britain and France both promoted but sometimes held back the development of the game. In Japan, rugby acquired national importance but international frustration. And in the USA and Canada, the sport regained some of the ground it had lost over the previous century.

Perhaps the most significant new horizon, however, was not one of geography but of gender, as women's rugby emerged and attempted to shift the game in one of the most fundamental ways imaginable.

21

EUROPEAN RUGBY AND THE RISE OF ITALY

At the end of the Second World War, Europe lay in ruins. Yet within a matter of months, the unity of nations that had defeated Hitler was shattered by the onset of the Cold War. Sport, like so many institutions, was torn between east and west, but in the midst of tensions that often threatened to escalate into nuclear war, 'oval diplomacy' criss-crossed a divided continent to create a vibrant rugby culture in both Eastern and Western Europe.

The popularity of rugby in post-war Europe was largely due to France. The French rugby union authorities wasted little time re-establishing the Fédération Internationale de Rugby Amateur (FIRA) after the end of the Second World War, despite the fact that Germany, Italy and Romania had fought on the opposing side, and FIRA was reconstituted at a meeting in Milan in 1948.

European matches had actually kicked off 18 months earlier when Czechoslovakia had travelled to the Netherlands to win 14-8. It was the Czechs who for a short time in the late 1940s became the post-war pioneers of the game, establishing a league competition in 1948 and travelling to Italy and Romania for matches before Cold War finally cut Europe in half, putting east–west sporting relations into a deep freeze until the mid-1950s.

The divisions were reflected in the first European Cup tournament that FIRA organised in 1952. Neither the Czechs nor the Romanians took part, leaving Belgium, Italy, Spain and West Germany to battle it out for the dubious right to play a full-strength France in the final. Italy emerged as the challenger, losing by a creditable 17-8 to a French side containing among others Roger Martine, Lucien Mias and Jean Prat. Nineteen fifty-four saw the addition of Portugal, but the final still featured Italy and France, who overcame the shock of a first-minute Italian try to win by a comfortable 39-12.

This was the last FIRA European Cup that would be played until 1965. Even by the time that the 1954 final was being played, the balance of European rugby was tipping towards the east.

The rise of Romania

The USSR and its Eastern European allies devoted significant resources to sporting activity and encouraged international sporting contacts to foster diplomatic links. The Soviet bloc's entry in the Olympic Games in 1952 had electrified the sporting world. The USSR finished second in the medals' table and then came first in Melbourne in 1956. Rugby, although a minor sport on a world scale, was none the less an important cultural component of Western European life and a way of overcoming Cold War divisions.

East Germany joined FIRA in 1956 after having played Czechoslovakia and Romania since 1951. The side was coached by Erwin Thiesies, a pre-war German international who became East Germany's first full-time rugby coach in 1953 when he was employed to coach a steelworks team in Henningsdorf, just outside Berlin. His team, BSG Stahl Hennigsdorf, won the inaugural East German championship in 1952 and dominated the competition until the unification of Germany in 1990. In 1957 Poland joined, although they had only just started a league competition and would not begin to play international rugby until 1958.

The same year that Poland joined FIRA, Moscow staged the Sixth World Festival of Youth and Students. The festival was a bi-annual celebration of sport and culture that had been staged by Eastern bloc countries since 1947. For the Soviets, now undergoing a post-Stalin 'thaw' under Nikita Khrushchev, it was an opportunity for foreigners to see the changes taking place in the USSR.

For the first time, the festival staged a rugby tournament featuring Czechoslovakia, Romania and, representing Britain, Welsh club side Llanelli. Italy and France were also invited. The Italians did not make it, but the French turned up with a full-strength side that contained Jean Prat, Michel Vannier, Henri Domec, Jean Dupuy and Amédée Domenech. When the other sides realised who they would have to face, the French were asked to withdraw from the tournament, leaving them to play a friendly against the Czechs that they won 36-18.

In the tournament itself, the Czechs lost to Romania and Llanelli, who drew 6-6 in their game, necessitating a play-off. Although Llanelli were the better organised side, the enthusiasm of the Romanians led to them scoring the only try of the match. Llanelli levelled with a penalty goal, but with ten minutes to go the Romanians made one of their few forays into the Welsh half and their full-back dropped a goal to win the game 6-3.[1]

As many in the game were already aware, the 1957 win demonstrated that the major rugby power in the east was Romania. Unbeaten in Eastern Europe since the war, earlier that year they had led France 15-6 with 15 minutes left of their match in Bucharest, only for the French to step up a gear to snatch the game 18-15.

The Romanians had their biggest impact in Britain. In August 1954 Swansea had played two matches in Romania as part of a pre-season tour. Eighteen months earlier Swansea had held the All Blacks to a 6-6 draw, but much to their surprise went down 23-12 to the Romanians in the second match in front of 60,000 in Bucharest. The following year a Romanian representative side played a four-match tour of England and Wales. Swansea were defeated once more, this time 19-3, Harlequins and Bristol were held to draws, leaving Cardiff the only side to defeat the tourists by a mere 6-3.

Coming hard on the heels of the Eastern European triumphs in the Olympics, the success of Romanian rugby seemed to confirm that the self-proclaimed socialist states of Eastern Europe had unlocked the secret of sporting success. A force in the Olympics, the East Europeans also presented problems for rugby union's amateur regulations. As in all Soviet bloc sports, elite athletes held down jobs but spent most of the time training and playing. Not only that, but the 1955 tourists were also paid winning bonuses. As the *Daily Mail* revealed, each member of the team received £100 for defeating Swansea and just missed out on £250 if they had beaten Cardiff.[2]

Despite the obvious gulf between the IRB and the Romanian definitions of amateurism, the rugby union authorities decided, not for the first time, to turn a blind eye to the issue. As Rowe Harding, Swansea's former Welsh captain and by then a prominent county court judge, explained, if rugby union was to 'pull down the iron curtain' and expel the Romanians, 'I have no doubt that the Rumanians will turn to rugby league, which will be a tragedy'.[3]

As Harding may have guessed, the Romanian Rugby Federation had already confidentially contacted the Rugby Football League in England. In December 1954, its secretary had written to the RFL asking to be sent rugby league rule books and information about the history of the game, saying that they were considering the 'initiation' of league in his country. Nothing had come of it, no doubt due in part to the IRB declining to implement its own amateur regulations against the Romanians' semi-professionalism.[4]

The Romanians weren't the only Eastern European country with an interest in rugby league. In 1953 the Yugoslavian Sports Association had invited two French rugby league student teams to play a four-match tour. The success of the matches led to the famous Partizan Belgrade sports club starting a league team, coached by former Romanian under-19 international Boris Blažević. In 1957 a league competition was started in Serbia and in 1961 Yugoslavia played the French national amateur team, losing by a respectable 13-0 in front of 5,000 at Banja Luka in Bosnia.

Rugby politics in Tito's Yugoslavia were uniquely fraternal at that time as both league, largely based in Serbia, and union, which was stronger in Croatia, were both administered by the Yugoslavian Rugby Federation (YRF). But in 1964, anxious to develop international contacts, the YRF applied to join FIRA and ended all rugby league competitions. Nada Split, the rugby league champions in its final two seasons, switched to union and went on to dominate the game. Not until 2001 would rugby league be revived.[5]

In soccer-mad Yugoslavia rugby had little political or social importance, but in Romania it had substantial government support and diplomatic importance. The Romanian leadership, despite its adherence to Stalinism, also had a somewhat arm's length relationship with Moscow and pursued a more independent foreign policy than other Soviet bloc nations. The Romanian government sought out allies in the West and Western countries were keen to exploit its partial breach with the USSR.

Rugby union became a conduit for diplomatic relations between Britain and Romania. In 1956 Harlequins toured Romania, led by the club president and by now prominent backbench Conservative MP Wavell Wakefield, and extensive discussions were held with Romanian ministers about trade links, scientific collaboration and even contacts between the Church of England and the Romanian Orthodox Church. In 1960, a parliamentary Anglo-Romanian Group was created, with Wakefield as chairman.[6]

Similar contacts took place with the French government and the growing political importance of rugby was reflected on the pitch. In 1960 the Romanians signalled that they were now European rugby's sixth power with an 11-5 win over France in Bucharest – the start of a three-year period in which Romania were unbeaten against the French, drawing twice in France and winning again at home in 1962. It was partly in recognition of the strength of Romania that FIRA started a new European tournament in 1965, the Nations Cup.

Romania's fall and Italy's rise

The first European Nations Cup began with just five teams and was won, not unexpectedly, by France, but by the time Romania lifted the trophy for the first time in 1969, 16 nations were competing. It was renamed the FIRA Trophy in 1973 and over the next ten years the Romanians were champions on four separate occasions, the only side other than France to win until a resurgent Italy did so in 1997.

By the late 1980s the USSR itself had become an emerging power in the second tier of European rugby, regularly finishing as runners-up in the FIRA Trophy. It had taken the Soviet game some time to gain momentum. In 1930 the Bolshevik commissar for education Anatoly Lunacharsky had dubbed rugby a game of 'gentlemanly combat', but despite his call for the game to be played in the Soviet Union there were several unsuccessful attempts to establish it in the 1920s and 1930s. A league had been created in Moscow in 1936 but closed at the beginning of the war in 1939.[7]

The game revived in the 1950s and by 1963 there were an estimated 150 rugby clubs in the USSR and a national championship was instigated in 1966.[8] The moving spirit of Russian rugby was Vladimir Ilyushin, the son of the famous Soviet aircraft designer and himself a lieutenant general in the Soviet air force, who oversaw the founding of the Soviet Rugby Federation in 1967. Partially due to the influence of Ilyushin, rugby gained a following in the air force, highlighted by leading clubs such as the Gagarin Air Force Academy and the Kiev Institute of Engineers of Civil Aviation.[9]

Official government recognition helped the game develop rapidly and in 1974 the USSR played their first international match. In 1991 they were even granted a match against an England XV at Twickenham, the first time a Russian had played at 'HQ' since Prince Alexander Oblonsky in 1936. This invitation from the RFU was perhaps as much a response to the establishment of rugby league in the Soviet Union in 1989 as it was due to a rise in Russian standards of play.

Much of the strength of Soviet rugby came from Georgia. Like many countries, Georgia had a tradition of rugby-style folk football going back centuries. The Georgian variation was called 'Lelo burti', Georgian for 'field ball', which it is claimed resembled modern rugby. Although there are reports of sporadic rugby matches being played in Georgia during the interwar years, it wasn't until 1959 that the game became established when Jacques Haspekian, a French-Armenian cyclist, introduced the game to students at the Georgian Polytechnical Institute in the capital Tbilisi, some of whom went on to form the country's first official rugby club, Qochebi.[10]

By 1964 there were four teams playing regularly and the Georgian Rugby Federation was created. As part of the Soviet Union at this time, Georgian clubs played in the Soviet championship. Lokomotiv Tbilisi finished third in 1968 and paved the way for Georgian teams' long record of success in the league. Indeed, by the mid-1980s Georgian sides dominated the championship and provided a substantial number of players for the Soviet national team.[11]

It wasn't until September 1989, when the Soviet Union started to break up, that Georgia played an international in their own right. Their opponents were Zimbabwe, who two years earlier had appeared in the inaugural World Cup, and the match ended in a surprise 16-3 victory to the Georgians. Over the course of the 1990s they established a position near the top of the second-tier nations, culminating in a 28-27 victory over Tonga in Tbilisi in 1999. Four years later they made their first appearance in the World Cup, the highlight of which was a creditable 19-46 loss to the Springboks. Their record improved in the next two tournaments, recording wins against Namibia in 2007 and

Romania in 2011 and proving that they were no pushovers in clashes with Ireland and Scotland.

As with all sports after the collapse of the former Soviet Union, Georgian rugby suffered from poverty and lack of resources. But this was partially offset by its links with France and the opportunities for Georgians to play professionally there – by 2013, 17 of the 28 members of the national side that toured Canada were playing for French clubs. By the end of the first decade of the 21st century, Georgia could justifiably claim to be the seventh strongest nation in European rugby, but its economic weakness and lack of a large television market means that despite its dominance of the European Nations Cup it is unlikely to be invited to sit at the top table of the Six Nations.

The rise of Georgia coincided with the decline of Romania. The Romanians had begun the 1980s with a narrow 14-6 loss to the All Blacks in 1981. They also won against both Scotland and Wales, most memorably in Cardiff in 1988, but the greatest moment in Romanian rugby history came in May 1990, when the team defeated France 12-6 in Auch in the Midi-Pyrénées. It marked the end of French coach Jacques Fouroux's national career, the humiliation of defeat being exacerbated by the fact that Auch was also the Little Corporal's birthplace. But within a few years, the seemingly irresistible rise of Romanian rugby was brought to a juddering halt.

The increasing professionalisation of rugby union in the late 1980s and early 1990s undermined the strength of the Romanian game. Its best players were attracted by the generous payments offered by French clubs, leaving domestic rugby bereft. Nor did the Romanian game have access to lucrative television deals. The fall of the Ceauşescu regime in 1989 and the poverty that ensued reduced Romanian rugby to a shadow of its former self.

The collapse of Romanian rugby could not have come at a worse time for the country. Discussions about expanding the Five Nations' tournament began after the game became professional in 1995. The prospect of increased revenue from the only other European nation that possessed both a rugby tradition and a highly developed television market was too great to resist. When the decision to include a new nation was made, it was no contest. Italy, rather than impoverished Romania, got the vote.

If the decision had been made in any other decade, it is unlikely that the Italians would have become the Sixth Nation. Rugby had struggled to regain popularity in post-war Italy, not least because of its associations with the old regime, and it was initially rare to find it played in Italian schools. It slowly regained popularity in smaller cities such as Treviso, Rovigo and L'Aquila that did not have traditions of success in soccer and where rugby could provide a focus for the local community. Rovigo even became known as *una città in mischia* (a city on the scrum). In 1955 the national side visited England to play London Counties in a creditable 22-11 loss at Twickenham but Italian rugby in the 1950s and 1960s lagged far behind the Romanians.[12]

This weakness was not unconnected with the fact that for most of the 1950s a war between union and league had wracked the Italian game. In 1949 a number of clubs had begun discussions with the RFL in England and in 1950 an Italian side led by the former captain of the Italian national rugby union team, Vincenzo Bertolotto, played a nine-match tour against league clubs in France and Britain. Bertolotto had previously captained the RSG Torino rugby union team that won the 1947 Italian championship, and eight of that side provided the backbone of the touring league side. For a short time a Torino team participated in the French rugby league and another tour of England took place in 1954. By that time the Italian league had 12 clubs but, as in France, the game was forbidden from calling itself rugby, instead being known as Gioco di XIII.

The league competition waxed and waned but underwent a revival in the late 1950s. In 1960 two matches took place against the touring Australians, with the Italians losing 37-15 in Padua and 67-22 in Treviso.

By 1961 the Italian league had grown to 18 teams. In May of that year Italian rugby league reached its highest point with a 13-10 victory over the French national amateur side. But pressure from the Federazione Italiana Rugby (FIR) caused the Ministry of Sport to refuse official recognition to the Federazione Amatori Italiani Gioco di XIII and, unable to access government funding, facilities or the schools' physical education curriculum, the league game disappeared and would not be revived until the late 1990s

The victory over league initially did little to improve the position of Italian rugby union. To increase the popularity of the union game, the FIR allowed clubs to recruit unlimited numbers of overseas players, especially *oriundi*, foreigners of Italian descent. By 1971 the Bologna team could boast seven Welshmen, including future British Lion Terry Cobner, while Treviso had numerous Oxford University alumni. There was little attempt to disguise the fact that these players were well remunerated.

To further strengthen the game, regional teams modelled on South African provinces were introduced and in 1975 Welshman Ray Bish was appointed national coach, the first non-Italian appointment. Coaching advice was given by Welsh master coach Carwyn James and French star Pierre Villepreux. But the most important change in the fortunes of Italian rugby would come from outside of the sport and was inadvertently caused by the Italian government's reform of the taxation system in the 1980s.[13]

As part of the liberalisation of the economy, the Ministry of Finance made it lucrative for businesses to sponsor sports teams and competitions by allowing a percentage of company turnover to be spent on tax-deductible 'community projects'. Rugby became a popular community project for some of the biggest names in Italian business. The most prominent example was the fashion company Benetton which essentially purchased the Treviso club, renaming it Benetton Treviso. Other teams' sponsors did not have the cachet of Benetton, one of them resulting in the wondrously titled Pastajolly Trevisum.[14] Brescia benefited from the largesse of future Italian prime minister Silvio Berlusconi's media companies.

This brought huge amounts of money into the Italian game, enabling clubs in the late 1980s to recruit global stars, such as Australian David Campese (who played for Brescia), New Zealander John Kirwan (Treviso) and South African Naas Botha (Rovigo). Although even Italian rugby union was still nominally amateur, this did not prevent the loquacious Campese claiming that Italy had made him rugby's first millionaire. Most importantly from a domestic perspective, the huge rise in playing standards also brought a host of top coaches to Italy and a much more competitive league structure.

The fruits of this new era in Italian rugby were seen in the first rugby union World Cup in 1987 in which the Italians defeated Fiji, heralding their rebirth on the international scene and nudging their way into the consciousness of the soccer-obsessed Italian sports media. The 1990s saw the national side make huge strides forward, beating Argentina in the 1995 World Cup and then defeating France and Ireland for the first time ever in 1997. The passing of the baton of European rugby was symbolically marked by the fact that of the nine matches between Italy and Romania in the 1990s, the Italians won seven. Italy were a shoe-in for the Six Nations.

And with that, rugby union became a little less Anglo-Saxon and a little more European.

22

ARGENTINA AND SOUTH AMERICA: RUGBY ON A SOCCER CONTINENT

If there is one sport for which Argentina is known around the world it is soccer. Perhaps after only Brazil and Italy it is a nation that is synonymous with the World Cup, with stars of incandescent brilliance such as Diego Maradona and Lionel Messi and a fan culture that is as expressive and as intense as any in Europe. Soccer is deeply ingrained within the cultural DNA of the Argentinian nation. Whether played in the sun or in the shade, it is a game loved by all Argentinians.

Yet Argentina's sporting passion could have been so very different. Its first soccer league began in 1891, and in its first ten years the title was won seven times by clubs that also played rugby. In 1899 two of those clubs, Lomas and Belgrano Athletic Club (AC), helped to found the River Plate Rugby Union (which became the Argentinian Rugby Union in 1951). The famous Buenos Aires FC started by playing soccer and then switched to rugby in 1874. As the 20th century dawned, rugby and soccer were neck and neck in the affections of the Argentinian sporting public.

So what went wrong for rugby?

Don't cry for rugby, Argentina

Since the early 1800s British merchants, engineers and businessmen had settled in Argentina to develop its agriculture, build railways and create a banking system to facilitate trade with Britain. Argentinian beef and wool were staples for British consumers across the imperial world. By 1900, it was universally acknowledged as being the most important outpost of what was called the informal British Empire.

Although Argentina was never an official British colony, in many ways its relationship with Britain was as close as that of Australia or Canada. By 1880 the British population of Buenos Aires and its surrounding regions was more than 40,000, boasting its own schools, clubs and networks, just like the British in India, Malaya or Kenya. In 1912 Harrods even opened a branch in Buenos Aires, the only place outside of Britain to be so honoured.

Sport inevitably had a role in this cultural export drive. Sporting clubs appeared in the 1860s as part of the expatriates' social and recreational networks. The first Buenos Aires Football Club started in 1867, as did the Rosario Athletic Club, which was initially founded in order to play cricket. Like Rosario, many were multi-sport clubs that offered British sports like soccer, rugby, cricket, hockey and later tennis and polo.

Naturally, much of the impetus for the adoption of sport came from British teachers. In 1882 one such individual, a Scot named Alexander Watson Hutton, who would become known as the 'father of Argentinian football', brought soccer to the continent's oldest British school, St Andrew's Scots School in Buenos Aires. Similarly evangelist teachers brought rugby with them alongside their copies of *Tom Brown's Schooldays* and the Muscular Christians' certainty of purpose.

As in Europe, sport was increasingly seen as an important aid to nation-building and in 1898 the Argentinian Minister of Justice and Public Instruction decreed that all schools, public or private, had to provide physical education and that each must establish a sports club for current and former pupils. It was the spark that would ignite the sporting passions of the entire population, whether they were Argentinian,

British-born or one of the many thousands of immigrants from Italy who were pouring into the country.[1]

Over the next decade some of the most famous clubs in Argentinian soccer were formed, many of which drew their players and support from outside the English-speaking community. Boca Juniors was founded by working-class Italian immigrants. Atlanta drew much of its support from the Jewish community. Some, such as Independiente and Estudiantes, were breakaways from older clubs. Soccer grew so rapidly in the first decade of the 20th century that in 1912 Argentina joined Chile as the first South American nations affiliated to FIFA.

Rugby stayed aloof from these developments. As working-class Argentinians and other non-British immigrants took up soccer, the British school and alumni clubs that played both football codes gradually abandoned soccer in favour of rugby. Even Alexander Watson Hutton's son, Arnaldo, played rugby as well as his father's soccer. When the first non-British rugby club was formed in 1904 it was by upper-class Argentinian engineering students. The differences between rugby and soccer were also illustrated by their leaders. After 1914, Argentinian soccer never had a British-born president. In contrast, Argentinian rugby had 20 presidents in its first 50 years of existence, only six of whom were were not British.

Two of those British presidents were Edinburgh's Gebbie brothers. Like many other young men from his background, Oswald Gebbie came to Argentina for business reasons, taking up a position with a firm of merchants. At home he had played rugby for Edinburgh Academicals and on arrival in 1902 joined Buenos Aires FC. He captained the Argentina side that played the touring British side in 1910. His brother Tom became president of the River Plate Rugby Union in 1915 and Oswald followed in his footsteps in 1939.[2]

It was not only British players who came. Buenos Aires was part of the global imperial network and attracted men from across the 'British world', especially South Africa. The most famous was Springbok great

Barry Heatlie, an early pioneer of the 3-4-1 scrum formation. 'Fairy', as he was nicknamed because of his imposing size, captained the Springboks in the historic third Test of 1903 when they defeated Britain 8-0 to win their first ever series. He moved to South Africa shortly after and joined the exclusive Gimnasia y Esgrima de Buenos Aires (Gymnastic and Fencing) multi-sport club, for whom he played and coached rugby until 1915.

Confirmation of the importance of Argentinian rugby came in 1910, when John Raphael captained an RFU-organised tour to Buenos Aires with a side consisting of 16 English players and three Scots. Aside from Raphael, only three other players were internationals. Labelled as a 'Combined British' team by their hosts, Raphael's men easily won all six matches, including a 28-3 victory in the international against Argentina. The Argentinian side consisted entirely of players of British origin, including Arnaldo Watson Hutton at scrum-half, and bolstered by Heatlie at number eight. Despite the defeats, the tour helped cement rugby's place in the culture of Argentina's elite.

By the time the next British tour took place in 1927, the game was no longer purely the sport of the English-speaking elite. More than half the Argentinian side that faced the British in the first Test match in 1927 came from Spanish-speaking families, and it was captained by Arturo Rodriguez Jurado, also a talented boxer who won the heavyweight gold medal at the 1928 Olympic Games. The tour was a social success but the Argentinians lost all four Tests heavily. In all, Argentinian sides scored a mere nine points against the tourists in nine games.

But such defeats did not matter. Rugby's roots were now deeply established in Argentina. The Buenos Aires' rugby *Torneo* (tournament) had become an important part of the interwar leisure world of the local professional classes. Nowhere was this truer than in San Isidro, the exclusive northern suburb of Buenos Aires. This was home to the Club Atlético San Isidro (CASI) that won an unprecedented 13 straight championships from 1917. As with other clubs, CASI also had a successful soccer side, but as soccer moved towards professionalism in the 1920s the club eventually abandoned the round-ball game.

In 1935 CASI was rocked by scandal when a group of players were suspended by the club for drunken behaviour during a post-match dinner. Although this was commonplace in rugger clubs around the world, the issue became a continuing source of friction and later that year the suspended players formed their own San Isidro Club (SIC). Eighteen months later the disgraced players gained revenge when the two clubs met for the first time and they won 3-0. The derby between CASI and SIC rapidly became the highlight of the Argentinian club season and continues to capture the imagination of rugby fans.

SIC would also gain fame as the club for which the young Che Guevara would play in the 1940s. Che would also play for Yporá, a club that was part of the Catholic League, an organisation of Buenos Aires rugby clubs outside the River Plate Rugby Union that had been formed by private Catholic schools.

The CASI split wasn't the only controversy that afflicted rugby in the 1930s. In 1932 the Junior Springboks played an eight-match tour of Argentina. At the end of the tour two South Africans, Rybeck Elliot and Wollie Wolheim, decided to return the following year to play for Buenos Aires' Hindú club. But the rugby authorities considered the use of overseas players a form of professionalism and suspended the Hindú club for a season. Elliot eventually returned to play for Hindú and turned out on the right wing for Argentina against the British touring side of 1936 and against Chile in 1938.

The rise of South American rugby

Club rugby in Argentina remained remarkably stable and static all the way through into the 21st century, but after the Second World War Argentina's relationship with Britain was no longer that of an informal outpost of empire. When Juan Perón came to power in 1946 he nationalised the banks and railways, in which British businesses had commanding interests, and sought an independent foreign policy. This was reflected in Argentine rugby's international relationships.

In 1949 France made their first tour of the country, winning all nine matches but only narrowly taking the two Test matches 5-0 and 12-3, thanks in large part to the kicking of the young Jean Prat. They returned again in 1954, winning the two Tests much more easily and ending the tour with a match against Chile. For those Argentinians who still valued the intimate link with Britain, a combined Oxford and Cambridge university side also toured in 1948 and 1955, the later tour witnessing the very first defeat of a touring side by an Argentinian team, when a combined Buenos Aries overcame the visitors 13-8.

The most important development was the staging in 1951 of the first South American nations tournament, El Sudamericano de Rugby, featuring Argentina, Uruguay, Chile and Brazil, which was held in Buenos Aires as part of the first Pan-American Games.

As in Argentina, rugby had been brought to the other three countries by the British and had become a feature of their elite English-speaking schools. Across the River Plate from Buenos Aires, Uruguay's proximity to its northern neighbour meant that it naturally had many shared cultural ties with Argentina and Britain – as generations of British consumers of Uruguayan Fray Bentos corned beef can testify.

Rugby is claimed to have been played in Uruguay's capital Montevideo as early as 1865 by members of the city's cricket club though there is more reliable evidence that a match between British and Uruguayan players took place in 1880. But rugby remained restricted to a small community of elite British expatriates, with Montevideo Cricket Club being the dominant side, and it wasn't until 1951 that the Unión de Rugby del Uruguay was founded.

Even in the 21st century the three most important Uruguayan clubs remain Carrasco Polo Club; Old Boys, a club of alumni of English-speaking schools; and Old Christians, a side formed by alumni of Stella

Maris College, a Roman Catholic school founded by Christian Brothers. Old Christians would find tragic fame in 1972 when the plane carrying them to a match against Old Grangonian in Chile crashed in the Andes, leaving survivors stranded for 72 days, during which they had to resort to eating human flesh to stay alive. (This grim story was the subject of a book, *Alive*, by Piers Paul Read (1974), and a subsequent film of the same name, released in 1993.)

Rugby seems to have been first played in Chile in the 1890s, once again because of British settlers who had moved to the capital Santiago and the major port of Valparaíso to develop trade links, railways and the copper industry. It was not until the interwar years that rugby clubs were formed and the Chilean Rugby Union was established in 1935. In 1936 Argentina visited Chile for the first time, winning both internationals easily.

In Brazil rugby was even more socially elite than in Argentina or Uruguay and the São Paulo Athletic Club became its major stronghold. This was the club that was introduced to soccer by Brazil's 'father of football', Charles Miller. As in Argentina, the popularity of soccer eventually proved too much for the British-educated elite that ran the club and it abandoned soccer in favour of rugby in 1912.

That first Sudamericano was played at the Gimnasia y Esgrima de Buenos Aires club and won, predictably, by Argentina. Indeed, with the exception of 1981, when they did not enter, Argentina have not only won every tournament but have never lost a single match in the competition. Despite reconfiguring the competition several times to reduce the dominance of Argentina, much of the interest has revolved around the battle for second place, which has historically been won by Uruguay or Chile. Brazil finished second in 1964, the only other side to clinch the runners-up spot.

Sadly, the tournament is perhaps most notable for its alarmingly one-sided scores, particularly in 2003 when Paraguay lost 144-0 to Argentina and 102-0 a week later to Chile. Fortunately, the

Paraguayans had a respite in the midweek match against Uruguay, losing by a mere 53-7.

Despite the ease with which the Argentinians dominated South American rugby, the regular round of international matches and incoming tours began to help them cohere into an organised, disciplined team. Better was to come, in large part due to the arrival of South African coach Izak van Heerden. He had been sent to Argentina by Danie Craven, to help them prepare for their tour to South Africa in 1965.

Van Heerden was an outstanding coach, noted for his discipline and attacking style of rugby, and he immediately set to work to improve the forwards' play in the loose and develop the combinations of the backs.[3] The fruit of his work was seen almost immediately. The Pumas, as they were nicknamed by South African journalists who allegedly misidentified the jaguar symbol on the team's shirts, won 11 of their 16 tour games in South Africa. And in the match that signified the start of the transformation of Argentinian rugby, they also defeated a strong Junior Springbok side 11-6 at Ellis Park.

A new era had begun for Argentine rugby. In 1966 the South African under-23 squad, the Gazelles, visited and only narrowly beat the national side in the two Test matches. Even better was to come in 1968 when the great John Dawes-led Welsh side toured, complete with J. P. R. Williams and Phil Bennett. The Pumas won the first Test 9-5 (although the Welsh Rugby Union did not award caps for these matches) and then drew the second 9-9. The following year Scotland toured, losing the first, again uncapped, Test 20-3 before regaining some pride with a 6-3 win. 'It was absolutely brutal,' recalled Scots' front-rower Ian McLauchlan, 'a lot of guys on that tour went out as boys and came back as men.'[4]

The 1970s saw a string of victories and draws with the major rugby powers, beginning with two defeats of Ireland in Buenos Aires and closing the decade with a 24-13 victory over Australia in Brisbane. Regular tours by the major rugby powers on an almost annual basis helped raise the standards of the national team, most notably demonstrated by a 21-21 draw with the All Blacks in Buenos Aires in November 1985.

The Pumas' rise to prominence was guided by their fly-half Hugo Porta, the first Argentinian to achieve international renown. A deadly kicker with gifted instinct for match management, Porta dominated Argentinian rugby in the 1970s and 1980s, eventually winning 58 caps.

He also captained the South American Jaguars team that toured South Africa three times in the 1980s in defiance of the Argentinian government's ban on sporting links with the apartheid regime. It was his seven goals that defeated South Africa 21-12 in 1982. Porta's standing was so high in South Africa that he was even selected for the South African Barbarians. In 1991, the year after his retirement from the game, he was appointed Argentinian ambassador to South Africa.

Porta's influence over Argentinian rugby was so profound that it changed in the way the Pumas played the game. His unerring boot – he averaged over ten points per match – led to the abandonment of the free-flowing play that had been coached by Van Heerden in favour of a forward game based on dominance in the scrum. Indeed, Argentinian forwards became noted for their technical expertise in the scrum, which provided the platform from which Porta's boot could punish opponents.

But the coming of the World Cup in the late 1980s coincided with a decline in Argentina's international standing. The Argentinian Rugby Union's resolute amateurism – at one point it deemed players who left Argentina to play overseas professionals and banned them – cut it off from the intense competitiveness of international rugby union in the early 1990s and it wasn't until 1999 that the side even qualified for the World Cup quarter-finals.

The start of the 21st century saw Argentinian players in high demand from professional rugby union clubs overseas, especially in France and Italy. It was Felipe Contepomi, a surgeon playing for Leinster, and Agustín Pichot, the CASI scrum-half who moved to Stade Français, who led the Pumas to their greatest heights when they finished in third place at the 2007 World Cup. A sign of how far rugby had advanced was the fact that when the quarter-final against Scotland clashed with the Boca Juniors versus River Plate Superclásico, the fiercest rivalry in Argentinian soccer, Boca brought forward their kick-off time to allow its fans to watch the Pumas.

Argentina was now unequivocally one of rugby's top-tier nations, a status that was underlined in 2012 when the Pumas joined with Australia, New Zealand and South Africa to transform the Tri-Nations into the Rugby Championship. In little more than a century, the Argentinian game had gone from being the pursuit of Argentina's elite to the newest member of world rugby's elite. And Latin America, at least in its south, was no longer an exclusively soccer continent.

23

EMPIRE OF THE SCRUM: JAPAN, ASIA AND AFRICA

In *The Singapore Grip*, J. G. Farrell's novel about the decline of the British Empire, the book's central character, Matthew Webb, walks through a hot and humid Singapore on the eve of the Japanese invasion in 1942. He is astonished to see 'thirty grown men engaged in a violently energetic game of rugby a mere few miles from the equator'.[1]

In fact, extreme heat rarely discouraged the numerous businessmen, civil servants, soldiers and sailors who took their passion for rugby with them as they went out to govern the British Empire in Asia and Africa. If trade followed the flag, an oval ball could often be found hard on its heels.

Unlike the 'white dominions' of the Empire, such as Australia, New Zealand and South Africa, rugby was largely a sport of expatriates and the educated elite in the rest of the British world. This was no more apparent than in India, where, despite matches being played in the early 1870s between teams from Royal Navy ships in Calcutta (now Kolkata) and Madras (Chennai), rugby achieved only minor support.

In 1873 a Calcutta Football Club was formed but disbanded due to lack of interest just four years later. The club's funds were withdrawn and the silver rupees melted down to make a 'Calcutta Cup' that was donated to the RFU as 'a challenge cup to be annually competed for by all rugby union clubs' along the lines of soccer's FA Cup. The RFU turned down the offer because of 'difficulties of all clubs playing together' but instead used it as the trophy for the England versus Scotland match.[2]

The game in India was revived by expatriate clubs such Bombay Gymkhana – a multi-sport and leisure club for the British colonial elite – and stimulated by the rotating presence of British Army regiments. In the early 1890s an All-India Cup tournament began and was won in its first season by the 2nd South Wales Borderers.

Bombay (Mumbai) won the cup the following year but over the next 15 years Welsh regiments dominated the competition, interrupted only by a reborn Calcutta club, the West Riding Regiment in 1907 and Madras Gymkhana in 1912. It was only after the First World War that rugby got off the ground in what would eventually become Pakistan, when the Karachi Rugby Union was formed in 1926.[3]

Nevertheless, rugby was confined to expatriate leisure circles throughout the 20th century. It is sometimes said that it was not widely played by Indians because, as a predominantly Hindu nation, religious belief forbade the touching of a leather ball. But this ignores the popularity of cricket and, to a lesser extent, soccer, both of which used a leather ball. The truth is that Indians were never encouraged to play rugby by the colonial elite who believed the game to be theirs and theirs only. It would not be until 1997 that an Indian national rugby team would take to the field, and only in 2003 did the Pakistani national side finally made its international debut.

The only part of the subcontinent in which rugby had a more substantial history was Sri Lanka (or Ceylon as it was known until 1972) where it was introduced by British plantation managers in in the 1870s. In 1874 a group of them working in Kandy in central Sri Lanka founded the Kandy Athletic, Boating, Cricket, Football and Dancing Club. The club became the social hub of the British expatriate population, and the first recorded game of rugby seems to have taken place there in 1876. Three years later a club was formed in Colombo, the capital, and by 1892 the game was popular enough to stage a Colombo versus 'Up Country' match.[4]

Many of Ceylon's elite schools, such as Kandy's Trinity and Kingswood colleges, were founded by Muscular Christian clergy who began to introduce rugby to the sons of local elites by the 1890s. In 1904 a match between Kandy and Colombo with teams of native Ceylonese players was played.

As in South Africa and Fiji, the sport remained racially segregated and when the Ceylon Rugby Football Union was founded in 1908, it concerned itself only with the game as played by the British. Regular rugby matches against visiting navy ships and army regiments became major social occasions for British colonial society in Ceylon. In 1910 the Second Leicestershire Regiment of the British Army played three matches on the island and both the 1930 and 1950 British rugby union Lions interrupted their journeys to play matches in Colombo. In 1955 the New Zealand Colts side played a five-match tour in Ceylon. A side including future All Black greats Colin Meads and Wilson Whineray had little trouble overcoming the opposition and won all five matches comfortably, conceding just eight points.

Within the subcontinent, the strength of Ceylonese rugby could be seen in 1929 when, just three years after entering the competition, Ceylon won the All-India Cup and would remain its strongest side until the 1960s. It was also powerful enough to start its own league competition in 1950, by which time rugby was dominated by native Ceylonese after the British had largely left following post-war independence.

Sri Lanka remains today an enthusiastic outpost of rugby union. At its most popular, important club matches can attract thousands of spectators. Although the national side has never so much as glimpsed a place in the World Cup finals, it is a stalwart of Asian rugby – and a testimony to the real yet often wasted potential of the game in the subcontinent.

Rugby in the 'British Far East'

Rugby's popularity in Sri Lanka was helped by its position on the arterial shipping routes of the British Empire. Those same links also made Malaya an imperial rugby outpost. Valued by the British because of its immense reserves of tin and rubber, Malaya came under British control in 1824. Rugby was imported by the colonial administrators and businessmen towards the end of the 19th century and until the 1920s remained a game played only by Europeans.

As in India, rugby was one of the sports provided by the social clubs founded for the colonists, the most prominent being the Royal Selangor Club in Kuala Lumpur that was formed in 1884 and would dominate rugby until the 1960s. The first club match was played in 1902 between Selangor and the Singapore Cricket Club. In 1921 the visiting British battleship HMS *Malaya* presented a trophy to be played for by Malayan rugby clubs. The annual North versus South Classic was the most important representative match from its inauguration in 1928.

Rugby was also introduced by British teachers into elite schools for native Malays at the start of the 20th century. In 1921 Zain Ariffin became the first Asian to play club rugby and in 1928 Lim Keng Chuan played in the North versus South Classic. But these players were exceptions, being educated in Britain, and Malayan rugby remained rigidly segregated.

The first Malay rugby team appears to have been the Omar club in Sitiawan, formed in 1923. The more famous Negri Sembilan All Blues side was founded two years later. Native Malay sides were excluded from the HMS *Malaya* Cup and in 1934 the All Blues Cup was started for Malay clubs. Perak beat Negri Sembilan 9-0 in the first final and the following year they were joined by teams from Singapore, Johore, Selangor, Kedah and Penang.[5]

Rugby union's place in Malayan society was consolidated during the civil war, or Malayan Emergency as it was known to the British, that engulfed the country between 1948 and 1960. The influx of British and

Commonwealth troops brought dozens of military sides. Most notable was the 1st Battalion Fiji Infantry Regiment which was stationed in Malaya from 1954 to 1956 and were unbeaten in 75 matches, scoring 2,890 points to a mere 293 in reply.

As the war came to an end and it became clear that independence was coming, the segregated structure of rugby started to break down. In 1959 Khek Cheow became the first Asian president of the Malayan Rugby Union. However, many of the former British colonists struggled to come to terms with the equality that independence brought. Leading player and former Malaysian Rugby Union secretary Ng Peng Kong recalled that 'beneath this veneer of sporting rivalry, there was the feeling of prejudice and enmity which commonly pervaded the relations between the Europeans and the locals. The [Selangor] club felt it needed a convincing victory to maintain its perceived superiority and the Asian, resenting this, wanted to turn the tables on the Europeans.'[6]

By the mid-1970s the expatriate community had vacated the leadership of rugby in Malaysia, as the country had become known in 1963, and this shift was symbolically acknowledged in 1975 when the HMS *Malaya* Cup was replaced as the country's leading tournament by the Malaysian Rugby Union Cup. The Singapore Rugby Union, created when Singapore separated from Malaya in 1965, became the home of expatriate rugby. Malaysia became a key component of Asia's rugby leadership, helping to found the Asian Rugby Football Union in 1968 and pioneering ten-a-side rugby as a version of the 15-a-side game.

The expansion of rugby to China followed a similar pattern to elsewhere in Asia. The two strongholds of the game were Shanghai and Hong Kong, the most important trade and financial centres of the British Empire in the Far East. A club was founded by British expatriates in Shanghai as early as 1867 but it was not until the 1870s that a game recognisable as rugby was played. By the 1880s the club was expressing a preference for rugby over soccer but it was only in 1907 that the Shanghai Rugby Union Football Club was formed.[7]

The first rugby match in Hong Kong appears to have taken place in 1885 when a Royal Navy team took on the newly formed Hong Kong Football Club, establishing a template for matches between military sides and local clubs, such as the Hong Kong and Shanghai Bank side, that would be the focus for rugby for much of the 20th century.

In 1910 the Triangular Tournament began as the highlight of the rugby, and social, seasons, pitting against each other the British Army, the Royal Navy and the best Hong Kong players. Of course, all players were European, and rugby remained segregated for decades.[8] The interwar period would be the golden era of rugby in China. In 1924 Shanghai played Hong Kong for the first time, a fixture that would take place 15 more times before 1949, with Hong Kong winning eight times to seven.

French sides also began playing in Shanghai, a port as important to the French Empire as it was the British, and in 1932 the first French club, L'Association Sportive Française, was founded. Touring sides from Australia, New Zealand and Japan were also regular visitors to both cities. The war brought rugby to an end as the Japanese occupation of China was extended into Shanghai's international settlement zone in December 1942 and Hong Kong was invaded.

After the war, the Chinese revolution led by Mao Zedong in 1949 prompted the abandonment of China by the former imperial powers and in 1952 the RFU was informed that Shanghai RFC had disbanded and its remaining funds would be transferred to them.[9] It would only be in the 1990s, when China began to promote sport as a way of improving international relations, that rugby began to be played again.

As the British Empire was being dismantled, Hong Kong's importance as a strategic hub for British business interests increased, and rugby's importance grew, too. In 1952 the Hong Kong Rugby Football Union was formed and the sport became a vital part of the expatriate community. By the 1960s Hong Kong was one of the leading

Asian rugby nations, and regularly finished in the top three of the Asian Rugby championship.

The game still remained an expatriates' sport, and it was not until the 1990–91 season that a native Chinese player was selected for a senior club. In 1994 Leung Yeung-kit became the first Chinese player to represent Hong Kong when he played for the under-24 side and in 1998 Chan Fuk Ping was the first Chinese to gain a full international cap for Hong Kong.[10]

The expatriate nature of Hong Kong provided rugby with its greatest innovation. The Hong Kong Sevens began in 1976, the idea of Ian Gow, a senior manager at Rothman's Tobacco. Sevens was used to raise the profile of the Rothmans brand and as an event for the Far East's business community to network. Cathay Pacific, the Hong Kong airline, jointly sponsored the first tournament which featured teams from Indonesia, South Korea, Australia, New Zealand, Tonga, Japan, Sri Lanka, Malaysia and Fiji.

The venture was an immediate success, becoming a magnet for business networking, corporate junketing and alcohol-fuelled socialising by visiting rugby players. By 1982 its popularity had grown so much that the matches were moved to the Government Stadium, which itself was rebuilt as a 40,000-seat venue in 1994 to accommodate the huge number of people wanting to be part of the tournament. Dominated by Fiji, who have appeared in 24 of the 39 finals, winning 14 of them, the competition has a high profile but little influence on the real business of international rugby union. Its real significance was that it demonstrated the commercial opportunities available to rugby union in the years before the game turned professional. In a very real sense, the Hong Kong Sevens were a microcosm of the future of the sport.

Japan: rugby the way of Bushido

Rugby gained its greatest influence in the Far East not in a colony of the British Empire but in a country that was one of Britain's imperial rivals and a future wartime enemy: Japan.

In 1868 Japan began a profound transformation – known as the Meiji Restoration – that started its journey from a feudal shogunate to a modern industrial nation. Schools and universities that could prepare their students for a new future were vital to the new regime, and Japan's rulers looked to the British education system as a model.

In 1886 the ministry of education introduced elite 'Higher Schools' based on British public schools. Sport became central to the curriculum. The familiar values of Muscular Christianity – stoicism, honour, duty and self-sacrifice – infused Japanese concepts of Bushido and *shitsujitsu gōken* (upright manliness) – and there was no better sport suited to this philosophy than rugby.[11]

British merchants, soldiers and sailors in Japan's major port of Yokohama had formed Yokohama Foot-Ball Club in 1866 which seems to have played rugby rules. In 1874 the London *Graphic* published an illustration of the club playing a match in the shadow of the snow-capped Mount Fujiyama.[12] But Yokohama was an expatriate club with no Japanese members and so rugby came to the Japanese through education. A small number of young men from the Japanese upper classes attended English public schools and universities in the late 1800s and some, like Ginnosuke Tanaka, who was educated at the Leys School in Cambridge and then at Cambridge University, returned home with a love of rugby.

In 1899 Ginnosuke Tanaka and Edward B. Clarke, who had been born in Yokohama but also went to Cambridge, formed a rugby club at Keio University in Tokyo, where Clarke was an English lecturer. In December 1901 the first Japanese rugby team took the field against Yokohama FC. By the end of the First World War rugby was being played throughout Japanese schools and universities. The national high school championship tournament began in 1918 and in the early 1920s regular university rugby matches began.

In 1926 the Japanese Rugby Football Union (JRFU) was founded, bringing together almost 500 schools and clubs in the Kwanto region in eastern Japan and the Seibu region in the west.[13] As well as Osaka, the Seibu region also included Taiwan and Korea, which were then occupied by the Japanese military. The JRFU enthusiastically promoted rugby tours to and from Japan and in 1927 a side from Waseda University toured Australia.

It lost all three of its matches but its main purpose was to develop the links between Japan and the British Empire. At the end of the tour the Japanese Consul-General in Sydney told Australian rugby union president H. D. Wood that 'that this game seems to singularly reflect the true spirit of the British people. Its encouragement, therefore, in my country will help to bring about a better understanding of that spirit by the Japanese people'.[14]

Rugby's popularity in Japan reflected the similarities between British and Japanese cultures. The Japanese zealously guarded the principle of amateurism, in contrast to the professionalism of Japanese baseball, and many of English club rugby's rituals were replicated. For many young Japanese men in the interwar years the game was the perfect introduction to the culture of the empire that still dominated the globe.

In the same year that Waseda went to Australia, Keio University visited Shanghai and was followed by Meiji University in 1928, Waseda University in 1933 and the Imperial Japanese Railways team in 1935. At least two Japanese sides were formed in Shanghai in the 1930s. In 1930 a representative team crossed the Pacific to British Columbia and managed a highly creditable 3-3 draw with the province's representative side in Vancouver.

Two years later the Canadian national side toured Japan and suffered a surprise 9-8 defeat against Japan in the first Test match. Shock turned to disbelief two weeks later when they were ripped apart by an astounding 38-5 in front of 35,000 people in Tokyo. The tour had been financed by the Canadian government to develop trade links and fortunately its off-field endeavours were much more successful than those on the field. At the second Test match the Canadians had been granted the rare privilege of meeting Prince Chichibu, the younger brother of Emperor Hirohito. Chichibu was, in fact, an Anglophile rugby fan, having been educated at Magdalen College, Oxford. After his death in 1953, Tokyo Rugby Stadium was renamed Chichibunomiya Rugby Stadium in his honour.

These international links were extended in 1934 by a touring Australian Universities side that was defeated 14-9 by Japan and in 1936 when a New Zealand Universities team was held to a 9-9 draw. But by this time relations in the Pacific between Britain, the USA and Japan were almost at breaking point.

Rugby was not played in Japan during the Second World War, yet within a few weeks of the Japanese surrender the game was restarted. Schools rugby was resurrected first in Kyoto and major companies like Toshiba and Ricoh followed the example set by the industrial conglomerate Kobe Steel in 1928 and started rugby teams for their workers. In 1949 there were enough company sides to begin a national championship.

Despite this growing importance of company teams, the schools and universities remained the cradle of the Japanese game. In 1952 and 1953 Oxford and then Cambridge universities toured Japan and a steady stream of university sides visited throughout the post-war decades. The All Japan High School Rugby Championship became arguably the most important competition in the game and the annual university match between Meiji and Waseda became the centrepiece of the rugby season, often attracting crowds in excess of 50,000.

The high tide of Japanese rugby occurred in the late 1960s and early 1970s. In 1968 the Cherry Blossoms, as the national side was nicknamed, toured New Zealand and defeated the Junior All Blacks 23-19 in Wellington. In 1971 an England XV toured Japan for the first time ever, and the Japanese narrowly lost the second match 3-6. In 1969 Tokyo hosted the first Asian Rugby Championship tournament, which Japan won. By 1971 there were more than 1,900 rugby clubs across the country.[15] In 1972 Japan defeated the touring Emerging Wallabies side 24-22 and then held them to a 17-17 draw. Japanese rugby was becoming a serious force.

But the Cherry Blossoms stalled in their development and remained rooted in the second tier of international rugby union. Despite its resolute defence of amateurism, by the 1980s Japanese rugby had become rugby's Italy of the East, a place where southern hemisphere players could go to circumvent the amateur regulations of rugby union. Players could be employed by Nippon Steel, Toyota, Toshiba, Suntory or a similar company, be paid a salary and star for the company team, all the while maintaining their amateur status. By the early 1990s, a player could earn in excess of 150,000 New Zealand dollars for a season in Japan with a leading team.[16]

Despite Japan beating Scotland 28-24 in 1989, the standards of the national side did not improve, graphically illustrated by the fact that, though they have appeared in every World Cup tournament since its inception, the Cherry Blossoms have never progressed beyond the group stages, recording just one win and one draw as well as suffering the tournament's heaviest ever defeat, a 145-17 loss to New Zealand in 1995.

Although a regular excuse for poor performance on the international stage is the supposedly smaller stature of Japanese players, the popularity of Sumo wrestling demonstrates that taller and heavier athletes are not rareties in Japan. In fact, it is the narrow segment of society from which Japanese rugby recruits its players that holds it back. As critics have pointed out, Japanese rugby still remains organised on the basis of social connection, with key positions going to those with the best networks rather than the greater skills.[17] In this, it continues the old traditions of amateurism, in which rugby union was primarily a social activity rather than a sporting endeavour.

In addition, Japanese rugby remains rooted in the past. It opposed the 1995 decision to take rugby union into the professional era and it was not until 2003 that its club competition was finally reorganised, with the 'Top League' becoming an elite division of the leading company clubs in an attempt to raise playing standards. In 2007 the JRFU finally appointed a foreigner, the former French international Jean-Pierre Elissalde, as national coach, several years after many top-tier national sides had dispensed with national qualifications for national coaches.

For a nation that modelled itself on the British traditions in order to modernise itself, its lingering commitment to those traditions now holds back its modernisation in the 21st century.

Rugby in French Africa

Just like the British, French colonists took rugby with them as part of their imperial mission, especially in Africa. By 1922, there were 27 clubs in French North Africa that belonged to the Fédération Française de Rugby (FFR), 17 of them in Algeria and the rest divided equally between Morocco and Tunisia.[18]

In Algeria, rugby became part of the sporting and educational world of the *Pied-Noirs*, the French colonial settlers who ran the country until independence in 1962. Its most famous son was Maurice Boyau, the pre-First World War Stade Bordelais player, French national captain and fighter pilot. But the sport's close links with French colonial power and soccer's association with the independence movement – most spectacularly when the Algerian Front de Libération Nationale created an independent national team in 1958 – meant that rugby remained at best a marginal sport in the country.

The game fared somewhat better in Tunisia, where it had been established in the decades after French annexation in 1881. In the early 1900s the game became part of the educational curriculum of the colonial settler colleges and the first club was founded in 1910 named Tunis-Stade Français. A league was formed in 1922 but rugby remained firmly a game for expatriates rather than the Tunisians, and the coming of independence in 1956 led to its collapse.

It was only in 1970, under the encouragement of the FFR, that rugby began again, a revival not unconnected with the French government's development of 'soft diplomacy' and cultural contacts with its former colonies. By the late 1970s, Tunisia was competing comfortably with third-tier European nations and in 1986 even scored a surprise 17-15 win over Romania.

The development of Moroccan rugby followed a similar pattern, although Morocco was strong enough in the 1930s to play and lose four internationals with Spain in 1931 and 1932. When Morocco gained independence in 1956, the Royal Moroccan Rugby Federation was created and joined FIRA, but it would not be until 1967 that it was strong enough to play internationals again, beginning once more with a defeat to Spain.

By the mid-1970s its standards had improved to the extent that Morocco could be included in the top division of the FIRA Trophy. A symbol of the quality of its players was back-row forward Abdelatif Benazzi, who played in the 1999 World Cup final for France and ended his career with 78 French caps after playing his first international rugby for his native Morocco.

Rugby was also taken to the French colonies of West Africa, but in Mali, Senegal and Cameroon the game languished in a very distant second place to the immense popularity of soccer. Ivory Coast fared a little better, reaching the 1995 World Cup in South Africa, but its maulings by Scotland, France and Tonga led to a questioning of the desirability of minor nations playing in the World Cup. Most tragically, Ivorian winger Max Brito broke his neck in a collapsed ruck in the match against Tonga, leaving him a paraplegic.

The one French colony where rugby did become a major force was perhaps the unlikeliest: Madagascar. The French annexed the island in 1896 and in the 1900s the occupying French army began to play rugby.

Civilian clubs were formed and in 1911 the Stade Olympique de l'Emyrne (SOE) club was founded in the Madagascan capital, Antananarivo. Unlike other clubs on the island, it allowed all races to join. By 1925 the club had 180 Malagasy and just two European members. Rugby quickly became popular across the whole population and playing standards rose rapidly, thanks to the influence of French coaches such as Georges Peyroutou, the French international fly-half who played in France's first ever Five Nations win against Scotland in 1911.[19]

By the 1920s Malagasy teams were regularly defeating expatriate sides, much to the irritation of the white colonial teams who felt that the Malagasys won because they were more violent, an echo of precisely the same debate that was taking place in French rugby at the same time, with talk of *Rugby a Muerte*. In 1933 the leading club of the colonists, Racing Club, decided that it no longer wanted to compete against Malagasy sides and withdrew from the championship.[20]

Even the imposition of the Vichy regime's 'National Revolution' on the island in 1941, which sought to return rugby to its 'traditional values', could not restore leadership of the game back to the old clubs. In 1947 an anti-colonial uprising took place to win independence for Madagascar, in which French administrators suspected rugby clubs of lending support to the rebels.

In 1953 a French national XV was sent to the island to play a two-match series against a Malagasy-only representative team. In front of 20,000 people, the French just scraped the first match 12-10, a result greeted ecstatically throughout Madagascar. Fours years later the Madagascar national side toured France for the first time. The Makis, as the team was nicknamed after the local ring-tailed lemur, defeated Toulon and Toulouse but the tour was remembered as much for its political importance as its rugby.

While in Toulouse, the team visited Joseph Ravoahangy Andrianavalona, a Malagasy nationalist leader who had been under house arrest since the 1947 rebellion. Then, in the last match of the tour against Racing Club de Paris, one of the Maki players, Raphaël Randriambahiny, was fatally injured when he hurled himself head-first at a Racing winger heading for the try line.

His body was brought back to be buried in Antananarivo and thousands followed his cortège to the funeral, which became not merely a tribute to a rugby player but a mass outpouring of nationalist feeling. Rugby had become one with native Malagasy pride and the nation's desire for independence.

The island became independent in 1960, but it was another decade before international matches were played. In that time local club rugby became intertwined with national culture, with club matches attracting thousands of spectators. The inauguration of the IRB's Africa Cup in 2000 at last offered the opportunity for regular international competition for Madagascar, one of the few countries in the world where rugby is not just the national sport but where it can also be said, in the words of national coach Bertin Rafalimanana, 'the colour of rugby is black'.[21]

Anglo-African rugby

In English-speaking Africa, rugby had been taken to Rhodesia (which became Zimbabwe in 1979) in the early 1890s when British colonists defeated the Ndebele people and took control of the region. England international William Milton, who, as we have seen, had been instrumental in rugby's emergence in South Africa, was a central figure in the creation of the new British colony and became 'administrator' – quasi-prime minister – in 1897. Not surprisingly rugby was encouraged and the Rhodesian RFU established in 1895. Three years later a Rhodesian team selected from clubs in the two major cities, Salisbury (now Harare) and Bulawayo entered the Currie Cup.[22]

Although touring sides to South Africa regularly visited Rhodesia, the first being the 1910 British Isles team, the country was seen as an extension of South Africa, not least by the South Africans themselves.

The Rhodesian RFU was a member of the South African Rugby Board, and the Springboks regularly cherry-picked from the best Rhodesian players. But this also worked to the advantage of the Rhodesians, as numerous South African rugby players ventured north to take jobs in the administration or business of the colony. This situation would be replicated in Namibia, formally South West Africa, where the game was started in 1916 when the territory was seized from Germany and which would also compete in the Currie Cup until independence in 1990.

Rhodesia's greatest rugby moment came in 1949 when they defeated the touring All Blacks 10-8 in their first match at Bulawayo and then drew 3-3 in the second at Salisbury. Two of the Rhodesian heroes of the series, barnstorming flanker Salty du Rand and centre Ryk van Schoor, were subsequently selected to play for the Springboks against the tourists, and du Rand went on to captain South Africa during the 1956 tour to New Zealand.

The 1949 series was the zenith of Rhodesian rugby: never again was Rhodesia able to defeat a touring side. Rugby remained a sport of the white colonial elite. Although majority rule was obtained in 1980, not until 1987 would a black player represent what was now Zimbabwe. Richard Tsimba made his international debut in 1987 when the Zimbabweans were included in the first rugby union World Cup as a representative of southern Africa, largely because the international sporting boycott of apartheid South Africa made it impossible to invite the Springboks. In 1998 Tsimba's fly-half brother Kennedy became his country's first black captain.[23] But rugby fell into decline in Zimbabwe and its last appearance in the World Cup came in 1991. Its place as the junior southern African representative in the World Cup was taken by Namibia, where rugby remained a predominantly white sport, and which has qualified for every tournament since 1999.

In East Africa, rugby followed a similar path to Rhodesia. It was a hugely popular sport among the British colonists in Kenya, Uganda and Tanzania, and a central part of the curriculum of elite schools. A Kenyan

Rugby Union was created in 1921 and the country soon became a popular destination for touring sides from both Britain and South Africa. In 1929 a strong South African Combined Universities side toured and visiting Royal Navy ships regularly played local clubs.[24]

In 1950 a representative East African side drawn from Kenya, Tanganyika and Uganda was selected for the first time to play the visiting Cape Town University tourists and in 1953 the East African RFU was formed to run the game in the region. As well as organising a touring side, nicknamed the Tuskers, the EARFU also staged representative matches against major touring sides throughout the 1950s and 1960s, including the British Lions, the Barbarians, South Africa and Wales.

The 1955 British Lions played East Africa at Nairobi on their way back from their historic tour of South Africa. They won 39-12 but the game became better remembered for the urban myth that future Ugandan dictator Idi Amin was a replacement on the East Africa team. Amin was indeed a rugby player, turning out for the Nile club and Kampala's Kobs club, but he had no involvement in the 1955 match.

At the start of the 1960s Kenya, Uganda and Tanzania won independence and slowly the nature of rugby began to change. At first, this was most notable in schools. In Kenya, segregated schooling was abolished and African students were admitted to the elite government schools, such as Nairobi School and Lenana School, in which rugby was played. These two schools developed an intense rivalry and incongruously took their nicknames – 'Patches' and 'Changes' – from the A and B sides of American soul singer Clarence Carter's 1970 hit single 'Patches'. It was Nairobi School that provided the first black player to represent East Africa, Mombasa winger Ted Kabetu in 1972, who two years later became the first African to captain a club in the region.[25]

These schools were also the cradle for Kenya's most important international successes, thanks to the creation in the 1960s of schools' sevens tournaments. The short-form game became tremendously popular, and by the late 1980s the Kenyan sevens side could compete seriously in the Hong Kong Sevens. At the end of the first decade of the 21st century Kenya was ranked in the top 12 of the world sevens' sides. Although the game had withered in Uganda and Tanzania, sevens offered Kenya the opportunity to make its mark on world rugby.

Empires may have crumbled and governments changed, but in the 21st century it had become even more common for grown men, and now women, to engage in an energetic game of rugby close to, and even on, the equator.

24

BIG HITS FROM THE SOUTH PACIFIC: FIJI, TONGA AND SAMOA

It started with little fanfare and even less expectation. In 1952 the Australian Rugby Union (ARU) somewhat grudgingly invited the Fijian national side to play a two-match Test series in Sydney. The Fijians had requested £250 to underwrite the expenses of the tour but the Australians saw them as an unproven box office attraction and refused. Despite the snub, the Fijians thought the chance to play their first Test series against a major rugby nation too good to miss.

When they arrived in Sydney in 1952, the tourists therefore had a point to prove. They had beaten the Maori representative team in New Zealand in 1951 and considered themselves ready to stake their claim among the elite of international rugby union.

The first Test match in Sydney seemed to support the reticence of the hosts. Barely 13,500 turned out to watch a rain-sodden match from which the Wallabies emerged 15-9 winners. But the Fijians' open running game appealed to an Australian public raised predominantly on rugby league and the tourists soon gained a reputation for exciting rugby.

Expectations were therefore high when the teams ran out on to the Sydney Cricket Ground on a fine Saturday afternoon in August 1952 to be greeted by 42,000 people ready to watch some spectacular rugby. They were not disappointed.

Just two minutes after the kick-off Fiji thought they had scored a try but the referee pulled them back. Even so, they went in 9-6 ahead at half-time thanks to an ambitious long passing game from their backs and dominance at the line-outs, where they smothered the Australian forwards on the few occasions they won the ball.

But the Wallabies gave as good as they got, outscoring the Fijians by three tries to one, and with just three minutes to go the scores were locked down at 12-12. Then the Fijians won a line-out some 30 yards from the Wallaby line.

They won the ball, fed it out quickly to five-eighth Wame Salabogi who shrugged off a tired tackle to touch down under the posts. His try was converted by Suliasi Vatubua to give Fiji a 17-12 lead as the final whistle approached.

It looked all over for the Wallabies when the Fijians pumped the ball back into touch at the Australian 25-yard line, but for once Australia won clean ball and, taking a leaf from the Fijian book, quickly shipped it wide and broke through the defence. Winger Eddie Stapleton was brought down just feet from line, but managed to lay the ball back to centre Herb Barker who passed it out to wing-forward Col Windon who crashed over in the corner.

It was now 17-15 with the conversion to come. Tension could not have been higher. One kick lay between Fiji and rugby history. Placing the ball almost adjacent to the touchline, Stapleton walked back, steadied himself and ran up to the ball, only to send it flapping weakly into the darkening Sydney sky. The overwhelmingly Australian crowd rose as one with the small coterie of Fijian fans to acclaim the victors.

It was the biggest shock yet in Test rugby. Fiji had won their first ever Test match at only their second attempt. 'By the time we return,' tour manager Les Martin told the *Sydney Morning Herald*, 'Fiji will be as strong as any union side in the world.'[1]

The fabulous fight of the Fijians

Fiji was a British colony from 1874 until it gained independence in 1970. Rugby came to the islands with the British and especially through teachers educated in the traditions of Muscular Christianity. The game had first been played on the islands in the 1880s, most notably when HMS *Diamond* docked in the capital Suva in July 1886, and surprisingly found themselves defeated by a makeshift team of European settlers.[2]

There were also a small but significant number of Fijians who had been educated in Australia and New Zealand and had brought their love of the game back home with them in the early 1900s. Most prominent was Ratu Jone Tabaiwalu, who returned from Wanganui in New Zealand where he had been a student in 1903 and introduced the game to Naililili, a town south of Suva.[3]

It wasn't until 1913 that organised clubs were formed by settlers, stimulated by a visit from the All Blacks on their way back from their high-scoring North American tour. Even a 67-3 drubbing by the tourists did nothing to dampen the enthusiasm for the game.

Rugby quickly became popular among all races on the islands but was divided into two governing bodies, the Fijian Rugby Union (for Europeans), founded in 1913, and the Fijian Native Rugby Union (for the native population), established in 1915. This was no different from the organisation of rugby in South Africa, but from the 1920s the division began to break down, not least because the European clubs quickly found themselves outnumbered by the native Fijian sides.

As part of colonisation the British also imported thousands of indentured labourers from India to work in the lucrative sugar cane industry. Although there were reports of Indian rugby clubs being formed, by the 1930s the sport had become primarily a native Fijian sport. In fact, from Fiji's first international matches in 1924 against Samoa and then Tonga, the national side always comprised native-born Fijians. Much was made by European journalists about the fact that native sides often played rugby in bare feet, but in reality this was a reflection of the poverty of most of the islanders, who could not afford rugby boots.

The game benefited hugely from Fiji's close ties to New Zealand. Auckland University's side visited regularly in the 1920s and rugby spread to every school in Fiji, helped by the fact that most teachers were trained in New Zealand colleges. The closeness of the link bore fruit most successfully in 1938 when the NZ Maori team visited Fiji and, demonstrating the high standard of rugby on the islands, the three-match series was drawn. The visit was reciprocated in 1939 and the Fijians returned home undefeated, winning seven and drawing one match, the crowning glory being the victory over the Maori by a relatively comfortable 14-4.

Following the Second World War, the Fijians scored further victories against the Maori and Tonga, and their reputation for free-flowing rugby earned them their invitation to Australia in 1952. Their fabulous victory in Sydney brought them another invitation in 1954, not least because the 1952 tour made a profit of £7,000, a consideration that radically altered the ARU's perception of the tourists. And once again they tied the Test series 1-1 thanks to another two-point victory at the Sydney Cricket Ground.

The fact that Sydney was a predominantly league city meant that the Fijians' exploits did not go unnoticed in 13-a-side circles around the world. In 1961 England's Rochdale Hornets placed an advertisement for rugby players in Fiji's leading newspaper, the *Fiji Times*. Much to their amazement, the first player to respond was Orisi Dawai, who played in the 1954 victory over Australia and later captained the Fijian national side. Dawai asked Rochdale if a cousin could join him on the journey to the north of England. The club agreed and Orisi arrived at

Manchester airport with none other than the great winger Joe Levula alongside him.

Despite the thousands of miles between the industrial north of England and the South Sea Islands, the two Fijians immediately found themselves at home. Another four Fijians moved to Rochdale over the course of the year, along with Kia Bose, who signed for Wigan, and Johnny Nabou, who joined Blackpool. In 1964 Huddersfield signed four Fijian players and Rochdale began a second wave of Fijian recruitment, most notably Mike Ratu. A small corner of northern England became a Fijian colony, as many of the players settled in Britain when they retired from playing.

Perhaps as a way of stemming the flow of players to rugby league, in 1964 the Fijians made their first ever tour to the northern hemisphere, playing in Wales, France and Canada. They won five of the 12 matches, losing to France and, narrowly, to a 'Wales XV' – the Welsh did not deign to give their game Test-match status – despite scoring six tries, before beating Canada on the way back home.

They were invited back to Britain by the RFU in 1970 as part of English rugby union's centenary celebrations, which also happened to coincide with Fiji finally being granted independence from Britain. They won six of their 14 games, including a memorable 29-6 demolition of a Barbarians side that contained Gareth Edwards, David Duckham, J. P. R. Williams and the nucleus of the British Lions team that would defeat New Zealand just eight months later. Perhaps most importantly, many of the tour games were televised by the BBC, earning the Fijians a global reputation as the entertainers of world rugby union.

Their stature in the game continued to grow. In 1974 they led a full-strength All Blacks side 7-4 at half-time in Suva until a last-gasp Ian Hurst try under the posts won it for the All Blacks by 14-13. Three years later Fiji scored perhaps its biggest triumph when the British Lions were defeated 25-21 in front of 20,000 people in Suva. The Lions were returning home from narrowly losing the 1977 series against the All

Blacks and were outplayed by the home side, who outscored them by five tries to three.

The apparently upward curve of Fijian rugby was halted in the 1980s, primarily because its population of less than a million people was not large enough for television advertisers, young players left for rugby scholarships in New Zealand and the major rugby nations were reluctant to commit to regular matches. The Fijians made it beyond the group stages in the 1987 and 1995 World Cups, only to fall at the first stage of the knock-out phase.

Fiji may have also spent too much time playing seven-a-side rugby. As the sevens circuit expanded in the 1980s, Fiji dominated the short-form game, winning the Hong Kong Sevens seven times in its first 20 years. Yet that was not translated into 15-a-side success. Living on a constant diet of wafer-thin defences and wide-open spaces did nothing to strengthen the national side for the rigours of an 80-minute, 15-a-side test of physical and mental strength. And despite sevens being a lucrative business for the IRB, the amateur regulations meant that little of that wealth found its way to the players.

In response, attracted by the burgeoning popularity of rugby league across the Pacific Islands and aware of widespread discontent among Fijian players, local rugby journalist Culden Kamea organised a Fiji seven-a-side team for the 1992 Nissan World Rugby League Sevens tournament held in Sydney.

Led by the national captain, Alivereti Dere, ten of Fiji's biggest rugby stars joined Kamea's team. League suited their playing style and they romped away with the bowl competition. Some players, like future Canberra star Noa Nadruku, joined Australian clubs but many returned to Fiji and started rugby league clubs themselves.

Three years later, the Fiji national team made its debut in the 1995 rugby league World Cup and astonished the game by crushing South Africa 52-6 in their first match. The growth of Pacific Islander immigration from the 1980s into Sydney and Auckland meant that the Bati, as the Fijian league side was nicknamed, could draw on large numbers of Fijian-heritage Australians and New Zealanders whose parents or grandparents were born in Fiji. Stars like Parramatta's Jarryd Hayne and Brisbane's Petero Civoniceva enabled the national side to reach the semi-finals of the 2008 and 2013 World Cups before eventually going down on both occasions to Australia.

As if to demonstrate that the two codes could be successful together, the high point of modern Fijian rugby union came at the same time as the rise of Fijian league, at the 2007 rugby union World Cup. Fiji scored a memorable 38-34 win over Wales, after racing to a 25-3 lead and then overcoming a Welsh fightback through a try by the prop Graham Dewes with just three minutes left to play.

It was one of the great World Cup matches and set Fiji up for a quarter-final with South Africa. Another shock seemed to be on the cards when the scores were level at 20-20 with 20 minutes to go, but the Springboks' big-match experience eventually told and they ran in two more tries to win 37-20, on their way to lifting the World Cup itself.

However, once again the Fijians could not build on this success. The 2011 World Cup saw them go home with nothing more than a solitary win over Namibia. Marginalised by the financial power of the major rugby nations and weakened by the loss of young players to overseas rugby and employment opportunities, the roller-coaster ride of Fijian rugby was set to continue.

Tongan trials

Twenty-one years after their famous 1952 victory over the Wallabies had marked the entrance of Fiji on to the stage of world rugby, another Pacific Island nation announced itself to the world with victory over Australia. This time it was Tonga, whose national team ran out on to the pitch at Brisbane's Ballymore Stadium on 30 June 1973 with just one previous Test match against a major nation and a squad widely reported to be tired and homesick. Invited to Australia to mark the golden jubilee of Tongan rugby, the team had lost 30-12 to the Australians in Sydney the previous week, but as soon as the ball was kicked off it was clear the story would be quite different this time.

The Tongans dominated from start to finish, controlling the rucks and carving up the Australian defence with deft long passes and dazzling combinations. Tries from centre Tali Kavapalu and winger Sami Latu saw them go in 8-7 up at half-time.

It got worse for Australia in the second half. The Tongans touched down twice more, squandered more opportunities and missed four more kicks at goal but still overwhelmed the Australians 16-11. It was the greatest day in Tonga's rugby history.

Indeed, rugby had a long history in Tonga. Although the islands were never officially a colony, as the British Empire extended its influence into the South Pacific in the 19th century the game was introduced to Tonga by British missionaries and teachers. Tupou College, Tonga's leading boarding school, was founded by English clergyman James Moulton, who had also been the first headmaster of Sydney's Newington College. Newington was one of the first Australian schools to play rugby and Moulton took its spirit of Muscular Christianity with him to the islands.

The years after the end of the First World War saw greater links being forged between New Zealand and the Pacific Islands, and the development of air travel and radio meant that regular international matches could be arranged between the island nations. In 1924 the first ever Pacific international series took place with Tonga and Fiji playing three matches in the Tongan capital Nuku'alofa. The series was drawn, each side winning one and the third finishing 0-0. The contests continued throughout the 1920s, most notoriously the third match of the 1928 series that was abandoned after a free-for-all broke out among the players in the second half.

Rugby soon came to occupy a central position in Tongan life. The Tongan Rugby Football Union was founded in 1923 and its first president was Prince Tugi, a senior member of the Tongan royal family. His son, who would eventually be crowned Tāufa'āhau Tupou IV, continued the rugby connection both as president of the TRFU and as a student at Newington College.[4]

For the next four decades the Tongans were restricted to matches against Fiji and Samoa. In 1960 they played and won their first game against New Zealand Maori and in 1969 they toured New Zealand but only playing provincial sides. It wasn't until 1973 that they were allowed a glimpse of the top table of international rugby when they were invited to Australia for what would turn out to be an historic tour.

Tonga's 1973 victory over the Wallabies meant that big things were expected from them in 1974 on their first tour to Britain. But despite having Carwyn James as their coaching adviser they won only one of their ten matches. On their way back home they despatched Canada 40-14, but for the next decade played only their traditional South Pacific opponents. Although they qualified for the first World Cup in 1987 the Tongans lost all three group matches and did not qualify for the 1991 tournament.

The promise of 1973 never materialised. The lack of a structured international season meant that the Tongans, like the other South Pacific nations, could not develop and measure themselves against the leading rugby nations. The increasing power of television money meant that, from the 1980s, internationals were always arranged with one eye on television ratings – and with a population of barely 100,000, Tonga was of little interest to TV schedulers or advertisers.

But the South Pacific Islands were also changing. From the 1960s the 'whites-only' immigration policies of Australia and New Zealand were reformed and, attracted by jobs and a higher standard of living, thousands of Tongans, Samoans, Fijians and other islanders made their way to cities like Sydney and Auckland. Many went in the opposite direction to the USA – leading to a number of Tongans, such as the Baltimore Ravens' Spencer Folau, playing American football in the NFL – and by 2004 around half of all Tongans lived abroad.

In the 1990s many of the children of this first wave of Tongan emigrants opted to play for the country of their birth rather than that of their heritage, perhaps most famously Jonah Lomu for the All Blacks in rugby union and Jim Dymock in rugby league for the Australian Kangaroos. It was the rise of the Tongan population living in Sydney, and to a lesser extent Auckland, that led to the development of rugby league in Tonga in the mid-1980s. Like Dymock, working-class Tongans living in Sydney largely gravitated to rugby league. Combined with the increased exposure of league on television, the experience of Tongan league players led to the establishment of the Tongan national rugby league side in 1986, when they reached the semi-final of league's Pacific Cup.

The increasing professionalism of rugby union in the 1980s also led to many talented Pacific Island rugby players emigrating to make the most of their skills. The famous Wallaby number eight Willie Ofahengaue played for New Zealand schoolboys but was forced to move to Australia, rather than return to Tonga, when the NZ immigration authorities refused to allow him back into the country in 1988. Scholarships were offered to Tongan schoolboys by elite rugby-playing schools in New Zealand, resulting in a talent drain of young players from the islands.

As is the case with European soccer clubs' recruitment of African footballers, many commentators sympathetic to Tonga and the other islands have accused New Zealand rugby union in particular of cherry-picking the best talent and tying young players to New Zealand instead of their homeland. Some have even compared the tactics of recruiters to 'blackbirding', the 19th-century practice of tricking Pacific Islanders into becoming indentured labourers and forcing them to work in the sugar cane fields of Fiji or Queensland in Australia.

When rugby union legalised professionalism in 1995 Tongan rugby was swept into a wild tempest of desperate lows, such as the 102-0 defeat at the hands of New Zealand in 2000, and dizzying highs, most notably their 19-14 win in the 2011 World Cup over the eventual runners-up, France. For a nation situated in the world's biggest ocean, such storms had become part of life, and so they would be in rugby.

A tale of two Samoas

Tonga had become a constitutional monarchy under British influence and, despite being nominally independent, had remained an integral part of the British South Pacific. But Western Samoa had suffered the bloody consequences of imperial rivalry.

Coveted by Britain, Germany and the USA for both strategic and economic reasons, in 1899 the Samoan islands were divided into American Samoa in the east and German Samoa in the west. But less than a month after the outbreak of world war in 1914, New Zealand annexed German Samoa to create its first colony, Western Samoa (which became Samoa in 1997).

New Zealand's occupation was disastrous for the Samoan people. Around a fifth of the population died of influenza in 1918 and 1919 as a result of a New Zealand ship being allowed to dock despite a quarantine order to combat the global influenza pandemic that followed the war. Then, in 1929, the police shot dead 11 peaceful demonstrators, among them high chief Tupua Tamasese Lealofi, who were demanding an end to colonial rule.

Unsurprisingly, New Zealand educators' attempts to introduce rugby were not immediately successful. Marist Brothers' teachers took the game to Catholic schools but the sport was slow to develop, despite a governing body being formed in the capital Apia in 1924. Only five Test matches, against Fiji and Tonga, were played between 1924 and 1955.

In fact, it would be the children of immigrants to New Zealand who became the first prominent Samoan rugby players. The first was Frank Solomon, who was born in American Samoa in 1906 and moved to Auckland in 1921. In 1931 he made his debut for the All Blacks and was part of the first New Zealand side to lift the inaugural Bledisloe Cup.

Significant immigration from the islands to New Zealand began in the 1950s. Among their number were the parents of Bryan Williams, who would become one of the All Blacks' greatest wingers. He was born in Auckland and like many Polynesians in the city began by playing rugby league. He switched to union and became an All Black in 1970 aged just 19. This was no ordinary All Black cap. Along with Maori Buff Milner, Blair Furlong and Sid Going, Williams was the first non-white player to be selected for an All Black tour to South Africa, when the South African government made Williams and his three Maori teammates 'honorary' whites for the duration of the 1970 tour. He scored a try on his debut in the first Test in Pretoria and went on to play a further 37 All Black Test matches. Known to all as Bee-Gee, he would become one of New Zealand's best-loved players.

Many other Aucklanders of Samoan heritage gravitated to the city's inner-city rugby league sides. Stand-off Fred Ah Kuoi had been born in Apia but moved to Auckland with his parents in 1962. He played for Auckland's Richmond club, made his debut for New Zealand in 1975 and then became one of the first global rugby warriors, playing for North Sydney Bears in Australia and Hull FC in Britain.

Similarly, Olsen Filipaina was born to Samoan parents and made his debut for the New Zealand league side in 1977. He then moved to Sydney to play for Balmain, Eastern Suburbs and North Sydney but in 1988 captained the Western Samoan team that reached the final of the rugby league Pacific Cup, a side composed predominantly of players from Samoan families in Auckland and Sydney.

By the 1990s, Samoa was an emerging power in both rugby codes. In 1986 Wales toured the South Pacific and defeated Western Samoa 32-14 in a match that was hard fought in every sense. Although the team was not invited to the 1987 World Cup, they qualified for the 1991 tournament. It was to be arguably the most memorable campaign in the competition's short history.

Based in Pool Three alongside Australia, Argentina and Wales, the Samoans were expected to finish last. Few expected anything but a home win when they took on the Welsh at Cardiff Arms Park. Eighty minutes later, Western Samoa had turned the rugby world upside down with a 16-13 victory. It could have easily been more. 'Thank God we weren't playing all of Samoa,' one Welsh wag wisecracked.

The men in blue then went toe-to-toe with Australia. Neither side could cross the other's line but Michael Lynagh's boot gave the eventual World Cup winners a 9-3 win. From demonstrating their defensive solidity, the Samoans then highlighted their attacking skills with a 35-12 demolition of Argentina. They were now in the quarter-finals to face Scotland, who had won their third Grand Slam the previous year. But it was a match too far for Samoa, who were defeated 28-6.

This was no flash in the pan. They reached the quarter-finals again in the 1995 and 1999 World Cups, defeating Wales once more in 1999. They scaled even greater heights in 2011 with an historic 32-23 victory over the Wallabies in Sydney, the obligatory humiliation of Australia that was the rite of passage for all the Pacific rugby nations.

And, once more proving that success could be achieved in both codes of rugby at the same time, the Samoan national league side rose to prominence in the 1990s. They played in their first rugby league World Cup in 1995, overwhelming France 56-10 and then losing to Wales 22-10 in Swansea in an epic encounter with a side bolstered by former All Blacks John Schuster and Inga Tuigamala, who was playing for his native country for the first time. The Samoans reached the World Cup quarter-finals in 2000 and 2013, and in 2014 became the first Pacific

Island nation to qualify for rugby league's Four Nations, alongside league's big three of Australia, England and New Zealand.

Unlike Fiji and Tonga, the Samoans weathered the storm of professionalism in rugby union without serious crises and had also maintained their place among league's leading second-tier nations. Yet the gap between Samoa and the leading rugby nations was no closer than it had ever been. For all the brilliance of the Pacific Islanders' play, the reality of rugby's brave new 21st century world of television-driven commercialism would lock them out of the riches they deserved.

25

THE USA AND CANADA: RUGBY'S NORTH AMERICAN DREAM

Rugby matches were few and far between in America in the 1930s. The one place where a fan could reliably see a game was in Los Angeles, where the British expatriate community around Hollywood had nurtured the game alongside cricket, strawberry jam and other reminders of their colder, greyer home five and half thousand miles away.

But, however surprised a casual observer may have been at the sight of a rugby match taking place among the palm trees and endless highways of LA, it was nothing to the shock they may have felt when they caught sight of one of the touch judges. For there, flag in hand running the line, they would have seen the man whose face would forever be known as that of Frankenstein's monster: Boris Karloff.

In fact, Karloff, who was born William Pratt in London and attended Merchant Taylor's School, was a well-known rugger fanatic. He had helped establish Hollywood RFC in the early 1930s and became president of the Southern Californian Rugby Union in 1937. Without his efforts and that of similarly dedicated individuals across the USA, rugby in America would have sunk without trace.

American rugby: From Boris Karloff to George W. Bush

If ever a sport experienced a complete evaporation of promise it was rugby in America. The US side that won the gold medal at the 1924 Olympics returned home to almost complete silence. If they had not had the tangible proof of their gold medals, their triumph against the odds in Paris could have seemed like a sporting daydream. The team arrived back in California and promptly disbanded. It would be another 52 years before an American national rugby team would take to the field.

Rugby was barely played in America in the 1920s. This was the golden age of college gridiron football, when the new medium of radio brought the game into the homes of millions of Americans, making colleges like Notre Dame, Georgia Tech and Nebraska household names. College football was also vocal about its amateur principles, if not necessarily their implementation, removing one of rugby's key claims to uniqueness.

When rugby revived in the 1930s, it was largely because of its British connections. In Southern California the game was resuscitated by members of the British expatriate community. In 1932 San Francisco-based players formed a Northern Californian RFU. On the East Coast, clubs were formed in 1930 in New York and at Harvard and Yale universities by Englishmen looking to play the game they had learned at home, and something of a regular season began to come into existence, supplemented by games with teams from Canada and, in the mid-1930s, annual spring break trips to Bermuda for its rugby tournament.[1] In 1934 seven sides formed the Eastern Rugby Union.[2]

In Chicago, the game was introduced in the early 1930s by way of the Illinois Cricket Association. Its president, Karl Auty, was a member of the rugby-playing Auty family of Yorkshire's Heavy Woollen District, of whom Wilf Auty had captained the Batley Northern Union team in the early 1900s and Richard Auty played rugby union for England in 1935. The British connection was also instrumental in the birth of rugby

359

in St Louis when history professor Edmond Hoogeworf arrived at the university from England in 1932 and set about organising the St Louis Ramblers rugby club.

In 1934, after being given permission by the IRB, Cambridge University, including Wilf Wooller who had made his debut for Wales the previous year, crossed the Atlantic to play four matches against three Ivy League universities – Harvard, Princeton and Yale – and an Eastern representative side.[3] Each was won easily by the Light Blues. Such was the success of the venture that plans were put in place to bring Oxford University over in 1935.

The proposal came to nothing and American rugby fragmented into unconnected regional groups. One of the sport's biggest advantages was its potential to provide meaningful international competition to the US, something that neither American football nor baseball could do, but the lack of an effective central organisation meant that no internationals could be organised. In 1938 the two Californian unions joined together, partly to consolidate the game in the state but also to stimulate international interest.

In June 1939, desperate to halt the decline of rugby and no doubt frustrated by the IRB's failure to provide an international profile for the American game, the secretary of the Californian Rugby Union David Nash wrote to the Rugby Football League in England. He explained that California was considering abandoning union for league and asked 'for the Council's views on the possibility of terms being arranged'.

At that year's annual RFL conference the chairman G. F. Hutchins declared that he was confident and happy 'at the prospect of America coming into the Rugby League'.[4] It was not to be. Less than two months after the annual conference, war broke out in Europe and so disappeared the possibility of Californian rugby switching to the 13-a-side game.

Nevertheless, the lure of international contests and the similarities between gridiron and the league game continued to exercise a fascination for American sports promoters in the 1950s. In 1952 former UCLA All Star lineman and budding sports entrepreneur Mike Dimitro put together a side with the intention of entering the inaugural Rugby League World Cup in 1954. Dimitro had seen rugby league in wartime Australia as a serviceman and in 1953 his 'American All Stars', a 22-strong team of gridiron converts, including the Pittsburgh Steelers starting quarterback Gary Kerkorian, arrived in Sydney for a tour of Australia and New Zealand. Despite never having played the game before, the All Stars won six of their 26 games.

Al Kirkland, their star player, adapted so well that he was signed by Parramatta and became a first-team regular for them in 1956 before emigrating to England to play briefly for Leeds. Vince Jones, the tourists' vice-captain, went on to play rugby union for Oxford University against Cambridge. But the All Stars were left out of the inaugural rugby league World Cup later that year, partly because the British league authorities were negotiating with Los Angeles journalist Ward Nash. Nash believed that rugby league could offer the US serious international competition and wanted to use American footballers to play international league matches in their off-season. Nash was also well connected. He was a friend of the vice-president of the USA, a former college football player, who wanted to meet with rugby league representatives. His name was Richard M. Nixon.[5]

Nixon never became involved in rugby and Nash never got further than organising a couple of exhibition matches between Australia and New Zealand in California in 1954. But by this time interest in rugby union was reviving, thanks to the visits of the 1948 Wallabies and the 1954 All Blacks. Both played two matches in California on the way home from their European tours and helped rekindle interest in the universities. In 1952 the Dartmouth College rugby club was re-established in New Hampshire and in 1958 they became the first American rugby team to tour Britain.

The Dartmouth tour to Britain was financed by President Eisenhower's 'People to People' cultural exchange programme. Part of the US government's Cold War diplomatic push to take American values to the rest of the world, Dartmouth's tour got significant publicity in the US press and demonstrated how other clubs could become part of rugby union's international network. From a handful of clubs in 1954, the Eastern Rugby Union grew to 29 by the start of the 1960s.[6] Over on the West Coast, the annual Monterey tournament was started in 1959 for clubs in California and British Columbia in Canada.[7]

The US game inadvertently had a major tactical impact on rugby, thanks to American Rhodes scholar Pete Dawkins. Dawkins played on the right wing for Oxford in the 1959 Varsity match, when it was still customary for wingers to throw the ball into the line-out. He decided to throw the ball from the shoulder, quarterback style, rather than the usual round-arm or under-arm throw. It proved to be highly accurate and helped Oxford win the match. Dubbed the torpedo throw by the British press, Dawkins' technique soon became the accepted way of throwing the ball into the line-out.[8]

The 1960s was a revolutionary decade around the world and a transformative period for American rugby union. The sport grew rapidly in American universities, finally finding itself a niche in collegiate sport. This was a time when American sport was in a state of upheaval. College sports were being desegregated and racial barriers removed. In this uncertain world, rugby seemed to represent a tradition free of political controversy. Much of its appeal was based on its reputation for being played by those for whom partying was at least as important as playing. It is thus not surprising that the most famous American to play rugby in the 1960s was Yale University full-back George W. Bush, the 43rd president of the United States.

Rugby also had the advantage that it was generally not part of the college-funded sports on university campuses. The introduction of the equal opportunity legislation called Title IX in 1972, which laid down that colleges had to spend equal amounts on men's and women's sports, meant that minority sports such as rugby often had their funding withdrawn. No longer answerable to college funding authorities, rugby could conduct itself as it chose.

In June 1975 the USA RFU, known today as USA Rugby, was founded, the first national governing body that American rugby had ever had. Existing league and regional structures were consolidated and greatly expanded over the next two years. The following year, America fielded an international rugby side once more when the Eagles, as it was nicknamed, played Australia in Los Angeles 64 years since the two sides had previously met at Berkeley.

The Eagles quickly became part of rugby union's expanding second-tier international circuit, regularly playing their Canadian rivals north of the border. In 1978 they recorded their first international win, a 12-7 victory over Canada in Baltimore. In little more than a decade the Eagles established a strong enough reputation for them to be invited to the inaugural 1987 Rugby World Cup. In their first match they defeated Japan 21-18 and competed well against Australia and England in their group. They defeated Japan again at the 2003 World Cup and in 2011 defeated their old superpower rival Russia 13-9. By that time there were over 88,000 registered rugby union players in the USA, slightly more than in Australia.

American rugby league also re-emerged in the late 1980s. In 1987 the first league international between the USA and Canada was staged and the national side took part in the 1995 and 2000 Rugby League World Cup Emerging Nations tournaments. In 2013 they reached the Rugby League World Cup proper, where, against all expectations, they topped their group and reached the quarter-finals. Yet, if union remained a marginal game on the American sports landscape, league's smaller footprint was confined to the margins of the margins.

Both union and league, as well as American football, also benefited from the rise in Polynesian immigration to the United States from the

1990s. American Samoans had long had unrestricted access but the increased pace of global population movement in the 21st century, as in Australian and New Zealand rugby, widened the pool of players available to the game beyond its traditional constituency of the universities and the university educated.

Perhaps most importantly, for a country in which the Olympics is the pinnacle of international sport, the entry of rugby sevens into the Olympic Games offers American rugby its greatest-ever opportunity. Yet as the profile of rugby grows, the seemingly unshakeable stranglehold of American football on the nation's sporting consciousness also continues to tighten. The efforts of American rugby, of whatever code, to gain a place in the nation's sporting consciousness remains as it always has been, an heroic struggle.

Maple-leaf rugby

As befits its geography, Canada in the 20th century found itself torn between the rugby that was played by its fellow 'white dominions' of the British Empire and the gridiron game that dominated its American neighbour to the south.

Indeed, for the first third of the 20th century there were two sports claiming the title of 'rugby': rugby union and Canadian gridiron football. To make things even more confusing, the governing body of Canadian football was called the Canadian Rugby Union, while the rugby organisation was called the Rugby Union of Canada.

By the 1920s the popularity of the native gridiron game had pushed what became known as 'English rugby' to the very fringes of the Canadian sporting scene, with it being played seriously only in British Columbia in the far west and Newfoundland and the Maritime Provinces on the east coast. In 1929 Canadian football severed its last link with its parent game and legalised the forward pass, bringing it closer to American football, but it was not until 1967 that it finally abandoned the title of Canadian Rugby Union.

The 1929 adoption of the forward pass coincided with the founding of the Rugby Union of Canada. A Canadian team had played in the 1919 King's Cup military tournament immediately after the First World War, but had fared badly, losing all five matches and scoring a solitary try to 31 conceded. The 1925 and 1936 All Black tourists stopped off in British Columbia to play two matches on their way home from Britain but these were essentially exhibition matches. The true level of Canadian rugby was seen in 1932 when, underwritten by the government, the national team toured Japan and lost both Test matches to the Cherry Blossoms.

Outside its British Columbia heartland, rugby floundered in the 1930s and 1940s. To some extent this reflected the gradual decline of Canada's imperial link with the British Empire. As its close ties to Britain began to fray, and the link with American culture and sport became stronger, rugby's importance also faded. Instead, nationalistically minded Canadians looked to ice hockey and Canadian football to express their patriotism.

In eastern Canada rugby union had been so decimated by Canadian football that in 1943 rugby officials in the Maritime Provinces decided to abandon rugby union for rugby league. In late 1943 the Rugby Football League in Leeds received a letter from John MacCarthy, the secretary of the Halifax (Nova Scotia) Rugby Union. He told the RFL that they had 'changed over from rugby union to rugby league' and asked for rule books to be sent to them.

However, the RFL couldn't provide any practical assistance until after the war and it wasn't until 1946 that the rugby strongholds of Nova Scotia, New Brunswick and Prince Edward Island made the switch as a whole. Nevertheless, the new game was quickly hailed as a success, having, in the word of the *Halifax Herald*, 'speeded up play and eliminated much that was deadly dull under the old Rugby Union code'.[9] Despite this positive start, rugby league also began to struggle in the 1950s as television helped Canadian football to increase its popularity. When British RFL secretary Bill Fallowfield visited in 1954, he found the game in very poor health and Canadian rugby league withered on the vine, finally dying out altogether in the early 1960s.[10]

But by this time, rugby union had started to reclaim some of the territory it had lost. In 1957 the Barbarians made a six-match tour of the country, taking in Ontario and Quebec as well as the British Columbia heartland. In March 1958 the Wallabies arrived in Vancouver, following in the footsteps of the 1948 Wallabies and the 1954 All Blacks. The 1948 and 1954 tourists had each easily won their games but this time, British Columbia triumphed over the Wallabies in one of the most surprising tour matches ever.

The Wallabies had lost all five Test matches in Europe and the match in Vancouver took place just six days and a long flight after a 19-0 defeat to France in Paris. The Canadians surprisingly led 5-0 at half-time and despite a fightback by the embarrassed Wallabies in the second half British Columbia hung on to win 11-8. The 6,643 crowd at Vancouver's Empire Stadium could barely believe their eyes. Canadian rugby had begun a new era.

Over the next decade, the game was reorganised and in 1962, 60 years after Canada's first and only tour to the British Isles, the national side undertook a 16-match tour of Britain. The Canadians managed just one victory and a draw but the tour raised the profile of the game at home. In 1965 the national rugby union, which had been dissolved in 1939, was re-established.

Part of this reinvigoration of the game was due to a new wave of British immigrants bringing their love of the sport with them, along with coaching and administration experience. Among English-speaking Canadians, the game started to claim its place in elite schools and among the professional classes. The ease of international travel meant that rugby also became a way of forging new links with the English-speaking world. Yet, despite the prominence of France in international rugby, the game made little headway among French-speaking Canadians, as a glance at the almost entirely Anglo-Saxon names of players in national sides over the years demonstrates.

The rebirth of Canadian rugby was announced in the most dramatic fashion on 14 September 1966, when, once again at the Empire Stadium, British Columbia defeated the British Lions, who were returning home from their tour of Australia and New Zealand. The British Columbia team boasted a number of players who played both rugby and Canadian football and who were not intimidated by the British pack, even one led by Irishman and future Lions' captain Willie John McBride.

As if to confirm the Canadian victory in the battle of the forwards, the decisive try of the game was scored by loose-head prop Peter Grantham. Scrum-half Ted Hunt stole the ball near the British Columbia try line and raced 80 yards before cross-kicking towards the Lions' goal, where the ball was scooped up and plonked down under the posts by Grantham. Full-back Don Burgess converted and the match ended in a historic 8-3 win to British Columbia.

It would not be the last time British Columbia would defeat a national side – they would also beat Scotland in 1985 and Japan in 1976 and 1989 – but this was a triumph that announced Canada as a serious rugby force. In 1983 the national team recorded its first win over a European side when it defeated Italy 19-13, and it was on the basis of its improving form that Canada was invited to take part in the inaugural Rugby World Cup in 1987.

The side started on the front foot with a completely unexpected and sweeping 37-4 victory over Tonga but they were brought down to earth with consecutive 40-point defeats by Ireland and Wales. But the vast improvement that had taken place over the previous two decades was highlighted in 1990 when Argentina were defeated home and away, and then at the 1991 World Cup when the side reached the quarter-finals.

The 1990s were the golden age of Canadian rugby. The success of the 1991 World Cup was followed by a victory over a touring England

XV in May 1993, a last-minute 26-24 victory over Wales in Cardiff in November 1993 and an 18-16 win over France the following year. At the heart of this rise to prominence was Gareth Rees, unquestionably the greatest Canadian to play the game.

Rees's Welsh parents had been part of the post-war wave of British immigration that had such an important impact on Canadian rugby. His father had played for London Welsh, and Rees himself had been educated at the self-described rugby powerhouse of St Michael's University School in British Columbia. He made his debut for Canada at 19 in 1986 against the USA and then played a key role in the 1987 World Cup campaign.

Rees was instrumental in shaping and guiding the Canadian team throughout the 1990s, playing in all of the first four World Cups and masterminding victories over the England XV, France, in which he kicked all of his side's points, and Wales, where he converted Alan Charron's try with the last kick of the game to win the match.

Much like Hugo Porta in Argentina, Rees's kicking ability and tactical nous meant that the Canadian strategy was based around him and his strengths as a kicker. But unlike Porta, who only ever played club rugby for Banco Nación, Rees became a major figure in British club rugby, playing for Wasps, Harlequins, Bedford and Newport, as well as a short spell in France with AS Mérignac.

His transnational career anticipated the globalised, professional careers that many players would follow after 1995 and the legalisation of professionalism. Yet the platform for Canadian rugby that Rees and his teammates had established in the 1990s did not turn out to be a springboard. As with so many other emerging nations, the advent of professionalism cut the ground from under the potential new rugby power.

Unable to compete in terms of finance and resources with Canadian football and ice hockey at home or the rugby superpowers abroad, the promise of the 1990s stalled.

New directions from North America

If the United States and Canada were unable to break into rugby's global elite, they did play a crucial role in challenging the very nature of the game. In 1976 a group of Canadian quadriplegic athletes in Winnipeg designed a new sport for wheelchair users, male and female. It was initially called Murderball because, unlike existing wheelchair sports, it allowed its players to crash their chairs into each other to stop their progress or to dislodge the ball. This was rugby – but on four wheels.

Wheelchair rugby quickly spread to the United States and the first team was formed at the University of North Dakota in 1981, the same year that the sport began in Australia. In 1989 Toronto hosted a triangular tournament between Canada, Britain and the United States and in 1993 the International Wheelchair Rugby Foundation was founded. It made its first appearance in the Paralympics in Atlanta in 1996 as a demonstration sport and is now a recognised medal sport at the Games. Furthermore, this was a sport that allowed the bone-crunching physical contact of rugby to be enjoyed by those who would otherwise be excluded from such pleasures.

In the late 1990s, the United States also became the centre for the emergence of gay-friendly rugby clubs, once again challenging some of the fundamental machismo traditions of the game. Although the London-based King's Cross Steelers were the world's first openly gay rugby club, formed in 1995, it was in America where the impact of shifting attitudes was strongest.[11] The Washington Renegades blazed a trail for American rugby in 1998, and in 2001 an invitational international sevens tournament was held for gay-friendly teams in Washington.

Organised by the newly founded International Gay Rugby Association and Board (IGRAB), it was renamed the Bingham Cup the following year after Mark Bingham, one of the stalwarts of the gay San Francisco Fog club who had been killed on United Airlines Flight

93 during the terrorist attacks of September 11 2001. Held every two years, the 2014 tournament attracted 15 teams from around the world, by which time IGRAB itself had grown to 51 member clubs in 15 countries.

Gay teams slowly emerged elsewhere, and in 2004 the Sydney Convicts became the southern hemisphere's first gay club. In 2005 the Union Cup began as a tournament for European clubs, and by 2013 had 17 clubs taking part. But the strength of gay-friendly rugby remains centred in the United States: almost half of IGRAB's member clubs are based there.

Beyond this, rugby has struggled to reflect changing attitudes towards sexuality. In 1995 Australian rugby league international Ian Roberts came out and played without incident as an openly gay player in the National Rugby League for the next four seasons. But it would be over a decade before another professional player felt able to do the same, when Gareth Thomas, the first man to win 100 caps for Wales, declared his sexuality in 2009, although leading Welsh referee Nigel Owens had also come out in 2007.

Given the thousands of professional players of both rugby codes, the fact that only two players felt comfortable enough in the game to be open about their sexuality shows how, despite an official stance of toleration, rugby is still largely trapped in the stereotypes of the past. In 2008, Johan Prinsloo, the then chief executive of the South African Rugby Union, said in an interview that 'being gay in the rugby world is like going to war and having a disco in the middle of the battlefield – it's inappropriate'.[12] Given such attitudes, it is perhaps not surprising that the impetus to challenge them has come from a country outside the traditional rugby-playing nations.

This willingness of North Americans to challenge traditions within rugby also provided the basis for possibly the greatest social change in the nature of the game around the world. Wheelchair rugby was a mixed sport that for the first time allowed men and women to play rugby seriously together. Gay-friendly teams questioned some of the macho conventions of the game, but perhaps the biggest breakthrough made in the United States and Canada was the emergence of women's rugby in the 1970s, a development that no doubt had the founders of the game spinning in their tombs.

26

WOMEN WILL HOLD UP
HALF THE GAME

It was the tightest World Cup final that had ever been played. In front of a record crowd, England and New Zealand tore into each other. Within the first half-hour, two New Zealanders had been sin-binned, yet England could not take advantage. Instead, with only 14 players, the Kiwis turned the tables when right-winger Hohepa stepped first outside and then inside struggling English defenders to touchdown 15 yards to the right of the posts. The try was converted and New Zealand went into half-time with a 7-0 lead and one hand on the trophy.

After half-time both sides scored penalties to make it 10-3. And then the English defence stood firm against sustained New Zealand pressure, repulsing wave after wave of seemingly irresistible attack. Hohepa made a clear break down the right and seemed certain to score a second try before English second-rower McGilchrist pulled off a miraculous covering tackle. But their impregnable defence gave England a psychological advantage and, when yet another Kiwi was sin-binned, the tide turned.

Now England piled on the pressure and it was New Zealand who had their backs to the wall. Sensing their opportunity the English won a penalty but declined to kick for goal. Three consecutive scrums on the Kiwis' line finally forced a hole through the defensive line and Barras crashed over for a try. The conversion was good and the game was locked at 10-10. Then, just as England were setting themselves for a final push, disaster struck. They were penalised for not releasing the ball while in possession, directly in front of their own goal.

Kiwi centre Brazier stepped up and calmly steered the ball between the posts to restore New Zealand to a 13-10 lead. With just over ten minutes left, New Zealand's big-match experience came to the fore and they calmly managed the match out, bringing the World Cup back to New Zealand for the fourth consecutive time. For England, even being part of arguably the greatest final so far was no consolation for a third successive loss in the final.

It was an epic clash but one that barely registered with the vast majority of rugby followers. This was because it was the Women's Rugby World Cup final of 2010, and players such as Carla Hohepa, Kelly Brazier, Joanna McGilchrist and Charlotte Barras remained almost entirely anonymous outside the women's game. Yet the growth of women's rugby of whatever code had been one of the great advances made by the game in the last decades of the 20th century.

The manly game?

The fact that women played the game at all would have been surprising to rugby's founders. 'We have no dealings with women here,' the Rev. Frank Marshall told a meeting of the Yorkshire Rugby Union in 1889. In 1932 former RFU president Percy Royds told the diamond jubilee dinner of Ealing RFC, 'ours is a game not founded for women. It seems to me to be the only game today in which women cannot compete – thank goodness.'[1]

In fact, one of the reasons for rugby's popularity among men was that it was a masculine kingdom in which men could socialise without women. In 1947 *Rugger* magazine asked 'what makes a sound XV?' to which it answered 'it is not sufficient for an individual to appear at the ground, change, play, wash and depart to the connubial company of the female of the species. Rather should a player join in the … genuine spirit of camaraderie that will pervade the ensuing cloud of alcoholic fumes and blue smoke.'[2] And, of course, drunken behaviour, initiation ceremonies, obscene songs and random acts of vandalism – usually dismissed as 'high jinks' – were all part of rugby union's obsessively male culture.

It was rare for women to play rugby in the first century of its existence. Reports of a women's 'football' team formed in Scotland in 1881 are unclear as to whether they played the association or rugby code, or neither.[3] We do know of one female player from this period, Emily Valentine. She was the daughter of the assistant headmaster of Portora Royal School in Enniskillen in Northern Ireland, the alma mater of both Samuel Beckett and Oscar Wilde. She recalled many years later how she got her chance to play in the late 1880s:

> It was just a school scratch match and they were one 'man' short. I was about ten years old. I plagued them to let me play, 'Oh, all right, come on then'. Off with my overcoat and hat – I always wore boys' boots any-how, so that was all right.
>
> I knew the rules. At last my chance came. I got the ball – I can still feel the damp leather and the smell of it, and see the tag of lacing at the open-ing. I grasped it and ran, dodging, darting, but I was so keen to score that try that I did not pass it, perhaps when I should; I still raced on, I could see the boy coming towards me; I dodged, yes I could, and breathless, with my heart thumping, my knees shaking a bit, I ran. Yes, I had done it, one last spurt and I touched down, right on the line.[4]

The thrill of the game remained unknown to almost all other women. Occasionally cartoons would appear in Victorian magazines and newspapers depicting women rugby players, yet these served more as 'humorous' warnings about the growth of the women's suffrage movement rather than any real evidence that women were playing the game. Indeed, such was the hostility to women taking part in rugby that the game missed out almost entirely on the tremendous boom in women's sport during the First World War.

While thousands of women were playing soccer in Britain by the end of the war, and even more watching them, there was almost no rugby played by women. In December 1917 women from Hancock's Brewery in Cardiff played a team of women from Lysaght's iron and steelworks in Newport at Cardiff Arms Park. The Lysaght's team won 6-0 but the game appears to have been a one-off.[5] This may have been connected with a widespread male chauvinist opposition to women playing rugby. In 1919 women in Featherstone, a mining village at the heart of rugby league country in the north of England, tried to play rugby league but were told by local men that they should play soccer because it was a more feminine game than rugby. The popularity of women's soccer in the Lancashire coalfields around Wigan and St Helens in the early 1920s can be explained to some extent by the fact that in these rugby league-playing areas such an attitude was commonplace.

Outside Britain, a little more headway was made, but not much. In September 1921, the Metropolitan Blues and Sydney Reds women's rugby league teams played in front of a crowd estimated at between 20,000 and 30,000 people at Sydney's Agricultural Showgrounds. The crowd was captivated by the skills of winger Maggie Maloney who scored four tries. Despite sponsorship and the support of Dally Messenger and the secretary of the NSW Rugby League, the proposed formation of a NSW Ladies Rugby Football League was stymied by the opposition of the NSWRL leadership, who banned any of their affiliated organisations or individuals from getting involved in the women's game. Starved of support, the women could not find the resources to continue.

That same year, women's rugby league sides were formed across the Tasman Sea in the Auckland suburb of Parnell and in Hornby, near Christchurch. As in England, a journalist in the Christchurch newspaper *The Press* suggested that the women would be more suited to the round-ball game. 'Let them play soccer,' he declared dismissively.[6] Even so, the Parnell club attracted 65 women interested in playing the game. In Wellington, a women's rugby union team was formed in July 1921. Partly these moves were a response to the start of women's soccer in New Zealand, although this too proved to be short-lived.

Such moves were also a reflection of how doing 'men's work' in factories during the First World War had broadened many young women's horizons. 'Women had successfully undertaken heavy work in the war [so] they could play the League game under the modified rules,' argued the *Auckland Star*.[7] It was to no avail. Opposition from both league and union authorities ensured that the movement never got off the ground. In 1930 there was another attempt to organise a women's rugby league match in Sydney but, once again, the opposition of the rugby league authorities nipped it in the bud. A charity match took place in Queensland in 1954 but, again, there were no subsequent matches.[8]

In contrast, French women made much more progress in playing their sport of choice. In 1917 the Fédération des Sociétés Féminines Sportives had been formed to encourage women to play all sports, including soccer. This encouraged some French women to play a 12-a-side version of *barette*, the form of touch rugby invented in the 1890s by Bordeaux's Philippe Tissié. By the late 1920s a national championship was being contested by sides from Paris, Bordeaux and Lille, but the competition had faded away by the start of the 1930s.

This is the modern world

Two decades were to pass before women would play a meaningful game of rugby again. This time it was in the rugby league hotbed of Workington in north-western England where three matches were organised as part of a carnival to celebrate the 1953 coronation of Queen Elizabeth II.[9] These matches were taken seriously by players and spectators alike, and like men's league became a focus for community support. Yet despite the athleticism and skills of the players, the matches were belittled by some newspaper reporters, a problem that would recur throughout the history of women's rugby.

League's strong community roots did allow a handful of women into coaching positions in schools; in English and Australian Catholic schools women coaches could occasionally be seen, such as Wakefield St Austin School's Winnie Powell, who later became a Carmelite nun. Individual trailblazers such as East Hull coach Kay Ibbetson and Whitehaven director Betty Haile also put down footprints in the 1960s that would only be followed decades later.

It would not be until the early 1960s that women began to play rugby union again. In 1962 attempts were made to start a women's team at Edinburgh University, in 1963 women students played against male students in London for charity and in 1966 Worthing RFC staged a similar event. Women's charity matches also began to be organised in France at the same time and in 1965 the first women's side, Les Violettes Bressanes, was formed in the town of Bourg-en-Bresse in eastern France. More clubs followed and in 1970 the Association Française de Rugby Féminin (AFRF) was founded, the world's first governing body for women's rugby. Three years later they approached the FFR for official recognition but had to wait another decade before it was granted.

It was in North American universities in the 1970s that women's rugby union first became a significant sport. The impact of the women's liberation movement and the passing of equal rights legislation inspired women in Canada and the United States to take up rugby. The men's game in those countries was, as we have seen, a marginal sport and so women faced less powerful institutional bias against them playing rugby.

Starting in 1972 at universities in Colorado, Illinois and Missouri, the game grew rapidly and by 1978 there were enough teams to organise the first national championship tournament in Chicago. Even so, there was little support from the men's game and an unofficial newsletter was founded to promote the women's game by players in Virginia and Florida.[10] In Canada, women's clubs had been formed in the mid-1970s in Alberta and Saskatchewan, leading to the first Western Canadian Women's Championship being held in Calgary in 1983. In 1987 the United States and Canada faced each other in their first international match.

In Europe, too, women's rugby grew in popularity in countries where men's rugby was not a major sport. In the Netherlands, students at Wageningen University started playing the game in 1975. Its popularity soon spread and by the early 1980s a ten-team league was in operation. In April 1982 the Netherlands ushered in the new era of women's rugby when they played in the first ever international match with France in Utrecht, losing 4-0. In 1979 Spanish and Italian women began to play the game.

Women's rugby continued to grow in the 1980s. New Zealand's first provincial match was played in 1980. In 1981 Japanese women staged their first rugby match and the Japanese Women's RFU was formed in 1988. By the end of the decade, women's rugby was being played across Europe, North America and the Pacific.

Great Britain lagged somewhat behind the rest of the rugby union world. It wasn't until the late 1970s that women began to play rugby seriously and university teams appeared, focused especially on universities with strong rugby traditions such as Loughbrough. The game progressed rapidly and in 1983 ten student sides formed the Women's Rugby Football Union (WRFU). A national league was started in 1985 and in 1987 the first England versus Wales international was staged, with England coached by Loughborough lecturer and former Scottish and British Lion Jim Greenwood. Wasps beat Richmond in the first women's cup in 1988 and by 1990 the WRFU had 90 member clubs.[11]

Although lacking the university infrastructure of their union cousins, women also began playing rugby league in the 1960s and 1970s. As early as 1966 women in Auckland had played competitive matches and in England in 1978 the British Amateur Rugby League Association allowed 13-year-old Elisabeth Beal to play for her local under-14s boys' side. By 1980, 'Ladies' clubs had been formed at Huddersfield, Leeds and at Pilkington's glassworks in St Helens. In 1984 Julie Fitzpatrick became the game's first woman referee when she officiated in the West Yorkshire amateur league and shortly after Julia Lee took charge of professional men's matches. By 1994, 21 women's clubs were playing the game in England, largely based in traditional rugby league towns. In 1993 the Australian Women's Rugby League was founded.

Going global

The 1980s saw rugby union's governing bodies begin to take women's rugby seriously and many national women's unions were recognised and assimilated by national men's unions. This gave women's rugby much more access to funding and resources, not to mention allowing the men's game to do something positive about its image as a bastion of unreconstructed male chauvinism. In 1990 the first international tournament was held in New Zealand, featuring the hosts, the USA, the Netherlands and the USSR, where women's rugby had been established only a couple of years earlier.

Although this first tournament was unsurprisingly won by New Zealand, it did not go unnoticed that the other nations did not have a strong men's rugby tradition and that the women's game did not simply follow the path of the men's. This was confirmed in 1991 when the first women's rugby union World Cup was staged in Wales. Only four of the competing 12 nations came from countries that were in the elite tier of the men's game and the final was won convincingly by the United States, captained by Kathy Flores, who would become one of American rugby's most important coaches.

The United States finished runners-up in the next two World Cups in 1994 and 1998, but by the turn of the century the balance of power had shifted substantially to the traditional nations of men's rugby. The first three of the finals staged in the 21st century were between the three times' victorious New Zealand Black Ferns and England, who had played in every final except one, and won the 2014 tournament. The same was true in women's rugby league, in which the Kiwi Ferns, as the women's league side was known, won the first three women's league World Cups and lost in the 2013 final to Australia.

Despite the tightening grip of the major nations, women's rugby continued to expand around the world. The opportunity for women to play a physically demanding and full-contact sport was simply too tempting. By the end of the 20th century there were 22 nations playing international matches. It had taken the game two decades of hard work to reach this total, but in the first decade of the new century 31 new countries began playing women's rugby union internationally.

The emergence of sevens as an important component of global rugby from the 1980s also helped the women's game. In 1997 a women's tournament was held at the Hong Kong Sevens for the first time. The fewer players required to play sevens meant that the game was an ideal introduction to the game for countries with no rugby tradition. In 2009, 16 teams competed in the first Women's Sevens World Cup in Dubai, which, although won by Australia, highlighted the increasingly global footprint of the game with teams qualifying from Brazil, China, Thailand and Uganda. The acceptance in 2009 of rugby union sevens for both men and women into the Olympic Games also helped to extend the range of the game to even more nations. By 2010, 99 national teams were playing women's sevens.

No better proof of the growing success of women's rugby could be found than the 2014 Women's Rugby World Cup that was held in Paris. With 14 competing sides, including Spain and Kazakhstan, the tournament set new standards of play and, perhaps most importantly, drama. The reigning champions, the Black Ferns, were astonishingly dumped out of the tournament by the hitherto unheralded Ireland, and the Canadians, who had never made it beyond the semi-finals, reached the final after a nail-biting 18-16 win over the hosts, France.

They faced England in the final in front of a sell-out 20,000 crowd in a match that was not settled until the 74th minute, when centre Emily Scarratt burst through the Canadian defence to score and then convert the game-sealing try for a 21-9 victory. It was as intense and as gripping a match as could be seen anywhere, and received huge media coverage, both in newspaper column inches and television viewers.

Flushed with success and confident of the game's future, a few days after England's win the RFU announced that it would offer 20 women professional contracts as part of the preparation for the 2016 Olympics' women's sevens tournament. But as the men's game discovered, professionalism brings its own problems. The advent of professionalism in rugby union had led to the strongest teams and nations becoming even stronger.

Greater media exposure for the women's game and increasing resources at the elite level has meant that the leading rugby-playing nations can attract better athletes and implement higher standards of coaching, leaving behind countries that lack extensive infrastructures. As professionalism advances, the women's game may find itself in the paradoxical position of more women playing rugby than ever before, but the chances of a player from a non-traditional country winning a World Cup being less than they were in the early 1990s.

Yet, regardless of the dangers the future may hold, of all the momentous changes that have taken place in rugby since the 1980s, the growth of the women's game will perhaps be seen by future generations as the most significant of all. And the heroes of women's rugby today, such as Julia Lee, Kathy Flores and Emily Scarratt, will become as important to the whole sport of rugby as are their male counterparts.

PART VII

TRADITION AND TRANSFORMATION

The burden of tradition weighed heavily on rugby's major nations. Amateurism had defined rugby union since the 1880s, but the changing world of the 1960s and 1970s threw old beliefs and conventions into question. Politics and sport became inseparable and the game's deep bond with South Africa wracked the game like never before. And its growing popularity brought intolerable new pressures.

Rugby league's century of professionalism was severely tested by the end of the old industrial world that had been its heartlands, and it, too, was forced to confront powerful new challenges.

As the wheels of history switched up gears, rugby was propelled into places that it had never before imagined. And just as 1895 was the game's decisive year of the previous century, 1995 would change rugby for ever.

27

SPRINGBOKS, ALL BLACKS AND THE POLITICS OF RUGBY

They were international rugby union's Romulus and Remus. The British may have invented the game, but South Africa and New Zealand transformed rugby from a trial of strength and skill to a test of national fitness, political advantage and diplomatic influence.

Richard Seddon, New Zealand's prime minister at the time of the 1905 All Black tour, basked in its reflected glory so much that he became known as the 'minister for football'. Paul Roos, the Afrikaner captain of the 1906 Springboks, was assiduous in his use of rugby to bring together Afrikaans- and English-speaking South Africans, and himself became a National Party MP in 1948.

Since their first meetings in the 1920s the two nations had quarrelled and disagreed like the mythical Roman twins. But unlike the Romans, neither one could kill off its rival sibling and rule alone. Both needed each other – and, as the second half of the 20th century would demonstrate, the rest of the rugby union world would become equally dependent on them.

The All Blacks' home defeat by the South Africans in the 1937 Test series left a deep scar on the psyche of New Zealand rugby. Its confidence and natural sense of superiority had been dealt a grievous blow. Revenge had to be taken, but the outbreak of war in 1939 led to the cancellation of the 1940 tour to South Africa. New Zealanders would have to wait more than a decade for the opportunity to put the record straight.

When the All Blacks finally arrived in South Africa on 29 April 1949 after a 26-day voyage across the Indian Ocean, anticipation could not have been higher. The success of the 1945–46 New Zealand Army team had laid down a challenge to the South Africans, not just for the unofficial world championship but also by the manner in which the game was played. Could the controlled forward game of the Springboks overcome the attacking verve of the New Zealanders, eight of whom were veterans of that 1945 team?

The All Blacks were extremely confident, so confident in fact that the New Zealand Rugby Union had arranged for Australia to visit New Zealand at the same time as the South Africa tour – and had scheduled the first Test match against the Wallabies in Wellington on the same day as the third Test against the Springboks in Durban. This could only be either a daring piece of bravura or a stunning act of hubris.

From the start of the tour the All Blacks appeared unsettled. In the matches before the first Test, the All Blacks lost two and drew one. The first match against the Springboks was going to be tight.

The All Blacks jumped out to an early lead, thanks to a try by winger Peter Henderson, but five penalties to prop Okey Geffin gave the Springboks a 15-11 win. The All Blacks had been outscrummaged, their inexperienced half-backs could not supply enough quick ball to the backs and the ominous presence of South African number eight Hennie Muller snuffed out almost all of the New Zealanders' set-piece moves.

Things then went from bad to worse. An exhausting train journey to Rhodesia for a two-match series saw the first lost 10-8 and the second drawn 3-3. On the way back the All Blacks' train crashed and, although no players were injured, one of the crew was killed, despite being attended by New Zealand centre and medical doctor Ron Elvidge.

On their return to South Africa, the 12-6 loss in the second Test confirmed that the All Blacks were no match for their opponents' scrummaging technique. If New Zealand rugby had honed its attacking technique over the previous decade, South African rugby had refined its scrummaging to an even greater extent. The New Zealand forwards simply could not cope with the Springboks' scrum. In perhaps the most humiliating episode in All Black history, their coach, 1905 All Black Alex MacDonald, asked his opposite number, Danie Craven, to help the New Zealand pack get to grips with the intricacies of the 3-4-1 scrum.

It made little difference. The third Test was lost 9-3 and the fourth 11-8 in a similar fashion to the first, with a New Zealand try being cancelled out by Geffin's kicking. The frustrated New Zealanders began to grumble that the South African referees were favouring the home side. Ninety-three penalties were awarded to the Springboks in the New Zealand half in the four Tests, eighteen on or inside the 25-yard line. Of the 63 won by New Zealand in the South African half, only one was on the 25-yard line.

Of course, as Danie Craven pointed out, the Springbok dominance of the scrum meant that the All Black pack probably gave away more penalties when under pressure in their own half, but the New Zealand *Rugby Almanack* was not convinced. 'The continued inflicting of penalties is disturbing and requires some explanation,' it said worriedly.[1] The *Almanack* also raised the perennial criticism that rugby union's scoring rules meant that the side scoring more tries, as the All Blacks had done in three of the Tests, could still lose to the side that kicked the most penalties.

But the reality was that the All Blacks had been out-thought and out-fought. Alex MacDonald was by common consent out of his depth as a coach and the players had arrived in South Africa unfit and unprepared for what was to come. The 4-0 defeat in the Test series was in no small part due to the overconfidence and lack of planning of the NZRU.

And for those who thought that things could not get any worse, they did. A week after the South Africans completed their whitewash, the Wallabies secured their second consecutive win over the All Black team that had been left behind, giving Australia the parallel Test series 2-0. In the matter of just two months, the mighty New Zealand had been humbled by South Africa, Australia and even Rhodesia.

As in life, so in sport. Hubris had brought New Zealand rugby union to its lowest point ever.

'Kill or be killed'

There are few things more motivating in life than humiliation. New Zealand rugby in the 1950s was driven by the overwhelming desire to undo the ignominy of the 1949 whitewash. When the 1950 British Isles side, the first rugby union tourists to be nicknamed the Lions by the press, the first to wear the now distinctive red shirt and the first to be picked entirely on merit, visited New Zealand they were narrowly but convincingly defeated 3-0 after drawing the first Test 9-9. A little Kiwi pride had been restored.

Three years later the All Blacks made their fourth tour of the northern hemisphere, winning three of the five Test matches but losing to Wales for the third time and, for the first time, France. But although there was some concern about the losses, by the time the tourists arrived back in New Zealand, few were interested in looking back. All eyes were now fixed on 1956 and the return of the Springboks.

The South Africans had also toured Britain and France in 1951, winning all their matches except a midweek fixture against a London Counties representative side, and achieving a Grand Slam in international matches, in the process destroying a hapless Scotland side 44-0 and sweeping away France 25-3. The results were not surprising, but the manner of the victories was. For although the Springboks' strategy was, as ever, to dominate their opponents in the forwards, the aim was now to provide a platform for the backs to cut free. Nine tries were scored against Scotland, four against Ireland and six against France. In the 1953 series against the visiting Wallabies, the Springboks scored 15 tries in winning the series 3-1.

The high point of the Springboks' new-found attacking effervescence came during the 1955 British and Irish Lions tour. The tourists possessed one of the finest sets of attacking players ever assembled. England's Jeff Butterfield, Wales' Cliff Morgan and Ireland's Tony O'Reilly were arguably their countries' greatest players in their positions. The tour would be one of the most memorable in rugby history.

The Lions went into the first Test at Ellis Park in Johannesburg with a run of 11 straight wins under their belts. The game see-sawed with the Springboks establishing an initial 11-3 lead. Then, in the second half, the course of the game flipped over completely and, inspired by Cliff Morgan, the Lions raced out to lead 23-11. By then, however, they were down to 14 men after English flanker Reg Higgins was stretchered off early in the second half.

Driven forward by 90,000 South African voices yelling them on, the Springboks sensed blood and fought back. Marshalled by scrum-half Tommy Gentles, at around five feet three inches tall one of the smallest men ever to play Test rugby, the home side took full advantage of the tiring seven-man Lions' pack. With the match well into injury time the Lions were clinging on at 23-19 but, as the referee looked to his watch, the Springboks created an overlap on the right and debutant right-winger Theunis Briers touched down halfway between the touchline and the posts.

Full-back Jack van der Schyff lined the ball up for the conversion and the win. A veteran of the 1949 All Black whitewash, Schyff had already kicked four goals that afternoon and this was well within his capability. But the ball went wide. The Lions had won and a dejected Schyff, shoulders hunched and head down, found himself on the front page of every South African newspaper the following morning. 'Shame!' was the headline in one. He never played for the Springboks again.

South Africa were in a different mood for the next Test and scored a record seven tries to steamroller the Lions 25-9. They dominated the set pieces and their three-quarters ripped the British defence to shreds, with

Tom van Vollenhoven on the left wing scoring a hat-trick against a nonplussed Tony O'Reilly.

There was more drama to come. In the third Test the Lions played a tight, controlled game in which their forwards for the first time established continuous dominance over their opponents. Cliff Morgan became a paragon touch-finder – there were 65 line-outs in the match – and the predominantly Welsh pack did the rest. A Jeff Butterfield drop goal saw the Lions go into half-time 3-0 ahead, and it was his try that proved decisive in the second half, giving the British Lions a 9-6 win.

They were now just one match away from being the first touring side to defeat the Springboks in the 20th century. The first 40 minutes in Port Elizabeth went the way of the previous Test match, with a tightly disciplined forward display giving the Lions a 5-3 half-time lead, but after the break the South Africans switched up a gear and ran in four tries to tie the Test series with a convincing 22-8 victory.

It was not merely a great series. If it confirmed South Africa as still the game's dominant power, it also demonstrated that the best of British rugby union could now compete at the very highest international level. It also suggested that the All Blacks, who had lost to South Africa, Australia, Wales and France in recent years, were quite probably merely the world's third best side.

New Zealanders could not allow such a state of affairs to last. Therefore, when the Springboks finally arrived in New Zealand in June 1956 the prize was far greater than mere rugby rivalry: New Zealand's national pride was at stake. The tour became the concern of the press, the Church and parliament. Newspapers obsessively reported the Springbok trials, hoping to gain an insight of what the All Blacks would have to face. School assemblies discussed the prospects of the tour and instructed their young charges on the vital importance of the Test series.[2]

The arrival of the tourists was greeted with the same enthusiasm as for a royal visit. A three and a half hour welcoming procession greeted them for the first match in Waikato. When the team's special train arrived in

Wanganui, the Springboks 'turned their procession in vintage cars and fire engines from the railway station to their hotel into a riotous comedy', with Western Province lock Jan Pickard squirting the admiring crowd with a water pistol.[3] Over the course of the four-month-long tour, roughly a third of New Zealand's population of two million went to watch a tour game.

The 40,000 who crammed into Dunedin's Carisbrook stadium for the first Test witnessed a tense and brutal match that was decided by an interception try from All Black winger Ronnie Jardon. Despite finding himself outnumbered by Springbok attackers on the left, he was able to grab an indecisive pass from Dawie Ackermann to race half the length of the field to score. Despite South African dominance in the scrum, the New Zealand forwards convincingly out-rucked their opponents, something that would become a feature of the tour.

The 14-10 scoreline told only half the story. The All Blacks finished with 14 men, while the Springboks had only 13 players on the pitch when the match ended. Hard play had become indistinguishable from foul play. Even the provincial matches had become vicious encounters, with each New Zealander seemingly desperate to prove that it was his individual responsibility to take revenge for the 1949 humiliation. National honour and personal pride appeared to be one and the same.

The atmosphere became so hostile that shortly before the second Test Springbok manager Danie Craven informed the New Zealand Rugby Union that his team would be cutting the tour short and returning home after the match. An 8-3 victory in Wellington persuaded him to change his mind, but the Springboks became increasingly irritated not just by the violence of their opponents but also by what they saw as unsympathetic refereeing and hurtfully partisan crowds.

If Craven thought his threat might encourage the NZRU to rein in their players he, and particularly his front-row forwards, were sorely disappointed. Within minutes of the third Test kicking off in

Christchurch the All Blacks signalled that they were going to put an end to Springbok forward domination by sheer physical intimidation.

The man who was primarily responsible was the former amateur heavyweight boxing champion of New Zealand, Otago prop Kevin Skinner. Called back into the side to stiffen the forwards, Skinner punched both South African props, Chris Koch and Japp Bekker, so hard that they were knocked to the ground. Skinner was unapologetic for the rest of his life. 'Once you pull on the Silver Fern, if you've got anything in you at all, that should give you all the kick you need,' he told the journalist Warwick Roger years later. 'You were, after all, in a kill or be killed situation.'[4]

The intimidation worked and the All Blacks took an 11-0 half-time lead. But the Springbok forwards were not going to lie down. They clawed their way back into the match and, with 20 minutes to go, the score was 11-10. Yet the All Blacks had the measure of their opponents and two tries in the last five minutes sealed a 17-10 New Zealand win. At 2-1 with one match to go, the Test series could not be lost. But not losing was not enough for wounded New Zealander pride. Victory was essential.

The fourth Test at Auckland was once again a ferocious, brutal battle. The 61,240 spectators who squeezed into Auckland's Eden Park were no less committed to victory than the players on the pitch. When Danie Craven walked out for a pre-match pitch inspection he was greeted by the thunder of hostile boos. Once again, the All Blacks lost the scrums but dominated the rucks, and this would prove decisive.

A penalty from full-back Don Clarke gave New Zealand a 3-0 half-time lead, but the decisive and series-sealing try came five minutes after the break. Springbok scrum-half 'Popeye' Strydom lost the ball in a tackle and New Zealand hooker Ron Hemi dribbled it forward. Number eight Peter Hilton-Jones kicked it on, South African full-back Bassie Viviers failed to gather the ball and it popped up into Hilton-Jones's hands for him to touch down. Clarke converted and then kicked another penalty to make it 11-0. Roy Dryburgh scored a converted consolation try in the dying seconds but the game finished 11-5 in the All Blacks' favour.

New Zealand had won the match, the series, the unofficial world championship and, most important of all, regained its national self-respect. But they had won no friends. Contrary to decades of tradition, not a single player on either side swapped a jersey at the end of the game.

Unfair play

The ferocity of the rugby on the 1956 tour was not simply a result of the two teams' desperation to win the series: it was also a reflection of two insecure and fearful nations, societies that had both been built on the domination of those with darker skins. For although both sides claimed that rugby had united their nations, the truth was often the opposite.

In 1948 the predominantly Afrikaner National Party won power for the first time in South Africa. It immediately began creating an apartheid system, which segregated the races, removed civil rights from the non-white population and punished those who transgressed its strict racial hierarchy. Most of these measures merely formalised practices or extended legislation that had been introduced under British rule, but the National Party claimed apartheid would lift Afrikaners to their rightful place in the world.

This rhetoric seemed to be confirmed in stunning fashion the following year when the Springboks whitewashed the 1949 All Blacks. The bond between Afrikaners and rugby union had grown increasingly strong in the interwar years and the dual political and sporting victories of 1948 and 1949 melded rugby and Afrikaner nationalism into one indivisible whole.

For rugby union, the racial discrimination that had been an informally accepted as part of the game now had the sanction of state policy. So when the NZRU selectors chose the 1949 touring team, it was once again an all-white side: no Maori players were chosen for the tour, despite widespread protests in New Zealand. For the NZRU the rugby bond they shared with the South Africans was more important than racial equality.

In contrast to the 1949 All Black tour, there were almost no protests in 1956, such was the suffocating hold that the desire to beat the Springboks had over the New Zealand nation. Only the Maori Women's Welfare League raised their voice in opposition. Yet the issue of race would not go away. Although white New Zealanders liked to proclaim that their country was free of racial prejudice, this was far from the truth.

Maori were at the bottom of the social and economic ladder, treated, at best, with patronising condescension. The famous journalist and broadcaster Winston McCarthy, the voice of New Zealand rugby union thanks to his iconic commentaries on All Black matches, could casually write that watching Maori players 'for the first or second time is like trying to pick out a particular sheep in a flock. They all look the same.'[5]

The Springboks did play the Maori representative team in 1956, the first time since the controversial 1921 match, surprisingly winning 37-0 in Auckland. Decades later the Maori full-back that day, and future Anglican bishop, Muru Walters, claimed that the side had been told to lose the match by the Minister for Maori Affairs, Ernest Corbett. Walters said that Corbett had told them a Maori victory would mean that the All Blacks would never be invited back to South Africa.[6]

The 1956 Springbok tour was the last for almost 40 years that took place without open political controversy. The increasing repression taking place in South Africa as apartheid laws were extended led to the emergence of an international anti-apartheid movement. So when in the summer of 1958 the NZRU announced it would tour South Africa in 1960, it was rocked by a wave of protest. More than 160,000 New Zealanders signed a petition organised by the Citizens' All Black

Tour Association (CABTA) backing their slogan of 'No Maoris, No Tour' and thousands of others marched in the streets. George Nepia sent a message to the CABTA saying, 'Best of luck. Let me know if you need a full-back'.[7] But the NZRU, backed by the government, refused to reverse its whites-only policy.

Not even events at Sharpeville on 21 March 1960, when South African police opened fire on unarmed demonstrators, killing 69 and wounding 180 men, women and children, caused the NZRU to change its mind. In response to nationwide protests, the National Party declared a state of emergency, arresting 18,000 people and banning the African National Congress. Two months after the Sharpeville massacre the All Blacks arrived to begin their third tour of South Africa.

The Springboks shut out the All Blacks 13-0 in the first Test, but the boot of Don Clarke proved decisive in the second when the All Blacks won 11-3. The third Test was drawn 11-11 after Clarke kicked a last-minute sideline conversion of a Frank McMullen try and so the series went down to the wire in the fourth Test at Port Elizabeth. The match, and the series, was only settled by a try to Transvaal flanker Martin Pelser.

In 1965 the Springboks visited Australasia, losing both Tests to Australia and three of four against the All Blacks. It was the most disastrous Springbok tour ever. The free-flowing rugby of the 1950s had long gone – as the political storm over apartheid intensified, it seemed that the team was taking its revenge on a hostile world by playing the dourest rugby possible. South African rugby could no longer pretend that it was not political. Its identification with the apartheid regime, whether symbolically or explicitly through the words of its players and officials, meant that the Springboks flew the flag of racism wherever they went. As Danie Craven explained, 'the Springboks are frontline soldiers and as such they must maintain open lines of communication between our country and other rugby countries'.[8] And until the protests became too loud to ignore, the rest of the rugby union world remained silent.

The IRB's response to South Africa's expulsion from the British Commonwealth in 1961 was to say that it gave them 'great pleasure to convey to South Africa the view shared by all the member countries that the change would not make any difference whatever in regard to South Africa's position in rugby'.[9] South Africa's exclusion from the 1964 and 1968 Olympics and the increasing international pressure to boycott sport with the apartheid regime had little impact on rugby's administrators.

Rugby union had become inextricably entwined with international politics – and for the next 25 years they would shape the internal politics of rugby.

28

GENTLEMEN AND PLAYERS: WALES AND ENGLAND 1945–95

'This is great stuff. Phil Bennett covering. Chased by Alistair Scown. Brilliant, Oh that's Brilliant. John Williams. Bryan Williams. Pullin. John Dawes ... great dummy. David, Tom David. The halfway line. Brilliant by Quinnell. This Is Gareth Edwards. A Dramatic Start. WHAT A SCORE!'

It was the most memorable commentary, the most memorable try and arguably the most memorable match in the history of rugby union. Gareth Edwards' try for the Barbarians two minutes and 25 seconds into the match against the seventh All Blacks in January 1973 captured the imagination like no other.

Phil Bennett's Nureyev-like sidesteps. J. P. R. Williams shipping the ball wide despite Bryan Williams' wild tackle around his throat. John Dawes' surge up the field that sliced open the New Zealand defence. The interpassing between forwards David and Quinnell. And Edwards' final unstoppable lunge after he appeared as if from thin air to take a pass apparently intended for the winger John Bevan and race 35 yards before finally hurling himself over the All Blacks' line for four points.

'If the greatest writer of the written word would have written that story, no one would have believed it,' exclaimed commentator Cliff Morgan as Edwards, who was nursing a sore hamstring before the match, walked back to his own half. It was a try that captured all the stirring possibilities that an oval ball and two teams could conjure up.

The game continued in the same spirit, with both sides opting to choose audacious attack instead of the dour defence that had often marked matches on this All Blacks' tour. By half-time the Barbarians led 17-0. The pace subsided slightly in the second half but the All Blacks could not reach the same state of rugby grace as Edwards and company and the game ended in a magnificent 23-11 win to the Barbarians.

It was a match rich in a symbolism that would grow over the decades that followed. The fact that the commentator was Cliff Morgan, arguably the greatest fly-half that Wales or the British Isles had ever produced, and himself a master of free-running rugby, gave the try the legitimacy of the pantheon.

The result of the match seemed to suggest that a scratch side assembled quickly with little time for training could defeat the mightiest of foes if its players were committed to the spirit of rugby. And it reinvigorated a belief in the transcendent qualities of the game. Whenever a match descended into stern and severe ten-man rugby, the memory of Edwards' try would refresh the weariest appetite for the game.

Of course, time has obscured much of the reality of the match. The Barbarian side was no band of itinerant warriors hastily gathered together. Twelve of them had been members of the British Lions' tour that had defeated New Zealand for the first time in a Test series in 1971. Two others, Phil Bennett and Tommy David, would play for the Lions on their all-conquering 1974 tour of South Africa. This was a team forged in the furnace of one of the greatest tours ever.

Conversely, the 1972–73 All Blacks disappointed many. Although they overcame England, Scotland and Wales, they drew with Ireland and Munster, and lost to Llanelli, North-Western Counties, Midland Counties (West) and France. The lowest point of the tour was reached when prop Keith Murdoch, who had scored the crucial try against Wales, was sent home after a series of alcohol-related incidents.

It was a time when rugby union was in turmoil off and on the field. It was haunted by the international campaign to isolate apartheid South Africa, and the 1972 Five Nations was not completed because of the troubles in Ireland, with both Wales and Scotland refusing to play in Dublin because of safety concerns.

And the game itself was changing. In 1971, the value of a try had been raised from three to four points, the first time in the history of the union code that a try had been worth more than a goal. The previous year kicking the ball directly into touch had been restricted to inside the kicker's 25-yard line, a 'dispensation' that had long existed in Australia. Substitutes for injured players had been allowed in 1968, reversing almost a century of RFU opposition to the idea.

Coaching, too, had ceased to be a dirty word. England appointed former international flanker Don White as its first national coach in 1969, and the Barbarians had been coached by a veritable giant of the genus, Carwyn James. A gradual shift in the tectonic plates of rugby tradition was underway that would lead all the way to the momentous changes of 1995.

Gareth Edwards' try and the Barbarians' victory highlighted what the Lions' 1971 triumph over the All Blacks had demonstrated – and what victory over the Springboks in 1974 would confirm. For the first time since international rugby tours had begun, British rugby union was on top of the world.

The dragon rampant

The beating heart of that dominance was Wales. Seven of the Barbarians' team were Welshmen. No fewer than seven of the 1971 Lions Test side in New Zealand were Welsh, including the captain John Dawes, as were six of the 1974 Test side in New Zealand. They also occupied the crucial positions of half-backs, full-back and number eight, providing the cerebral cortex of the side.

For the best part of two decades, beginning in 1964 when they shared the Five Nations Championship with Scotland and ending with a seventh Triple Crown in 1979, Wales were the nonpareils of northern hemisphere rugby. They won the Five Nations outright eight times and shared it twice more, winning three memorable Grand Slams along the way. Decades later, Gareth Edwards, Barry John, Phil Bennett, Gerald Davies and J. P. R. – no need for a surname – would still be household names not merely in Wales but wherever the game was played. It was undoubtedly the greatest generation of Welsh rugby.

There had been a hint of what might come in the early 1950s. The Grand Slam had been won in 1950 and 1952 by a side that combined the virtues of resolute forward play and breathtaking back play. Led by John Gwilliam, a tower of strength at number eight as much as he was a pillar of rectitude in his career as a school headmaster, Wales proved to be frustratingly difficult to score against – they conceded a mere eight points in their four games in 1950 – and devilishly hard to prevent from scoring.

In 1953 Wales once again defeated the touring All Blacks by 13-8, not least due to a try by the searingly fast winger Ken Jones. The national side followed the lead of Bleddyn Williams' Cardiff, who also defeated the tourists 8-3. Swansea almost accounted for the New Zealanders, too, that year, drawing 6-6. A Welsh tour of New Zealand was suggested but the logistics proved insurmountable.

The national side was blessed with a bountiful host of talent in the middle of the field. For the first Grand Slam in 1950 the fly-half was the deceptively paced Billy Cleaver, a player who could switch from being a siege-gun kicker when the conditions demanded ten-man rugby into a fleet of foot ball-runner when the ground was hard.

By the time of the 1952 triumph, Cliff Morgan had stepped into the fly-half position. Morgan was a man who ran with all the freedom and vigour of an excited puppy, someone who played every match with the enthusiasm of his first. As the South Africans discovered when he starred on the 1955 Lions tour, this made him almost impossible to contain.

In the centres, Wales could boast Jack Matthews and Bleddyn Williams, the perfect combination of iron and steel. Matthews had once held future world-heavyweight champion Rocky Marciano to a draw in a wartime boxing match and presented a fearsome sight for any would-be tackler. So, too, did Williams, but this was because of his elegant speed and elusiveness, qualities which earned him the title of the 'Prince of Centres' indicating that he belonged in the same exalted company as the similarly titled Gwyn Nichols who masterminded Wales' 1905 defeat of the All Blacks.

And then there was the Golden Boy. Lewis Jones was a schoolboy prodigy who could play any position from full-back to fly-half with equal brilliance. He made his debut for Wales as full-back at Twickenham in 1950 aged just 18 years, nine months and ten days. As half-time approached with England leading, he gathered up an England punt and, instead of kicking for touch, bamboozled several surprised English defenders to set up a try for Cliff Davies. By the end of the match Wales had won 11-5 and a new star had been born. Less than five months later he flew out to New Zealand as a replacement on the British Lions' tour of Australia and New Zealand. He returned home as the tourists' leading points' scorer.

At first glance Jones appeared to the embodiment of the nonchalant gentleman amateur. Unhurried, sometimes seemingly uninterested in the play, he would pick his moment to insert himself into the game, usually with magnificent consequences. At half-time in even the biggest matches, he would sometimes relax with a cigarette, much to the surprise of his less laid-back teammates.

In fact, Jones was a rebel. His self-confidence stemmed from his inexhaustible reservoir of talent, and he had no time for hierarchies of status that dominated Welsh rugby off the field. In 1952, after playing a leading role in Wales' second post-war Grand Slam, he decided that he had enough of deference and unemployment and signed to play rugby league for Leeds for a record £6,000. He became just as big a star in league, returning to Australia and New Zealand with the league Lions in 1954 and 1957 and eventually being inducted into the British rugby league Hall of Fame.

Jones was merely the most prominent of dozens of Welshmen who would go north in the 1960s and 1970s. Alongside him, the most famous name to make his home in the rugby league heartlands was Billy Boston, a winger with the power of an express train. Boston signed for Wigan as a 19-year-old in 1953 and within a year was flying out with Jones on the 1954 rugby league tour Down Under. He had been born in Cardiff's Tiger Bay, the son of a Welsh-Irish mother and a Sierra Leonean father, and learned his rugby playing for Cardiff Internationals, a multi-racial club based in Cardiff's docklands.

As his union career progressed he came to understand that, regardless of talent, it was highly unlikely that anyone with his dark skin would play for Wales – in fact, it was not until 1986 that Glen Webbe became the first black Welsh international. Boston was not the only black Welshman who looked to league to fulfil his ambitions. Players like Johnny Freeman, Colin Dixon, Frank Wilson and Clive Sullivan made their way north to play at the very highest levels of the game, with Sullivan becoming the first black player to captain any British national sports team when he led Great Britain to victory in the 1972 Rugby League World Cup.

The rise of black Welsh players, albeit in the league game, was an indication of how Welsh society was changing in the 1950s. The number of miners winning Welsh caps fell from 43 in the interwar years to just ten in the post-war era before professionalism, reflecting the precipitous decline of the industry that, more than any other, had made modern Wales. In contrast, the number of teachers playing for Wales more than tripled from 23 to 73 in the same period. Twenty-five teachers won caps in the 1950s alone and a third of the side that beat the 1953 All Blacks was in the profession.

Young Welshmen had traditionally benefited from the sporting and career opportunities offered by the Welsh educational system, which was historically more open than that in England, but the 1950s saw the beginning of a huge expansion of higher education that would bring tremendous benefits to Wales. Universities and physical education colleges such as Loughborough and St Luke's in Exeter produced teams and players that spent considerable time training and studying the game. In the 1960s Loughborough University's side could field future stars such as Gerald Davies, John Dawes, John Taylor and John Mantle.

As the Welsh students graduated, they took the same philosophy to their clubs and ultimately to Wales and the British Lions. Many of them gravitated to London Welsh, a club comprised of exiles who were studying or pursuing professional careers in the capital and which provided a testing ground for what was to become the characteristically Welsh style of rugby.

By the time Wales shared the 1964 Five Nations Championship with Scotland, the national side was composed of players whose education, health care and social mobility were largely the product of the welfare state that had been established after the Second World War. With almost full employment and a social safety net, Wales underwent a revival of cultural nationalism.

On the rugby pitch, the buccaneering style of the Welsh national team seemed to reflect the new sense of Welsh self-confidence. Barry John, the supremely talented fly-half of the later 1960s and early 1970s, was nicknamed King John, an example of journalistic licence that also spoke volumes about the position of the team in Welsh society.

Carwyn James, the visionary Welsh coach who masterminded the 1971 Lions' victory in New Zealand but who never coached his national side – he did not believe the coach should be subordinate to a selection committee – even stood as a Plaid Cymru candidate in the 1970 general election, albeit in vain. Booing 'God Save The Queen' at internationals became de rigueur. Yet Wales was actually in thrall to a cultural, rather than a separatist political, nationalism. In 1979 a referendum rejected devolution by a four to one margin. By and large, the Welsh appeared to be nationalists only for the 80 minutes that an international rugby match lasted.

But what an 80 minutes it often was. Few countries could match Wales during the 1960s and 1970s. They lost just seven Five Nations' matches in the entire 1970s. It was not simply the manner in which Wales won, it was also about the men who engineered their victories. The Welsh fly-half factory turned out three of its greatest products in the space of a generation. David Watkins went north and was replaced by Barry John, who tired of life in the celebrity spotlight and retired at just 27; he in turn was succeeded by the lightning-paced Phil Bennett.

Forwards like Mervyn Davies and John Taylor brought a verve and energy to the pack rarely seen in Britain. On the wings Gerald Davies and J. J. Williams headed a litany of world-class three-quarters. And, of course, Gareth Edwards and J. P. R. Williams were simply the best in their positions that Wales, or probably anywhere else, had ever produced. Together, the side was capable of playing a soaring rugby that few could emulate.

The team's rise to greatness coincided with the introduction of colour television in Britain in 1967. The BBC's first live television broadcast of a rugby match had taken place as long ago as 1938 when Scotland's Calcutta Cup win was shown and the Five Nations had become a bedrock of the corporation's winter sports coverage in the 1950s. In 1966 it started the magazine show *Rugby Special* on BBC2, the channel on which colour television was first introduced. To see the red jerseys of the Welsh pack streaming forward and then to watch a blur of red as Gerald Davies or J. J. Williams sped towards the try line was for many one of their earliest experiences of the new format

And as Gareth Edwards' classic try for Barbarians showed, colour also meant that highlights could have a timeless quality and be replayed over and over again, unlike the dated patina of monochrome. Misty memories and grainy black and white footage were now replaced by living colour.

For Welsh supporters this easy access to the past would prove to be a good thing. Between 1979 and the coming of professionalism in 1995, they would have little more than their memories and video cassettes to remind them of how glory felt. Wales would win only one more Triple Crown, when they shared the championship with France in 1988, and one outright championship in 1994.

If things were bleak on the rugby field, they were far bleaker off it. These were the years during which Wales suffered the full devastation of de-industrialisation. After a heroic year-long effort by miners to stop the closure of pits, the Welsh coal industry essentially died. The steel industry suffered a similar fate. Mass unemployment on a scale not seen since the 1930s returned to the Valleys and with it rugby suffered.

In the late 1980s the dire state of the Welsh economy and the endless politicking of the WRU saw a new generation of players rediscovering the road north, with stars like Jonathan Davies, Scott Gibbs and John Devereux finding fame, fortune and considerable scope for their skills in rugby league. For the first time since the 1950s, the Welsh national rugby league team attracted large crowds and challenged the established league nations, most notably in the 1995 Rugby League World Cup when they reached the semi-finals at Old Trafford, which reverberated for the first time to thousands of Welsh citizens singing 'Hen Wlad Fy Nhadau', the official national anthem of Wales.

A full generation would pass before the glories of the 1970s would be revisited again, only this time it would be in the era of professionalism.

England's rise and fall …

If there was one thing more frustrating in the 1990s for Welsh rugby union supporters than seeing Wales' best players in the 13-a-side game, it was the fact that the Five Nations was now dominated by the English. In 1977 Phil Bennett, by then captain of Wales, made a memorable speech to his team before they played England at Cardiff Arms Park:

> Look what these bastards have done to Wales. They've taken our coal, our water, our steel. They buy our homes and live in them for a fortnight every year. What have they given us? Absolutely nothing. We've been exploited, raped, controlled and punished by the English – and that's who you are playing this afternoon.[1]

It was a reflection of the antagonism that the Welsh felt towards what they felt were the arrogant and condescending English. Many in English rugby union reciprocated this dislike. Richard Sharp, England's artful fly-half of the early 1960s, felt uncomfortable with the intensity of Welsh supporters: 'when you win they make you feel that you are lucky, and if you lose they are patronising.'[2]

This rivalry's high point, or its lowest depending on one's perspective, was the 1980 Twickenham encounter when Bill Beaumont's England side stood toe-to-toe with Jeff Squire's Wales. Thirty-four penalties were awarded by the referee David Burnett, who twice stopped the match to warn the captains about foul play and then, after 14 minutes, sent off Wales' Paul Ringer for a dangerous tackle on England fly-half John Horton.

The Welsh scored two tries to England's none and looked to have the match sewn up when Elgan Rees touched down with three minutes to go but the conversion was unsuccessful. In injury time, the Welsh infringed near their right touchline and the metronymic Dusty Hare stepped up to kick his third penalty goal of the match and hand England a 9-6 victory. It was, said the *Daily Telegraph*'s John Mason, a match in which 'too many people concerned have cause to be ashamed'.[3]

Ashamed or not, England, who had already beaten France and Ireland, then went to Scotland and scored five tries to secure their first Grand Slam since 1957. The post-war years had largely been barren for the English. The 1980 triumph was only England's fifth outright Five Nations win in the previous 34 years. From the mid-1960s there was little but bleakness, recrimination and soul-searching.

Yet the fifties had started out well. Captained by Nim Hall and containing two future RFU presidents in Albert Agar and John Kendall-Carpenter, England had won its first outright Five Nations since the war in 1953. The team was graced by the wing play of Ted Woodward, a fast, burly winger who blazed a trail from which Peter Jackson and later David Duckham would weave their magic, and saw the debut of centre Jeff Butterfield, a grammar school boy who had learned the arts of the game by watching Welsh stand-off Willie Davies carve up defences for Bradford Northern.

Butterfield and hooker Eric Evans, another northerner but from Manchester, would become the cogs around which England's 1957 Grand Slam side would revolve. With the experienced Evans now captaining the side, England achieved the optimum balance of a dominating pack of forwards, such as Peter Robins and David Marques, with an incisive back line, exemplified by the right-wing partnership of Butterfield and Peter Jackson. In a moment of journalistic history, 1957 marked the first time that winning all four Five Nations matches became known, by *The Times* at least, as the Grand Slam.[4]

England were undefeated again the following year but draws against Wales and Scotland meant that they could not claim another Grand Slam. A shared title with France followed in 1960 but it wasn't until 1963 that another championship was won. This time the architect and captain was fly-half Richard Sharp, who had made his England debut while still a student at Balliol College, Oxford. Tall, blond and unmistakeable on the pitch, for opposing defenders the problem was not so much recognising him but recognising what he would do when he had the ball in his hands.

It was this unpredictability that brought England their championship when, losing 8-5 in the final match against Scotland, Sharp received the ball from a scrum 40 yards out and dummied his way past defenders three times to squeeze in at the side of the posts. The try was converted and England hung on to seal their title.

Although Sharp's background was very much that of the archetypal rugger player of previous decades, English rugby union was changing. 'The blood coming in now is not quite as blue as it used to be and lots of them are not going into the established rugby clubs,' explained a delegate at the RFU's 1960 annual general meeting. He was correct. Between 1945 and 1970, 63 cent of England internationals were privately educated, down from 82 per cent in the interwar period. Between 1970 and 1995 this process accelerated, with privately educated players dropping to 44 per cent but grammar schools increasing their representation to 34 per cent. The number of players educated at non-grammar state schools rose to 23 per cent – its highest ever proportion.[5]

In the meritocratic 1960s Harlequins, Richmond and Blackheath, the traditional big three of club rugby, found their dominance challenged by clubs such as Bedford, Leicester, Coventry and Moseley in the Midlands, south-western clubs such as Bath, Bristol and Gloucester, and northern sides like Gosforth, Orrell and Headingley. The emergence of these clubs in the front ranks of the game was not unconnected to shifting attitudes in society, which gave them the self-confidence to challenge the RFU's authority.

It was thus hardly surprising when some of these clubs began to call for national cup and league competitions. The idea of a knock-out cup tournament – not seriously discussed by the RFU committee since 1878 when it decided not to use the Calcutta Cup for a national cup tournament – was raised by Bedford at the RFU's 1967 annual general meeting. The following year a dozen northern clubs proposed the formation of a northern league comprising clubs in Cheshire, Lancashire,

Northumberland and Yorkshire. Both ideas were turned down flat by the RFU.[6]

But attitudes to sport and especially to amateurism were changing in Britain. Cricket did away with the amateur divide in 1962, leading to the end of the 'Gentlemen versus Players' match. The Lawn Tennis Association abandoned amateurism in 1967 when Wimbledon went 'open'. Even the description 'amateur' became one of the words that symbolised the problems of post-war British society. When Edward Heath became leader of the Conservative Party in 1966, the *Observer Magazine* told its readers that he deplored 'the amateurishness of British politics'.[7]

Rugby union spent considerable time in the 1960s defending its amateur ethos from what it saw as the threat of commercialism. In 1965 players were banned from accepting awards 'presented by a commercial firm' and in 1969 the International Board reiterated that 'commercial sponsorship is contrary to amateur principles. No gift or financial support should be accepted by any union or affiliated body from a commercial firm or any individual in his commercial capacity.'[8]

Yet the pressure from companies seeking to sponsor rugby was intense. Just two years after ruling that sponsorship was impossible, the RFU changed its mind and decided that 'patronage and commercial assistance are acceptable provided they benefit the game'. By the end of 1972 it had attracted, with almost no effort, eleven commercial sponsors.

The RFU also backtracked on the question of a knock-out tournament. In 1971 a new 'RFU Club Competition' kicked off with 32 teams taking part. It proved to be both a financial and sporting success, complete with giant-killing exploits from Wilmslow who knocked out Harlequins in the quarter-finals. Providing further proof that power was shifting to provincial clubs, the cup was dominated by Gloucester, Bristol, Coventry, Bedford, Gosforth, Leicester and Bath. In 1975 it became the John Player Cup thanks to Imperial Tobacco's three-year £100,000 sponsorship, replicating its similar deal with rugby league.

The introduction of leagues was not so easy. Historically, the RFU had viewed leagues as the gateway to professionalism and had turned down a number of proposals from clubs in the 1970s. But pressure for leagues did not just come from the clubs, it also arose from England's fall from grace.

England's playing record collapsed after the 1963 Five Nations' victory and reached a nadir in the 1970s when the side won just 11 Five Nations' matches. This caused many in the game to call for drastic action to raise national standards. England's slump – like Wales' rise – also happened at precisely the moment that television was becoming the most important medium for sports coverage. It brought the political and national rivalries of international sport into the living rooms of millions. Live coverage of England matches, with one or two honourable exceptions, simply highlighted the weakness of the national side.

In 1975 Peter West of *The Times* argued for leagues because 'there is a great yearning in England to see their international side consistently winning again. ... The case for a league rests on the contention that the cream – both corporate and individual – comes out on top – and on merit.'[9] The ship of state was turning, but slowly, and it would be another decade before English rugby union introduced a league system.

... and rise

By the time Bill Beaumont was carried shoulder high from the field at Murrayfield in celebration of England's 1980 Grand Slam, Britain was on the verge of radical change. And money was at its heart.

On his way back from a match at Llanelli in 1975, Bedford and England winger Derek Wyatt mulled over the state of rugby. 'The crowd must have been 12,000 or more; the car park, which had a capacity of perhaps 800 cars, was full; the programmes were sold out; the bars were packed. Where, I pondered, was the money going?' He was not the only one. Speaking in the month of Margaret Thatcher's election victory in 1979, Leicester official Kevin Andrews told an RFU meeting that 'there is an enormous amount of money available' and asked 'whether we, in rugby football, were getting our fair share of it'.[10]

This was the spirit of the age. English society's slow move away from traditional gentlemanly values reached maximum velocity following Margaret Thatcher's arrival in Downing Street in 1979. It was most spectacularly seen in one of English rugby union's traditional bastions, the City of London, which in October 1986 experienced the 'Big Bang', which replaced the old boy networks and codes of behaviour with deregulation and 'free market' principles in which money, rather than status, was the determining principle.

Those who played and administered rugby union were part of this changing world. Indeed, Thatcher's husband Denis had been a senior referee and ran the line at the 1956 France versus England match in Paris. England internationals such as Rob Andrew, Peter Winterbottom, Tony Underwood, Brian Moore, Simon Halliday and David Pears all worked in the City, and major matches became part of the financial sector's social and corporate entertainment world.

The changed attitudes towards competition were reflected in the introduction finally in 1987 of a full league structure for the English game. Sponsored by the brewers Courage, more than one thousand teams were organised in a league of 108 divisions. The Courage leagues boosted crowds, club income and playing standards.

English rugby union's new age was dominated by Bath. With gifted backs such as Jeremy Guscott and Stuart Barnes, and a forward pack of characters like Gareth Chilcott and Victor Ubogu, who were as well suited to the new celebrity age as they were for rugby's increasingly power-driven set pieces, Bath carried off the league title five times before the professional era and won the cup nine times in 12 seasons. They were effectively a professional side and their success increased the pressures on other clubs to recruit and retain the best players. Well-founded rumours of payments to players, signing-on fees and sudden moves from less fashionable to more glamorous clubs abounded.

But the leagues also had a positive impact on the England national team. In 1990 the RFU president Michael Pearey explained that 'the resurgence of England Rugby over the last two years has been due in large measure to the introduction of leagues'.[11] The added competitive toughness that the leagues brought to the England side was complemented by the methods of national coach Geoff Cooke.

Thanks to the lingering amateur distrust of training, the England side did not have a coach until 1969 when former Northampton and England forward Don White was appointed. A succession of coaches made little difference to England's performances until Cooke took over in 1987, following a disastrous Five Nations and an anonymous first World Cup campaign.

In his first major move, Cooke surprised everyone by appointing 22-year-old Will Carling captain of the side in October 1988. Carling was the very model of the modern rugger man, combining a public school and military background with an easy familiarity with the City and its new-found brashness. Under Carling's leadership, England blossomed in a way that had not been seen since the days of Wavell Wakefield in the 1920s, who like Carling was a product of Sedbergh School.

Cooke refashioned the team around a tight, aggressive pack featuring fearsome players like Brian Moore, Dean Richards and Jason Leonard, the kicking of Rob Andrew and a flowing three-quarter line including Jeremy Guscott and the flying Underwood brothers, Rory and Tony. He overturned RFU traditions, demanding total control of the side and overriding the committees that had previously controlled the national side. He brought in his own backroom staff as part of what he termed 'professionalising' the way England played the game.

Over the next eight seasons, England won three Grand Slams and another Five Nations Championship in 1996. In 1991 they reached the World Cup final, losing narrowly to Australia. The success that the English game had demanded had been achieved, but amateurism, the principle that the RFU had traditionally held dearer than all others, had been abandoned.

It was a deal that most rugby people accepted without demur. And it would lay the basis for even greater England triumphs in the new era ahead.

29

BRAVEHEARTS, TIGERS AND LIONS: SCOTLAND AND IRELAND IN THE POST-WAR YEARS

Scottish rugby union had made a tradition of being traditional. It had long opposed all attempts to relax the game's amateur regulations. It suspected that international tours were a form of undercover professionalism – and refused to play the 1908 Wallabies and the 1924 All Blacks because of this. It was the last country to abandon the old 3-2-3 scrum formation and it wasn't until 1932 that it allowed players to wear numbers on their shirts.

Such conservatism ran deep. Melrose lock-forward Frank Coutts recalled turning up for a national trial after the war and standing in line to be weighed. When it came for him to step on to the scales, he was asked for a penny to put in the weighing machine. Still believing that rugby was primarily a recreation for players, the Scottish Rugby Union (SRU) itself did not even have its own offices; its secretary Harry Simson had to work from a local solicitors' firm.[1]

Yet it was the conservative Scots who became the most innovative of the British rugby nations in the post-war years. In 1960 they became the first nation from the British Isles to undertake an international tour when they travelled to South Africa. The Test against the Springboks was lost by a creditable 18-10 but the tour was judged an overall success, inspiring England to visit Australia and New Zealand in 1963 and Wales to tour South Africa the following year.

More surprisingly, the SRU was the first to introduce leagues into domestic rugby, overcoming their fear that such a move would open the door to professionalism. In 1973 the club game was organised into six national divisions, with a network of district leagues below them. The inaugural title was won by Hawick, who went through the season undefeated until they lost their final match to the second-placed West of Scotland.

The reason for the SRU's radicalism was easy to fathom. Between 1950, when a last-minute Allan Sloan try was converted in torrential rain by Northampton full-back Tommy Gray to give Scotland a 13-11 victory over England, they did not defeat the auld enemy for another 14 years. It was the last respite before a bleak decade and a half. Between 1951 and 1955 Scotland lost 17 consecutive matches. The lowest point was a 44-0 drubbing in 1952 by the touring Springboks, a match that went down in infamy as the 'Murrayfield Massacre'.

To some extent the reason for the Scots' decline was demographic. The rugby-playing population of Scotland, concentrated primarily among the former pupils of the country's elite schools and in the Borders towns, had always been smaller than that of the other home nations. The expansion of grammar school and university education in England and Wales in the 1950s and 1960s, which increased the pool of players in those countries, meant that the Scots lagged even further behind. The Scots also suffered due to the legacy of their strict adherence to the letter of the amateur regulations. In a world where sport was becoming intensely competitive, the Scottish brand of amateur fastidiousness was somewhat counter-productive.

However, as the 1960s dawned the Scots were no longer perennially propping up the Five Nations table. Partly this was down to a willingness of the players to learn from their opponents, but it was also due to the Inter-District Championship, which had been introduced in 1953 as a tournament to bridge the gap between club rugby and the international game, starting to pay dividends.

A flavour of the possibilities that lay ahead came in 1958 when a dominant Scottish pack subdued the Wallabies by 12-8. But it wouldn't be until 1964 that the flower of Scotland truly began to bloom again, when the Scots drew 0-0 with the touring New Zealanders, the only home nation not to lose to the All Blacks, won the Calcutta Cup for the first time since 1950, and shared the Five Nations Championship with Wales, their first taste of the title since 1938.

In 1966 and 1968 they again defeated Australia but the crowning glory was two victories against the Springbok tourists, 8-5 in 1965 and 6-3 in 1969. Perhaps most satisfyingly to those Scots who nursed ancient rivalries, England were defeated six times in eight meetings at the start of the 1970s, including a record-equalling streak of four consecutive victories from 1970.

As with England and Wales earlier, the Scottish side also began to benefit from an influx of players who had graduated from physical education colleges. Key men such as Ian McGeechan (who studied at Carnegie College in his hometown of Leeds), the inspirational prop Ian McLaughlan (Jordanhill College in Glasgow) and Jim Telfer (Moray House School of Education in Edinburgh) brought a level of sophistication to the side that allowed them to compete on equal terms with even the great Welsh team of the 1970s. All three would play for the Lions and provide an important legacy for the Scottish side.

Even the SRU came to recognise the importance of coaching, formerly viewed as one of slipperiest slopes to professionalism, and in 1971 it appointed Bill Dickinson, the coach of Jordanhill College, as the national team coach. But still beholden to the ambiguities of amateurism, the SRU gave him the title of 'adviser to the captain' and did not pay him a salary.

It would not be until the 1980s that the full fruits of Scotland's new attitudes became evident. As in Wales, Scottish national feeling had grown since the 1960s. In 1967 Winnie Ewing had become the Scottish National Party's first Member of Parliament and at the October 1974 general election the SNP won more than 39 per cent of the Scottish vote. The 1979 referendum had narrowly failed to endorse Scottish devolution but the social unrest of the Thatcher years in the 1980s exacerbated Scotland's sense of alienation from its neighbours in the south. Reflecting this changing attitude, the Scottish side adopted 'Flower of Scotland' as their unofficial national anthem in the mid-1970s and in 1990 it was sung for the first time as the official anthem before Five Nations games. Scotland's playing standards began to rise on the tide of nationalism.

Jim Telfer was appointed as Scotland's coach in 1980 and set about building a team that would be professional in attitude, if not in monetary terms. In 1984 a sparkling Scottish side won the Triple Crown at a canter before coming face-to-face with an unbeaten France at Murrayfield in what was sudden-death play-off for the Grand Slam.

For the first hour of the match, it looked as if the French would take the title. A try from scrum-half Jérôme Gallion capped a period of back-line brilliance and at 9-3 the Scots were on their heels. Then Gallion was stretchered off after colliding with one of his own players. French indiscipline gave full-back Peter Dods, his right eye almost closed, the opportunity to square the match with penalties and then Finlay Calder, the stand-out among a pack that eventually dominated their French opposite numbers, delivered the *coup de grâce*. His try was converted and Scotland had won 21-12. It was their first Grand Slam for 59 years.

In 1986 Scotland shared the title with the French but Telfer had moved on and the end of the 1980s proved to be lean times. A disappointing first World Cup in 1987 saw them crash out 30-3 in the quarter-finals to New Zealand. The following year Ian McGeechan became national coach. It was to be a turning point for Scotland, for McGeechan himself and for British rugby as whole, as he came to be arguably the most influential coach in the history of British rugby at both the club and national level.

In 1990 McGeechan's men strode through the Five Nations. France were put to the sword 21-0 at Murrayfield, a post-1914 record. But as Scotland strode, England rampaged, racking up 83 points in their defeats of the other three nations. The title would be decided when the two sides met in their final match of the tournament at Murrayfield, six years to the day since the men in blue won their last Grand Slam.

It was perhaps the greatest Scottish performance since the 1920s. Their forwards faced down one of the best English packs of all time – featuring Brian Moore, Peter Winterbottom, Mike Teague and a host of others who had never taken a backward step – repelling wave after wave of determined drives. Scotland led 6-0 but England scored the first try through Guscott though Simon Hodgkinson missed the conversion, as he would do with two later penalties. Craig Chalmers had a steadier day with the boot and at half-time Scotland had the noses in front by nine points to four.

The match was decided by an amazing turn of events at the start of the second half. Scotland's kick-off sailed out of play on the full and England chose to put a scrum down on the centre spot. Richard Hill fed the ball and Moore raked it back quickly. But it was too quick for the England back row and the ball didn't come out.

When the scrum was put down again, Scotland had the put-in. John Jeffrey picked it up from the base of the scrum, fed scrum-half Gary Armstrong who passed to Gavin Hastings to chip-kick into the corner for Tony Stanger to touch down. England only managed a solitary Hodgkinson penalty. When the New Zealand referee David Bishop finally blew his whistle for no-side, Murrayfield, Edinburgh and much of Scotland exploded with joy.

This was not just a win over England, not merely a Grand Slam triumph, it was a victory for the Scottish nation. At the end of a decade that had seen Scotland suffer more than most from social unrest and political neglect, politics, society and sport had come together in one incredible 80-minute period. It was a moment that would live on through the ages. And it would have to – because the magic of Murrayfield in 1990 marked not only the high point but also the end of a golden era of Scottish rugby.

From Kyle's heroes to Celtic Tigers

If the years after the end of the Second World War were some of the darkest ever for Scotland, the opposite was true for Ireland. In the space of just four years from 1948 to 1951 the Irish team won the Five Nations Championship outright three times, one of which included its first ever Grand Slam in 1948. In the previous 65 years, they had won the championship outright on only four occasions. This was truly a team for the ages.

Captained by hooker Karl Mullen, Irish success was built on an aggressive, mobile back row of Bill McKay, Jim McCarthy and Des O'Brien. But the jewel was a young Ulster medical student, Jack Kyle. Kyle had the speed, the sidestep and the sensitivity to the rhythms of a match that allowed him to sniff out the merest whiff of a try-scoring opportunity.

Kyle was a fly-half who could not have played ten-man rugby even if he had wanted to. His instinct was to get the ball in his hands and challenge defenders to make decisions about how to stop him. And once they had decided, he would do the opposite. Kyle's legacy would inadvertently be bequeathed in large part to Wales. He was the idol of the young Cliff Morgan, who modelled his game on Kyle's, and trace elements of Kyle's fly-half style could also be seen in Barry John and Phil Bennett. In 1951, Kyle scored a brilliant try at Cardiff Arms Park that almost took a second Grand Slam across the Irish Sea but the conversion was missed and Ireland had to settle for a 3-3 draw and a mere championship.

But the side that won the Grand Slam broke up quickly and the glory that they had earned slipped away. This was partly because the Irish were already an old side by the late 1940s – only three of the Grand Slam side were born after 1925. Eire had remained neutral during the Second World War and, unlike rugby in Britain, the game had continued more or less unaffected, allowing many Republic of Ireland players the opportunity to develop without the dislocations of war and reach their peak in the late 1940s.

Despite the continuing presence of Kyle until 1958, Ireland struggled to make an impact on the Five Nations. This was not necessarily due to a dearth of talent. From the mid-1950s, the side could boast outstanding wingers in Tony O'Reilly, who combined playing international rugby with revivifying the Irish butter industry by inventing the Kerrygold brand, and Niall Brophy, both of whom played for the Lions. Indeed, all three Lions' tours of the 1950s were captained by Irishmen. But as with the Scots, the Irish had yet to enter the modern rugby world and brought a style of play that was known somewhat disparagingly as 'all boot, bollock and bite'.

And despite the sporting unity that existed between the two nations in Ireland, tensions bubbled under the surface. Irish internationals had traditionally been played at Lansdowne Road, Dublin, the spiritual home of middle-class Irish Catholic rugby, and Belfast's Ravenhill Park, the mecca for Northern Ireland's middle-class Protestant rugby aficionados.

However, in 1954, the unity of the team was rattled when the 11 players from the Republic objected to singing 'God Save the Queen' before the Ravenhill match against Scotland. Captain Jim McCarthy informed the secretary of the Irish RFU that all 11 would not line up for the national anthems if the British national anthem was played for Ireland.

Realising that the players would not compromise, the IRFU met with the 11 dissidents on the morning of the match and agreed not only to the players' request but also that no further internationals would be played in Belfast, a decision that no doubt also pleased the IRFU's treasurer, who was not alone in realising that Ravenhill was far too small to accommodate the size of crowds now wanting to see Ireland play. Having scored a victory in the morning, the players took the field and beat Scotland 6-0.[2]

Irish society itself began to change in the 1960s, typified by Sean Lemass's reforming government, and rugby, too, cast off some of its old conservatism. Coaching ceased to be a dirty word and Ireland toured South Africa in 1961 for the first time and then Australia in 1967. Although they continued to struggle in the Five Nations, the Irish defeated Australia four times between 1958 and 1968, beat the Springboks in 1965 and then drew with them in 1970, and lost by a single point to the 1965 All Blacks and earned a stirring comeback draw against them in 1973.

Politics once more intervened in 1972. On 30 January, the day after Ireland recorded a historic 14-9 win over France at the Parc des Princes, 13 people were shot dead by the British Army in Northern Ireland on what became known as Bloody Sunday. Britain and Ireland were thrown into turmoil, and Wales and Scotland both pulled out of their matches scheduled to be played at Lansdowne Road for security reasons. The Five Nations was suspended for the first time outside of the two world wars. The following year the title was shared by all five teams for the first, and only, time. Ireland's 18-9 defeat of John Pullin's England in Dublin is probably less remembered for the game than for Pullin's after-match remark, 'we may not be very good, but at least we turned up'.

The five-way tie in 1973 was the nearest Ireland had got to a title since 1951. The following year, they finally got their hands on the championship again. The decisive match came at Twickenham, when a free-flowing Irish side outscored England by four tries to one to win 26-21, the third of five successive victories over the English. The star of the match was Mike Gibson, a slight but devastatingly talented centre or fly-half.

Gibson had the pace to glide around would-be tacklers but also a clairvoyant's ability to read the play and pop up in support of the merest half-break. As he proved on five British Lions tours, especially during the 1971 Test matches against New Zealand, he was the equal of any three-quarter in the world.

The brilliance of Gibson aside, it was the Irish pack, led by fellow Ulsterman Willie John McBride, that laid the basis for the 1974 championship, and it would be the pack that provided the thread of continuity between 1974 and Ireland's next championship in 1982. Moss Keane and Fergus Slattery, two veterans of the McBride era, were the twin pillars of the 1982 pack, building the platform for the unerring kicking of fly-half Ollie Campbell that led to the Triple Crown going back to Dublin for the first time since 1949.

They repeated this again in 1985, although by this time Campbell's boot had been replaced by that of Michael Kiernan. It was Kiernan's cool head and steady eye that, with two minutes to go against England at Lansdowne Road and the game tied at 10-10, received the ball from a line-out and nervelessly slotted the ball between the posts to lift another Triple Crown.

It would be almost a quarter of a century before Ireland would rise to such heights again, although this would come in the brave new world of professionalism. Like the rest of the rugby world, the Irish were inching their way into the future. In 1978 the IRFU formed a Game Development Committee to spread the coaching gospel and, in 1991, the All Ireland League was created to raise the club game to the higher standards required for the increasingly competitive new age. As the Irish economy was becoming transformed into a free-market, low-tax 'Celtic Tiger', rugby followed in its wake.

Yet perhaps the memory of Irish rugby that would burn brightest from the last decades of the 20th century come not from the national side, but from a provincial side, Munster.

Ireland had never beaten the All Blacks; their 10-10 draw in 1973 was the nearest they had come. But they weren't the only Irish side that the New Zealanders could not defeat that year. Munster also held the tourists 3-3. The 1978 All Blacks were a tougher proposition than their predecessors. They swept through the British Isles, defeating all the national sides and despatching their regional opponents. Apart from one.

On the last day of October 1978, 12,000 spectators crammed into Limerick's Thomond Park to see if Munster could repeat their moral victory of 1973. But marshalled by Tony Ward, who vied with Ollie Campbell for the Irish number ten jersey, the red shirts of Munster ripped into their opponents, putting the All Blacks on the back foot from the kick-off. Christy Cantillon ran through the All Blacks defence to score a try. Ward's conversion and a drop-goal gave Munster a 9-0 lead at half-time and then another Ward drop-goal deep into the second half sealed the game for a historic 12-0 win.

Superficially, it seemed like a victory for traditional local rugby values, but Munster coach Tom Kiernan, who had captained the Lions on the 1968 South Africa tour, had planned meticulously for the match. He intensified the side's training regime to ensure their fitness, used videos of the All Blacks to study their tactics in detail and took the side on a four-match tour of London to prepare them. It was a foretaste of the technocratic and managerial rugby that was to come.

Yet the evening's sporting drama was eclipsed that evening by personal tragedy. As Munster completed their final lap of honour that night at Thomond Park, captain Donal Canniffe was told that his father had collapsed and been taken to hospital. By the time Canniffe got to his car to go to hospital it was too late. His father had died of a heart attack while listening to the game on the radio.

Four goes into one

Although for most of the post-war period Ireland and Scotland had to play second fiddle to Wales and to a lesser extent England in the Five Nations, when it came to the British Lions the Scots and the Irish had the upper hand, at least as far as captaincy was concerned. Ten of the captains who led the 13 Lions tours between 1950 and 1993 were either Irish or Scots.

Karl Mullen, the hooker who led the Irish through their glory years of the late 1940s and early 1950s, captained the first tour to Australia and New Zealand in 1950. The shared experiences of combat between 1939 and 1945 led to a greater feeling of Britishness in the post-war years. In 1947 the Rugby Football League had officially changed the name of the national rugby league side to Great Britain and similar sentiments were reflected in the enthusiasm of the players and supporters for the rugby union Lions.

Even for players from the Republic of Ireland, this transnational unity was appealing. Although many players in every Lions' side shared a similar background of elite schools and university education, grudges and rivalries held over from matches sometimes presented problems. Carwyn James explained to his 1971 Lions how his vision of rugby multi-culturalism worked:

> I don't want Irishmen to pretend to be English, or English to be Celts, or Scots to be less than Scots. You Irish must be the supreme ideologists off the field and, on it, fighters like Kilkenny cats. You English, stiffen your upper lips and simply be superior. And you Welsh, just continue to be Triple Crown aspirants in your own cocksure, bloody-minded way.[3]

The 1950 squad was selected to represent the very best talent across the British Isles, unlike previous tours which had been chosen on the basis of availability rather than talent. The 1930 tourists had been required to possess a dinner jacket and a minimum of £80 cash on tour to cover their own expenses, and all pre-Second World War touring sides were weaker than the stronger home nations.

But with backs like Jack Kyle, Bleddyn Williams and Lewis Jones and forwards like Mullen and Wales' Roy John and John Robbins, there could be little argument that this side represented the cream of British rugby union. After an encouraging 9-9 draw in the first Test against the All Blacks, the side succumbed to the greater power of the New Zealanders and lost the next three Tests. Although Australia were beaten twice as the Lions returned home, there was widespread disappointment with the tour.

The opposite was the case with the tour to South Africa five years later. It opened with a 23-22 British victory in front of 95,000 at Johannesburg's Ellis Park. Neither side could establish dominance and they drew a thrilling series 2-2. This rising standard of British play was highlighted by the 1959 tour Down Under. After the now customary series win over the Wallabies, the Lions came face-to-face with the All Blacks. Or, rather, with Don Clarke's boot. Although the tourists lost the series 3-1, they scored ten tries to New Zealand's seven, for whom Clarke scored 39 of their 57 points. Most controversially, the Lions lost the first Test 18-17 despite scoring four tries to nil.

The 1960s were a lean time for the Lions. Other than against Australia, they did not win a single match during those years. Their tours became more famous for on- and off-field controversies than for their quality of rugby. Violence was an ever-present threat. Springbok centre 'Mannetjies' Roux broke Lions' fly-half Richard Sharp's jaw in the tourists' match against Northern Transvaal in 1962, and the 1968 tour was marked by continuous ill feeling between the Lions and their hosts, not least because of the tourists' loutish behaviour.

To some extent these national tensions reflected the changing political times. The old ties of the British Empire were dissolving. New Zealand had lost its traditional favoured relationship with Britain, as successive British governments sought to join the European Common

Market, thus putting an end to the special economic relationship between the two countries. Tightening immigration controls aimed at curbing migrants from India and Pakistan also impacted on white New Zealanders, and Australians, who were no longer eligible for unrestricted entry into what once had been but no longer was the Mother Country.

The situation in South Africa was far worse. Following the Sharpeville massacre in March 1960, South Africa had declared itself a republic in 1961 and been expelled from the British Commonwealth, which had been created in 1949 as a way of maintaining relationships between the countries of the former British Empire. Rugby became an arena in which political and national antipathies would be played out, on and off the field.

Violence also became an issue on the two greatest Lions tours, to New Zealand in 1971 and South Africa in 1974. Orchestrated by Carwyn James and blessed with a great Welsh back line augmented by Mike Gibson and David Duckham, the 1971 Lions had played brilliant rugby to win the series 2-1, alongside the drawn final Test.

Apart from the second Test defeat in Christchurch, they went through New Zealand undefeated to become arguably the greatest Lions' team ever. But, forearmed by their previous experience on the 1966 tour, they were completely uncompromising. Carwyn James' characteristically paradoxical instruction to 'get your retaliation in first' became their watchword.

That same lesson was applied with even more vigour three years later when the Lions returned to South Africa. Winning the series 3-0 alongside a drawn final Test, they literally fought their way to their first series win in South Africa since 1896, helped by the famous – or infamous – rallying cry of '99' to signal an all-in brawl. 'The Lions went through South Africa like latter-day Genghis Khans,' wrote the normally unshockable journalist John Reason. 'Some of the teams, like Orange Free State, [that] they left behind looked as if they had been in a road accident.' On the eve of the third and deciding Test, captain Willie John McBride told the Lions 'there is no escape. We will take no prisoners!'[4]

By 1974 Lions' tours had become about much more than rugby. Tours had begun in an age when Britannia ruled the waves and sport was part of the cultural bond that held Britain and its colonies together. Now the Empire was dead, the nations of the Mother Country were pulling apart and the traditions of the past were being challenged around the world. And that included those of rugby union.

30

THE FRANCE THAT WINS …

It is barely an hour's drive from Orthez to Mont-de-Marsan. On the banks of the Gave de Pau river, Orthez is a small medieval town nestled in the heart of Aquitaine rugby country. On 31 December 1967 the local club, perennial Cinderellas whose only taste of glory was a second division championship in 1935, played a friendly match against Stade Montois, the glamour club from Mont-de-Marsan whose champagne rugby had brought them the *Bouclier de Brennus* in 1963.

The undeniable star of Stade Montois was Guy Boniface, the handsome, fearless centre who embodied the spirit of open rugby. Along with his brother and centre partner André, Boniface was at the heart not only of Montois' success but that of France itself.

He made his debut for the French team that shared the 1960 Five Nations Championship, starred for the championship-winning side of 1961 and eventually won 35 international caps. His style and looks had made him the face of French rugby, a combination of the romantic hero of La Belle Époque and the media-friendly celebrity of the 1960s television age.

As he got into his car to drive back home to Mont-de-Marsan late that New Year's Eve, he knew his life was entering a period of transition. He had not played for France since the heartbreaking final match of the 1966 Five Nations, when the French had led 8-6 with just minutes separating them from a fourth outright championship.

As they pushed forward for a final try to seal the game, fly-half Jean Gachassin spotted an overlap on the left and threw out a looping pass to

Stade Montois winger Christian Darrouy. But Darrouy's opposite number Stuart Watkins intercepted the pass and ran 75 yards upfield to score a try and snatch the championship for Wales.

The Boniface brothers were blamed for not playing safe. Champagne rugby had gone to their heads, claimed the critics. This was not a little unfair. Full-back Claude Lacaze had missed a conversion from almost in front of the Welsh posts and just before full-time he had also missed a difficult but kickable penalty. Gachassin had thrown the pass but was not dropped. Yet it was the Boniface brothers who shouldered the responsibility for the loss. Neither was selected for the 1967 Five Nations.

As Guy Boniface drove north on the RN133 he contemplated what the approaching New Year would bring. A return to international rugby? A move into coaching? Or a new career in the media? For a man of his fame and charisma, the future seemed to be limitless.

It was not to be. As Boniface reached the village of Hagetmau, less than 20 miles from home, he lost control of his car and crashed. He was rushed to hospital but died of his injuries in the early hours of 1968.

Three days later the tragedy deepened when Bègles' young winger Jean-Michel Capendeguy, who had made his international debut against the 1967 All Black tourists, was killed in another car accident. For many, it appeared that the age of the rugby Musketeer had come to a catastrophic end.

The deaths of Boniface and Capendeguy were a tragic start to a momentous year in the history of France and its rugby. Eleven days after thousands had turned out for Boniface's funeral, France kicked off the 1968 Five Nations with a 9-8 win at Murrayfield. Efficient victories against England and Ireland took them to the top of the table, so by the time they arrived at Cardiff Arms Park for the final match the only question that remained the Grand Slam.

This time there were no mistakes. Although Wales led 9-3 at half-time, another pair of brothers, the half-backs Guy and Lilian Camberabero, led the French to the summit that the Boniface brothers could not. Whereas the Boniface instinct was to pass before thinking of kicking, the Camberabero style was to kick before thinking of passing.

It was Lilian Camberabero's half-blocked drop-goal attempt that led to France's first try and then Lilian himself went in for the try that took France ahead. Guy then landed a penalty and minutes later the game was over. For the first time since it entered the Five Nations in 1910, France had won the Grand Slam.

The irresistible rise of French rugby

Regardless of the other successes that France would have on the rugby pitch – in 1954 they defeated the All Blacks for the first time and in 1958 became the first touring side in the 20th century to win a series in South Africa – the quest for the Grand Slam was at the very heart of French rugby union. It was this more than any other consideration that had shaped the policies and practices of the Fédération Française de Rugby (FFR) ever since they re-entered the Five Nations after the Second World War.

France were invited back into the tournament in March 1939 but the war delayed their return until the Five Nations restarted in 1947. However, the French game continued to be dogged by controversy. During the 1948 Five Nations the British press had reported that France's scrum-half, Yves Bergougnan, had in fact been a rugby league player, having signed a contract in 1944 with Toulouse Olympique before switching to code and city rivals Stade Toulousain.

Bergougnan, who would become the last player to land a four-point drop goal in international rugby in that year's match with England, was one of 99 former league players who were now playing union, contrary to the amateur regulations that the FFR had agreed to uphold as part of their acceptance back into the international fold.[1] Scottish centre Russell Bruce recalled many years later asking Bergougnan why he had

430

switched from league to union; 'it was more lucrative,' the scrum-half replied.[2]

By 1951 the situation in France had become so disquieting that the International Board wrote a confidential letter to the FFR, reminding them of the terms of the agreement that had allowed France back into the Five Nations. The first of these was that 'no player who has been proved guilty of receiving payment other than actual out-of-pocket travelling and hotel expenses is ever allowed to play Rugby football again or to act in any official capacity in connection with any rugby football club'.[3]

As with most rugby union-playing nations, the FFR had no problem agreeing to the amateur regulations, safe in the knowledge that 'social aid', as French clubs called their provision of jobs and housing to players, would continue, but discreetly.

The IRB also demanded the ending of the French Championship, something that everyone knew was impossible. Even so, the FFR was so fearful of being expelled again that it voted in 1952 to comply with the IRB request and end its flagship tournament. Having satisfied the IRB, the FFR presented the resolution to that year's annual meeting of the clubs, who promptly voted against the move by 745 votes to none. Despite the huffing and puffing of the IRB and the deferential posturing of the FFR, nothing changed and the polite cross-Channel gavotte continued.

One crucial reason why the British nations did not push the FFR over the brink as they had in 1931 was the continuing threat of the reborn French rugby league. Even before the liberation of Paris in August 1944, rugby league had begun to be played again. But when Paul Barrière, the future president of the French Rugby League, went to Paris in September 1944 on behalf of the Ligue Française de Rugby à Treize to ask the Comité National des Sports for government support for the rebirth of league, he was told that there was no reason to alter the Vichy decision to ban the game.[4] None of the assets seized by Vichy would be returned.

In fact, the Comité National des Sports remained firmly under the control of officials who had been appointed under Vichy. In post-war France as a whole, little was done to purge the French body politic of those who had collaborated with the Nazis. Sport was left almost untouched by even the superficial cleansing of French political life that took place after 1945. Moreover, the head of the Comité National des Sports with whom Barrière was negotiating was Alfred Eluère, who also just happened to be the president of the FFR.

Rugby league was therefore allowed to be played but under very restrictive circumstances. It could not be played in schools, no more than 200 professional players could be engaged and, perhaps worst of all, was forbidden to call itself rugby. Instead, it had to go by the name of *jeu à treize*, or 'game of thirteen'. The sport which had suffered the most under Vichy was treated as if it had been the guilty party.

Even so, the game sprang to life with an enthusiasm and vitality that belied the obstacles placed in its way. Carcassonne, boasting the 20-year-old prodigy Puig Aubert, won the first championship in 1945 and the next year carried off the league and cup double, the first time it had been achieved in French rugby league. They would appear in the first six championship finals after the war, winning three. In the first year in which they did not make it to the final, the title was won by FC Lyon, which had switched codes from union to league in 1946, the last club to do so.

It was not just at home that French league surged ahead of its powerful union rival. In 1949 France, led by Puig Aubert, not only won rugby league's European Championship but it also achieved what the French national rugby union had never done in more than 30 years: defeat England in England. And not merely in England but at Wembley Stadium itself, as Aubert guided his men to an historic 12-5 victory over a strong English side. The championship success was repeated in 1951 and 1952.

Even better was to come two years after the Wembley win. Making their first tour to Australia in 1951, Aubert's men once again played dazzling league football. Although they had not defeated Australia in four previous meetings, the French took the first Test 26-15, a margin that could have been considerably more if they had not relaxed after going into half-time 16-2 ahead.

Australia took the second Test in Brisbane but in the final one at the Sydney Cricket Ground the French blew their hosts away, running in seven tries to two, with the great scrum-half Jo Crespo picking up a hat-trick. They were acclaimed as one of the greatest sides ever to visit Australia, and arrived back in France to be welcomed by thousands lining the streets of Marseille. In 1953, the Kangaroo touring team failed to avenge their defeat and the French won a home series against the Australians for the first time ever.

The following year, in 1954, France staged the first Rugby League World Cup. Masterminded by Paul Barrière who first suggested it in the 1940s, the tournament brought together the four rugby league nations for the first time. By now, the French were acknowledged as the unofficial world champions of the game and were heavy favourites to take the tournament, especially after Britain and Australia were missing key players after a hard Test series during the summer. But in front of 30,000 people at the Parc des Princes, Puig Aubert and his men were outfoxed 16-12 by a wily British side and it was the Scotsman Dave Valentine who would lift the very first rugby World Cup trophy.

It was the one failure in Aubert's long sequence of success in the 1940s and 1950s that brought him five championships, four cups and 46 French caps. Universally known as 'Pipette' for the prodigious smoking habit that would eventually kill him – legend had it that during dull matches he would pull out a cigarette for a quick smoke – he became one of those rare players that transcend sport to become a cultural symbol of their community. As his biographer Bernard Pratviel points out, Aubert's qualities as a player became the basis for a number of everyday phrases used in south-west France, such as '*Hé, maladroit, achète les gants de Pipette!* ('Hey, clumsy, buy some Pipette gloves!') and *'Tu as le panache de Pipette!*' ('You have the verve of Pipette!').[5]

Pipette missed the 1955 tour to Australia due to injury, but Jacques Merquey's team repeated the success of the 1951 tourists, taking the final two Tests after the Australians won the opening match of the series. Although no one could guess at the time, this was to be the high water mark of French rugby league. The sport's post-war success had been built on a generation that had learned the game as youngsters and who continued the indomitable spirit of defiance that the experience of the war had taught the *Treizistes*.

But, due to the ban on league in schools and the restrictions placed on the game, there was a shrinking pool of players from which to replace the Puig Aubert generation. What's more, the growing strength of rugby union offered far greater financial rewards than league, leading to talented young league players such as Jo Maso, the son of a Carcassonne league international who himself had played representative league against England, switching to the supposedly amateur game.

Rugby union's greater financial clout was not simply due to the FFR's creative interpretation of the code's amateur regulations. Like league, it too was experiencing a surge in its fortunes on and off the field, not least because of the institutional advantages it had carried over from Vichy. In 1951 the national team emulated its league cousins' famous Wembley triumph over England by winning for the first time at Twickenham.

On a mud heap of a pitch, the French pack completely outplayed the English forwards, who at one point were so battered by the ferocity of their opponents that they were reduced to six scrummagers due to injuries. The French back row turned the screw, scoring all of their side's point. Captain Guy Basquet touched down for the first try that was converted by Jean Prat, who also scored the next try and sealed the game 11-3 with a drop goal five minutes from time. France's only defeat that year was to the great Ireland side that was on its way to its third championship in four years.

Better was to come in 1954. Now captained by Prat, France won three of their Five Nations matches to share the title for the first time in their history. Perhaps even more significantly, they also recorded their first ever defeat of the touring All Blacks, thanks to a Prat try that gave them a tight 3-0 victory.

Just like Puig Aubert in league, Jean Prat became the totemic figure in French rugby union in the 1950s. Nicknamed *Monsieur Rugby*, Prat was a back-rower who had mastered all the skills of the game. Just as importantly, he was an inspirational leader. With France desperately hanging on to a two-point lead as the clock ticked down against a rampant Welsh side during their 1949 international at Stade Colombes, Prat told his teammates, 'these British have pissed on you for a hundred years, you can hold out for five minutes'.[6] They held on to win 5-3.

Prat and his centre-three-quarter brother Maurice were two of the pillars of their home town club, FC Lourdes. In 1928, the year Maurice was born, their father, a local farmer, sold some of his land to enable the club to build a stadium. Lying in the foothills of the Pyrenees, the town had become famous as a site of Catholic pilgrimage after a local girl reported seeing the Virgin Mary there in 1858. Yet it was the vision of Jean Prat and his fellow Lourdais forwards pounding down the pitch on land that had once belonged to his father that caused opposing players to pray during the 1950s.

From 1948, the year of their first French championship, to 1960, when they won their seventh title, FC Lourdes did not lose a single match at home. They completed a hat-trick of championships between 1956 and 1958, the first side to do so since Stade Toulousain in the early 1920s.

The club's success was no miracle. It was based on set moves, such as the 'lourdaise' which involved the flanker and the scrum-half swapping positions, and combinations that were endlessly rehearsed in training, an ethic of hard work and involvement of all players, and a powerful set of forwards who were confident with the ball in hand, the exemplar of which was Prat himself. Moreover, its players trained and prepared in a professional manner thanks to the assistance of the club patron, Antoine Béguère.

Béguère had played for the club as a young man but his greatest contribution was as a businessman and mayor of the town. As a building contractor at a time, Béguère was able to offer 'social aid' to Lourdes' players in the form of jobs in his building company, thus allowing them to devote their energies to rugby on a full-time basis. After Béguère collapsed and died of a heart attack during a Lourdes versus Agen match in October 1960, the club would win only one further championship.

The impact of Lourdes' domination of French rugby union was as important internationally as it was domestically. It was no coincidence that France rose to be considered a major rugby-playing nation in the 1950s. Between 1948 and 1958 the national side played only one major international match without a player from Lourdes. In the 1958 Five Nations the French side contained no fewer than seven of the club's players.

Lourdes' players occupied central roles in one of French rugby union's greatest achievements when the national side toured South Africa in 1958. This was a weakened side, missing for various reasons Maurice Prat and the Boniface brothers, and tour manager Serge Saulnier sought to bind the squad together through an emotional appeal to patriotism. He reminded them that this was their first visit to a former British dominion and that the South Africans believed the French had ceased to be a world power. 'You will be able to demonstrate that France is still a great power,' he told his players.[7]

The first Test was drawn 3-3 after a Pierre Danos drop goal had given France a 3-0 half-time lead, but most commentators felt that the French had the best of the match. Three weeks later the two sides met again in the deciding game. France opened the scoring with a penalty goal from

Lourdes full-back Pierre Lacaze but a converted Loftie Fourie try saw the Springboks lead 5-3 at half-time.

The second half saw the French pack, led by captain Lucien Mias playing the game of his life, dominate the match. Lacaze dropped a goal to put the French ahead and then with seven minutes remaining his elegant Lourdes' teammate Roger Martine dropped the goal to win the series. Although all the points were scored by backs, it was Mias and the forwards who were the heroes of the day, leaving South Africa defeated in a home Test series for the first time since 1896. France were now unquestionably a member of rugby union's international elite.

'The France that wins'

The victory in South Africa took place at the same time as France itself was undergoing a profound political crisis. Forced to withdraw ignominiously from its former colony Vietnam, humiliated by the failure of the Anglo-French attempt to seize the Suez Canal in 1956 and paralysed by a revolving door system of government, matters came to a head when the French army seized power in Algeria in May 1958 in an attempt to stop Algerian independence.

The leaders of the coup called for Charles de Gaulle to return to power and on 1 June 1958 he was made prime minister with emergency powers. In November his proposals for a new constitution were passed and a new, fifth, republic was proclaimed. In a country that had flirted with the possibility of civil war, de Gaulle needed symbols of national unity and international prestige to legitimise his regime. He called for *La France qui gagne* ('The France that wins') and his new government put sport at the centre of French life. 'The best [youths] must be taken in hand to prove the continuity of French vigour and its rebirth in international competition,' he wrote in 1960.[8]

There was no sport better placed than rugby union to fulfil this national role. Rugby league had no diplomatic weight and French soccer was not a power in world football. And, as luck would have it, two days after de Gaulle had become president of the new French republic on 8 January 1959, France defeated Scotland in the first match of the campaign that took the Five Nations title across the Channel as the sole property of the French for the first time.

The championship was shared with England the following year, thanks to a 3-3 draw with the English in Paris, but in 1961 and 1962 the title was won outright yet again. As de Gaulle's quest to restore France's status on the world stage continued – in 1960 it became the fourth nuclear power when it exploded an atomic bomb in the Sahara, the same year that French gross domestic product overtook that of Britain for the first time – rugby became the sporting symbol of French success.

The game was boosted by the rise of television. French television had first broadcast international matches in 1955 and the annual cycle of the Five Nations became a regular focus for viewers to convert their homes into 80-minute citadels of Gallic patriotic fervour. French technological expertise also meant that the national side's 1961 tour to New Zealand was broadcast live on French television via satellite, the first time ever for a rugby tour, although a 3-0 whitewash in the Test series was perhaps not the best way to showcase the new technology.

As the popularity of rugby reached new heights, stars such as Guy Boniface became celebrities. Boniface was as likely to appear in *Paris Match*, the weekly colour magazine that combined news, celebrities and lifestyles, as he was in *L'Equipe*. President de Gaulle allegedly did not allow cabinet meetings to be held if they clashed with Five Nations matches. When France won the championship in 1967, the captain of the side Christian Darrouy sent a telegram to the Elysée Palace declaring 'Mission Accomplished!'. The game simultaneously represented Gaullist modernity while still symbolising the unchanging *vérités* of traditional rural France, *la France profonde*.

Yet, as the controversy surrounding Boniface and the failure to play conservatively in the closing stages of the Welsh match showed, French rugby faced a dilemma. Had its desire for international success led to the abandonment of the philosophy of *rugby champagne*, open, attacking rugby? Many feared that it had, and with good reason.

The successes of the late 1950s had not been based on flowing back-line moves but, as was pointed out by one of French rugby's leading journalists, Denis Lalanne, on the scrum. 'We know where rugby begins and where it must begin all over again. It certainly does not begin in the back row. It begins in the FRONT ROW,' he explained in his classic account of the triumphant South African tour, *The Great Fight of the French Fifteen*.[9]

The historic Five Nations Championship win of 1959 also followed this philosophy to the letter. E. W. Swanton noted of France's 11-3 win over Wales which clinched the title that 'William Webb Ellis himself might almost have wondered whether his revolution had been achieved in vain, for there was certainly not a great deal of picking up the ball and running with it.'[10]

As with most beliefs about national playing styles in sport, French commitment to open rugby had a mythic quality to it. The great Lourdes side of the 1950s was based on strong forward play, as was the success of the national side in the same decade. Clearly the French had a preference for a daring, dashing rugby played through the hands, but so too did almost every rugby nation.

Even England, from whom the French took their scrummaging expertise, believed deep down that the true spirit of the English game was expressed by Ronald Poulton Palmer and David Duckham rather than the aggressive forward play that was the traditional source of English success. Like all narratives about national character – such as America's belief that it was the land of opportunity or Australia's vision of itself as the lucky country – views about the national ways of playing rugby tell us more about how nations wished to see themselves than how they actually were. But the French myth helped to anchor rugby in the national culture. The French may not have invented rugby, but they believed that only they knew truly how to play the game.

Yet the simple truth for the French, as much as for anyone else, was that once winning became the imperative, the rules of rugby union meant that every side defaulted to a safety-first approach that, in the words of Lalanne, began in the front row of the scrum. And despite protestations to the contrary, this was a lesson that would not forgotten by French *rugbymen*.

Thus the 1968 Grand Slam was achieved by a ruthlessly attritional pack driving forward to give the Camberabero brothers the time and space to launch the ball upfield. In the aftermath of the Grand Slam there was no attempt to return to *rugby champagne*. Instead, the forward-dominated, territorial game was refined and perfected. It became the style that made France the only challenger to Welsh superiority in the Five Nations in the 1970s and the most successful northern hemisphere nation of the 1980s.

It also dominated French domestic rugby, most notably through the stranglehold that AS Béziers maintained on the championship in the 1970s and early 1980s. Playing the same powerful forward game, they carried off the *Bouclier* ten times in 14 seasons from 1970. In some ways, this functional, almost technocratic, style reflected the conservatism of French society in the aftermath of May 1968. De Gaulle's successor, Georges Pompidou, appointed the former rugby union international Jacques Chaban-Delmas as his prime minister, and the game was seen as a unifying force in a society that had been split from top to bottom by *les événements* of 1968.

In 1977 the essence of that utilitarian style was refined to it purest, when a second Grand Slam was achieved by a French side that comprised the same 15 players in each of the four matches and which did not concede a single try. Its star was the blond, brave and charismatic flanker Jean-Pierre Rives, who seemed to embody the suppressed spirit of French rugby.

But as valuable as Rives was, and he became national captain in 1978, the field marshal of the side was *le petit caporal*, the scrum-half Jacques Fouroux, a man whose similarity to Napoleon extended beyond his nickname to both his diminutive height and his limitless ego. He was appointed national coach in 1981 and quickly established total control of the side, basing his tactics on ruthless forward play and attritional territorial advantage. His strategy met with complete success. He carried off a Grand Slam in his first season in charge, another in 1987, won an outright Five Nations Championship in 1989 and shared it on three more occasions. In his ten years of generalship, he lost just ten Five Nations matches.

He was much less successful against Australia and New Zealand, recording just a single win against the All Blacks, but his regime is perhaps best, if uncharacteristically, remembered for the inaugural 1987 rugby union World Cup. After an opening draw with Scotland, Fouroux's men played sparkling rugby to reach the semi-final, where they played the joint hosts Australia.

In one of the greatest ever matches, the Wallabies held the lead for most of the match but the French, like a marathon runner following a pacemaker, refused to let them out of their sight. With minutes remaining on the clock, Didier Camberabero landed a penalty to level the scores at 24-24. Extra-time loomed. But then, from an Australian line-out deep in French territory, the Wallabies were harried off the ball. It was inelegantly passed out wide by full-back Serge Blanco and hoofed downfield by Patrice Lagisquet.

Everyone knew that this was France's last throw of the dice. The ball then moved through 11 pairs of French hands, first to the right and then finally to the left where Blanco suddenly appeared to finish off the move he had started in his own half and score in the corner. Camberabero converted to make it 30-24.

There was just time for the kick-off. The ball was caught by the French and fed back to Franck Mesnel who booted it into touch, whereupon the referee blew for no-side. Against all expectations, France would meet the All Blacks in the World Cup final.

The two sides were to meet at a time when France–New Zealand relations were at the lowest point they had ever been. In 1985 French secret service agents had sunk the Greenpeace ship *Rainbow Warrior* in Auckland harbour to stop its protests against France's testing of nuclear weapons in the Pacific. Just as French foreign policy towards Britain could be contained in a single Five Nations match, now its interests in the Pacific were encapsulated in a World Cup final.

But history took its revenge on Fouroux and the All Blacks snuffed out France by playing the way of the Little Corporal: a tight, controlled forward game dominated by the positional and goal kicking of Kiwi fly-half Grant Fox. In a match that was as dour as the semi-final had been exciting, the All Blacks took the World Cup by 29-9.

The 1987 World Cup marked the beginning of the end for amateurism in rugby union. In France, the process was far less traumatic than it would be for the English-speaking rugby nations. In 1965 *Rugby World* magazine explained that '*amateur* may be a French word, but in the rugby clubs of France and elsewhere on the continent attitudes are borrowed from professional sport that would make the turf at Twickers bristle'.[11]

By the mid-1970s the benefits on offer in France were such that players began to make their way across the Channel to play rugby, most notably England lock Nigel Horton who joined Toulouse in 1977 and worked as a bar manager.[12] Nor was there now any shame, or discretion, about signing rugby league players, as had happened most notoriously in 1980 and 1981 with league internationals Jean-Marc Bourret and Jean-Marc Gonzalez. The advent of professionalism in August 1995 was the signal to put the French game on a sounder business and financial footing.

The open poaching of two of its star players said much about French rugby league's fall from grace since the 1950s. Although the national side had reached the final of the 1968 Rugby League World Cup and hosted the 1972 tournament, the game lacked financial and institutional power of the union code and it began to contract. Even Test series wins against Australia in 1968 and 1978 did little to raise its national profile. Lack of television coverage and its inability to project an international image for France restricted the appeal of the game to its heartland. And the bitter opposition of the FFR to rugby league continued long after the code had ceased to be a threat to the popularity of rugby union.

In 1981 league finally garnered the national headlines it had wanted, but for all the wrong reasons when the championship final between Villeneuve and Perpignan's XIII Catalan was abandoned after the referee was unable to stop the fighting between the two teams. The game remained rooted in its traditional localities and fostered its strong sense of injustice and defiance of the status quo, which reflected the position of both the sport and its communities in the South of France.

In 1991, thanks to a determined campaign by its supporters, the sport finally won back the right to call itself *rugby à treize*, rather than *jeu à treize*, although reparations for its assets confiscated under Vichy have never been paid. Despite Jacques Fouroux's short-lived attempt to revivify the game in 1995, it would not be until the present century and the introduction of the Perpignan-based Catalans Dragons into the British Super League that French rugby league would begin to recover the ground it had lost.

31

RUGBY LEAGUE: A PEOPLE'S GAME IN A TELEVISION AGE

As in Greek tragedy, it is the athlete's curse that their triumphs and tragedies are played out under the gaze of the public. Such was the fate of Wakefield Trinity prop Don Fox in the 1968 Rugby League Challenge Cup final against Leeds at Wembley.

Torrential rain before the kick-off covered the pitch in standing water. After 15 minutes Wakefield led 7-4, thanks to two Fox goals and a Ken Hirst try set up by long, raking Fox kick that bamboozled the Leeds defence. But then the heavens opened again and the two teams struggled to cope with the nearest thing to a monsoon that Wembley had ever seen.

Then, on 69 minutes, the game came alive. Leeds winger John Atkinson was awarded a disputed penalty try and Bev Risman's conversion gave Leeds a 9-7 lead. Two minutes from time, Risman slotted over another penalty to give Leeds a commanding if unlikely 11-7 lead.

And then the drama began.

Fox, realising that something extraordinary had to happen, took the kick-off quickly and landed the ball just in front of the Leeds defenders. It slipped under the foot of Leeds centre Bernard Watson and was hacked on towards the posts by Hirst. He flew past five startled Leeds players and dived on the skidding ball just before it slid over the dead-ball line between the posts. Leeds now led 11-10, with a conversion to come from under the posts.

It was the 80th and final minute. The conversion would be the last act of the match. Up strode Fox, the architect of Wakefield's fightback, to take the kick. In his 15 years as a professional rugby league player, he had kicked almost 700 goals, most of them far more difficult than the one he now faced.

Conscious of the appalling conditions, he took his time setting the ball on a small mound of mud. He placed his right foot carefully against the ball and walked backwards, slowly and precisely measuring out his customary five and a half paces.

He was the most experienced man on the pitch. He was one of the most respected players in the game. And he knew that it was now his duty to win the cup for his team and his town.

Many of the Leeds side stood with their backs to him, not wishing to witness the moment that the cup would be prised from their grasp. The crowd, too, knew that the cup would soon be on its way to Wakefield.

Fox ran up to convert just as he had hundreds of times before. But this time the slipperiness of the ball and the wet toe of his right boot did not make perfect contact. The ball flew off to the right of the posts. The match, the final and the cup were lost.

And so was Fox. In frustration he turned and flung himself to the ground, his fists slamming the wet grass that had denied him. On BBC TV, commentator Eddie Waring's Yorkshire tones supplied the Greek chorus for the tragic scene as he exclaimed, 'he's a poor lad'.

Moments later, it was announced that Don Fox had been awarded the Lance Todd trophy as the man of the match.

His greatest triumph and his greatest tragedy had become one and the same.

From boom to bust to boom

Fox was born in Sharlston in the heart of the West Yorkshire coalfield, the birthplace of interwar league legend Jonty Parkin. Like Parkin, he had been a half-back but as he aged he had moved into the forwards.

Like his father, he started his career with the local Sharlston club and worked at the nearby pit. And like his brothers, the illustrious Neil and the astute coach Peter, he earned his own place in rugby league immortality.

In 1953 he made his debut for Featherstone Rovers as an 18-year-old at the apex of rugby league's post-war popularity. As with all British sports, the immediate post-war years were a boom time for rugby league. The war was over but rationing remained and austerity reigned. Sport offered a shaft of sunlight amidst the gloom of 1940s Britain.

Spectator numbers at league games rocketed to a peak of 6.8 million in the 1948–49 and 1949–50 seasons. The Challenge Cup final at Wembley sold out its 95,000 capacity for the first time in 1948. In 1954, the year after Fox made his professional debut, 102,569 people were officially recorded as attending the Challenge Cup final replay between Warrington and Halifax at Bradford's Odsal Stadium. Many thousands of others were uncounted in the confusion of the unstoppable flood of spectators.

If crowds were high, the game's stars had rarely shone brighter in the firmament. Two generations of the greatest rugby players ever lit up the sky. Bradford's Ernest Ward, Barrow's Willie Horne and Wigan's Eric Ashton were orchestral conductors in all but name, and each captained Great Britain. Powerhouse forwards such as Vince Karalius, Ken Gee and Derek Turner were as skilful as they were intimidating.

But perhaps the greatest talent to emerge in the post-war years was Alex Murphy, the St Helens' scrum-half whose lightning speed off the mark was matched only by his quickness of thought. Murphy had been signed by St Helens at one minute past midnight on his 16th birthday in 1955 and as an 18-year-old had starred on the 1958 British tour to Australia. After winning everything with St Helens, he moved to Leigh and guided the club as player-coach to their only Wembley win in a 24-7 upset over odds-on favourites Leeds in 1971. He then moved to Warrington, playing and coaching them to Wembley glory in 1974.

It was not just home-grown players who rose to prominence. Lewis Jones and Billy Boston were just two of dozens of Welshman who made their way north for rugby glory and an honest day's pay. Some stars had trekked even further. Until 1947, when an international transfer ban was introduced, British clubs cherry-picked the best of post-war Antipodean talent, among them Brian Bevan, Harry Bath, Arthur Clues, Lionel Cooper, Pat Devery, and Johnny Hunter. Possibly even more than the preceding two generations of Australian exiles, this group left an indelible mark on the game.

Sydney-born Bevan's 796 tries made him rugby's most prolific try scorer ever, and today a statue dedicated to his memory stands in his adopted home of Warrington. Hunter, Devery and Cooper became the crucial triumvirate in Huddersfield success of the early 1950s. Arthur Clues and a complete three-quarter line of fellow Australians raised Leeds back to the heights they had conquered under their previous generation of imports.

By the end of the 1950s the boom years were over for British rugby league. Between 1950 and 1960 the average league match crowd fell from 9,600 to 4,829. The trend became alarming in the 1960s and by the early 1970s total annual attendances were barely more than a million for all games. It was not the only sport to suffer a decline. English soccer crowds fell by almost a third between 1950 and 1965 and cricket crowds by almost two-thirds. Britain also underwent profound economic changes, especially in rugby league's northern industrial heartland. Between 1947 and 1970, more than two-thirds of all coal mines were closed. In 1984 the number of people employed in the textile industry was little more than 10 per cent of its 1954 total. The soil in which rugby league had flourished was rapidly becoming barren.

The decline in attendances led to a crisis of confidence and considerable debate about the rules of the game. It was widely believed that negative tactics were driving away spectators, the most notable example being that of the 'creeping barrage'. This involved the acting half-back picking the ball up from the play-the-ball and running forward without passing until he was tackled. This would be repeated ad infinitum to minimise the risk of losing possession. Bill Fallowfield, the prickly secretary of the RFL, had campaigned to change the play-the-ball rule since the early 1950s, but the issue was finally settled by a decision to borrow from American football. At the 1966 meeting of the Rugby League International Board, Fallowfield suggested limiting possession to four tackles per team. The proposal was passed unanimously and within weeks the new rule was being hailed as a turning point for the game.

The rule was extended to six tackles in 1972 in order to allow greater opportunities for attack, and gradually other rules were streamlined to encourage faster, more open play. In 1974 the value of the drop goal was reduced from two points to one. The problem of constantly resetting the scrum was gradually solved by allowing, albeit informally, the scrum-half to feed the ball to his own forwards, and in 1983 a handover of the ball to the opposing side, rather than a scrum, was introduced when the attacking side was tackled on the sixth tackle. The principle cherished by the founders of the Northern Union, that theirs would be 'a game without monotony', had never been more apparent.

Despite such positive changes, rugby league also continued to suffer at the hands of rugby union. Until the late 1980s, anyone who played league, paid or not, was automatically banned from the union game. Faced with threat of sporting and social ostracism, very few players dared change codes. Sometimes players joining a rugby union club were asked to sign a declaration stating, 'I have not taken part in rugby league football, either as an amateur or a professional, nor have I signed any rugby league form, after reaching my 18th birthday'.

Although this was officially explained as combating professionalism, everyone understood that the enemy was not professional sport but rugby league itself, as the IRB admitted in 1958: 'there is in general no objection to persons who are or have been ranked as professionals in games other than Rugby League football being permitted to play Rugby Union football or to participate in the affairs of rugby union clubs'.[1] This nonsense would only finally end in 1995, when union itself openly embraced the dreaded professionalism.

The decline in rugby league's fortunes was only arrested in the mid-1970s. Off the field, the development of commercial sponsorship, which the game had pioneered in 1961, brought new money into the sport. In November 1971 the inaugural Player's No. 6 Trophy competition kicked off and in May 1974 the RFL agreed to allow clubs to carry advertising on their shirts, something which had first been seen in the 1960s in French rugby league.

This rugby league renaissance was led by the two Hull clubs, Hull FC and Hull Kingston Rovers. Together, they dominated the game in the late 1970s and 1980s, winning championships and challenge cups and jointly contesting the major finals six times in six seasons. Their mantle was then taken up by Wigan who revolutionised the game by becoming the first club to employ players on a full-time basis in the mid-1980s.

This enabled them to sign many of the biggest stars in the game, including Martin Offiah, Joe Lydon, Andy Gregory and Ellery Hanley, and from 1985 they dominated the game in a way not seen since Harold Wagstaff's Huddersfield. In 11 seasons they won the Challenge Cup nine times and the championship eight.

The renewed interest in the game was taken to new heights by the 1982 Australian Kangaroos' tour, which not only saw the Great Britain side humiliated but also brought crowds flocking to witness the brilliance of the Kangaroos' play. For the first time since the 1950s Australian players became household names across the north of England.

Like the England soccer team's eye-opening 6-3 defeat by Hungary in November 1953, the shock at the scale of the 1982 series' whitewash was traumatic and, desperate to learn from their conquerors, the league authorities lifted the international transfer ban in 1983. In the following ten years, 757 Australian players came to play for British clubs. Many became local icons, among them Mal Meninga at St Helens, Peter Sterling at Hull, Brett Kenny and John Ferguson at Wigan. The high point of this invasion was undoubtedly the 1985 Challenge Cup final between Wigan and Hull, which brought the sublime skills of Kenny, Sterling and John Ferguson to the attention of a national public in a thrilling 28-24 Wigan victory.

But as the British game reached new heights domestically, it fell to a new low internationally. Britain had last won the Ashes in 1970 but was humiliated in 1979 when, for the first time ever, it lost a series 3-0. The same happened in the next four Ashes series. It would be nine years before Great Britain would win another Test match against Australia. As even the most one-eyed British supporter had to admit, Australia was now the world's dominant rugby league power on and off the field.

Down Under on top

This was a considerable turnaround. At the end of the Second World War, Australian rugby league had no doubt that it was the junior partner to the British game. In October 1945 Australian Foreign Minister H. V. Evatt persuaded the RFL to send a British touring team Down Under in 1946 telling them that Lions' tours 'ought to be resumed as soon as possible, in the best interests of rugby league football and of the Empire'.[2] E. S. Brown, the manager of the 1954 Australian World Cup squad, was even more explicit, telling the RFL that 'there is a strong desire in Australia to get along with England from every point of view'.[3]

In 1950, 30 years after they had last won them, Australia finally regained the Ashes at a muddy Sydney Cricket Ground when winger Ron Roberts found himself the extra man on an overlap and dived over in the corner 15 minutes from time to give his side a series-winning 5-2 victory. Normality was restored in 1952 when Britain retook the crown but they faltered in 1954 when, in one of the most thrilling and free-scoring series, Clive Churchill once again captained the Australians to success.

Britain retained the Ashes for the rest of the decade but in the 1963 series, in a portent of what was to come, Australia shocked even themselves and took the Ashes by winning the first two matches by 28-2 and 50-12, the first time any side had scored 50 points in an Ashes match.

Australia's growing power on the pitch reflected increasing economic clout off it. The legalisation of poker machines in New South Wales in 1956 introduced a considerable new source of income for rugby league clubs, and led to the creation of 'leagues clubs', which combined gambling, restaurants and community activities, allowing clubs to subsidise their on-field activities lavishly. Coupled with the abandonment of the local residential qualification for players in 1959, which meant that players no longer had to live in the immediate area of their club, Sydney clubs were now able to compete financially with the British.

Now the tide of rugby league emigration turned, to flow in the opposite direction. In March 1963 Derek Hallas became the first player in the modern era to move Down Under when he went from Keighley to Parramatta. He was followed by major stars such as St Helens' Dick Huddart and Tommy Bishop, who, together with a host of other top players, migrated in the 1960s. Britain's 1970 Ashes victory accelerated the exodus, as Australian clubs clamoured to sign the victorious British stars. In 1971 Manly paid a then world record £15,000 to Castleford to sign their awesome loose forward Malcolm Reilly.

The wave of British imports of the 1960s and 1970s brought new skills and approaches to the Australian game. Wigan's Dave Bolton went to Balmain and redefined stand-off play. Reilly brought a whole new combination of all-sided technical ability and uncompromising ferociousness. His Manly teammate, Hull KR's Phil Lowe, built on Dick Huddart's legacy as a free-running second-row forward: 'as the aircraft carrier made the battleship obsolete, Phil Lowe established that the lumbering forward was about to join the mastodons in extinction,' wrote an admiring Thomas Keneally.[4]

The loss of British players to Australian clubs was one symptom of how rugby league was being revolutionised in Australia. Thanks to immigration by 'Ten Pound Poms' (an expression used to described Britons who emigrated to Australia after the war on an assisted passage scheme) from Britain and by southern Europeans, the country's population doubled in the 30 years following the Second World War and, as the dominant sport in NSW and Queensland, rugby league grew hugely in popularity among both players and spectators in the post-war years. New clubs were admitted to the NSW premiership in 1947 and 1967 and between 1959 and 1967 crowds attending matches in Sydney doubled to more than 1.5 million per season.

The popularity of the game was, perhaps paradoxically, spurred by the dominance of South Sydney in the early 1950s and then by St George from 1956 to 1966. Souths, based in working-class, inner-city Sydney, dominated the premiership in the interwar years and resumed that role in the early 1950s. Nicknamed the 'Rabbitohs', allegedly because players were so poor they sold rabbits around the district, the side was captained by Clive Churchill, a full-back who redefined the role, turning it from a stentorian last line of defence to a fifth three-quarter.

Souths' domination did not last. St George, based in the rapidly expanding southern suburbs of Sydney, quickly outstripped the achievements of the Rabbitohs by winning the premiership for 11 successive seasons from 1956 to 1966. They were able to capitalise financially on the now legal presence of poker machines and the growing local population to build a huge leagues club that quickly became known as the 'Taj Mahal' for its size and opulence.

This apparently never-ending flow of revenue allowed St George to buy the very best talent. Much of the success of St George's record-breaking championship-winning run was due to the influence of British playing methods learned by returning players such as Harry Bath, who had emigrated to play for Warrington between 1948 and 1956, and hooker Ken Kearney, who played for Leeds between 1948 and 1952. By the mid-1960s, the influence of players and coaches who had played in England had helped to raise the Australian game to the same level as the traditionally dominant British.

Australian attitudes to the Mother Country were also changing. Britain's application to join the European Common Market in 1961 without consulting Australia and the ending of free entry into the UK for Australians in 1962 led to growing alienation. Many began to look to the United States, among them rugby league coaches seeking an advantage in the increasingly competitive Sydney competition. Two young coaches, Terry Fearnley and Jack Gibson, went to America to study American football coaching methods in the NFL, especially those of the all-conquering Green Bay Packers' legendary coach Vince Lombardi.

Gibson, in particular, would have tremendous success in the 1970s and 1980s, first with Sydney's Roosters and then with the Parramatta Eels. By the time that Gibson's Parramatta completed a hat-trick of premierships in 1983, Australian rugby league had become a major entertainment industry in its own right. The importance of the British link to the game had withered and, as British teams struggled to remain competitive, the importance and intensity of Anglo-Australian Test matches was replaced by the annual NSW versus Queensland 'State of Origin' series.

State of Origin began in 1980 and quickly became a centrepiece of the Australian sporting winter. By selecting only players born in each state – hence 'origin' – the three-match series rekindled regional passions and raised rugby league to new heights. In 1988 the New South Wales Rugby League became a national league with the addition of teams from Queensland, in particular the Brisbane Broncos, and for the first time the very best Australian players all played in the same league. Together, the new Australian Rugby League (ARL) and State of Origin commanded massive public interest and huge television audiences. The ARL was now the world's most important club competition in either rugby code. As the game entered the 1990s, a bright future seemed assured.

Super war

The ever-increasing popularity of Australian rugby league was not confined to Australia. Its rising tide had also lifted the game in New Zealand. In the 1970s, the increasing wealth of league in Sydney lured a number of top Kiwi players over the Tasman. In the 1980s regular televising of Australian club matches began in New Zealand. Most importantly, from 1983 onwards the New Zealand Kiwis played a series of physically intense and nail-biting matches against the Kangaroos. At a time when Great Britain struggled to score tries against Australia, let alone beat them, the Kiwis were formidable opponents.

In 1988 they reached the final of the Rugby League World Cup for the first time in their history, only to lose disappointingly to Australia. Despite this the team's top players, such as Mark Graham and Kevin Tamati, became national celebrities. Even more astounding for a nation fixated with rugby union, a steady stream of All Blacks switched to league, including John Gallagher, Marc Ellis and John Schuster. Kiwi stars became crucial components of Australian club sides and in 1992 it was announced that a team from Auckland, the traditional power base of New Zealand league, would join the ARL in 1995.

The 1988 World Cup also saw the inclusion of Papua New Guinea for the first time. League had been established in PNG by Australian servicemen during the Second World War and, as Australia began to colonise the country in the 1950s and 1960s, the popularity of the game grew among the indigenous population. By the 1970s it had become the undisputed national sport of PNG, highlighted in 1975 by the visit by England on their way to the 1975 World Cup in Australia.

Two years later, the Kumuls (named for the indigenous bird of paradise) pulled off one of the biggest shocks ever in rugby league by walloping France 37-6 in Port Moresby, the PNG capital. It would be another nine years before they would record another victory, a 24-22 win over a full-strength New Zealand team, but by this time PNG had been accepted as the fifth international side of rugby league. The increasing penetration of television in a largely underdeveloped and, in some places, still unexplored country only served to increase the popularity of the game and establish it as PNG's national sport.

The emergence of satellite television in the 1980s also led to greater worldwide exposure for league around the world. By 1995, the number of countries playing the sport had grown so much that the Centenary Rugby League World Cup held that year saw ten teams participating, including Fiji, Tonga and Samoa for the first time, and another seven in an Emerging Nations tournament that was held at the same time.

The growing popularity of rugby league, especially as measured by television audiences, had not gone unnoticed by those outside the sport. The 1980s had brought deregulation to the television industry around the world and the development of satellite and digital technology led to the emergence of an entirely new market of consumer pay-TV. And, as media moguls such as Rupert Murdoch and his arch-rival Kerry Packer very quickly realised, sport was, in Murdoch's famous words, 'a battering ram' to be used to establish pay-TV networks.[5]

Such prescience did not extend to the leaders of Australian rugby league. In 1993 they had signed a deal with Kerry Packer's free-to-air Channel 9 that paid the ARL A$80 million for TV rights for the next seven years. Pay-TV rights were also included in the deal for free. The previous year English soccer's newly formed Premier League had been paid £191.5 million for pay-TV rights by Murdoch's BSkyB. When Murdoch's Australian News Ltd company approached the ARL to open discussions about acquiring pay-TV rights in 1994, the ARL told them to speak to Packer.

To make matter worse, the expansion of the Australian Rugby League had also led to friction between the traditional Sydney clubs and the newer clubs, especially the Brisbane Broncos. In early 1994, the Broncos' chief executive, former Australian winger John Ribot, met Rupert Murdoch and proposed the formation of a 'Super League' tailored to suit the needs of News Ltd's satellite television network which included mergers of clubs in Sydney. Locked into a weak bargaining position thanks to its Channel 9 deal, the ARL found itself in the middle of a battle between the two media barons with little means of self-defence. Discussions continued between the ARL and Ribot's Super League supporters throughout late 1994 and 1995 but Ribot's hopes that the ARL would compromise came to naught, partly because Kerry Packer did not want an agreement with Rupert Murdoch.

Finally, at the end of March 1995, negotiations broke down completely. Ribot, assisted by Lachlan Murdoch (Robert Murdoch's eldest son and deputy chief executive of News Ltd), rolled out a battle plan and began to sign players for their new Super League, largely through the simple expedient of offering them more money than they had ever seen in their lives. Within weeks Murdoch's men had also signed up all the professional clubs in England, who agreed to switch to a summer season as part of an £87 million deal. The global war for rugby league was on – and within weeks it would also have a momentous impact on rugby union.

Rugby league had never seen so much money nor such commercial interest in it. Yet the sport's very existence was now at stake. Just like Don Fox at Wembley in 1968, what should have been its moment of greatest triumph became the moment of its greatest disaster.

32

RUGBY'S ROAD TO 1995

On 24 June 1995, the Springboks and the All Blacks walked out to do battle for rugby union's World Cup in front of 63,000 people at Ellis Park, Johannesburg. They had fought for the unofficial championship of the world many times before, but now there could be no doubt that the victors would truly be the best team in the world.

In the week before the final, expectations vied with paranoia for headlines as accusations of listening devices, early morning car alarms and a bout of food poisoning contracted by some All Blacks dominated pre-match discussions. Tensions ran high. This was perhaps the most important rugby match that had ever taken place.

After 80 minutes, nothing separated the two sides. Each had scored a drop goal and two penalties. For the first time in a final, the match went into extra-time. Once again, both sides swapped penalties. And then, with seven minutes left to play, the Springboks won a scrum on the New Zealand 22-metre line, ten metres in from touch.

Springbok captain François Piennar called for a back-row move, but, sensing the need to put points on the board, fly-half Joel Stransky shouted at his half-back partner Joost van der Westhuizen for the ball.

The ball emerged from the scrum and Westhuizen fed it back to Stransky, standing a few metres back to the right of the New Zealand posts. It was clean ball and as the New Zealand defenders raced forward at him, Stransky's right boot hit the ball strongly, sweetly and successfully between the posts. 'I don't think I've ever kicked a ball as well as that,' he later remembered.

It was 15-12 and it seemed like the whole of South Africa held its breath for the next few minutes. Then, after time seemed to stand still for hours, referee Ed Morrison looked at his watch and blew the whistle for full-time. At last, the Springboks were the official, acknowledged and undisputed champions of the world.

Even more importantly, the match had been a triumph for South Africa's first black president, Nelson Mandela. Aware of the importance that the game had for white South Africans and especially Afrikaans speakers, Mandela had built up a relationship with the Springbok side and had addressed the team in the dressing room before kick-off. He arrived at the stadium wearing a replica of captain Francois Piennar's number six jersey and was still wearing it when he presented the World Cup to Pienaar himself.

Barely a decade earlier, no self-respecting black South African would have considered supporting the Springboks, let alone wearing one of the symbols of apartheid sport. Mandela's gesture signalled that rugby would not be forced to change and that its potent symbolism would be left untouched. Both South Africa and rugby union had been transformed but, as the following years would demonstrate, old traditions and structures were not so easily displaced.

Oval-shaped politics

By the end of the 1960s, the issue of South African apartheid dominated rugby politics. In 1969 the Springboks arrived in London for their sixth European tour of Britain. The British Lions had toured South Africa twice in the 1960s, losing both the 1962 and the 1968 series, but it was not until the 1969 tour that British rugby union came face-to-face with the consequences of its South African connection.

The stage had been set by the proposed England cricket tour to South Africa in 1968 and the non-selection of Basil d'Oliveira, the Cape Town-born all-rounder who had emigrated to England in 1960 and was now eligible for the national team. Under pressure from South Africa he was not selected for England but was later brought into the side as a replacement. The South African government refused to accept him and the tour was cancelled.[1] Anti-apartheid campaigners led by Peter Hain switched their attention to the 1969 South African tour of Britain.

As soon as the Springboks touched down at Heathrow airport they were greeted by demonstrators chanting 'Don't Scrum with a Racist Bum'. Tour manager Corrie Bornman immediately inflamed the situation by telling journalists that his players would mix with all races 'provided they are rugby players'.[2] As had been predicted, the Springboks' matches were met by thousands of demonstrators and interrupted by continual pitch invasions. The tour reached its nadir on 15 November at Swansea when stewards mercilessly laid into demonstrators, sending 20 anti-apartheid campaigners to hospital, five of whom were knocked unconscious. Home Secretary James Callaghan called for a report on the events and a week later banned club stewards from being used against demonstrators.[3]

The Springboks trudged sourly through Britain, outwitted by demonstrators and largely outplayed by their international opponents, drawing with Wales and Ireland and losing to England and Scotland. But the results were incidental. The tour had, in the words of All Black captain Chris Laidlaw, ensured that 'rugby has gained international infamy as the key activity by which South Africa seeks to legitimise its doubtful sporting and cultural links with the rest of the European world'.[4]

Worse was to come when the 1971 Springboks toured Australia. Tens of thousands of demonstrators turned out to oppose the tourists wherever they played. The Australian Council of Trade Unions declared a boycott of anything connected with the tour. Airline and airport workers refused to fly the Springboks around Australia, the Waterside Workers' Federation boycotted all South African ships and 4,000 Melbourne dockers went on strike for a week in protest at the tour.

There was also a significant breach in the game's wall of disdain for the protests. Six Wallabies – Tony Abrahams, Paul Darvenzia, Terry Foreman, Barry McDonald, James Roxborough and Bruce Taafe – refused to play against the Springboks, following the example set by Wales' John Taylor in 1969. But by and large the leadership of the sport remained united in support of the Springboks.

Matches were played behind police cordons and barbed wire to stop demonstrators invading the pitch. Hundreds of protesters were arrested. When the team arrived in Queensland for four matches, the scale of the protests was so large that the prime minister Joh Bjelke-Petersen declared a month-long state of emergency, effectively granting himself the same police-state measures employed by the South African government.[5] Despite the fierce opposition off the pitch, the Springboks found their on-field opponents to be rather less ferocious and went through the tour undefeated, winning all three Test matches comfortably.

In between the social unrest of the 1969 and 1971 tours, the Springboks had hosted the 1970 All Blacks, after the South African government agreed to make Sid Going, Blair Furlong, Buff Milner and Bryan Williams, Maori all, 'honorary whites' for the duration of the tour. Even this was less of a concession than it appeared. As New Zealand's leading rugby writer Terry McLean revealed, South African prime minister John Vorster met New Zealand's deputy prime minister John Marshall in late 1967 to lay down conditions for the acceptance of Maori players. 'There should not be too many Maoris, they should not be too "black" and no violent controversy should attend their selection,' he insisted.[6] The New Zealanders went along with the conditions – but still lost the series 3-1.

It was not only politics that dimmed the lustre of Springbok–All Black contests. As the historic 1971 British Lions series win in

New Zealand confirmed, the southern hemisphere superpowers were not the only claimants to the title of world champion. The brilliance of the Welsh and the rising standards of British play meant that the Lions could legitimately claim to be the best side in the world. Indeed, when they went through their 1974 tour of South Africa undefeated and only missed out on a 4-0 Test shut-out of the Springboks thanks to referee Max Baise disallowing Fergal Slattery's last-minute try in the final Test, there could be no doubt who the world's best side was.

When the All Blacks returned to South Africa in June 1976, there was a sense that this was a contest for world rugby union's silver medal. Since they had last met in 1970 the All Blacks had lost to the Lions, England and France. Now they fared no better against the Springboks, losing the series 3-1. But the tour would not be remembered for the rugby that was played, but for the circumstances and consequences of its playing.

The All Blacks arrived in South Africa less than two weeks after police had shot dead 176 people and wounded hundreds at a demonstration in the Johannesburg township of Soweto. South Africa was gripped by strikes, protests and demonstrations. With the 1976 Montreal Olympic Games fast approaching, African nations began calling for the New Zealand Olympic team to be barred from the games due to the All Blacks' breach of the sporting boycott of South Africa. The International Olympic Committee refused to exclude New Zealand so 27 countries boycotted the Games. The rugby bond between South Africa and New Zealand was ripping apart world sport.

And that would soon be the case within New Zealand itself. In 1973, fearful that the scenes of civil unrest seen in Britain and Australia would be repeated at home, the Labour government cancelled the Springbok tour at the last minute because the South African Rugby Board (SARB) refused to change its white-only selection policy. But National Party prime minister Robert Muldoon subsequently made welcoming a

Springboks' tour a key issue in his platform and in 1981, after an absence of 16 years a South African touring side finally returned to New Zealand.

Among the touring party was 31-year-old Errol Tobias, who had become the first 'coloured' player to play for the Springboks earlier that year, but no one was fooled that his selection was anything but window dressing and he did not play in any of the Test matches. But almost as soon as Tobias and his teammates touched down on New Zealand soil, the country exploded.

Demonstrators took to the streets in their thousands, while as many others stood firmly in support of the tourists. Every match was protected by hundreds of riot police, the first time these had been seen in New Zealand. Two matches were cancelled because of the actions of protestors and the final Test in Auckland was disrupted by demonstrators dropping flour bombs on to the Eden Park pitch from an aeroplane. It was the nearest thing to civil war the country had ever experienced. When it was over, no one really cared that the All Blacks had won the series by two Tests to one.

South Africa and the road to professionalism

The importance of South Africa to rugby union and the sport's inability to break the link not only thrust the game to the forefront of international politics in the 1970s and 1980s; it also set in train the process that would eventually lead to rugby union becoming professional.

Before the Second World War, South African rugby was the southern hemisphere nation that was most deferential to the RFU. But as SARB came under the control of Afrikaans speakers in the 1950s – many of them members of the Broederbond, an Afrikaner equivalent of the Freemasons – it became increasingly critical of the RFU's leadership of the IRB. From the mid-1950s it began to propose alterations to the rules and was criticised openly by the IRB for allowing substitutes, then strictly against the rules, during the 1958 French tour of South Africa.[7]

Most importantly, attitudes towards players' payments were diverging, too. In 1963 SARB president Danie Craven called for higher expenses' payments to touring players and offered to make 'out of pocket' payments to players going to South Africa for its 75th anniversary celebrations.[8] Although SARB proclaimed its adherence to amateurism, it was apparent that many Afrikaners did not entirely share the enthusiasm of the Anglo-Saxons.

Moreover, the late 1950s saw attempts to bring rugby league to South Africa and a number of prominent Springboks, such as Tom van Vollenhoven, Wilf Rosenberg and Tommy Gentles, left to play for English league clubs. Martin Pelser, one of those who turned to league, stated bluntly: 'I cannot recount the many days of unpaid leave I had to take for the sake of amateur rugby … Amateur rugby, and especially Springbok rugby, is a game for rich men's sons. I, and others like me, could no longer afford it.'[9]

Numerous black and mixed-race players also left South Africa to play in British rugby league. Goolam Abed, Louis Neumann, Salie Schroeder, Llewellyn Maganda, Green Vigo and Dave Barends were among many who left home to find fame and fortune in the north of England. Cape Town-born Barends, who had played for the South African 'Coloured' team in the 1960s, became the first non-British-born player to play rugby league for Great Britain when he toured Australia in 1979.

League in South Africa never got off the ground, thanks to SARB's virulent opposition. Danie Craven himself declared that he wanted to 'prevent another Huddersfield' in reference to the site of the 1895 meeting that split English rugby, and approvingly described union's attitude to league as being 'the strictest form of apartheid'.[10]

But South Africa's increasing international isolation allowed SARB to claim a greater degree of flexibility towards amateurism. The commercialisation of the South African game grew throughout the 1960s, especially sponsorship from breweries and tobacco companies.

In 1969, SARB opposed the IRB ruling that 'commercial sponsorship is contrary to amateur principles' and the IRB wrote to SARB querying the extent of commercial involvement in the sport.[11] By 1976 the British unions were sufficiently concerned to register their alarm at the number of players 'being invited, in some cases with their wives and families, to South Africa to play and coach in what would normally be their close season'.[12] The meaning was clear – players in South Africa were being paid to play.

But by the late 1970s, the IRB was unwilling and unable to act against such violations of their amateur code. Unwilling because they had invested considerable political capital in supporting SARB against the movement to boycott the apartheid regime. Unable because they knew that decisive action against SARB would lead to an international split. Danie Craven, as wily an SARB president as he had been a Springbok scrum-half, exploited this to the full, telling politicians what they wanted to hear while pursuing his agenda of keeping South Africa within the ranks of international rugby union.

Part of Craven's power came from his ability to exploit the fear of professionalism. The example of cricket and the establishment of Kerry Packer's television-driven World Series Cricket competition in 1977 demonstrated what could also happen to rugby union. Indeed, plans for a Packer-style professional rugby union circuit in New Zealand were mooted in 1977 and in 1979 SARB was approached by businessmen to discuss a professional tournament.[13]

Most importantly, South Africa's desire for international competition in the 1980s led to the extravagant financing of so-called 'rebel' tours. Thanks in large part to Craven's astute political manoeuvring, the threat of a professional breakaway led by South Africa never materialised, despite being in almost complete international sporting isolation by the mid-1980s. England toured in 1984 but the All Blacks' projected 1986 tour was banned by the New Zealand High Court, forcing SARB to invite so-called rebel touring teams.

In April 1986 the unofficial New Zealand 'Cavaliers' arrived in Johannesburg, boasting 28 of the 30 players originally picked for the banned All Black tour, all of whom were paid. Three years later a World XV toured to celebrate SARB's centenary which, although sanctioned by the IRB, was no less a professional side than the Cavaliers had been. As a Welsh Rugby Union inquiry into the tour discovered, the players were paid around £30,000 each. 'SARB,' the inquiry went noted drily, 'was prepared to tolerate the making of financial inducements to players to tour'.

More generally, the Welsh inquiry found cynicism and deceit to be widespread in the sport. 'While individual lack of circumspection or even deceitful behaviour might be explicable, the vitally disturbing feature was that such behaviour seemed so widespread as to be almost endemic to the whole system and its operation'. The only criterion used by the players when deciding whether to accept illegal payments was the likelihood of being 'discovered or penalized'.[14] Amateurism had rotted from the inside.

When RFU president Denis Easby returned from England's 1994 tour of South Africa, he revealed that he no longer had any doubt 'that South Africa paid its players and its referees contrary to the regulations'.[15] The end of rugby union as he knew it was nigh.

Advance Australia where?

The decisive blow that ended rugby union's amateur age would eventually come from Australia, a prospect that a couple of generations earlier would have horrified Australian rugby union. Indeed, for a nation that prided itself on being outspoken and forthright, the Australian game was remarkably deferential to the Mother Country and the RFU.

So when the British unions invited Australia to become the first side to tour Britain after the Second World War, it was greeted with unrestrained joy in Sydney. On arrival in Britain in September 1947, the Wallabies were welcomed with equal enthusiasm. In the post-war gloom of austerity Britain, their brand of rugby, like that of the 1945 New Zealand Army team, offered an exciting alternative to the somewhat stodgy rations that most British sides still offered. 'They relax into light-heartedness and schoolboy zest when they pull on their boots for football,' reported British journalist Denzil Batchelor.[16]

In the Test matches, none of the British sides crossed their line, yet the Wallabies scored four tries against both Ireland and Scotland and three against England. They succumbed to Wales, who forced them to play a forward-oriented game that nullified their attacking might, and were beaten at their own game by France, who outscored them three tries to nil.

Playing was just one part of the story. The tour was treated as almost an official state visit, with audiences being granted with the royal family, the Duke of Gloucester, the prime minister Clement Atlee and Irish President Eamon de Valera, not to mention official visits to the Houses of Parliament and other historic buildings. It was a triumph for Australian rugby union on and off the field.

For once the feeling was mutual, as was demonstrated in 1948 when Australia, along with New Zealand and South Africa, was finally given a seat on the International Rugby Board. At last, Australia would sit on the IRB as equals with the British. And even better was to come 18 months later, when the Wallabies won a Test series in New Zealand for the first time ever. It was truly a green and golden age.

No sooner had it begun than it was over. The three decades that followed could not have been bleaker. In the 1950s, Australia won just seven of 35 Test matches, losing to every Test nation as well as the New Zealand Maori and, most famously, twice to Fiji. The Wallabies lost all five Test matches on the 1957 tour to Europe and barely managed to win half their tour games.

Things were no better in the 1960s when just 11 of 40 Test matches were won. The drawn 1963 series in South Africa and then a series win over the Springboks in 1965 were the only high points.

Perhaps the lowest point came on the 1967 European tour when hooker Ross Cullen was sent home after just the third match of the tour for taking a bite out of Oxford prop Ollie Waldron's ear.

Australian society was changing, yet rugby union was not. Millions of immigrants had moved to Australia since the end of the Second World War, and for many of them the road to integration led through sports with large working-class constituencies such as rugby league, Australian Rules football and to a lesser extent soccer. Rugby union remained confined to the private schools and the professions and so had little to offer most 'New Australians'.

In the southern state of Victoria, which had provided four Wallabies in 1939, the game almost disappeared, and the few thousand people who watched Sydney's Shute Shield final were dwarfed by the tens of thousands who gathered every weekend for rugby league matches. Rugby union remained largely the preserve of the elite private schools, unable to attract new circles of support or broader numbers of players.

By the 1970s it had become apparent that the game's malaise was part of Australian sport's broader international decline. In 1976 the Australian Olympic team had returned from the Montreal Games without a single gold medal, and in 1980 the government created the Australian Institute of Sport with the explicit aim of putting Australia back in the elite of world sport.

Although rugby union did not become part of the AIS until 1988, the increased national focus on sports science, coaching and professional administration across all Australian sport shook the game out of its torpor. Learning from American school sport, the private rugby union-playing schools in Sydney and Brisbane started pro-actively to recruit talented teenage players. In 1980 the Wallabies defeated the All Black tourists in a series for the first time since 1949. Change was in the air.

This was highlighted most brilliantly on the Wallabies' 1984 tour to Britain and Ireland when they achieved a Grand Slam whitewash of all the home nations. Even a muddy Cardiff Arms Park could not halt them and they ran in four tries to a solitary David Bishop touchdown, the only Test try they conceded. Two years later, they won the Test series in New Zealand for the first time since the 1940s.

As the 1984 tour suggested, one of the paradoxical reasons for the Wallabies' re-emergence was the growing strength of Australian rugby league. Key members of the tour party, such as David Campese and Mark Ella, had grown up playing league and brought some of those skills to union. Moreover, the quantum leap forward that Australian rugby league had taken in the 1970s and 1980s not only rubbed off on the 15-a-side game in terms of coaching and tactics, but also created a vacuum in international league that the Wallabies filled.

Whereas once Australia versus Great Britain rugby league matches had dominated sport in New South Wales and Queensland, the anaemic performances of the British had severely undermined the credibility of international league. One-sided league Tests could not offer the excitement of a reborn Wallabies' side now challenging for the title of best rugby union team in the world, and they became Australia's premier team in global sport.

And over the next two decades Australia was arguably the world's dominant international rugby union side. In 1991 the Wallabies defeated England 12-6 in the World Cup final at Twickenham. In 1999 they returned to Britain to win the trophy once more, this time defeating France 35-12 in Cardiff.

The structures that were put in place in the late 1970s and 1980s produced two generations of great players. The strategic and organisational skills that Nick Farr-Jones and Michael Lynagh brought to the 1991 side were replicated in 1999 by Stephen Larkham and George Gregan. The 1991 pack that reversed the traditional disdain for Australian forward play was repeated by the 1999 side, with continuity provided by the great lock John Eales. In 2003 they came within seconds of a third World Cup but were foiled by Jonny Wilkinson's last-minute drop goal that took the cup back to England.

There was one more reason why Australian rugby union rose to such prominence in the 1990s. It was better prepared to deal with the immense changes that took place during the decade in which the amateur game turned professional. Indeed, in many ways it led the movement away from amateurism.

The Australians first broached the idea of a World Cup in 1983, partly as a way to control what many saw as an inevitable move to professionalism, fuelled in part by direct experience of Kerry Packer's creation of World Series Cricket in 1977. As if to confirm their fears, in April 1983 Australian journalist and sports promoter David Lord announced that he had signed up 200 of the world's leading players to take part in a global professional rugby union tournament based on Packer's model. Lord soon discovered that it was not so simple to organise a mutiny and his scheme was dead before the end of the year.

For the supporters of the World Cup concept, Lord was crucial in strengthening their case. He demonstrated that if the IRB did not organise a World Cup, someone else would. 'If we were to save our game and not lose it to some entrepreneur, we would have to act promptly and organise a world cup', argued Nick Shehadie, a 1947 Wallaby and then president of the Australian Rugby Union.[17] In June 1984 New Zealand once again raised the issue and in March 1985 the IRB voted 10–6 to stage a World Cup in Australia and New Zealand in 1987.

The success of the inaugural World Cup was repeated on a grander scale in England in 1991. Huge television audiences, burgeoning sponsor interest and an increasingly profit-based approach from within the game itself swept away all of the old concerns about the dangers of commercialism. Amateurism was on its death bed, and it was only a matter of time before someone would deliver the *coup de grâce*.

Endgame/new game?

The funeral of what was once rugby union's most sacred shibboleth was held in South Africa at the 1995 World Cup. Not merely were South

African rugby and the fate of amateurism around the world intimately entwined, but the singularity of rugby and Afrikaner identity meant that the game would play an important role in the future of the nation itself.

In 1986 secret negotiations began between Nelson Mandela's African National Congress and the South African government. It had become clear to many in the white elite that the never-ending cycle of township revolts and the growing radicalism of black trade unions were making South Africa ungovernable. Investment from foreign banks was drying up and there was a huge flight of domestic capital out of the country.

Echoing the phraseology of Giuseppe di Lampedusa in his novel *The Leopard*, there was a widespread belief that if white South Africans wanted things to stay the same, things would have to change. In 1990 Nelson Mandela was released from jail after 27 years and the ANC legalised. Four years later, on 27 April 1994, in South Africa's first ever election under universal suffrage, the ANC was voted into government and Mandela elected president.

Rugby union was a major symbolic part of this process, both at home and internationally. In 1987 South Africa had not been invited to the inaugural World Cup because of the boycott of apartheid. The following year Danie Craven secretly met the ANC to discuss terms to allow the Springboks to return to international rugby. In March 1992, one of the major conditions of those talks, the unification of SARB and the non-white rugby federations into the South African Rugby Football Union (SARFU), took place and South Africa re-entered the world of international rugby. In August that year the Springboks played the All Blacks and the world champion Wallabies in official Test matches for the first time since the 1970s.

They lost both, demonstrating the effects of almost two decades of isolation, but the matches also highlighted the extent to which rugby remained the last redoubt of unapologetic apartheid. Angry at the replacement of the national anthem with a two-minute silence for peace and reconciliation, spectators defiantly sang 'Die Stem van Suid-Afrika', the national anthem of the old South Africa. For Mandela and the ANC, if they didn't know it before, it was clear that the political future of South Africa would be fought out under the shadow of the oval ball.

Conversely, the future of rugby union would be decided in the shadow of South Africa. Despite recognising that something had to be done, the IRB had no clear plans for the future of the game. In 1994 it had set up a 'working party' to discuss the future of amateurism. When it reported back in February 1995, it could not even explain why rugby union was an amateur sport. 'As to quite why it was considered that the question of compensation for bona fide loss of time was thought to be contrary to "the true interest of the game and its spirit", is not made clear in the surviving documentation of that time,' it declared incorrectly.

The report went on to argue that if the game had been founded 'in the latter part of the 20th century, then [its amateur principles] would be considered socially unacceptable and divisive'.[18] This was nothing less than an admission that the Northern Union had been right in 1895. The reality was that rugby union no longer had use for the formal social segregation of amateurism. Indeed, in the battle against rugby league's new-found riches, amateurism was now an obstacle. As in the wider world, the gentlemanly traditions that had shaped rugby union in the past had been displaced by the demands of the 'marketplace' and the wealth now available to sport.

All it took to bring the amateur house tumbling down was an energetic push – and it was Australian rugby league that inadvertently did the pushing. In February 1995, News Corporation's proposal to create a rugby league 'Super League' was vetoed by the Australian Rugby League (ARL) authorities and rugby civil war broke out in the game. Momentary *Schadenfreude* in rugby union ranks rapidly dissolved when it became clear that union players could also be tempted by the hundreds of millions of dollars pouring into both sides in the rugby league war. 'We don't want our players sitting there like lambs to the slaughter. The advent of Super League could force us to move to professionalism much quicker than we were going,' warned NZRU chairman Richie Guy.[19]

Guy's words were echoed by former Wallaby Ross Turnbull. 'To protect ourselves from Super League, we must take the game global, we must become professional'.[20] On 8 April representatives from the Australian and New Zealand rugby unions decided that the only realistic course of action was to approach News Corporation for a deal. Four days later, the New South Wales Rugby Union officially announced that rugby union was no longer an amateur sport.

Two days before the Springboks and the All Blacks met to contest the World Cup final, the Australian, New Zealand and South African unions signed a US$550 million ten-year deal with News Corporation. 'For some time rugby union has appeared to be threatened by other codes, almost like a wounded impala limping through the bushveld with lions nearby,' declared SARFU president Louis Luyt. 'This agreement allows these unions to retain control of their destinies.'[21]

The future of rugby union and, in no small way, that of the South African nation had been decided at the 1995 World Cup. All that remained was for the IRB to formally ratify the decision to legalise professionalism. On 27 August 1995 it did precisely that. It was just two days short of the one hundredth anniversary of the split that had established rugby league and the original form of professionalism in rugby.

PART VIII

INTO THE 21ST CENTURY

The events of 1995 catapulted rugby of both codes into the 21st century. Wherever it was played the game was subject to new pressures and new responsibilities but also new opportunities. Ahead of it lay a future far different from that which any of the game's founders could have imagined.

And yet, the game's appeal remained as powerful as it ever had, for in an age of rapid technological changes, scientific advances and burgeoning corporate interests, the pleasures of the oval ball grew ever more compelling ...

33

SHRINKING WORLD, GLOBAL OVAL

When England ran out in front of a packed Millennium Stadium on the first Saturday of February 2005 history was made before the ball had even been kicked off. Leading his men into the cauldron against a Wales that would win its first Grand Slam since 1978 was Jason Robinson, the first black player ever to captain England.

This in itself was remarkable. Apart from Bristol's Jimmy Peters, who played five times for England between 1906 and 1908, the first black England rugby union international had been Chris Oti who made his international debut in 1988. But unlike Oti, who had been educated at Durham and Cambridge, Robinson had been born to a single mother in south Leeds and attended a local comprehensive. For him to become captain of England showed just how much rugby union had changed in little more than two decades.

But Robinson embodied much more. His prodigious rugby skills had been honed not at Old Deer Park, Welford Road or any of the other traditional grounds of English rugby union, but at Central Park, Wheldon Road and all points north. Jason Robinson had been born and bred a rugby league player. And for a black ex-professional international rugby league player to lead the England rugby union side was as unthinkable as anything could have been just a decade earlier.

He was not the only league player who found himself in demand by the 15-man code. When he had lined up to face Australia in the 2003

World Cup final, he had come face-to-face with three other league internationals, Mat Rogers, Wendell Sailor and Lote Tuqiri. In the quarter-final against Wales he had come up against fellow league international Iestyn Harris. Even the All Blacks had recruited lock Brad Thorn from the Brisbane Broncos. And the coaching booths of almost all the major nations contained at least one coach who had been trained in league.

The oval world seemed to have flipped on its axis.

A world in union

If the RFU's decision to oppose professionalism in 1895 was a game-changer, the IRB's decision to support professionalism exactly one hundred years later was no less momentous in its consequences for the game.

As in 1895, the path to professionalism was not straightforward. Indeed, the plans of the southern hemisphere giants, who had come together to form South African, New Zealand and Australian Rugby (SANZAR), ran into problems even before the IRB made the decision to abandon amateurism. Flushed with their own self-satisfaction in reaching a deal with Rupert Murdoch, SANZAR failed to consult their players or notice that Ross Turnbull's World Rugby Corporation (WRC), backed by Kerry Packer, had already secretly signed up most of the cream of rugby union talent from under their noses.

To what extent Packer was genuinely interested in Turnbull's WRC rather than simply poking a sharp stick into the eye of Murdoch is open to question. As players like Welsh captain Ieuan Evans discovered, signing with WRC entitled them to nothing more than a promise of a down payment three months later and the responsibility of paying for their own match insurance. The WRC's plans finally collapsed when Murdoch's general, Sam Chisholm, personally persuaded Springbok captain Francois Pienaar to switch sides and

Ross Turnbull was publicly humiliated on South African television by the Murdoch-supporting Louis Luyt.[1]

Having despatched its rival, SANZAR set to work organising its two flagship competitions. The Tri-Nations international series between the three countries was modelled on the northern hemisphere's Five Nations while the Super 12 competition would be a regional tournament, comprising five New Zealand sides, four South African and three Australian, with the Australian Capital Territory Brumbies from Canberra joining Queensland and New South Wales.

When they kicked off in 1996 the Tri-Nations and the Super 12 were greeted with huge enthusiasm. Both tournaments were initially dominated by New Zealand with Auckland's Blues and then the Canterbury Crusaders lifting the first five Super 12 titles. Indeed, the two sides dominated the first 13 years, with only the Brumbies and Pretoria's Bulls interrupting their run of successes.

The defining team of Super Rugby, and the backbone of the equally successful All Blacks side, were the Crusaders. Over two generations of players, from Justin Marshall and Reuben Thorne to Richie McCaw and Dan Carter, the side dominated the game, playing open, attacking rugby that most teams found almost impossible to defend against. Indeed, in 2002 they went through the entire season unbeaten, including an epic 96–19 win over the NSW Waratahs.

The All Blacks shared much of the philosophy of the Crusaders' free-flowing game. Despite Australia and South Africa's better World Cup records, New Zealand won ten of the 16 Tri-Nations series up to 2011 and then a further two following the inclusion of Argentina in the tournament and its rebranding as the Rugby Championship.

But what really mattered was winning the World Cup. Whereas once New Zealanders valued their rivalry with South Africa above all else, the desire to be the world champions now focused on the World Cup – and the Tri-Nations was seen ultimately as preparation for it. So by the time New Zealand hosted the World Cup in 2011, the fact that it had not lifted the trophy since the very first competition in 1987 was weighing heavily on its collective sporting consciousness.

The extra-time loss to the Springboks in 1995, the inexplicable collapse against the French in the 1999 semi-final, and then the smash and grab win by the French again in the 2007 quarter-final seemed to suggest that the All Blacks might have a World Cup hoodoo. The All Blacks were a team of champions, but were they a champion side?

The answer would come on 23 October 2011 when the New Zealanders lined up against their nemesis France in the World Cup final. They had already beaten the French in the group stages but their opponents' form had been so erratic – Tonga had also defeated them in a group match – that the outcome seemed to defy logical prediction. It turned out to be a final of move and counter-move, an attritional battle of position with each side probing to find that decisive weakness.

Both sides scored a single try but the decisive score was Stephen Donald's 46th minute penalty which would ultimately give the All Blacks an 8-7 victory. Twenty-four years after winning the first cup final, New Zealand were once more the undisputed world champions. No more talk of hoodoos.

The South Africans had no such concerns about superstition. The triumph of 1995 had been followed by a narrow extra-time loss in the 1999 semi-final, thanks to Wallaby Stephen Larkham booting his first ever international drop goal from 48 metres. In 2003 no one expected much of coach Rudi Straeuli's weak Springbok side and the team unsurprisingly bowed out at the quarter-final stage.

But under Jake White, who had been appointed in 2004 to modernise Springbok play, the South Africans had been almost unstoppable in the 2007 group and knock-out stages. In the final they suffocated England to win 15-6 and lift their second World Cup in four attempts.

Professionalism had little direct impact on South African rugby. For most of the top players, the changes of 1995 were largely about putting informal agreements on a contractual basis and abandoning the need to use the language of amateurism. South African rugby had always been organised on a top-down basis which meant that the provincial structure of the game was able to absorb the impact of professionalism without the inconvenience of club owners seeking to impose themselves on the direction of the game, something which would bedevil the English and, to a lesser extent, the French games.

The strength of South Africa's domestic game also meant that the Super 12 did not command the same importance as it did in Australia and New Zealand. The Currie Cup was not diminished by Super Rugby, as had happened to New Zealand's National Provincial Championship, and the fact that South Africa commanded the biggest market for sponsors and television networks meant that it held most of the aces when dictating the terms of the competition.

This lack of fundamental change was reflected in the racism that still affected South African rugby. Controversy broke out shortly before the 2003 World Cup when Geo Cronje allegedly refused to share a room with Western Province's black lock-forward Quinton Davids. In 2006 Jake White had claimed that he had been forced to pick non-white players for political reasons. And despite the political rights now enjoyed by South Africa's majority non-white population, the 2007 World Cup-winning team including just two non-white players, J. P. Pietersen on the right wing and the wonderfully talented Bryan Habana on the left.

This was an increase of precisely one over the number of non-white players in the 1995 World Cup-winning side. That player was Chester Williams, who had no illusions about his experiences at the highest level of Springbok rugby: 'the one-nation factor lasted about a week after the [World Cup] final before South Africa, its society and its rugby lapsed back into racism,' he told the *Sunday Times* in 2002.[2]

The fact that South Africa won the Tri-Nations only three times since it began highlighted how the World Cup has changed the focus of international rugby. Now that there is an official rugby World Cup, Test matches against the All Blacks no longer occupy quite the same position in the South African rugby pantheon. The unquenchable thirst of television networks for live sport has also diminished the rarity value of Springbok versus All Blacks clashes. In the 50 years following their first meeting in 1921 the two sides played each other 30 times – yet between 2000 and 2014 they played 31 matches against each other. Familiarity often breeds indifference.

As well as the World Cup there was one other exception to the seemingly never-ending diet of international matches and tours. That was the British and Irish Lions. When the game went professional many questioned the future of the Lions. The demands of clubs and national unions on players seemed to suggest that the new age of rugby would have no place for a concept from Victorian times.

But the 1997 tour to South Africa demonstrated the continuing power of the Lions. Bolstered by the return to rugby union from league of Scott Gibbs, John Bentley, Alan Tait and Allan Bateman, the Lions defeated the Springboks two Tests to one. The public interest generated by the tour removed any doubts about the future and in 2001 the Lions went to Australia. Captained for the second time by England's Martin Johnson, the Lions lost the series, despite the emergence of Jason Robinson on his first tour since switching from league, but the huge crowds and impressive rugby played by both sides captured the imagination of rugby followers around the world.

Led by former England coach Clive Woodward, the 2005 Lions went to New Zealand with hopes as high as Woodward's back room staff was large. Forty-four players were selected for the tour and 26 coaches and advisers accompanied them. Such hubris seemed to be inviting trouble and it all came crashing down once the Test matches began and the All Blacks' whitewashed the Lions 3-0. Ian McGeechan took the Lions back to South Africa in 2009 and, although they lost 2-1, the tour went down as one of the greatest, with the second Test earning a place in posterity as one of the most exciting, and for the players most physically punishing, ever played.

The triumphant 2013 tour of Australia highlighted how the Lions could evoke much deeper emotions in the rugby and sporting community than were generated by tours from the individual nations of the British Isles. Part of this was due to the fact, for obvious reasons, that the standard of play of the Lions was usually much higher. But for the three former dominions of the British Empire who hosted Lions' tours, the opportunity to test themselves against their former colonial British masters kindled their sense of national identity and historic grievances like nothing else. Professionalism had altered many things in rugby, but the game's deeper connections of community and continuity remained largely unchanged.

The importance of the World Cup and Lions' tours was even more pronounced for Australian rugby union. The triumphs of 1991 and 1999 had raised the game in Australia to new heights and the Wallabies had become Australia's most important national winter sports team, rivalled only by the dominant run of success of the national cricket side in the 1990s. The smooth transition to professionalism and the rise of the ACT Brumbies, led by the Wallaby playmakers of George Gregan and Stephen Larkham, meant that Australia had become a rugby union superpower in its own right.

The success both on and off the field of the 2003 World Cup seemed to promise even more success. But the euphoria did not translate into domestic expansion. Rugby union found itself competing for third place in the football hierarchy, as both league and Australian Rules signed huge television deals. In 2005 soccer launched the 'A-League' on the back of a golden generation of Australian-born soccer players and the success of the 'Socceroos' in qualifying for three successive World Cup tournaments meant that they replaced the Wallabies as Australia's leading national side.

The only expansion that the game was able to sustain was the addition of two more Super 14 franchises, Perth's Western Force in 2006 and the Melbourne Rebels in 2011. The reality was that rugby union's roots were still embedded deeply in the Australian private school system and the worlds of business and the professions. It could not compete with the mass appeal of rugby league or Australian Rules – and nor did many of its supporters want it to.

Twenty-first-century league

The mass appeal of rugby league in Australia was nowhere more apparent than on Sunday 12 November 2000, when 80,000 people marched the two miles from the inner-city Sydney suburb of Redfern to Sydney Town Hall at the heart of the city's business district. It was the biggest demonstration that the city had seen since the protests against the Vietnam War 30 years earlier. Yet the demonstrators were not protesting about war or peace, or any other political cause.

They were demonstrating in support of rugby league and in particular against the plan of Rupert Murdoch's News Limited to remove South Sydney Rabbitohs from Australia's National Rugby League competition. If anyone doubted the ability of sport to move people, both figuratively and literally, the thousands of men, women and children who turned out that Sunday afternoon proved otherwise. The passions generated by the Super League war brought to the surface the game's deep emotional resonance with supporters and their communities.

That same fervour was aroused wherever rugby league was played in the decade after 1995. The sport had been in turmoil ever since negotiations between Murdoch and the Australian Rugby League collapsed in February 1995. In 1997 both sides staged their own competitions, complete with grand finals, State of Origin representative matches and international Tests. At the 1995 Rugby League World Cup, held to coincide with the sport's centenary, Australia sent a team comprising only those players who had refused to sign with Murdoch's Super League.

When British rugby league in Britain aligned itself with Murdoch's Sky TV in the UK thousands of people protested in the streets and stadiums of the north of England against Murdoch-inspired plans to merge clubs. 'They've taken our jobs, now they want to take away our leisure,' one demonstrator argued, and the strength of the protests was so fierce that ultimately no mergers took place.[3]

But the price of the civil war proved to be far too high. In Australia, the two leagues survived as separate entities for just one season, as neither side could afford the continuous haemorrhaging of millions of dollars. A compromise was reached and the National Rugby League (NRL) formed in 1998. But it would take the best part of two decades for the bitterness between the two factions to subside. In Britain, there was no split but the high-handed and undemocratic creation of Super League led to a well of resentment that was at least as deep as that which existed in Australia.

The focus for opposition was South Sydney. The club had been excluded from the NRL as part of the peace settlement between the warring factions. But the loss of the Rabbitohs touched a deep nerve in the sport and in Sydney itself. The fact that the club was also the traditional team of Sydney's indigenous Aboriginal community made the loss even more profound. But the campaign paid off and finally, following a legal appeal, South Sydney were readmitted back into the NRL in 2002. The civil war was almost over, but it had cost Rupert Murdoch an estimated A$560 million, lost untold hundreds of millions of dollars for Kerry Packer's rival media empire and almost robbed the game of its soul.[4]

Unsurprisingly, the fractured landscape of rugby league in both Australia and Britain led to many outside the sport, and some inside, to claim that it was dying. In 2001, the *Guardian*'s leading sports journalist Frank Keating confidently predicted that league would be dead by 2006: 'it is only a matter of time before rugby league in Britain is forced to merge with a voracious union. I give it five years, and that is being generous.'[5] Many other rugby union writers in both hemispheres made similar prognoses.

Yet this was to profoundly misunderstand the nature of rugby league, and indeed the appeal of any sport. The intricate web of communal, cultural and emotional ties that bind a sport to its supporters is far stronger than it may appear to an outsider, stretching across time, space and generations. Sport connects friends and families, grandparents and grandchildren, allies and acquaintances, and offers a profound sense of belonging and kinship. Forged over decades, such deep bonds are not easily broken or lost.

And so it proved with rugby league. The first decade of the 21st century became one of the most successful in the history of the sport. The NRL recorded the biggest aggregate crowds in its history, the leading British clubs saw attendances rise to levels not seen since the early 1960s and even French rugby league, thanks to the entry of Perpignan's Catalans Dragons into the Super League in 2006, saw a revival of fortune after decades of decline. On the pitch, a new generation of New Zealand league stars, such as stand-off Benji Marshall, finally put an end to Australia's 30-year domination of the World Cup with a thrilling 30-24 win in the final of the 2008 tournament, the first time in 54 years that the Kiwis had lifted the trophy.

The final was held in Brisbane, home to the Queensland State of Origin side, arguably the most dominant side of either rugby code since the mid-2000s. From 2006 to 2013 they won the series against New South Wales eight consecutive times, thanks to five of the most gifted players ever to pick up an oval ball. With the exception of Johnathan Thurston, all played for Melbourne Storm, a side created by Murdoch's News Limited to expand rugby league into Australia's second biggest city in 1998. The wily hooker Cameron Smith, the cerebral half-back Cooper Cronk, the rapier full-back Billy Slater and the majestic centre Greg Inglis, who would later move to South Sydney, created a dynasty in Queensland and Melbourne.

After winning the NRL title in only their second season, the Storm's inspirational quartet steered them to win a further three grand finals up to 2011. Even a salary cap avoidance scandal in 2010 that resulted in them being stripped of two of those titles did little to slow their momentum or the elegance of their rugby. The rise of Melbourne was symbolic of the recovery of Australian rugby league as a whole. By the start of the second decade of the new century the game had never been healthier, as highlighted in August 2012, the NRL announced that it had signed a five-year television deal worth $1.025 billion, a record for the rugby codes.

As had been the case since the 1960s, British rugby league invariably lagged behind its Antipodean cousin. The restructuring of the game into a summer sport and the creation of the Super League led to a consolidation at the top – only four clubs, Bradford, Leeds, St Helens and Wigan, have won the Super League title since 1996 – but also an expansion of the game at grass roots level around Britain. By 2005 every county in England had at least one rugby league club, something that would have been unthinkable in the 1970s, and there were now domestic competitions in Ireland, Scotland and Wales.

This expansion was partially due to rugby union's turn to professionalism in 1995. Union had abandoned its draconian sanctions against league, allowing players to change or alternate between codes without fear. But it was also a reflection of the way in which the switch to a summer season had helped the game move away from the stereotypical image that it was a game played in the mud of the grim industrial north of England. Hard grounds and the warmth of a summer sun gave players a greater scope to display and develop their skills, the perfect stage for performers such as Leeds Kevin Sinfield or Wigan's Sam Tomkins.

Yet there remained one unavoidable problem for British rugby league. Its national side could not consistently compete with Australia. The Great Britain side did not win another Ashes series against the

Kangaroos after 1970 and did not reach another World Cup final after narrowly losing in 1995 to the Australians. Indeed, England, as the national team had been rebranded, clearly ranked third in the rugby league world after Australia and New Zealand.

Despite this international imbalance, the 21st century also saw league played in more countries than ever before. Fourteen sides contested the 2013 World Cup, ranging from the Cook Islands to the USA, and the matches attracted record crowds for the competition. Taken as a whole, the sport had never been stronger, commanding crowds and an international presence that would have shocked and surprised its administrators of the 1970s, let alone the founders of the game in 1895.

Britain and Ireland face-to-face with the future

It was not just rugby league that was wracked by civil war in the years after 1995. Almost immediately after the legalisation of professionalism in 1995, a three-sided war broke out in England between the RFU, its grass roots clubs and the professional teams, most of which had been taken over by multi-millionaire businessmen who wanted to run them like soccer's Premier League clubs. Only a series of negotiations that would have taxed the patience of even the most seasoned Foreign Office mandarin eventually led to agreements that allowed peace to break out.

But the market logic of the new era had a brutal impact on the English club game. Richmond, now owned by millionaire Ashley Levett, signed England forward Ben Clarke in what was reputedly rugby union's first £1 million transfer. Yet by 1999 Levett decided that he could no longer continue to underwrite the club and it was 'merged' with London Irish. Other former powerhouses of the game, such as London Scottish, Orrell, West Hartlepool, Moseley and Nottingham were simply unable to compete financially. Even Bath, the flagship of the pre-professional era, found it financially impossible to continue its dominance of the game.

With the exception of Harlequins, London's surviving elite clubs no longer played in their historic locality. London Irish played in Reading, London Welsh in Oxford, Saracens established themselves in Watford until moving back to London in 2012 and Wasps became High Wycombe's club before moving to Coventry in December 2014. Leicester Tigers, buttressed by the club's deep social and business roots in the East Midlands, came to dominate the English Premiership and won the Heineken Cup in two of its five appearances. Eventually, a degree of equilibrium in the club game was reached by the mid-2000s, underpinned to a great extent by rising attendances in the Premiership and the success of the England side.

England's World Cup victory in Sydney in 2003 was crucial to the successful transformation of English rugby union. The success that had begun under Geoff Cooke continued under his successors. Jack Rowell, the architect of the dominant Bath side of the 1980s and 1990s, won a Grand Slam in the last season before professionalism and picked up the Triple Crown the following season. But in between, England had a disappointing World Cup campaign in South Africa, failing to build on the promise of their 1991 final appearance, and crashed out heavily to New Zealand in the semi-finals.

At the end of the 1997 season Rowell was replaced by Clive Woodward who, in keeping with the new professional ethos, transformed the management and coaching of the squad into something resembling a corporate structure. But although it was Woodward's managerialist approach and rigorous planning that caught the headlines, his biggest asset was that he inherited a squad that was reaching full maturity and was continuously refreshed by young talent forged in the increasingly competitive environment of the English Premiership.

Players like Martin Johnson, Lawrence Dallaglio and Jonny Wilkinson were among the finest English players ever in their positions.

Woodward even had a wildcard unavailable to any previous England coach – rugby league international winger Jason Robinson. As capable of flair as they were, this was a side that paid meticulous attention to the game plan and based its success on its ability to control every facet of the game. In 2003 they completed a Grand Slam in the spring and then strode confidently into the World Cup final in the autumn.

So when the clock ticked down to the last minute of extra-time in the final with England drawing 17-17 with hosts Australia, everyone watching knew that England's forward drive aimed to create the space for a Jonny Wilkinson drop goal. The Wallabies knew it as well, but there was little they could do to prevent the inevitable as first Dawson, then skipper Martin Johnson took the ball closer and closer to the Australian posts.

Eventually the ball was released and flung back to Wilkinson standing just outside the 22 metre-line. With just 29 seconds remaining of extra-time, he stroked the ball through the Australian uprights with his unfavoured right boot to win the World Cup. It was undoubtedly England's greatest-ever victory.

Woodward left the following year, and by the time of the 2007 World Cup, Brian Ashton, the son of a Leigh rugby league player, had taken charge of England, and they once again reached the final. This time they met a South African side even more skilled at controlling a game and were suffocated 15-6 in a tryless match of gruelling intensity.

By then the great side of 2003 had begun to fade away. In the following years England seemed to revert back to an earlier time, recording just a single Six Nations title since 2003's Six Nations and World Cup triumph. World Cup glory had unified the English game, yet the tensions between club rugby and the national side continued to simmer under the surface.

In Wales, a country where obsession with rugby politics often seems to rank as high as the national passion for the game itself, the post-1995 landscape was even more complex than that in England. The expectation that the clubs in the Welsh Premiership league would continue as before but with players simply switching to professionalism immediately fell victim to the adage that no battle plan survives contact with the enemy. In this case, the enemy was the deindustrialisation of the Welsh economy and the simple fact that South Wales possessed neither the population nor the wealth to sustain nine professional premiership sides.

By the turn of the century the Welsh game was on its knees, at both club and international level. The professional era coincided with one of the worst slumps ever for the Welsh national side. Victory in the 1994 Five Nations was followed by disappointment, frustration and occasionally abject humiliation. Something had to be done. In 1998 the Welsh Rugby Union (WRU) appointed New Zealander Graham Henry as head coach of the national team. Hailed as the Great Redeemer, a reference to the first line of 'Cwm Rhondda', 'Guide Me, O Thou Great Redeemer', Henry was also an advocate for restructuring Welsh rugby on a regional basis similar to the provincial system in his native New Zealand.

Although the redeemer departed early in 2002, the WRU unveiled its plans to restructure the game into four regions. To no one's surprise, uproar ensued but eventually WRU chief executive David Moffett, a serial CEO who had been at the helm of the NSW Rugby Union, the New Zealand Rugby Union, Australia's National Rugby League and Sport England over the course of the previous decade, brokered a deal that created five regional teams. With the exception of Llanelli and Cardiff, the other three regions were formed through club mergers.

Things did not go to plan. Celtic Warriors, the merger of Bridgend and Pontypridd, folded at the end of their first season, leaving the Welsh Valleys with no senior club side, and Ebbw Vale pulled out of their joint venture with Newport. That left three of the historic clubs of Welsh rugby union – Cardiff, Llanelli and Newport – rebranded as regional sides, with the Ospreys, the child of Swansea and Neath, as the only survivor of the original regional plan.

The new structure did little to solve the financial problems of the clubs or bring success in the Heineken Cup. With the exception of Cardiff in the very first tournament, no Welsh side has ever reached the final, let alone won it. Yet for the national side, the era was one of the most startlingly successful periods in Welsh history. Wales won three Grand Slams in just eight years between 2005 and 2012, emulating the glorious side of the 1970s that won three Grand Slams between 1971 and 1978.

The answer to this conundrum was perhaps that Welsh rugby could provide enough players for one exceptionally strong squad but no more – but without the vibrant club rugby that had been the rock upon which Welsh rugby had traditionally built its national side, there was the merest echo of hollowness about the roars that greeted these triumphs in the Six Nations.

The Scottish Rugby Union was more prepared than the Welsh for the coming of the professional era. It realised that the existing club structure could not support fully commercialised rugby and in 1996 launched four regional franchises. Two were based in the traditional hotbeds of Edinburgh and the Borders, but the other two were in Glasgow and in northern Scotland, where the Caledonia Reds played out of Perth and Aberdeen. But the Reds did not survive and, despite a number of attempts, professionalism could not be sustained in the Borders. By 2008 only the Edinburgh and Glasgow teams remained.

But unlike in Wales, the concentration of Scottish talent did not result in international success. Scotland narrowly won the final Five Nations' tournament in 1999 – Italy were included to make it Six Nations the following season – but it was a solitary diamond in two decades of rocks. Part of the problem for Scottish rugby was self-inflicted. The redevelopment of Murrayfield in the 1990s had saddled the SRU with a debt of around £20 million, which meant that the new regional clubs had to be largely self-reliant in their difficult early years.

But there was also a deeper structural problem in Scotland that professionalism had exacerbated. Scottish rugby union had a very narrow playing population. Even at the height of its popularity it never had more than 15,000 adult players, around half the number of players in Wales and Ireland and barely 10 per cent of those in England.[6] In the days of amateurism when all players had jobs and couldn't train full-time the numerical advantage did not translate into a massive skills gap between nations. But professionalism was a ruthless master that discarded all but the very best players. The Scots simply didn't have the playing capital to match their rivals. Outside the small Borders towns, rugby was unknown in working-class areas and soccer reigned supreme. With no new native stocks of players to replenish elite rugby, Scotland increasingly came to rely on players born abroad, especially the so-called 'Kilted Kiwis'. It would be the central issue that would face the Scottish game in the 21st century.

If Scotland's prescient move to regional teams was not rewarded with on-field success, in Ireland the opposite was true. For the Irish Rugby Football Union (IRFU), despite its initial opposition to the game going professional, 1995 heralded the start of Irish rugby's greatest ever era. Indeed, professionalism could not have come at a better time, as it coincided precisely with new vitality of the Irish economy.

As with the economy itself, the tremendous growth in the popularity of rugby was fuelled by overseas investment, this time in the form of Rupert Murdoch's Sky Sports whose millions had underwritten the move to professionalism across the English-speaking world, and facilitated by the wholesale dismantling of corporate controls, in this case the ending of amateur regulations. In Dublin especially, rugby became closely associated with the huge wealth that was now available to the privately educated professional classes.

The traditional school powerhouses of the game – Blackrock, Belvedere, Terenure and Clongowes Wood – not only provided many provincial and international players, such as Cian Healy, Luke Fitzgerald and the incomparable Brian O'Driscoll, but also a revivified and expanding audience for the game. The many thousands who followed Irish sides across Europe in the Heineken Cup were symbols as well as beneficiaries of the growing globalisation of rugby union and the Irish economy.

It was also an era when the fruit machine of genetic luck paid out a jackpot. The cohort of players who represented Ireland in the late 1990s and 2000s were a golden generation of Irish rugby. O'Driscoll himself stood alongside Mike Gibson, Bleddyn Williams and Gwyn Nicholls as one of the northern hemisphere's greatest centre-three-quarters. Ronan O'Gara rivalled Jonny Wilkinson in the modern pantheon of fly-halves and bore comparison to Jack Kyle, while players like Geordan Murphy and Gordon D'Arcy would walk into any hall of fame. The depth and quality of talent in Irish rugby could be seen in the fact that the Lions took 12 Irishmen with them to New Zealand in 2005 and 16 to South Africa in 2009.

Lions' selections were icing the cake on a decade and a half of overwhelming success. Irish teams won the Heineken Cup six times between 1999 and 2012. The 2012 final was an all-Ireland affair, between Leinster and Ulster. Only Connaght, rugby's outpost in the Gaelic football hotbed of the West of Ireland, failed to lift Europe's ultimate prize.

Provincial success was magnified by the national team. The Irish side carried off four Triple Crowns in the decade from 2004, and in 2009 O'Driscoll's men achieved the holy grail: winning Ireland's first Grand Slam since Jack Kyle's side in 1948, making them only the second Irish side ever to do it. There had almost never been a better time to be an Irish rugby player or supporter.

'Almost' – because there was also a sad downside to the rise of the professional provincial teams. Club rugby went into rapid decline, even in its Munster heartlands. In 1991, 11,000 people watched the Senior Cup final between Shannon and Young Munster but when the two teams met in the 2002 final just 4,000 turned out. Even the All-Ireland League that had been set up in 1991 to promote club rugby was quickly marginalised by the success of the provinces and crowds dwindled.[7]

As in Wales, professionalism had sucked the life from the club game. Without a vibrant club structure, it remains an open question whether Irish success can be sustained after the gilded generation has taken its final bow and the economic collapse of 2008 has declawed the Celtic Tiger.

A European union

In an increasingly global sports world, it became clear to many that the future of rugby could not be constrained by national borders. The formation of the Celtic League in 2001 was an attempt to bring the regular competition and rivalries of the club game to the new provincial sides of Irish, Scottish and Welsh sides. Although its first season included all nine Welsh Premiership clubs, they were replaced in the second by the new Welsh regional sides, and in 2003 the Celtic League became the single professional league of all three countries. In 2010 it followed in the wake of the Five Nations and added an Italian presence with Benetton Treviso and Aironi, whose spot was taken over by Parma-based Zebre in 2012.

But the league suffered in the shadow of the Heineken Cup and the Six Nations. It changed its name according to each new sponsor and Irish sides in particular had little compunction about fielding second-string sides when major Heineken Cup games were in the offing. It struggled to attract crowds, never achieving a seasonal average in five figures – and even that average was boosted by annual blockbuster crowds for Leinster versus Munster clashes.

The Heineken Cup itself suffered no such problems. Inspired by the popularity and commercial success of soccer's UEFA Champions League, it was launched as the first major initiative of the post-professional era in the northern hemisphere in 1995 and, despite a low-key first season which was boycotted by English and Scottish clubs, the tournament quickly captured the imagination of the media and the public.

The first final attracted 21,800 to see Toulouse pull off a late 21-18 extra-time win over Cardiff at the Arms Park. Ten years later, 74,534 watched Munster overcome Biarritz 23-19, again in Cardiff but this time at the WRU's new Millennium Stadium. By this time, the final had become a carnival of rugby, with supporters travelling to the match in their droves and creating a symphony of sound and colour unique in world rugby union.

As well as record crowds, the Heineken Cup helped to forge new rivalries, such as that between Leicester and Toulouse, refresh old ones, such as Munster and Leinster, and take the game to pastures new, with matches in Geneva, Brussels and San Sebastián. It brought an international glamour to club rugby and allowed many of the national feelings evoked by the Six Nations to spill over into the club game.

First among such emotions was rivalry with the French. Partly this was due to longstanding enmities that could be seen every year in internationals but it was also due to French success in the tournament. French clubs contested 13 of the 19 tournaments held up to 2014. They won the H Cup, as it was officially known in France because of the government's ban on alcohol advertising, seven times. Four of those finals were all-French affairs.

Indeed, the tournament highlighted the fact that France had become the superpower of European club rugby. That rugby union dominated the sporting landscape of southern France – even after the French soccer side's victory in the 1998 FIFA World Cup – made it the world's largest single market for rugby. The rebirth of Stade Français and the merger of Racing and US Métro in 2001 to form Racing Métro 92 led to Paris becoming an important and lucrative rugby market. The money available to clubs from television companies and sponsors was significantly higher than elsewhere. In 2011 Toulouse announced a projected turnover of €30 million, placing them comfortably ahead of the NRL's Brisbane Broncos and England's Leicester Tigers as the richest rugby club in the world of either code.[8]

But such riches also brought their own problems. Attracted by the huge salaries available – in 2011 the average player in France was earning 25 per cent more than his counterpart in England – and the French lifestyle, overseas players flocked to the Top 14 league, as the French Championship became known after a decade of reform.[9] In 2014 there were 220 non-French players active in the Top 14, and only Clermont and Toulouse had squads that were more than 60 per cent French.[10] For wealthy club owners such as Toulon's Mourad Boudjellal and Stade Français's Max Guazzini, acquiring international stars such as Jonny Wilkinson, Morné Steyn or Sonny-Bill Williams not only brought success on the field but prestige off it.

It also meant something of a roller-coaster ride for the French national side. Since the start of the century France have won three Grand Slams in the Six Nations but also finished rock bottom in 2013, second from bottom in 2001 and suffered ignominious defeats to Italy in 2011 and 2013. French national coaches invariably blamed the number of foreign players in the Top 14 for their woes. The imposition of a salary cap and a quota system for French-qualified players did little in the short term to redress the problem.

Yet French inconsistency in the Six Nations once more showed how the competition itself had been diminished by the growing importance of the World Cup. A poor season in the northern hemisphere's premier international competition could now be dismissed as being irrelevant for the biggest prize was elsewhere. And when it came to the World Cup, the French did everything but win it. They reached the final in 1999 – the same year that they also finished bottom of the then Five Nations – but lost heavily to Australia after knocking out the favourites New Zealand, and fell by a single point to the All Blacks in Auckland in 2011. In 2003 and 2007 the pain of semi-final defeat was made worse because it was administered on both occasions by *les rosbifs*.

Given the domestic strength of French rugby, it is not likely that a World Cup victory would have significantly extended the game's appeal to the rest of French society. As many commentators pointed at the time of France's victory in the 1998 FIFA World Cup, Zinedine Zidaine's multi-racial team contrasted starkly with the nation's largely white rugby union side. Although black players played for France as early as 1906, when Georges Jérome and André Verges played against the All Blacks, rugby identified with an older, more traditional rural vision of the nation, in contrast to the modern, multicultural reality of urban France. Indeed, for many of its supporters, rugby union's representation of *la France profonde* was one of its most valuable characteristics. In the 21st-century world of shifting populations and multinational cultures, it remains to be seen if French rugby's greatest strength will eventually turn out to be its Achilles heel.

The French game was perhaps the best example of how the globalisation of rugby in the 21st century gave rise to new opportunities for rugby players to ply their trade around the world. This was especially true for Pacific Islanders. Forty-eight of the 220 overseas players in France in 2014 were from Fiji, Samoa and Tonga. Similar numbers could be found in British union and league, while the number of Pacific Island heritage players in Australia's NRL amounted to 38 per cent of all players in 2013. The importance of rugby skills to the economies of the Pacific Islands can be gauged by the fact that in 2006 earnings from Fijian overseas rugby players accounted for 11 per cent of money sent home to Fiji.[11]

But the global spread of their players did little to help Pacific nations compete consistently at international level. Professionalism saw them go backwards as the powerful nations became more powerful and many of the best Pacific players switched to the bigger nations. Apart from a single appearance by Fiji in 2007, no Pacific Islands side has reached the quarter-finals of the World Cup in the professional era.

To overcome this weakness, in 2001 the Pacific Islands Rugby Alliance (PIRA) was formed with the intention of uniting Fiji, Samoa and Tonga in a rugby union version of the way in which the West Indies cricket team represents the cricketing nations of the Caribbean. But it was no more successful than the individual nations, losing eight of its nine international matches before being wound up in 2009. The brutal logic of professionalism dictated that without resources or attractive television markets, the weaker rugby nations got weaker while the strong got stronger.

The more the rugby world changed, the more it stayed the same.

CONCLUSION

THE SOUL OF THE GAME

On 9 October 2009, Pierre de Coubertin's twin passions of rugby and the Olympics were once more united. The International Olympic Committee met in Copenhagen and voted to include Rugby Sevens in the 2016 Olympic Games in Rio de Janeiro.

The IOC's decision immediately opened new vistas for the expansion of rugby union. Governments had long viewed the Olympics as such an important indicator of national prestige that a sport's inclusion in the Games guaranteed state support in most of the IOC's 204 member countries.

Discussions about rugby union becoming part of the Olympics had begun in the 1990s, and the IRB was officially recognised as a participating international federation in 1994. As the last major international sporting bodies to abandon amateurism, the two organisations had much in common.

However, the IOC baulked at including 15-a-side rugby and instead suggested that the seven-a-side game was more appropriate. Eventually, after the IRB agreed to abandon its Sevens' World Cup and promote the Olympics as the highest level of short-form rugby, the game was given the green light.

Acceptance by the IOC was the culmination of the expansion of sevens that had begun in Hong Kong in the 1970s. The IRB's Sevens World Series began in 1999 and quickly became a global tour, visiting ten or more major world cities each season. The IRB had been assiduous in promoting sevens to the world's major multi-sport festivals and it is now played in the Pan American Games, Asian Games, Pacific Games and the Commonwealth Games.

Despite the expansion of sevens, it remains to be seen whether it will lead to an expansion of 15-a-side rugby. The sevens circuit is dominated by specialist players, few of whom have made any impact on the full game. And the sport itself lacks the tactical complexity, breadth of skills and physical intensity of its bigger brother.

The inclusion of sevens rather than the 15-a-side game in the Olympics highlighted a dilemma that continued to face the sport. IOC president Jacques Rogge, who himself had played international rugby union for Belgium, was sharply critical of the full game. Interviewed after the 2007 World Cup final he told the BBC, 'I'm not happy about the quality of play … I think the lawmakers have to think about making the game more open'.[1]

He was voicing an old complaint that had grown louder since the adoption of professionalism. In the 1960s the growing importance of television led to pressure to reform the rules. In 1970 kicking the ball directly into touch from outside the kicker's 25 was punished by the ball being returned to the opposition at the point from which it was kicked. The following year, as we have seen, the value of a try was raised to four points. In 1972 the RFU's laws committee even discussed abolishing the line-out.[2]

Such reforms were given renewed momentum by the start of the Rugby World Cup in 1987. Global media interest and the demands of television networks brought into focus the need to provide a spectacle. In April 1992 tries were increased to five points by the IRB and the ruck and maul rules were changed to force teams in possession of the ball to open up play. The emphasis was on providing entertainment. Steve Bale of the *Independent* described the 1992 changes as 'the first official acknowledgement that rugby union is no longer exclusively a players' game'.[3] This was only the beginning.

The coming of professionalism in 1995 was accompanied by almost continuous attempts to improve the game as a spectacle, from the legalisation of lifting in the line-out to yet more tinkering with the ruck and the maul to ensure more continuous play. In 1995 there were even experimental games of 13-a-side played in Scotland. In 2008 rugby union was plunged into controversy by a trial of the 'Experimental Law Variations' in the Super 14 tournament, some of which found eventually their way into the rule book.

Professionalism itself had increased the speed of the sport. A 2005 IRB report showed that over the previous 20 years the average number of line-outs in internationals had fallen from 52 to 37, and scrums from 31 to 19. The number of passes had risen but kicks had fallen. Penalty goals had decreased and try-scoring had increased. The rate of change over the previous 20 years had been greater than entirety of the previous century.[4]

There was, of course, a spectre hovering behind all discussions about rugby's rules. Rugby union's reinvigorated evolutionary impulse was confronting exactly the same problems that rugby league had faced a century earlier. League itself had evolved on a pragmatic basis by providing answers to the very same problems union was grappling. The ruck and the maul were replaced with the play-the-ball. Excessive touch kicking had been curbed by penalising direct kicking into touch. The domination of the scrum was reduced by removing two forwards and cutting the opportunities for scrummaging. Indeed, many of union's rule changes followed the pattern that league had laid down in previous decades.

Just as they had once been in league, scrums became the focus for much of rugby union's angst about its rules. The simple truth was that no matter how precisely the contest at the scrum was legislated, players and coaches would always find ways to circumvent or undermine the rules. As professionalism advanced, the 'struggle for possession', a shibboleth of the union code, was slowly disappearing. The 2005 IRB study found that the side in possession now retained the ball 13 out of 14 times at the breakdown, nine times out of ten at the scrum and eight out of ten at the line-out.[5] Just as league had, union was evolving into a struggle for territory and position.

This apparent convergence between the two games has led to speculation about the eventual reunification of the codes. The ending of rugby union's ban on league players changed the sporting landscape, allowing stars like Jason Robinson and Lote Tuquiri to flourish across both codes. Perhaps even more significant was the flood of rugby league coaches into union after 1995. Of the eight 2003 World Cup quarter-finalists, only New Zealand did not have any former league personnel on their coaching staff.

Yet although rugby union is heading down the same road as rugby league had earlier taken, the two sports travelled in very different vehicles. Tradition weighs heavily on both, in the ways that they play rugby and the ways in which they see the game. The split that had cleaved rugby apart in Victorian times created two separate and distinct sports.

One only has to discuss the essence of rugby with supporters of each game to realise the struggle for the ball by the forwards is at the spiritual heart of the union game, whereas for league it is the open, passing game that is its soul. These two philosophies have remained constant ever since they first appeared in the 19th century.

Even more importantly, each game has its own deep heritage that transcends the shifting exigencies of the rule book. Names like Harold Wagstaff and Wavell Wakefield, Clive Churchill and Danie Craven, Puig Aubert and Guy Boniface mean everything to their own code and nothing to the other. Whatever similarities there may be on the field, the rugby codes are no closer to each other off the field than they are to any other sport. These are not merely two different games. They are different cultures.

And so they will remain for the foreseeable future. Each game will continue to grow in its own different way. We can be certain that women's rugby of both codes will extend its appeal. The fact that rugby offers an intense physicality unlike other team sports gives it a distinctive appeal to girls and women who have traditionally been excluded from robust contact sports. World Cups will get bigger, as befits a sport that pioneered trans-hemispheric competition decades before the word globalisation had been coined. And digital and television networks will bring new fans to rugby, either as committed supporters or, more likely, as those for whom rugby is one more enjoyable strand among many of their entertainment lives. But the game will not challenge soccer's grip on the global sporting imagination.

Nor should we want it to. Because almost two centuries after the birth of the original game, rugby in all its forms has developed a unique, never-ending capacity to generate passion, pride and meaning for everyone who plays and watches the game. Whether pupils at Rugby School, factory workers in Rochdale, farmers from Rotorua or women sevens' players in Rio, rugby brings them not just recreation but also significance to their lives and that of the communities to which they belong.

Since it emerged in the middle of the 19th century, rugby has been many things: a tool of educationalists, an instrument of governments and a plaything of adventurers. It has been used to promote the best in humanity and to support the worst. It has brought hope and joy, and sadness and despair. It has encompassed all human emotions, noble and otherwise. For countless numbers of people, it helps them make sense of the world and, sometimes, of life itself.

Yet none of this, not the great tournaments, not the passionate engagement with the game, not even the deep significance that rugby has for so many different communities around the world, would be possible were it not for humanity's endless fascination with the limitless possibilities presented by a simple oval ball.

NOTES

Part I Kick-off

1 The Tradition

1 Barbara Tuchman, *Practicing History: Selected Essays*, New York, Ballantine, 1991, p. 234.

2 Quoted in John Stow, *Survey of London (1598)*, London, Everyman edition, 1970, p. 507.

3 John Robertson, *Uppies and Doonies: The Story of the Kirkwall Ba' Game*, Aberdeen, Aberdeen University Press, 1997, p. 129. Joseph Strutt, *The Sports and Pastimes of the People of England* (1801), London: Methuen edition, 1903, p. 93. *London Gazette*, 4–7 April 1719.

4 The Cumberland match is in *Bell's Life in London* [hereafter *Bell's Life*], 7 October 1849. Examples of four-a-side can be found in *Bell's Life*, 8 February 1846, and one-a-side in 9 and 16 February 1845 and 10 January 1847.

5 For a description, see Edward Moor, *Suffolk words and phrases; or, An attempt to collect the lingual localisms of that county*, Woodbridge, London, R. Hunter, 1823, pp. 63–6. David Dymond, 'A Lost Social Institution: The Camping Close', *Rural History*, vol. 1, no. 2, October 1990, pp. 165–92.

6 Richard Carew, *Survey of Cornwall* (1710), London, Faulder edition, 1811, p. 197.

7 Hugh Hornby, *Uppies and Downies: The Extraordinary Football Games of Britain*, London, English Heritage, 2008, pp. 142–53.

8 John Goulstone, *Football's Secret History*, London, Catford, 2001, pp. 29–30.

9 Goulstone, p. 39.

10 Goulstone, p. 27.

11 Hull & East Riding Athlete, 27 November 1889. Robert Malcolmson, *Popular Recreations in English Society, 1700–1850*, Cambridge, Cambridge University Press, 1973, p. 85.

12 Stan Chadwick, *Claret and Gold: History of Huddersfield Rugby League Club*, Huddersfield, Venturer's Press, 1946, p. 1.

13 *Bell's Life*, 2 January 1842.

14 Goulstone, p. 32.

15 *Yorkshire Post*, 10 February 1896. A. E. Wright and T. E. Jones, *British Calendar Customs*, London, Folklore Society, 1936, p. 27.

16 Gareth Williams, 'The dramatic turbulence of some irrecoverable football game', in Grant Jarvie (ed.), *Sport in the Making of Celtic Culture*, Leicester, Leicester University Press, 1999, p. 58.

17 Montague Shearman, *Athletics and Football*, London, Longmans, 1887, p. 260.

2 A School Called Rugby

1 *The Times*, 9 October 1857.

2 Jennifer Macrory, *Running with the Ball: Birth of Rugby Football*, London, Collins, 1991, p. 14.

3 *Bell's Life*, 21 December 1845.

4 *Bell's Life*, 7 May 1843.

5 *Derby and Chesterfield Reporter*, 23 February 1832 and 7 February 1845.

6 Quoted in Lytton Strachey, *Eminent Victorians*, London, Folio Society edition, 1986, p. 171.

7 F. D. M., 'Thoughts on ourselves, our position and our prospects', *The Rugby Miscellany*, no. 7, February 1846, pp. 226–8.

8 *Report of the Commissioners on the Revenues and Management of Certain Colleges and Schools*, British Parliamentary Papers. Public Schools and Colleges, vol. XX, Education, General 9, 1864, p. 266.

9 *Football Rules*, Rugby, 1845, p. 13.

10 Sydney Selfe, *Chapters from the History of Rugby School*, Rugby, Lawrence, 1910, p. 139.

11 Anon., 'Reminiscences', *The New Rugbeian*, vol. 3, no. 2, November 1860, p. 80.

12 Selfe, *Chapters...*, p. 61.

13 Macrory, *Running with the Ball*, p. 93.

3 What Tom Brown Did Next

1 H. H. Almond 'Athletics and Education' *Macmillan's Magazine*, 43, November 1880–April 1881, p. 283.

2 *Yorkshire Post*, 11 April 1864.

3 Hugh Cunningham, *The Volunteer Force: A Social and Political History, 1859–1908*, Brighton, Croom Helm, 1975.

4 On the earliest clubs see Adrian Harvey, 'The Oldest Rugby Football Club in the World?', *Sport in History*, vol. 26, no. 1, April 2006, pp. 150–52.

5 For Wellington and other schools adoption of Rugby School rules, see Rev. Frank Marshall and L. R. Tosswill (eds), *Football: the Rugby Union Game*, London, Cassell, 2nd edition, 1925, p. 33.

6 Rev. Frank Marshall (ed.), *Football: The Rugby Union Game*, London, Cassell, 1892, pp. 77–8. W. H. H. Hutchinson in *Yorkshire Evening Post*, 1 December 1900. Hull FC in *Yorkshire Evening Post*, 20 February 1904. Marshall and Tosswill (eds), *Football: The Rugby Union Game*, 2nd edition, p. 21.

7 For Rochdale see C. W. Alcock (ed.), *Football Annual*, London: Lilywhite, 1868. For Sale see M. Barak, *A Century of Rugby at Sale*, Sale, Sale FC, 1962. For Preston see A. Marsden, *Preston Grasshoppers' Centenary Brochure*, Preston, The Club, 1969. For Bradford see *Yorkshire Evening Post*, 15 November, 1902. For St Peter's see A. Raine, *History of St Peter's School*, London, Bell, 1926, p. 134.

8 *Yorkshire Evening Post*, 9 February 1901.

9 The rules agreed at this meeting are published in *Bell's Life*, 28 November 1863. For a comprehensive account and analysis of the voting patterns at the FA's foundation meetings, see Adrian Harvey, *Football: The First Hundred Years*, Abingdon: Routledge, 2005, pp. 143–9.

10 *Bell's Life*, 5 December 1863.

11 *Bell's Life*, 2 January 1864.

12 *Bell's Life*, 7 January 1871.

13 Graham Curry, 'The Cambridge Connection', *The Sports Historian*, 22 (2), 2002, pp. 46–73.

14 *The Times*, 23 November 1870.

15 *Bell's Life*, 24 December 1870.

16 Rugby Football Union minutes, 26 January 1871. A report of the first meeting is in *Bell's Life*, 28 January, 1871.

17 The first laws are reproduced in O. L. Owen, *The History of the Rugby Football Union*, London, 1955, pp. 59–72.

18 Alcock, *Football Annual*, 1875, pp. 48–9.

19 Macrory, *Running with the Ball*, pp. 103–5.

20 https://web.archive.org/web/20121103223545/http://www.richardlindon.com/4.html, accessed 25 November 2012.

4 Rugby's Great Split

1 *The Yorkshireman,* 3 February 1887.

2 *The Times,* 12 November 1880.

3 Alcock (ed.), *Football Annual,* 1880, pp. 73–5. Graham Williams, *Glory Days: The History of English Rugby Union Cup Finals,* Leeds, 1998.

4 Arthur Budd, 'The Rugby Union Game', in Alcock (ed.), *Football Annual,* 1880, p. 52.

5 *Yorkshire Post,* 5 October 1886.

6 *Athletic News Football Annual,* Manchester, Athletic News, 1893, p. 149.

7 *The Yorkshireman,* 18 September 1889.

8 *Oldham Evening Chronicle,* 13 October 1890.

9 For example, see the letter of S. A. Austin of Belgrave RFC, 26 August 1908, to the Midland Counties RFU (Leicestershire County Archives, DE3097/32).

10 *Yorkshire Post,* 11 April 1891.

11 Ibid., 29 September 1897.

12 *Leeds Mercury,* 21 September 1893.

13 *Yorkshire Post,* 8 January 1894.

Part II Towards Five Nations

5 Scotland: 'Rugby Football: The Real Game of the Two Countries'

1 *Bell's Life,* 25 March 1871. Player details from Andy Mitchell, *First Elevens: The Birth of International Football,* Glasgow, CreateSpace, 2012.

2 Marshall (ed.), *Football. The Rugby Union Game,* p. 99.

3 *Bell's Life,* 8 December 1870.

4 Mitchell, *First Elevens,* p. 156.

5 *Bell's Life,* 1 April 1871.

6 Ibid., 1 April 1871.

7 Ibid., 25 March and 1 April 1871.

8 Marshall (ed.), *Football. The Rugby Union Game,* p. 140.

9 R. J. Phillips, *The Story of Scottish Rugby,* Edinburgh, Foulis, 1925, p. 89.

10 Marshall (ed.), *Football. The Rugby Union Game,* p. 202.

11 Phillips, *The Story of Scottish Rugby,* p. 94.

12 Tom Devine, *The Scottish Nation,* Harmondsworth: Penguin, 1999, pp. 285–92.

13 Phillips, *The Story of Scottish Rugby,* p. 102.

14 Neil Tranter, 'The First Football Club', *International Journal of the History of Sport*, vol. 10, no. 1, pp. 104–9.

15 *The Edinburgh Academy FC Centenary History*, Edinburgh, Pillans & Wilson, 1958, p. 10.

16 A. M. C. Thorburn, *The History of Scottish Rugby*, London, Johnson & Bacon, 1980, pp. 28–30.

17 Ibid., p. 14–16. Marshall (ed.), *Football. The Rugby Union Game*, p. 54.

18 *Glasgow Herald*, 25 December 1871.

19 Rugby Football Union minutes, 15 January 1872.

20 Marshall (ed.), *Football. The Rugby Union Game*, p. 148.

21 *The Times*, 3 March 1884. The RFU statement on the matter is printed in *The Times*, 16 April 1885.

22 *The Times*, 7 May 1888, 30 December 1889 and 29 April 1890.

23 E. H. D Sewell, 'Rugby Football', in *Fortnightly Review*, vol. 85, no. 8, 1909, p. 989.

6 Ireland: A National Identity

1 Elizabeth Miller and Dacre Stoker (eds), *The Lost Journal of Bram Stoker*, London: Robson Press, 2012, p. 152. I am grateful to Victoria Dawson for bringing this reference to my attention. Marshall (ed.), *Football. The Rugby Union Game*, p. 225. Details of Irish international doctors from Willow Murray, 'Doctors who played for Ireland', *Touchlines*, December 2006, p. 10.

2 Liam O'Callaghan, *Rugby in Munster: A Social and Cultural History*, Cork: Cork University Press, 2011.

3 Harvey, 'The Oldest Rugby Football Club in the World?' *Sport in History*, vol. 26, no. 1, April 2006, pp. 150–52.

4 Neal Garnham, *The Origins and Development of Football in Ireland*, Belfast, Ulster Historical Association, 1999, pp. 3–5.

5 *Belfast News-Letter*, 18 January 1869.

6 *Glasgow Herald*, 25 December 1871. Marshall (ed.), *Football. The Rugby Union Game*, p. 226.

7 Garnham, *The Origins and Development of Football*, p. 59.

8 *Bell's Life*, 20 February 1875.

9 Marshall (ed.), *Football. The Rugby Union Game*, p. 229.

10 Ibid., p. 241.

11 O'Callaghan, *Rugby in Munster*, p. 43.

12 James Joyce, *A Portrait of the Artist as a Young Man*, London, Wordsworth, 1992, p. 4.

13 O'Callaghan, *Rugby in Munster*, p. 77.

14 Garnham, *The Origins and Development of Football*, p. 12.

15 Ibid., pp. 8–9.

16 Michael Cusack, 'A Word About Irish Athletics', *Irishman*, 11 October 1884.

17 O'Callaghan, *Rugby in Munster*, p. 16.

18 Ibid., pp. 145–6.

19 I am grateful to the esteemed rugby historian the late Piers Morgan for telling me this story.

20 *Athletic News*, 21 September 1914.

7 Wales: The Dragon's Embrace

1 David Smith and Gareth Williams, *Fields of Praise*, Cardiff, University of Wales, 1980, p. 161.

2 Ibid., p. 124.

3 Gwyn Prescott, *'This Rugby Spellbound People': Rugby Football in Nineteenth-century Cardiff and South Wales*, Cardiff, Welsh Academic Press, 2011, pp. 42–5.

4 Ibid., p. 69.

5 *South Wales Daily News*, 15 December 1879.

6 Prescott, *'This Rugby Spellbound People'*, p. 147.

7 Ibid., p. 46.

8 Gareth Williams, *1905 and All That*, Llandysul: Gomer Press, 1991, p. 155.

9 Elias Jones, 'The Palmy days of Welsh Rugby 1886–1895', reprinted in Gareth Hughes, *One Hundred Years of Scarlet*, Llanelli, Llanelli RFC, 1983.

10 *The Yorkshireman*, 3 March 1887.

11 *Yorkshire Post*, 6 October 1893.

12 Ibid., 12 January, 7 February and 3 March 1898. *The Times*, 18 October 1897.

8 France: The Baron, The Red Virgin and Rugby's Belle Époque

1 Jean-Pierre Bodis, 'Le rugby en France jusqu'a` la seconde guerre mondiale. Aspects politiques et sociaux', *Revue de Pau et du Béarn*, 17, 1990, p. 221.

2 Pierre de Coubertin, 'Notes sur le foot-ball', *La Nature*, 8 May 1897.

3 Ulrich Hesse-Lichtenberger, *Tor! The Story of German Football*, London: WSC, 2003, p. 19.

4 *The New Rugbeian*, November 1861, p. 313. *Wakefield Express*, 23 November 1872.

5 Richard Holt, *Sport and Society in Modern France*, London, Macmillan, 1981, p. 46.

6 Quoted in John A. Lucas, 'Victorian Muscular Christianity, Prologue to the Olympic Games Philosophy', *Olympic Review*, no. 99, January–February 1976, p. 50.

7 Thiery Terret, 'Learning to be a Man', in John Nauright and Timothy Chandler (eds), *Making the Rugby World*, London, Cass, p. 75.

8 Sébastien Darbon, *Une Brève Histoire du Rugby*, Paris: L'Oeil Neuf, 2007, pp. 81–2.

9 Philip Dine, *French Rugby Football: A Cultural History*, Oxford, Berg, 2001, p. 45.

10 Stendhal, *Love*, Harmondsworth, Penguin, 1975, p. 190

11 Northern Union General Council minutes, 12 November 1912.

12 http://rugby-pioneers.blogs.com/rugby/2007/06/percy_bush_from.html – accessed 18 January 2014.

13 http://rugby-pioneers.blogs.com/rugby/2010/09/a-welshman-in-bordeaux-and-some-legal-stuff.html. P. Lafond and J-P Bodis, *Encyclopédie du Rugby Français*, Paris: Dehedin, 1989. E. H. D. Sewell, 'The State of the Game', *Fortnightly Review*, vol. 89 (1911), pp. 933–48.

14 Henri Garcia, *La Fabuleuse Histoire du Rugby*, Paris: Martinière, 2004, p. 24.

15 *The Yorkshireman*, 24 November 1894.

16 *The Graphic*, 1 December 1894. I am grateful to Dave Pendleton for bringing this to my attention.

17 *The Press* (Auckland), 15 February 1906.

18 *Daily Telegraph*, quoted in *The Press*, 15 February 1906.

Part III Making a Rugby World

9 New Zealand: All Blacks in the Land of the Long White Cloud

1 'Britain of the South' was a common phrase of the 19th century, see, for example, the *Sydney Telegraph*, 14 June 1884.

2 *Lyttleton Times*, 20 December 1854.

3 *The Press*, 29 August 1863.

4 Rex Thomson, 'Provincial Rugby in New Zealand: Otago's Academic Pioneers', *Journal of Sport History*, Fall 1996 (23:2), pp. 211–27.

5 Alan Turley, *Rugby: The Pioneer Years*, Auckland, HarperCollins, 2009, p. 105.

6 *Sydney Telegraph*, 14 June 1884.

7 *New Zealand Herald*, 7 May 1884.

8 Ibid., 5 June 1886.

9 Greg Ryan, *Forerunners of the All Blacks*, Christchurch, Canterbury University Press, 1993, p. 15.

10 Ryan, *Forerunners*, p. 17.

11 Greg Ryan, 'The Paradox of Māori Rugby, in Greg Ryan (ed.), *Tackling Rugby Myths*, Dunedin, Otago University Press, 2005.

12 *The Press* (Auckland), 8 January 1889.

13 *Otago Daily Times*, 4 December 1888.

14 Ryan, *Forerunners*, p. 94.

15 Quoted in Ryan, *Forerunners*, p. 85.

16 *Leeds Mercury*, 18 February 1889.

17 Tom Ellison, *The Art of Rugby Football*, Wellington, Geddis & Blomfield, 1902, p. 68.

18 Quoted in Ryan, *Forerunners*, p. 94.

19 Greg Ryan, *The Contest for Rugby Supremacy: Accounting for the 1905 All Blacks*, Christchurch, Canterbury University Press, 2005, p. 33.

20 Quoted in Sean Fagan, *Rugby Rebellion*, Sydney, Hachette Livre, 2005, p. 29.

21 H. M. Moran, *Viewless Winds. Being the Recollections and Digressions of an Australian Surgeon*, London, Peter Davies, 1939, p. 46.

22 *New Zealand Herald*, 15 August 1904.

23 Ryan, *Contest*, pp. 57–9.

24 Details of the tour are from Ryan, *Contest*.

25 *The Times*, 20 November 1905.

10 South Africa: From Gog's Game to Springboks

1 Details of the battle can be found in the *Cape Times*, 13 March 1900. Morkel biographical details are at *The Missing Brothers of Sommie and Douglas Morkel* at http://family.morkel.net/wp-content/uploads/Missing-Brothers-of-Sommie-and-Dougie-Morkel1.pdf, accessed 21 April 2014.

2 Floris J. G. van der Merwe, 'Rugby in the Prisoner-of-War Camps During the Anglo-Boer War of 1899–1902', *Football Studies,* vol. 1, no. 1, 1998, pp. 76–83.

3 F. N. Piggott, *The Springboks. History of the Tour, 1906-7*, Cape Town, Dawson, 1907, p. 96.

4 Floris J. G. van der Merwe, 'Gog's Game: The Predecessor of Rugby Football at the Cape, and the implications thereof', paper presented to the 35th Conference on Social Science in Sport, Ljubljana, Slovenia, 24–27 August 2006. For a description of Gog's Game, see Ivor D. Difford, *The History of South African Rugby Football 1875–1932*, Wynberg, Speciality Press, 1933, p. 501.

5 Lloyd B. Hill, 'Reflections on the 1862 Football Match in Port Elizabeth', *South African Journal for Research in Sport, Physical Education and Recreation*, vol. 33, no. 1, 2011, pp. 81–98.

6 *Cape Argus*, 8 September 1862, quoted in Jonty Winch, 'Unlocking the Cape Code: Establishing British Football in South Africa', *Sport in History*, vol. 30, no. 4, 2010, p. 503.

7 Jonty Winch, *Sir William Milton: A Leading Figure in Public School Games, Colonial Politics and Imperial Expansion, 1877–1914*, unpublished PhD, University of Stellenbosch, 2013.

8 Difford, *History of South African Rugby Football*, p. 457.

9 Ibid., p. 563.

10 Quoted in André Odendaal, '"The thing that is not round": The untold history of black rugby in South Africa', in Albert Grundlingh, André Odendaal and Burridge Spies (eds), *Beyond the Tryline: Rugby and South African Society*, Johannesburg, Ravan Press, 1995, p. 24.

11 Quoted in Winch, 'Unlocking the Cape Code', p. 517.

12 Details of the history of non-white rugby in this section are taken from Odendaal, 'The thing that is not round', *passim*.

13 Difford, *History of South African Rugby Football*, p. 470.

14 Albert Grundlingh, 'Playing for Power? Rugby, Afrikaner Nationalism and Masculinity in South. Africa, C.1900–C.1970', in Nauright and Chandler (eds), *Making Men: Rugby and Masculine Identity*, Abingdon, Routledge, 1996, p. 181.

15 *The Times*, 12 October 1926.

16 Marshall (ed.), *Football: The Rugby Union Game*, p. 112.

17 Ibid.

18 Burridge Spies, 'The imperial heritage: Rugby and white English speaking South Africa', in Grundlingh, Odendaal and Spies (eds), *Beyond the Tryline*, p. 72.

19 Van der Merwe, 'Rugby in the Prisoner-of-War Camps', p. 81.

20 Ibid., p. 80.

21 G. R. Hill quoted in *Rugby Football: a weekly record of the game*, 17 November 1923. p. 273.

22 Dean Allen, '"Captain Diplomacy": Paul Roos and the Creation of South Africa's Rugby Springboks', *Sport in History*, 33:4, December 2013, pp. 568–94.

23 *The Times*, 25 September 1906.

24 Allen, 'Captain Diplomacy', p. 575.

25 Jonty Winch, '"There Were a Fine Manly Lot of Fellows": Cricket, Rugby and Rhodesian Society during William Milton's Administration, 1896–1914', *Sport in History*, 28:4, December 2008, p. 596.

26 *Guardian*, 17 December 1906.

27 Piggott, *The Springboks*, p. 105.

11 Australia: Wallaroos and Kangaroos

1 Mollie Gillen, *The Founders of Australia: A Biographical Dictionary of the First Fleet*, 1989, p. 445. The precise figures have never been established.

2 Sean Fagan, *The First Lions of Rugby*, Melbourne, Slattery, 2013, p. 80.

3 Fagan, *First Lions*, p. 76.

4 *Otago Witness*, 31 August 1888.

5 Lionel Frost, *Australian Cities in Comparative View*, Victoria, Penguin, 1990, p. 4.

6 Tony Collins, 'The Invention of Sporting Traditions: National Myths, Imperial Pasts and the Origins of Australian Rules Football', in Stephen Wagg (ed.), *Myths and Milestones in the History of Sport*, London, Palgrave, 2011, pp. 8–31.

7 Asa Briggs, *Victorian Cities*, London, Odhams, 1963, pp. 218–19.

8 Thomas Hickie, *They Ran with the Ball: How Rugby Football Began in Australia*, Melbourne, Longman, 1993, p. 2.

9 Ibid., p. 111.

10 For the details of Queensland rugby's early history, see http://jottingsonrugby. wordpress.com/rugby-in-australia/rugby-in-queensland/

11 Maxwell L. Howell and Reet A. Howell, 'The First Intercolonial Rugby Tour in 1882', *Journal of the Royal Historical Society of Queensland*, vol. 11, issue 4, pp. 126–38, and P. Horton, 'A History of Rugby Union Football in Queensland, 1882–1891', unpublished PhD thesis, University of Queensland, 1989.

12 Sean Fagan, 'Rugby's Whistler's Call the Tune', http://www.theroar.com. au/2013/02/22/rugbys-whistlers-call-tune/

13 *Yorkshire Post*, 14 January 1888.

14 Letter of Arthur Shrewsbury to Alfred Shaw, 18 January 1888. I am grateful to Peter Wynne-Thomas at Nottinghamshire CCC archive, Trent Bridge, and Trevor Delaney for making available copies of Shrewsbury's correspondence.

15 See Tony Collins, *Rugby's Great Split*, London, Cass, 1998, pp. 57–8.

16 Fagan, *First Lions*, p. 214.

17 Ibid., p. 225

18 Fagan, *Rugby Rebellion*, p. 126.

19 *Australian Star*, 8 October 1907.

20 Fagan, *Rugby Rebellion*, pp. 112–15.

21 Ibid., p. 197.

12 From Rugby to Gridiron: The United States and Canada

1 Mark Ryan, *For the Glory. Two Olympics. Two Wars. Two Heroes*, London, JR Books, 2009, p. 199.

2 Gary Magee and Andrew Thompson, *Empire and Globalisation*, Cambridge, Cambridge University Press, 2010, p. 69.

3 *New York World*, 17 November 1872.

4 *New York Times*, 5 June 1857.

5 Parke H. Davis, *Football. The American Intercollegiate Game*, New York: Charles Scribner, 1911, p. 24.

6 Walter Camp, 'The Game and Laws of American Football', *Outing*, October 1886, p. 72.

7 Proceedings of the Convention of the Intercollegiate Football Association (IFA), 23 November 1876, reprinted in Davis, *Football*, pp. 461–7.

8 *Boston Daily Globe*, 25 November 1877.

9 Proceedings of the Convention of the IFA, 12 October 1880, reprinted in Davis, *Football*, p. 468.

10 A. G. Guillemard, 'Foundation and progress of the Rugby Football Union', in Marshall (ed.), *Football. The Rugby Union Game*, p. 71. Anon, 'Football as played at Rugby in the sixties', *Rugby Football*, 3 November 1923.

11 *New York Times*, 2 December 1893.

12 Ibid., 9 April 1882.

13 John Watterson, 'The Gridiron Crisis of 1905: Was It Really a Crisis?' *Journal of Sport History*, vol. 27, no. 2, Summer 2000, p. 294.

14 John J. Miller, *The Big Scrum: How Teddy Roosevelt Saved Football*, New York, HarperCollins, 2011.

15 Roberta Park, 'From Football to Rugby – and Back, 1906–1919: The University of California-Stanford University Response to the Football Crisis of 1905', *Journal of Sport History*, vol. 11, no. 3, Winter 1984, p. 20.

16 Joseph R Hickey (ed.), *Spalding's Official Rugby Football Guide 1910*, American Sports Publishing Co., NY, 1910, pp. 31–5. Greg Ryan, 'Brawn against Brains: Australia, New Zealand and the American Football Crisis, 1906-13', *Sporting Traditions*, vol. 20, no. 2, May 2004, pp. 19–38. *New York Times*, 15 April 1906.

17 G. P. Taylor, 'New Zealand, the Anglo-Japanese Alliance and the 1908 Visit of the American Fleet', *Australian Journal of Politics and History*, vol. 15, no. 1, 1969, pp. 55–76.

18 *Sunday Call*, 14 August 1910.

19 Park, 'From Football to Rugby', p. 33.

20 Walter Camp, 'Rugby Football in America', *Outing*, March 1911, p. 710.

21 Park, 'From Football to Rugby', p. 74

22 I am grateful to Doug Sturrock for allowing me to see an early draft of his excellent research on the history of Canadian rugby.

23 Michel Vigneault, *La Naissance d'un sport organiséau Canada: Le hockey à Montreal,1875–1917*, unpublished PhD thesis, Université Laval, Québec, 2001.

24 *Toronto Daily Globe*, 12 November 1875.

25 Doug Sturrock, *Rugby in British Columbia: An Abbreviated History*, http://www.bcrugby.com/history/history/, accessed 27 August 2013.

26 *The Times*, 1 December 1902.

27 *San Francisco Call*, 3 January 1912.

28 Max Howell, *Born to Lead: Wallaby Test Captains*, Celebrity Books, Auckland, NZ, 2005, p. 52.

Part IV Golden Years Amidst the Gathering Storm

13 Harold Wagstaff and the Phantoms of Baskerville

1 *Sydney Morning Herald*, 4 July 1914.

2 Clifford and Wagstaff quotes in *Sports Post* (Leeds), 4 May 1935.

3 *Sydney Morning Herald*, 6 July 1914.

4 Handwritten MSS note on the 1914 match, in the Douglas Clark Collection at the Imperial War Museum, London.

5 *Sports Post* (Leeds), 4 May 1935.

6 *Athletic News*, 16 September 1906.

7 *The Yorkshireman*, 23 August 1893.

8 Rugby Football Union AGM minutes, 28 May 1909.

9 A. J. P. Taylor, *Essays in English History*, London, Penguin, 1976, p. 309.

10   *Daily Graphic*, 18 April 1910.

11   Fagan, *Rugby Rebellion*, pp. 99–101.

12   *Yorkshire Post*, 10 April and 12 September 1907.

13   Ibid., 5 September 1907.

14   *Athletic News*, 7 October 1907.

15   *Yorkshire Post*, 2 October 1907.

16   Bill Greenwood, *Class Conflict and Clash of the Codes: the Introduction of Rugby League to New Zealand 1908 to 1920*, PhD, Massey University (2008), p.123.

17   G. T. Vincent and T. Harfield, 'Repression and Reform: Responses Within New Zealand Rugby to the Arrival of the "Northern Game, 1907–8"', *New Zealand Journal of History* vol. 31, no. 2 (1997), p. 238.

18   John Haynes, *From All Blacks to All Golds*, Christchurch, Ryan and Haynes, 1996, pp. 149–51.

19   Hamish Stuart in the *Otago Witness*, 3 January, 1909, quoted in Greg Ryan, 'A Lack of Esprit du Corps: The 1908 Wallaby Tour of Britain', *Sporting Traditions*, vol. 17, no. 1, November 2000, p. 45.

20   McMahon in *The Referee*, 31 March 1909.

21   *The Times*, 27 October 1908.

22   *Yorkshire Post*, 5 February 1909.

23   Fagan, *Rugby Rebellion*, p. 312.

24   Undated press clipping (*c.*July 1914) in J. C. Davis collection, box 51, item 4, Mitchell Library, Sydney.

25   *Rugby League News* (Sydney), 7 June 1941.

14 British Rugby Before 1914: Stoop to Conquer

1   Quoted in Huw Richards, *The Red and The White*, Aurum Press, London, 2009, p. 48.

2   See Ryan, *Contest*, 2005.

3   *Yorkshire Post*, 20 February 1909. Marriott letter reprinted in *Yorkshire Post*, 19 January 1909, RFU and IB decisions in *Yorkshire Post*, 1 and 20 February 1909.

4   Huw Richards, *A Game for Hooligans*, Edinburgh, Mainstream, 2006, p. 95.

5   The *Guardian*, 17 December 1906.

6   For Stoop's life see Ian Cooper, *Immortal Harlequin*, Tempus, Stroud, 2004.

7   *Daily Mail*, 20 September 1910, quoted in James Martens, 'They Stooped to Conquer: Rugby Union Football 1895–1914', *Journal of Sport History*, vol. 20, no. 1, Spring 1993, p. 36.

8   H. B. T. Wakelam, *The Game Goes On*, London, Arthur Barker, 1936, p. 57.

9   James Corsan, *For Poulton and England*, Matador, London, 2009, p. 125.

15 A Greater Game? Rugby and the First World War

1   I am grateful to George Franki for providing background information on Darb Hickey.

2   Thomas Hughes, *Tom Brown's Schooldays*, Oxford: Oxford University Press edition, 1989, p. 104.

3   *The Times*, 4 March 1919.

4   Marriott's circular is in the *Yorkshire Rugby Football Union Commemoration Book*, Leeds, YRU, 1919, p. 266.

5   Smith and Williams, *Fields of Praise*, p. 201.

6   Letter of 28 August 1914, in E. B. Poulton, *The Life of Ronald Poulton*, London, Sidgwick & Jackson, 1919, p. 308.

7   Harper, letter of 7 September 1914. A. M. C. Thorburn, *The Scottish Rugby Union, Official History*, Edinburgh, Scottish Rugby Union and Collins Publishers, 1985, p. 117.

8   NUGC minutes, 8 September 1914.

9   *Athletic News*, 13 April 1915.

10 Manly District Rugby Union Football Club, *10th Annual Report and Balance Sheet for Season*, 1915. NSWRU *Annual Report*, 1915.

11 Ian Collis and Alan Whittaker, *100 Years of Rugby League*, Sydney, New Holland, 2007, p. 52.

12 See, for example, *Sydney Morning Herald*, 23 August 1915.

13 *The Referee*, 7 September 1910, quoted in Fagan, *Rugby Rebellion*, p. 322.

14 *Athletic News*, 11 January and 1 February 1915.

15 *Yorkshire Post*, 10 February 1917. *The Times*, 12 and 15 February 1917.

16 Arnaud Waquet and Joris Vincent, 'Wartime Rugby and Football: Sports Elites, French Military Teams and International Meets During the First World War', *International Journal of the History of Sport*, vol. 28, no. 3–4, 2011, pp. 379–81.

17 *The Times*, 5 October 1916.

18 *Athletic News*, 18 January and 18 October 1915. Edmund McCabe, 'Rugby and the Great War', *Stand To!*, 52, 1998, pp. 41–4. Lyn Macdonald, *Somme*, London, Michael Joseph, 1983, p. 319. Poulton, *Life of Ronald Poulton*, p. 311. Robert Graves, *Goodbye to All That*, Harmondsworth, Penguin, 1960, p. 149.

19 Quoted in Dine, *French Rugby Football*, p. 53.

20 Rodney Noonan, 'Offside: Rugby League, the Great War and Australian Patriotism', *International Journal of the History of Sport*, vol. 26, no. 15, pp. 2209–10

21 Douglas Clark, MS diary, Imperial War Museum, 90/21/1.

22 Paul Jones, *War Letters of a Public School Boy*, London, Cassell and Company, 1918, p. 157.

23 Letter of Jellicoe reprinted in E. H. D. Sewell, *The Log of a Sportsman*, London, Fisher Unwin, 1923, p. 164.

24 Quoted in *Athletic News*, 18 January 1915.

25 *The Times*, 21 April 1919.

26 *Athletic News*, 21 December 1914.

27 Anne Pallant, *A Sporting Century*, Plymouth, 1997, p. 144.

28 Ruth Elwyn Harris, *Billie: the Nevill Letters 1914-1916*, London, Macrae, 1991, p. 7.

29 Jones, *War Letters*, p. 198.

30 Tony Collins, 'English Rugby Union and the First World War', *The Historical Journal*, vol. 45, no. 4, 2002, pp. 809. *Athletic News*, 10 and 17 March 1919.

31 Eastern Suburbs District Football Club, *16th Annual Report and Balance Sheet*, 1919. Jean-Pierre Bodis, 'Le rugby en France jusqu'a la seconde guerre mondiale: aspects politiques et sociaux', *Revue de Pau et du Bearn*, no. 17, 1990, pp. 217–44.

32 *The Times*, 26 February 1919.

33 *Athletic News*, 10 and 17 March 1919. Simon Inglis, *League Football and the Men Who Made It*, London, Collins Willow, 1988, p. 100.

34 *Yorkshire Rugby Football Union Commemoration Book*, p. 272.

35 See *Athletic News*, 8 May 1916.

Part V Challenge and Change in the Interwar Years

16 All Blacks versus Springboks: Battle for the World

1 *Daily Mail*, 21 December 1918. *The Times*, 21 January 1919.

2 G. H. Goddard, *Soldiers and Sportsmen*, London, A. I. F. Sports Control Board, 1919, p. 22.

3 *The Times*, 22 March 1919.

4 Paul Dobson, *Rugby's Greatest Rivalry: South Africa vs New Zealand, 1921–1995*, Cape Town, Human & Rousseau, 1996, p. 13.

5 *Feilding Star* (New Zealand), 10 September 1919.

6 *Natal Witness*, 27 August, 1919, quoted in F. G. van der Merwe, 'Race and South African Rugby: a Review of the 1919 All Black Tour', *South African Journal for Research in Sport, Physical Education and Recreation*, vol. 32, no. 2, 2010, pp. 161–9.

7 SARB minutes in Van der Merwe, *Race and South African Rugby*.

8 *New Zealand Herald*, 18 March 1919.

9 *Evening Post*, 30 August 1921.

10 Quoted in Ryan (ed.), *Tackling Rugby Myths*, p. 106.

11 Difford, *History of South African Rugby Football*, pp. 543–63, 637–42.

12 *New Zealand Truth*, 19 July 1928.

13 George Nepia, *I, George Nepia*, London, LLP, 2002, p. 112.

14 *New Zealand Herald*, 8 July 1921.

15 Wakelam, *The Game Goes On*, 2nd edition, 1954, p. 203.

16 *Evening Post*, 24 September 1937.

17 Ibid., 27 September 1937.

17 *Rugby de muerte, à treize* and *à la Vichy*

1 Quoted in Richard Escot and Jacques Riviere, *Un Siècle de Rugby*, Paris, Calmann-Levy, 1997, p. 58.

2 Dine, *French Rugby Football*, p. 61

3 *Rugby Football*, 17 October 1923. *La Dépêche du Midi*, 6 May 1925.

4 Mike Rylance, *The Forbidden Game*, Brighouse, League Publications, 1999, p. 14.

5 International Board statement, 13 February 1931.

6 *Rugger*, 26 September 1931.

7 Details from Rylance, *The Forbidden Game*, chapters 1–3.

8 Dine, *French Rugby Football*, p. 90.

9 Quoted in *La France*, 22 August 1940, quoted in Rylance, *The Forbidden Game*, p. 128.

10 The report was published in Voivenel's *Mon Beau Rugby*, 1942. See Rylance, *The Forbidden Game*, pp. 132–3.

11 Rylance, *The Forbidden Game*, p. 150.

18 Britain's Rush to Rugby

1 Peter MacIntyre in Sydney Grammar School magazine *The Torch-Bearer*, vol. 29, no. 1, May 1924, p. 37.

2   *The Times*, 26 February 1919.

3   Figures from RFU *Handbooks* for 1919–20 and 1929–30.

4   W. W. Wakefield and Howard Marshall, *Rugger*, London, Longman, 1927, p. 106.

5   Ibid., p. 105.

6   International Board minutes, 19 March 1921.

7   Liam O'Callaghan, 'Rugby Football and Identity Politics in Free State Ireland', *Éire-Ireland*, vol. 48, no. 1 & 2, 2013, pp. 158–60.

8   Ibid., p. 163.

9   Christopher Brooke, *A History of the University of Cambridge, vol. 4, 1870–1990*, Cambridge, Cambridge University Press, 1993, p. 517.

10 Gareth Williams, 'From Grand Slam to Great Slump: Economy, Society and Rugby Football in Wales during the Depression', *Welsh Historical Review*, vol. 11, 1983, pp. 339–57.

19 Leagues Apart: 1919–39

1   Ian Heads, *The Kangaroos*, Sydney, Lester Townsend, 1990, p. 67.

2   Richard Hoggart, *The Uses of Literacy*, Oxford, Oxford University Press, 1957, p. 78.

3   Max and Reet Howell, *The Greatest Game Under the Sun*, Brisbane, QRL, 1989, p. 47.

4   E. G. Shaw and A. C. Wallace, *Report of the tour of the NSWRU representative team The Waratahs 1927–28*, 27 March 1928, p. 18 (Australian Rugby Union archives, Sydney).

5   'Editorial', *Rugby News*, 12 May 1928, p. 4.

6   Australian Rugby League Board of Control minutes, 21 July 1950.

7   John Coffey and Bernie Wood, *Auckland: 100 Years of Rugby League*, Auckland, Huia, 2009, p. 60.

20 Rugby in the Second World War

1   Dine, *French Rugby Football*, p.109.

2   RFU Finance and Emergency Committee minutes, 11 December 1933. RFU Committee minutes, 20 December 1935. S. F. Coopper to J. V. Waite of the USA Rugby Union, 26 February 1936.

3   *The Times*, 10 July 1929.

4   IRB minutes, 17 March 1933.

5 Sport-Libre's underground journal can be found at http://gallica.bnf.fr/
ark:/12148/cb328719335/date.

6 For rugby and the Resistance see Rylance, *The Forbidden Game*, pp. 153–4, and,
more generally, Jean-Louis Gay-Lescot, *Sport et Éducation sous Vichy, 1940–1944*,
Lyon, Presses Universitaires de Lyon, 1992.

7 Albert Grundlingh, 'Playing for Power', in Grundlingh, Odendaal and Spies
(eds), *Beyond the Tryline*, pp. 120–21.

8 *Daily Mail*, 15 November 1939.

9 Gus Risman, *Rugby Renegade*, London, Stanley Paul, 1958, p. 35.

10 Howard Marshall, *Oxford v Cambridge*, London, Clarke & Cochran, 1951,
pp. 246–56. *Old Alleynian RFC 1898–1948*, London, Clowes, 1948, p. 94.
Dave Hammond, *The Club: Life and Times of Blackheath F.C.*, London,
MacAitch, 1999, p. 126.

11 Tony Collins, *Rugby League in Twentieth Century Britain*, Abingdon, Routledge,
2006, p. 82.

12 Collis and Whittaker, *100 Years of Rugby League*, pp. 156 and 172.

13 See, for example, Paul Donoghue, *Rommel versus Rugby*, Petone, Apex Print, 1961.

14 Graham Jooste, *Rugby Stories from the Platteland*, Johannesburg, South
Publishers, 2005, pp. 122–3.

15 Brendan Gallagher, 'Geffin takes name mystery to the grave', *Daily Telegraph*,
21 October 2004.

Part VI Rugby's New Horizons

21 European Rugby and the Rise of Italy

1 *The Times*, 10 September 1957.

2 *Daily Mail*, 8 January 1956.

3 Harding to Ward, 30 January 1956, TNA FO 371/122750.

4 I. Denicky to W. Fallowfield, 8 December 1954. RFL Archives, University of
Huddersfield.

5 *Open Rugby*, November 1989, pp. 42–3.

6 'Confidential Report from British Legation in Bucharest', 17 May 1956, TNA FO
371/122750.

7 *Thoughts on Sport*, Moscow, Ogenek, 1930, p. 72, in James Riordan, *Sport in
Soviet Society*, Cambridge, Cambridge University Press, 1980, p. 104.

8 Victor E. Louis and Jennifer M. Louis, *Sport in the Soviet Union*, Oxford,
Pergamon, 1980, chapter 2.

9 *Western Mail*, 28 December 1963. 'Ilyushin first Russian in IRB Hall of Fame', http://www.irb.com/history/halloffame/newsid=2065514.html, accessed 27 July 2014.

10 http://www.rugbyworldcup.com/home/news/newsid=2013819.html, accessed 24 June 2014.

11 Louis and Louis, *Sport in the Soviet Union*, pp. 39–40.

12 Gherardo Bonin, 'Rugby: The game for "Real Italian men"', in T. J. L. Chandler and John Nauright (eds), *Making the Rugby World. Race, Gender, Commerce*, London, Cass, 1999, pp. 88–104.

13 J-P. Bodis, *Histoire Mondiale du Rugby*, Toulouse, Editions Privat, 1987, pp. 395–6.

14 *Rugby World & Post*, September 1993.

22 Argentina and South America: Rugby on a Soccer Continent

1 Tony Mason, *Passion of the People*, London, Verso, 1995, pp. 3–7.

2 David Barnes, *The Accies*, Edinburgh, Birlinn, 2008, p. 117.

3 UAR Annual Report 1965 (http://uar.com.ar/pdf/memorias/1965.pdf), p. 6.

4 David Barnes and Peter Burns, *Behind the Thistle*, Edinburgh, Birlinn, 2010, p. 51.

23 Empire of the Scrum: Japan, Asia and Africa

1 J. G. Farrell, *The Singapore Grip*, London, Fontana, 1978, p. 328.

2 RFU committee minutes, 22 January 1878.

3 Richards, *A Game for Hooligans*, p. 59.

4 E. W. Foenander (ed.), *A Guide to Ceylonese Football*, Colombo, privately published, 1911, pp. 3–6.

5 Ng Peng Kong, *Rugby: A Malaysian Chapter*, Kuala Lumpur, privately published, 2003, pp. 60–2.

6 Ibid., pp. 41–2.

7 Simon Drakeford, *It's A Rough Game But Good Sport*, Hong Kong, Earneshaw Books, 2014.

8 Leigh Jones and Nicky Lewis, 'Emergence, Cessation and Resurgence during the Evolution of Rugby Union in Hong Kong', *International Journal of the History of Sport*, vol. 29, no. 9, 2012, pp. 1344–62.

9 RFU minutes, 6 June 1952.

10 Hong Kong Rugby Football Union launches Hall of Fame, http://www.hkrugby.com/eng/news/4152.php, dated 16 May 2014 23:04:00.

11 Keiko Ikeda, 'Ryōsai-kembo, Liberal Education and Maternal Feminism under Fascism: Women and Sport in Modern Japan', *International Journal of the History of Sport*, vol. 27, no. 3, 2010, pp. 537–52.

12 Mike Galbraith, '1866 and all that: the untold early history of rugby in Japan', *Japan Times*, 15 March 2014.

13 *Rugby News* (Sydney), 12 September 1936.

14 Ibid., 3 September 1927.

15 Bodis, *Histoire Mondiale*, p. 389.

16 Shiggy Kono to Max Mannix 2.8.94, David Hinchliffe archive, RFL Archives, University of Huddersfield.

17 R. Light, H. Hirai and H. Ebishima, 'Professionalism and tensions in Japanese rugby', in G. Ryan (ed.), *The Changing Face of Rugby: The Union Game and Professionalism since 1995*, Cambridge, Cambridge Scholars Press, 2008.

18 Bodis, *Histoire Mondiale*, pp. 200.

19 Evelyne Combeau-Mari, 'Vitality of Associations and the Expansion of Sport: Sporting Associations, an Opportunity for Freedom for the Malagasy (1920–1939)', *International Journal of the History of Sport*, vol. 28, no. 12, 2011, pp. 1605–24.

20 Evelyne Combeau-Mari, 'Rugby on the High Plateaus: A Physical Culture of Combat and Emancipation', *International Journal of the History of Sport*, vol. 28, no. 12, 2011, pp. 1703–15.

21 Quoted in Combeau-Mari, 'Rugby on the High Plateaus', p. 1712.

22 Jonty Winch, 'There Were a Fine Manly Lot of Fellows', pp. 583–604.

23 'Tsimba brothers enter IRB Hall of Fame', http://www.irb.com/history/halloffame/newsid=2063965.html#tsimba+brothers+enter+irb+hall+fame, 25 October 2012.

24 M. Campbell and E. J. Cohen, *Rugby Football in East Africa 1909–1959*, Nairobi, King and Charles, 1960.

25 Gishinga Njoroge, 'Renaissance of Kenyan Rugby', *The Nairobian*, 2 November 2013.

24 Big Hits from the South Pacific: Fiji, Tonga and Samoa

1 *Sydney Morning Herald*, 12 August 1952.

2 *Suva Times*, 24 July 1886.

3 Robert F. Dewey, 'Embracing Rugby and Negotiating Inequalities in the Pacific Islands', in J. S. Te Rito and S. M. Healy (eds), *Conference Proceedings of Te*

NOTES

Tatau Pounamu: The Greenstone Door Traditional Knowledge and Gateways to Balanced Relationships, Auckland, Ngā Pae o te Māramatanga, 2008, p. 158.

4 Dewey, 'Embracing Rugby', pp. 158–65.

25 The USA and Canada: Rugby's North American Dream

1 *New York Times*, 29 March 1936.
2 Ibid., 23 May 1934. I am grateful to Scott Cantrell for his insights on American rugby in the 1930s.
3 International Rugby Football Board minutes, 29 July 1931.
4 RFL Council minutes, 24 June 1939.
5 See Gavin Willacy, *No Helmets Required*, Durrington, Pitch Publishing, 2013.
6 T. J. L. Chandler, 'Recognition Through Resistance: Rugby in the USA', in T. J. L. Chandler and John Nauright, *Making the Rugby World: Race, Gender, Commerce*, London, Cass, 1999, p. 52.
7 *Sports Illustrated*, 17 March 1980.
8 Ibid., 21 December 1959.
9 Undated letter from John MacCarthy of Halifax Nova Scotia in RFL Archives, University of Huddersfield.
10 RFL Council minutes, 2 February 1955.
11 Rachel Cooke, 'The Groundbreakers', the *Observer*, 4 May 2003.
12 Quoted in Simon Borchardt, 'Don't Ask, Don't Tell', keo.co.za, 27 May 2008, http://keo.co.za/2008/05/27/dont-ask-dont-tell/ accessed 14.00, 10 March 2014.

26 Women Will Hold Up Half the Game

1 *The Yorkshireman*, 18 December 1889. *Rugger*, 6 February 1932.
2 *Rugger*, 15 January 1947.
3 See newspaper reports at http://www.donmouth.co.uk/womens_football/1881.html
4 Extract from the memoirs of Emily Galwey, Museum of World Rugby exhibition, Twickenham, September 2010.
5 Arron Jones, 'A Short History of Women's Rugby', *Touchlines*, October 2003. Collins, *Rugby League in Twentieth Century Britain*, pp. 154–6.
6 Quoted in John Coffey, *Canterbury 13*, Christchurch, self-published, 1987, pp. 53–4.

7 July 1921, quoted in Barbara Cox, 'The Rise and Fall of "The Girl Footballer" in New Zealand during 1921', in *International Journal of the History of Sport*, vol. 29, no. 3, March 2012, p. 449.

8 *Courier-Mail* (Brisbane), 20 September 1954.

9 Victoria Dawson, 'Workington's Wonder Women', *Forty-20*, September 2013, pp. 38–9.

10 Megan Taylor Shockley, 'Southern Women in the Scrums', *Journal of Sport History*, vol. 33, no. 2, 2006, pp. 127–55.

11 'Girls Just Want to Have Fun', *Rugby News*, June 1990.

Part VII Tradition and Transformation

27 Springboks, All Blacks and the Politics of Rugby

1 A. H. Carman, A. C. Swan and R. Masters (eds), *The Rugby Almanack of New Zealand 1950*, Wellington, Sporting Publications, 1950, p. 30.

2 Trevor Richards, *Dancing On Our Bones*, Wellington, Bridget Williams, 1999, p. 18.

3 M. N. Pearson, 'Heads in the Sand: the 1956 Springbok Tour to New Zealand in Perspective', in R. Cashman and M. McKernan (eds), *Sport in History*, Brisbane, University of Queensland Press, 1979, pp. 272–92.

4 Barry Donovan, 'Turning silver to gold', *New Zealand Herald*, 23 October 2011.

5 Winston McCarthy, *Haka: The All Blacks Story*, London, Pelham, 1968, p. 257.

6 'Rugby: Maori told to throw match against Boks', *New Zealand Herald*, 13 April 2010.

7 Richards, *Dancing On Our Bones*, p. 20

8 Quoted in Bodis, *Histoire Mondiale*, p. 358.

9 IRB minutes, 17/18 March 1961.

28 Gentlemen and Players: Wales and England 1945–95

1 Phil Bennett, *The Autobiography*, London, Willow, 2003, p. 275.

2 Quoted in Martin Johnes, 'A Prince, a King and a Referendum: Rugby, Politics and Nationhood in Wales, 1969–1979', *Journal of British Studies*, vol. 47, no. 1, 2008, p. 144.

3 *Daily Telegraph*, 18 February 1980.

4 *The Times*, 16 March 1957.

5 All quotes and figures are from Tony Collins, *A Social History of English Rugby Union*, London, Rouledge, 2009, p. 103.

6 RFU Executive minutes, 5 May 1968, 17 January, 14 May and 6 June 1969.

7 Quoted in Christopher Booker, *The Neophiliacs*, London, Fontana, 1970, p. 28.

8 International Board minutes, 19 March 1965 and 13/14 March 1969.

9 *The Times*, 1 November 1975.

10 Derek Wyatt, *Rugby Disunion*, London, Gollancz, 1995, p. 19. RFU Forward Planning sub-committee, 3 May 1979.

11 Tony and Mitchell Williams, *The Official Rugby Union Club Directory 1990–91*, London: Burlington, 1990, p. 6.

29 Bravehearts, Tigers and Lions: Scotland and Ireland in the Post-war Years

1 Barnes and Burns, *Behind the Thistle*, p. 5.

2 Frank Keating, 'How Ravenhill rebels made an issue out of an anthem', the *Guardian*, 27 February 2007.

3 Frank Keating, 'Be Your Own Men', *The Spectator*, 20 March 1993.

4 John Reason and Carwyn James, *The World of Rugby*, London, BBC, 1979, p. 224.

30 The France That Wins

1 'Arbitration on the conflict between the FFR and the FFJXIII', Gaston Roux, General Director of Sports, 10 July 1947, document in RFL Archives, University of Huddersfield.

2 Barnes and Burns, *Behind the Thistle*, p. 4.

3 Confidential letter to FFR from IRB 20 March 1951, RFU Archives, Twickenham.

4 Robert Fassolette, 'Rugby League Football in France 1934–54' *Sport in History*, vol. 27, no. 3, 2007, p. 391.

5 Bernard Pratviel, *Immortel Pipette*, Portet, Imprint Publishing, 2004, p. 94.

6 Valérie Bonnet, 'Le stéréotype dans la presse sportive: vision de l'identité à travers l'altérité', *Signes, Discours et Sociétés* [en ligne], 4. Visions du monde et spécificité des discours, 11 janvier 2010, at www.revue-signes.info/document.php?id=1417. ISSN 1308-8378. Accessed 14 March 2014.

7 Collectif Midi Olympique, *Cent ans de XV de France*, Toulouse, Midi Olympique, 2005, p. 86.

8 Quoted in Lindsay Sarah Krasnoff, 'The Evolution of French Sports Policy', in Richard Holt, Alan Tomlinson and Christopher Young (eds), *Sport and the Transformation of Modern Europe*, Abingdon: Routledge, 2011, p. 70.

9 Denis Lalanne, *The Great Fight of the French Fifteen*, Wellington, Reed, 1960, p. 200 [capitals in original].

10 *Daily Telegraph*, 6 April 1959.

11 *Rugby World*, September 1965.

12 Richards, *A Game for Hooligans*, p. 197.

31 Rugby League: A People's Game in a Television Age

1 Huddersfield RUFC membership application form, c. 1972, at TNA AT 25/234. IRB minutes, 14 March 1958.

2 RFL Council minutes, 10 October 1945.

3 Ibid., 18 November 1954.

4 Thomas Keneally, 'The Other Code', *Esquire*, November 1991.

5 The *Independent*, 16 October 1996.

32 Rugby's Road to 1995

1 Peter Oborne, *Basil D'Oliveira: Cricket and Controversy*, London, Little, Brown, 2004.

2 The *Guardian*, 31 October 1969.

3 Ibid., 17, 19 and 25 November 1969 and 15 November 1999 for Frank Keating's recollections.

4 Chris Laidlaw, *Mud in Your Eye*, London, Pelham, 1973, p. 1.

5 Tom Hickie, *A Sense of Union*, Sydney, 1998, chapters 12 and 13.

6 Quoted in Richards, *Dancing On Our Bones*, p. 36.

7 See IB minutes, 21 March 1959, 15 March 1963 and 6 January 1964.

8 IRB minutes, 15 March 1963.

9 The *Sportsman*, March 1966, quoted in A. Grundlingh, 'Playing for Power', in Grundlingh, Odendaal and Spies (eds), *Beyond the Tryline*, p. 116.

10 Hendrik Snyders, 'Preventing Huddersfield: The Rise and Decline of Rugby League in South Africa', *International Journal of the History of Sport*, vol. 28, no. 1, January 2011, pp. 9–31. Craven quote from *The Times*, 23 December 1985.

11 IRB minutes, 15 March 1963, 6 January 1964, 13/14 March 1969 and 19/20 March 1970.

12 IRB minutes, 11/12 March 1976.

13 *The Times*, 17 and 18 January 1978. IB minutes 21/22 March 1979.

14 Welsh Rugby Union, 'Report of Inquiry into the Involvement of Welsh Players in the Centenary Celebrations of the South African Rugby Board: Conclusions and Recommendations', August 1989, Cardiff, 1991, pp. 3–5. David Hinchliffe archives, University of Huddersfield.

15 RFU annual general meeting, 8 July 1994.

16 K. Pelmear (ed.), *Rugby Football: An Anthology*, London, Allen & Unwin, 1958, p. 260.

17 *The Times*, 28 May 1983, and *Sydney Morning Herald*, 16 October 2003.

18 Bernard Lapasset, F. C. H. McLeod, Rob Fisher and Vernon Pugh, 'Report of the IRB Amateurism Working Party', February 1995, pp. 3-4.

19 Stuart Barnes, *The Year of Living Dangerously*, London, Richard Cohen, 1995, p. 153.

20 Peter Fitzsimons, *The Rugby War*, Sydney, HarperCollins, 1996, p. 312.

21 Ibid., *The Rugby War*, pp. 15–20. *Daily Telegraph*, 24 June 1995.

Part VIII Into the 21st Century

33 Shrinking World, Global Oval

1 Ieuan Evans and Peter Jackson, *Bread of Heaven*, Edinburgh, Mainstream, 1995, p. 202

2 Quoted in *Sydney Morning Herald*, 22 October 2002.

3 Ian Clayton, Ian Daley and Brian Lewis (eds), *Merging on the Ridiculous*, Pontefract, YAC, 1995, p. 14.

4 *Australian Financial Review*, 5 August 2005.

5 The *Guardian*, 7 May 2001.

6 *The Times*, 7 January 2009.

7 O'Callaghan, *Rugby in Munster*, pp. 212–18.

8 Mark Evans, 'Is French Club Rugby a Bubble Waiting to Burst?', *Running Rugby*, September 2011.

9 Bruce Crumley, 'Gloom over French Soccer Contrasts With Rugby's Rise', *Time*, 16 May 2010.

10 'Too Many Foreign Players in the Top 14? 'Bullsh*t' says Boudjellal', *Irish Independent*, 30 June 2014.

11 Yoko Kanemasu and Gyozo Molnar, 'Life after Rugby: Issues of Being an "Ex" in Fiji Rugby', *International Journal of the History of Sport*, vol. 31, no. 11, 2013, p. 1390.

Conclusion The Soul of the Game

1 'Rogge voices Olympic rugby doubts', 30 October 2007, http://news.bbc.
   co.uk/sport1/hi/rugby_union/7061471.stm – accessed 11:18, 21 July 2014.
2 RFU laws committee minutes, 5 July 1972.
3 The *Independent*, 17 April 1992.
4 IRB, *Changes in the Playing of International Rugby Over a Twenty Year Period*,
   September, 2005, p. 6.
5 Ibid., p. 4.

INDEX

INDEX

INDEX

INDEX